the
THEORY and
MANAGEMENT
of SYSTEMS

McGRAW-HILL SERIES IN MANAGEMENT

Keith Davis, *Consulting Editor*

the
THEORY and
MANAGEMENT
of SYSTEMS

Third Edition

Richard A. Johnson

Fremont E. Kast

James E. Rosenzweig

Graduate School of Business Administration
University of Washington

McGRAW-HILL BOOK COMPANY
New York   St. Louis   San Francisco   Düsseldorf   Johannesburg
Kuala Lumpur   London   Mexico   Montreal   New Delhi   Panama
Rio de Janeiro   Singapore   Sydney   Toronto

THE THEORY AND MANAGEMENT OF SYSTEMS

34567890 DODO 79876

*This book was set in Palatino by Black Dot, Inc. The editors
were Richard F. Dojny and Annette Hall; the designer was
Hartmuth Bender; and the production supervisor was Sally
Ellyson. The drawings were done by John Cordes, J & R
Technical Services, Inc.*

Library of Congress Cataloging in Publication Data

Johnson, Richard Arvid, 1917.
  The theory and management of systems.

  Bibliography: p.
  1. Operations research.   2. Industrial management.
3. System analysis.   I. Kast, Fremont Ellsworth,
1926–   joint author.   II. Rosenzweig, James
Erwin, 1929–   joint author.   III. Title.
HD20.5.J6   1973   658.4'032   72–5618
ISBN 0-07-032634-7

To the "New" Blondie, Dolly, and Zelda
and more Twilight Golf

Contents

Preface

The systems approach to the management of organizations has passed its infancy and is approaching adolescence. Over the past two decades it has emerged as a vigorous, lively, and sometimes undefinable teen-ager. We are bombarded with references to systems: environmental systems, urban systems, transportation systems, ecological systems, systems dynamics, systems analysis, etc., etc., etc. . . . When the manuscript for the first edition of this book was completed in 1962, we were apprehensive that the systems approach might not "catch on." Now we are apprehensive in the opposite direction. It has not only caught on but is running rampant. Everything is a system, and systems thinking is the by-word.

In this revised edition we have reacted to this ubiquitous use of the term *systems approach* and have attempted to refine our thinking. We go beyond the view that "the systems approach is a way of thinking" toward a more precise understanding of the relevant concepts and their applications. We still emphasize the importance of "systems thinking" but have tried to suggest more precise terminology applicable at different levels of analysis. Consequently we have refined the systems approach into three levels of consideration: (1) systems philosophy, (2) systems design and analysis, and (3) systems management. The book has been revised to present these three foci of the systems approach more precisely.

Systems philosophy takes its frame of reference from general systems theory and provides a way of thinking about complex systems and the relationship between components. Over the past ten years we have been aware of the utilization of a systems philosophy in other disciplines. Part of this comes from our increased interest in these fields; but we are convinced that there has been an actual expansion in systems thinking in these areas as well. In many fields, particularly the social sciences, the concentration over the past several decades has been on analytical, fact-finding approaches. This has been useful in helping to develop knowledge and to understand the details of specific but limited subjects. At some stage, however, there should be a period of synthesis, reconciliation, and integration, so that the analytical and fact-finding developments are unified into broader, multi-dimensional theories. There is evidence that every field of human knowledge passes alternatively through phases of analysis and fact-finding to periods of synthesis and integration. In his presidential address to the American Sociological Association in 1965, Pitirim Sorokin stated:

> If sociology is going to grow as a basic science of sociocultural phenomena, it is bound to pass into a new synthesizing-generalizing phase. Empirical signs indicate that for several reasons this transition has already begun. Stipulating certain conditions, we can reasonably expect a synthesizing sociology, unifying into a rich, logically and empirically valid system all the sound parts of the existing analytical theories and integrating all the little and "middle-range" uniformities of today's sociology.[1]

In psychology also the systems approach is gaining adherents. For example, Katz and Kahn in their study of organizational processes have moved from the traditional emphasis on individual psychology and interpersonal relations to systems constructs. They suggest that classical organization theory implicitly assumes a "closed" system and that the development of open-system theory furnishes a much more dynamic and adequate framework for the study of organizations. They conclude:

> In some respects open-system theory is not a theory at all; it does not pretend to the specific sequences of cause and effect, the specific hypotheses and tests of hypotheses which are the basic elements of theory. Open-system theory is rather a framework, a meta-theory, a model in the broadest sense of that overused term. Open-system theory is an approach and a conceptual language for understanding and describing many kinds and levels of phenomena. It is used to describe and explain the behavior of living or-

---

[1]Pitirim A. Sorokin, "Sociology of Yesterday, Today and Tomorrow," *American Sociological Review*, December 1965, p. 883.

ganisms and combinations of organisms, but it is applicable to any dynamic, recurring process, any patterned sequence of events.

It is such a recurrent pattern of events, differentiated from but dependent upon the larger stream of life in which it occurs and recurs, that constitutes an open system. All such systems involve the flow of energy from the environment through the system itself and back into the environment. They involve not only a flow of energy but a transformation of it, an alteration in energic form the precise nature of which is one definition of the system itself.[2]

This view not only indicates the interest of psychologists in using the systems approach in the study of organizations, but also reinforces our own ideas of the importance of these concepts as a framework for thinking rather than a rigid theory.

There is additional evidence of the use of the systems approach in the integration of psychology with advanced technology. In the foreword to *Psychological Principles in System Development*, Arthur Melton says: "This book has the distinction of being the first of its kind, and a very significant first indeed. It marks the coming of age of a systematic conception of the application of psychological principles to the invention, development, and use of complex man-machine systems."[3] This book emphasizes that "in our society, some of the most important and spectacular developments of the current age are *systems*."[4] It suggests that many of our technological developments, such as the electric light and telephone, started off as product inventions but led to the development of complex man-machine systems.

The same trends toward synthesis and systems thinking are evident in business. Culliton suggests that we are moving from the "age of analysis" to the "age of synthesis." "Quietly, necessarily, and inevitably we are entering a period that forces man to find more accurate answers to questions involving the 'wholeness' of an operation."[5] This "age of synthesis" forces management to think and act in new and different ways—as suggested by the systems approach. In this view the whole is not merely a combination of the subsystems but is distinct from its parts.

The systems approach has become the underlying basis for the application of many new methods and techniques such as

---

[2]Daniel Katz and Robert L. Kahn, *The Social Psychology of Organizations,* John Wiley & Sons, Inc., New York, 1966, pp. 452–453.
[3]Arthur W. Melton in Robert M. Gagné (ed.), *Psychological Principles in System Development,* Holt, Rinehart and Winston, Inc., New York, 1962, p. v.
[4]Robert M. Gagné, ibid., p. 1.
[5]James W. Culliton, "Age of Synthesis," *Harvard Business Review,* September–October 1962, pp. 36–38.

electronic data processing. In discussing the application of these techniques in an American Management Association research bulletin, Higginson says:

> These new techniques are resulting not from a reaffirmation of old concepts but from an emergence of new ones. The conversion from the traditional to the new is considered by many to be more evolutionary than revolutionary, because the elements of management have not been modified drastically. What is novel is that these elements are being considered as a dynamic totality. The whole is deemed more important than the parts and the process more vital than the basic elements. As one data-processing executive remarked, companies are discovering that the interaction of parts is more important than the parts themselves. Companies are becoming systems-oriented.[6]

Thus, the systems approach is having a profound effect upon business operations and requires a new and different perspective on the part of managers.

This thinking in terms of systems instead of parts or components is aptly expressed by Ellis and Ludwig:

> Newspapers are apt to characterize our age as the "Jet Age," "Space Age," or the "Atomic Age." People more familiar with the details of modern technological concepts, however, probably would choose "The Systems Era" as being a more accurate descriptive phrase. The jet engine and nuclear weapon, for example, become part of a "weapons system," and the nuclear reactor part of a "power distribution system." Management makes use of "systems concept," "systems philosophy," and "systems approach." Engineers and physical scientists speak of "systems analysis," "systems engineering," and "systems theory." Medical, biological, and behavioral scientists discuss "nervous systems," "homeostatic systems," and "social systems."[7]

Although to speak of our time as the "systems era" may be presumptuous, we are impressed by the extent to which systems approaches are being used by the various disciplines as a basis for dealing with the integration and synthesis essential in a complex world. We have tried to capture the spirit of this new thinking in our revision.

On the other hand, we do not see the systems approach as a panacea for managers. It does not simplify the task necessarily;

---

[6]M. Valliant Higginson, *Managing With EDP: A Look at the State of the Art*, American Management Association, Inc., New York, 1965, p. 9.
[7]David O. Ellis and Fred J. Ludwig, *Systems Philosophy*, Prentice-Hall, Inc., Englewood Cliffs, N.J., 1962, p. 2.

but it does facilitate understanding and coping with complex situations. Philosophers and managers have long sought concepts and methods which fit any and all situations—the one best way.

> Our great weakness is the habit of reducing the most complex issues to the most simplistic moralisms. About Communism. About Capitalism. About Crime. About Corruption. About Likker. About Pot. About Race Horses. About the SST. Name it.
>
> A century ago the Swiss historian Jacob Burckhardt foresaw that ours would be the age of "the great simplifiers," and that the essence of tyranny was the denial of complexity. He was right. This is the single great temptation of the time. It is the great corruptor, and must be resisted with purpose and with energy.
>
> What we need are great complexifiers, men who will not only seek to understand what it is they are about, but who will also dare to share that understanding with those for whom they act.[8]

Toffler expresses the same idea as follows:

> Finally, we have the Super-Simplifier. With old heroes and institutions toppling, with strikes, riots, and demonstrations stabbing at his consciousness, he seeks a single neat equation that will explain all the complex novelties threatening to engulf him. Grasping erratically at this idea or that, he becomes a temporary true believer.[9]

We are true believers in the systems approach as an aid for complexifiers. Systems of systems are pervasive—whether explicit or implicit. The ability to recognize them, to understand their interrelationships and to anticipate the repercussions of changes in a subsystem is a function of man's cognitive complexity—an important attribute of effective managers.

> It is men with . . . expanded views of reality who will exert the greatest influence on man's organizations. The views, insights, and attitudes that reflect understanding of these concepts are the qualities of systems thinking, and the guide to the systems approach. . . .
>
> A total system inevitably exists at the start. It is already there. Systems design, or *redesign* certainly deals with the whole to the extent that man's present knowledge permits him to do so; but the objective is to deal not only with the total system but also with its own internal subsystems and with its relationship to other systems. The idea is to improve the system that is the whole, by

[8]Daniel P. Moynihan, "Remarks," Dec. 21, 1970.
[9]Alvin Toffler, *Future Shock*, Bantam Books, Inc., New York, 1971, p. 361.

redesign of the whole and its parts, in relationship to the external systems that constitute its environment.[10]

Modern managers must be capable of coping with larger and more complex systems than ever before. Conceptual ability, tolerance for ambiguity, and a sense of the situation are becoming essential for managerial effectiveness. The systems approach fosters the development and refinement of these skills.

In this edition of *The Theory and Management of Systems* we have expanded our discussion to include all complex organizations. We have looked to both the behavioral and the quantitative sciences in developing many new inputs. Dynamic advancements in these basic disciplines have provided new ideas and information.

The systems approach continues to be applied increasingly in human affairs—from the view of the individual as a complex system of interacting components to large-scale, man-machine systems involving many organizations. Systems thinking has proved appropriate and useful in a wide variety of contexts: military missions, space explorations, pollution control, urban mass transit, ecological balance, law-justice systems, and many others. The systems approach provides a way of addressing these complex problem areas at three levels. Systems analysis provides a framework within which problems are identified, alternative solutions are evaluated, and difficult choices are made in the allocation of resources. At the philosophical level, the systems approach fosters a way of thinking which maintains the total system (law-justice, for example) as the focal point so that solutions which improve subsystems at the expense of other subsystems or the total will be deemphasized. Systems management couples the philosophical frame of reference with logical, systematic, analytical methods while developing ways to coordinate program activity which will meet established objectives.

The main objectives of the first edition were to provide a conceptual model for the systems approach, to suggest certain applications, and to explore some of the means of implementing this approach. It was primarily a conceptual treatise rather than a textbook; however, it has been used extensively in the classroom. Since that time we have experimented with its use and have solicited feedback from colleagues elsewhere. In later editions we have maintained the theoretical and conceptual approach, but we

[10]John A. Beckett, *Management Dynamics*, McGraw-Hill Book Company, New York, 1971, p. 106.

also have tried to make it a more appropriate book for the classroom. We have added questions at the end of each chapter and
have included a number of cases to illustrate methods and applications.

Because of the rapid accumulation of knowledge in the field,
each of the chapters has been revised substantially, and the titles
of several have been changed accordingly. A new chapter has been
included on planning-programming-budgeting systems (PPBS).
Also, several new cases have been added. As a result of these
changes the book has been lengthened somewhat, and we hope
it has been significantly improved.

We wish to thank our colleagues who have reviewed and
criticized earlier editions. We are grateful to Professors Albert N.
Schrieber, Robert C. Meier, William T. Newell, and Henry C.
Fischer who gave us permission to use several cases. We wish to
thank the Boeing Company and the Weyerhaeuser Company for
providing materials. We are grateful to the secretaries in the Graduate School of Business Administration, and particularly to Jane
Smith and Nona Pedersen who typed and proofread most of the
revised manuscript. Finally, we would like to thank the students
who served as a laboratory for our ideas and case material.

Richard A. Johnson
Fremont E. Kast
James E. Rosenzweig

the
THEORY and
MANAGEMENT
of SYSTEMS

PART 1

Observe how system into system runs,
What other planets circle other suns.

Alexander Pope, *An Essay on Man*

All philosophers find
Some favorite system to their mind
In every point to make it fit
Will force all nature to submit.

T. L. Peacock, *Headlong Hall*

Systems Theory and Concepts

INTRODUCTION The vast growth in size, complexity, and diversity of operations of the modern organization has made the managerial task exceedingly difficult, but more essential to the success of the enterprise. It is our contention that today's large-scale organization should apply the *systems approach* to cope with the growing complexities and proliferation of operations. It provides a framework within which the manager can integrate his operations more effectively.

In Part 1 we develop the theoretical framework for the systems approach and set the stage for a more detailed and practical discussion of systems application later in the book. Chapter 1 sets forth conceptual foundations and shows how general systems theory has applicability as a framework for scientific investigation and understanding in a wide variety of fields or disciplines. It then traces the transition from a general systems theory to systems concepts for management. Attention is focused on the relationship of the systems approach to organizational subsystems —strategic, coordinative, and operating.

In the next four chapters we discuss the relationship between systems concepts and the primary managerial functions. Chapter 2 looks at *organization,* Chapter 3 covers the *planning* function, Chapter 4 considers the *control* function, and Chapter 5 discusses *information* and *communication* processes. It will be shown that systems concepts are important in the effective performance of these functions.

In Chapter 6 the ideas on the utilization of systems concepts in various managerial functions are drawn together to form an integrated systems approach for organizations. It is in this chapter that we merge general theory with practical applications. Part 1 provides the intellectual stepping-stone to move from a broad, general theory of systems to the practical application of the systems approach in organizations.

CHAPTER 1

Conceptual Foundations for the Systems Approach

The systems approach is a way of thinking about the job of managing. It provides a framework for visualizing internal and external environmental factors as an integrated whole. It allows recognition of the function of subsystems, as well as the complex supra-systems within which organizations must operate. Systems concepts foster a way of thinking which, on the one hand, helps to dissolve some of the complexity and, on the other, helps the manager to recognize the nature of complex problems and thereby to operate within the perceived environment. It is important to recognize the integrated nature of specific systems, including the fact that each system has both inputs and outputs and can be viewed as a self-contained unit. But it is also important to recognize that business systems are a part of larger systems—possibly industrywide, or including several, maybe many, companies and/or industries, or even society as a whole. Further, business systems are in a constant state of change—they are created, operated, revised, and often eliminated.

In this book we shall develop a foundation for management by system. However, before turning to aspects concerned primarily with organizations and their management, it will be necessary to set the stage with certain introductory materials relating to systems in general and concerning an evolving body of knowledge called "general systems theory." This background material will provide the basis for relating systems theory to organizations and for the integration of systems concepts and management.

The discussion in this chapter is centered on the following topics:

> Systems defined
> General systems theory
> Systems theory and organizations
> Systems concepts and management
> The systems approach
> Plan of the book

SYSTEMS DEFINED

A system is *an organized or complex whole; an assemblage or combination of things or parts forming a complex or unitary whole.* It is a "set of interrelated elements."[1] The sequence of terms is significant because the systems approach emphasizes wholeness (set) first, then moves to consideration of parts and subsystems (elements), including interactions (interrelationships) among them and between the parts and the total.

The term *system* covers an extremely broad spectrum of concepts. For example, we have mountain systems, river systems, and the solar system as part of our physical surroundings. The body itself is a complex organism including the skeletal system, the circulatory system, and the nervous system. We come into daily contact with such phenomena as transportation systems, communication systems (telephone, telegraph, etc.), and economic systems.

A science often is described as a systematic body of knowledge; a complete array of essential principles or facts, arranged in a rational dependence or connection; a complex of ideas, principles, laws, forming a coherent whole. Scientists endeavor to develop, organize, and classify material into interconnected disciplines. Sir Isaac Newton set forth what he called the "system of the world." Two relatively well-known works which represent attempts to integrate a large amount of material are Darwin's *The Origin of Species* and Keynes's *General Theory of Employment, Interest, and Money.* Darwin, in his theory of evolution, integrated

---

[1]Russell L. Ackoff, "Towards a System of Systems Concepts," *Management Science,* July 1971, p. 661.

all life into a "system of nature" and indicated how the myriad of living subsystems were interrelated. Keynes, in his general theory of employment, interest, and money, connected many complicated natural and man-made forces which make up an entire economy. Both men had a major impact on man's thinking because they were able to conceptualize interrelationships among complex phenomena and integrate them into a systematic whole. The word *system* connotes plan, method, order, and arrangement. Hence it is no wonder that scientists and researchers have made the term so pervasive.

The antonym of systematic is chaotic. A chaotic situation might be described as one where "everything depends on everything else," but where the connecting system is not understood. Since two major goals of science and research in any subject area are explanation and prediction, such a condition cannot be tolerated. Therefore there is considerable incentive to develop bodies of knowledge that can be organized into a complex whole, within which subparts or subsystems can be interrelated.

There is an obvious hierarchy of suprasystems that can be created; that is, systems, systems of systems, and systems of systems of systems. For example, the universe is a system of heavenly bodies which includes many subsystems of stars called *galaxies.* Within one such galaxy, the Milky Way, there is the solar system, one of many planetary systems. Similarly, an organism is a system of mutually dependent parts each of which might include many subsystems. Human life is composed of microorganisms which form larger systems that are subsystems of the organism as a whole.

While much research has been focused on the analysis of minute segments of knowledge, there has been increasing interest in developing larger frames of reference for synthesizing the results of such research. Thus attention has been focused more and more on overall systems as frames of reference for analytical work in various areas. Eddington describes this process as follows:

> From the point of view of the philosophy of science the conception associated with entropy must I think be ranked as the great contribution of the 19th century to scientific thought. It marked a reaction from the view that everything to which science need pay attention is discovered by microscopic dissection of objects. It provided an alternative standpoint in which the centre of interest is shifted from the entities reached by the customary analysis (atoms, electric potentials, etc.) to qualities possessed by the system as a whole, which cannot be split up and located—a little here and a little bit there. . . .

> We often think that when we have completed our study of *one* we know all about *two,* because "two" is "one and one." We forget that we still have to make a study of "and." Secondary physics is the study of "and"—that is to say, of organization.[2]

The problem of AND is a legitimate one for scientists because detailed knowledge of each element of a compound— hydrogen (H) and oxygen (O), for example—does not ensure understanding of the combination—water (H_2O). But it is also legitimate for scientists to concentrate on individual parts in pushing back the frontiers of knowledge, leaving to others the task of integrating results. For managers, however, the problem of AND is central. The essence of management is coordination; it is our contention that a similar synthesizing process can be useful for managers. Whereas managers have often focused attention on particular specialized areas, they may lose sight of the overall objectives of the business and the role of their particular business in even larger systems. These individuals can do a better job of carrying out their own responsibilities if they are aware of the "big picture." It is the familiar problem of not being able to see the forest for the trees.

This disregard of the total system may be deliberate in the sense that departmental or subsystem managers are inclined to enhance their own performance at the expense of the total operation. However, it is more likely that such disregard is unintentional, resulting from the inability of decision makers in isolated segments to comprehend the interaction of their decisions with other segments of the organization. The focus of the systems approach is on providing a better picture of the network of subsystems and interrelated parts which go together to form a complex whole.

GENERAL SYSTEMS THEORY[3]

General systems theory is concerned with developing a systematic, theoretical framework for describing general relationships of the empirical world. Buckley describes its role as follows:

[2]Sir Arthur Eddington, *The Nature of the Physical World,* University of Michigan Press, Ann Arbor, Mich., 1958, pp. 103–104.
[3]Four sources provide the basis for this section: Ludwig von Bertalanffy, *General System Theory,* George Braziller, Inc., New York, 1968; Kenneth Boulding, "General Systems Theory: The Skeleton of Science," *Management Science,* April 1956, pp. 197–208; James G. Miller, "Living Systems: Basic Concepts," *Behavioral Science,* July 1965, pp. 193–237; and Walter Buckley (ed.), *Modern Systems Research for the Behavioral Scientist,* Aldine Publishing Company, Chicago, 1968.

> A whole which functions as a whole by virtue of the interdependence of its parts is called a *system,* and the method which aims at discovering how this is brought about in the widest variety of systems has been called general system theory. General system theory seeks to classify systems by the way their components are *organized* (interrelated) and to derive the "laws," or typical patterns of behavior, for the different classes of systems singled out by the taxonomy.[4]

There are a number of potential applications for such a framework. For example, there are existing similarities in research methods and the categorization of knowledge in various disciplines. Models can be developed which are applicable to many systems, whether physical, biological, behavioral, or social. An ultimate but distant goal will be a framework (or system of systems of systems) which will tie all disciplines together in a meaningful relationship.

One of the most important indications of the need for a general systems theory is the problem of communication between the various disciplines. Although there is similarity between general methods of approach—the scientific method—the results of research efforts are not often communicated across discipline boundaries. Hence conceptualizing and hypothesizing done in one area seldom carries over into other areas where it could conceivably point the way toward a significant breakthrough. Specialists do not seem to communicate with one another. For example:

> Hence physicists only talk to physicists, economists to economists —worse still, nuclear physicists talk only to nuclear physicists and econometricians to econometricians. One wonders sometimes if science will not grind to a stop in an assemblage of walled-in hermits, each mumbling to himself words in a private language that only he can understand.[5]

Of course, the conflict of ideas and difficulties of communication are even greater between the various cultures—the scientific, the social sciences, and the humanistic. This conflict has been intensified during the twentieth century.[6]

On the brighter side there has been some development of interdisciplinary studies. Areas such as social psychology, biochemistry, astrophysics, social anthropology, economic psychology, and economic sociology have been developed in order to emphasize the interrelationships of previously isolated dis-

[4]Buckley, op. cit., p. xvii.
[5]Boulding, op. cit., p. 198.
[6]C. P. Snow, *The Two Cultures and the Scientific Revolution,* Cambridge University Press, London, 1959.

ciplines. More recently, areas of study and research have been developed which call on numerous subfields. For example, cybernetics, the science of communication and control, calls on electrical engineering, neurophysiology, physics, biology, and other fields. Operations research is often pointed to as a multidisciplinary approach to problem solving. Information theory is another discipline which calls on numerous subfields. Organization theory embraces economics, sociology, engineering, psychology, physiology, and anthropology. Problem solving and decision making are becoming focal points for study and research, drawing on numerous fields. Unfortunately the "new" cross-disciplines often create a jargon or "in" language that compounds the communication problem further.

With all these examples of interdisciplinary approaches, it is easy to recognize a surge of interest in larger-scale, systematic bodies of knowledge. However, this trend calls for the development of an overall framework within which the various subparts can be integrated. In order that the *interdisciplinary* movement may not degenerate into *undisciplined* approaches, it is important that some structure be developed to integrate the various separate disciplines while retaining the type of discipline which distinguishes them. One approach to providing an overall framework (general systems theory) would be to pick out phenomena common to many different disciplines and to develop general models which would include such phenomena. A second approach would include the structuring of a hierarchy of levels of complexity for the basic units of behavior in the various empirical fields. It would also involve development of a level of abstraction to represent each stage.

We shall explore the second approach, a hierarchy of levels, in more detail since it can lead toward a system of systems which has application in most businesses and other organizations. The reader can undoubtedly call to mind examples of familiar systems at each level of the following model.

1. The first level is that of static structure. It might be called the level of *frameworks*. This is the geography and anatomy of the universe. . . . The accurate description of these frameworks is the beginning of organized theoretical knowledge in almost any field, for without accuracy in this description of static relationships no accurate functional or dynamic theory is possible.
2. The next level of systematic analysis is that of the simple dynamic system with predetermined, necessary motions. This might be called the level of *clockworks*. The solar system itself

is of course the great clock of the universe from man's point of view, and the deliciously exact predictions of the astronomers are a testimony to the excellence of the clock which they study. . . . The greater part of the theoretical structure of physics, chemistry, and even of economics falls into this category.

3. The next level is that of the control mechanism or cybernetic system, which might be nicknamed the level of the *thermostat*. This differs from the simple stable equilibrium system mainly in the fact that the transmission and interpretation of information is an essential part of the system. . . . The homeostasis model, which is of such importance in physiology, is an example of a cybernetic mechanism, and such mechanisms exist through the whole empirical world of the biologist and the social scientist.

4. The fourth level is that of the "open system," or self-maintaining structure. This is the level at which life begins to differentiate itself from not-life: it might be called the level of the *cell.*

5. The fifth level might be called the genetic-societal level; it is typified by the *plant,* and it dominates the empirical world of the botanists.

6. As we move upward from the plant world towards the animal kingdom we gradually pass over into a new level, the "animal" level, characterized by increased mobility, teleological behavior, and self-awareness. Here we have the development of specialized information-receptors (eyes, ears, etc.) leading to an enormous increase in intake of information; we also have a great development of nervous systems, leading ultimately to the brain, as an organizer of the information intake into a knowledge structure or "image." Increasingly as we ascend the scale of animal life, behavior is response not to a specific stimulus but to an "image" or knowledge structure or view of the environment as a whole. . . . The difficulties in the prediction of the behavior of these systems arises largely because of this intervention of the image between the stimulus and the response.

7. The next level is the "human" level, that is, of the individual human being considered as a system. In addition to all, or nearly all, of the characteristics of animal systems man possesses self-consciousness, which is something different from mere awareness. His image, besides being much more complex than that even of the higher animals, has a self-reflective quality—he not only knows, but knows that he knows. This property is probably bound up with the phenomenon of language and symbolism. It is the capacity for speech—the ability to produce, absorb, and interpret *symbols,* as opposed to mere signs like the warning cry of an animal—which most clearly marks man off from his humbler brethren.

8. Because of the vital importance for the individual man of symbolic images in behavior based on them it is not easy to separate

clearly the level of the individual human organism from the next level, that of social organizations. . . . Nevertheless it is convenient for some purposes to distinguish the individual human as a system from the social systems which surround him, and in this sense social organizations may be said to constitute another level of organization. . . . At this level we must concern ourselves with the content and meaning of messages, the nature and dimensions of value systems, the transcription of images into historical record, the subtle symbolizations of art, music, and poetry, and the complex gamut of human emotion.

9. To complete the structure of systems we should add a final turret for transcendental systems, even if we may be accused at this point of having built Babel to the clouds. There are however the ultimates and absolutes and the inescapables and unknowables, and they also exhibit systematic structure and relationship. It will be a sad day for man when nobody is allowed to ask questions that do not have any answers.[7]

Obviously, the first level is most pervasive. Descriptions of static structures are widespread. However, this descriptive cataloguing is helpful in providing a framework for additional analysis and synthesis. Dynamic "clockwork" systems, where prediction is a strong element, are evident in the classical natural sciences such as physics and astronomy; yet even here there are important gaps. Adequate theoretical models are not apparent at higher levels. However, in recent years closed-loop cybernetic, or "thermostat," systems have received increasing attention. At the same time, work is progressing on open-loop systems with self-maintaining structures and reproduction facilities. Beyond the fourth level we hardly have a beginning of theory, and yet system description via computer models may foster progress even at these levels in the complex of general systems theory.

Regardless of the degree of progress at any particular level in the above scheme, the important point is the concept of a general systems theory. Clearly, the spectrum, or hierarchy, of systems varies over a considerable range. However, since systems concepts represent a point of view rather than a particular method or content area, progress can be made as research proceeds in various specialized areas but within an overall system context. General systems theory provides for scientists at large a useful framework within which to carry out specialized activity. It

[7]Boulding, op. cit., pp. 202–205.

allows researchers to relate findings and compare concepts with similar findings and concepts in other disciplines.[8]

Systems theory has had significant impact within many basic disciplines because it provides a useful framework for analyzing and understanding complex, dynamic phenomena. Emphasis is on wholism and interactions which typically reverberate throughout living systems. This approach is particularly useful for studying social organizations.

> The development and contagion of the modern systems perspective can be traced in part to the concern of several disciplines to treat their subject matter—whether the organism, the species, or the social group—as a whole, an entity in its own right, with unique properties understandable only in terms of the whole, especially in the face of a more traditional reductionistic or mechanistic focus on the separate parts and simplistic notions of how these parts fit together.[9]

The term *functionalism* has been used to describe the analysis of social and cultural life from the standpoint of wholes or systems. This point of view has been manifest in all the social sciences "from psychology through sociology, political science, economics, and anthropology to geography, jurisprudence and linguistics."[10] Although there are several connotations of the word *functionalism*, its most important aspect is the emphasis upon systems of relationships and the integration of parts and subsystems into a whole.[11] General systems theory and the functionalistic point of view (including dynamic equilibrium concepts from economics) offer a theoretical framework for the study of organizations.

SYSTEMS THEORY AND ORGANIZATIONS

An important aspect of general systems theory is the distinction between closed and open systems. An example of an open system is a living organism which is not a conglomeration of separate elements but a definite system, possessing organization and wholeness. An organism is an open system which maintains itself

[8]Joseph D. McGrath, Peter G. Nordlie, and W. S. Vaughn, Jr., *A Systematic Framework for Comparison of System Research Methods,* Human Sciences Research, Inc., Arlington, Va., November 1959, p. 2.
[9]Buckley, op. cit., p. xxiii.
[10]Don Martindale, *Functionalism in the Social Sciences,* Monograph 5, American Academy of Political and Social Science, February 1965, pp. viii–ix.
[11]Robert K. Merton discusses various connotations of the word *function* in *Social Theory and Social Structure,* The Free Press of Glencoe, New York, 1957, pp. 20–22.

while the matter and energy which enter it keep changing. The organism is influenced by, and influences, its environment and reaches a state of dynamic equilibrium in this environment.[12] Such a description of a system adequately fits the typical social organization. For example, the business organization is a man-made system which has a dynamic interplay with its environment—customers, competitors, labor organizations, suppliers, government, and many other agencies. Furthermore, the business organization is a system of interrelated parts working in conjunction with each other in order to accomplish a number of goals, both those of the organization and those of individual participants.

At times scholars in the field of management have depicted organizations as smoothly running machines. This would coincide with Boulding's second level in the general systems theory, that of "clockwork" systems. Organizations were described as highly mechanistic and predictable, and the various resources available—men, material, and machines—were manipulated in just that way.

Another common analogy was the comparison of the organization to the human body, with the skeletal and muscle systems representing the operating line elements and the circulatory system as a necessary staff function. The nervous system stood for the communication system. The brain symbolized top-level management, or the executive committee. In this sense an organization was represented as a self-maintaining structure, one which could reproduce. Such an analysis hints at the type of framework which would be useful as a systems theory for business —one which is developed as a system of systems and which can focus attention at the proper points in the organization for rational decision making, from the standpoint both of the individual and of the organization.

The scientific management movement utilized the concept of a man-machine system but concentrated primarily at the shop level. The so-called "efficiency experts" attempted to establish procedures covering the work situation and providing an opportunity for all those involved to benefit—employees, managers, and owners. The human relationists, the movement stemming from the Hawthorne–Western Electric studies, shifted some of the focus away from the man-machine system per se to motivation and interrelationships among individuals in the organization.

[12]A closed system, by definition, has no interaction with its environment. Rather than using a dichotomy of open-closed, it is more useful to think of systems in terms of the degree to which they are open (or closed).

Recognition of the effect of interpersonal relationships, human behavior, and small groups resulted in a relatively widespread reevaluation of managerial approaches and techniques.

The concept of the business enterprise as a social system also has received considerable attention in recent years. The social-system school looks upon management as a system of cultural interrelationships. The concept of a social system draws heavily on sociology and involves recognition of such elements as formal and informal organization within a total integrated system. Moreover, the organization or enterprise is subject to external pressure from the cultural environment. In effect, the enterprise system is recognized as a part of a larger environmental system.

Over the years, mathematics has been applied to a variety of business problems, primarily internal. Since World War II, operations-research techniques have been applied to large, complex systems of variables. They have been helpful in shop scheduling, and other similar problems. Queuing models have been developed for a wide variety of traffic- and service-type situations where it is necessary to program the optimum number of "servers" for the expected "customer" flow. Operations research techniques have been applied to the solution of many complex problems involving a large number of variables. However, by their very nature, these techniques must structure the analysis by quantifying system elements and often narrowing and isolating the focus of attention. This process of abstraction frequently simplifies the problem and takes it out of the real world. The solution of the problem may not be applicable in the actual situation because it cannot be integrated.

Simple models of maximizing behavior no longer suffice in analyzing business organizations. The relatively mechanical models apparent in the "scientific management" era gave way to theories represented by the "human relations" movement. Emphasis has developed around "decision making" as a primary focus of attention, relating communication systems, organization structure, questions of growth, and conditions of uncertainty. This approach recognizes the more complex models of administrative behavior and should lead to more encompassing systems that will provide the framework within which to fit the results of specialized investigations of analysts.

The aim of systems theory for organizations is to facilitate better understanding in a complex environment; that is, if the system within which managers make decisions can be provided as a more explicit framework, then such decision making should be easier to handle. But what are the elements of this systems theory which can be used as a framework for integrated decision making? Will it require wholesale change on the part of organization structure and administrative behavior? Or can it be fit into existing situations? In general, the new concepts can be applied to existing situations. Organizations will remain recognizable. Simon makes this point when he says:

1. Organizations will still be constructed in three layers; an underlying *system* of physical production and distribution processes, a layer of programmed (and probably largely automated) decision processes for governing the routine day-to-day operation of the physical *system,* and a layer of nonprogrammed decision processes (carried out in a man-machine system) for monitoring the first-level processes, redesigning them, and changing parameter values.
2. Organizations will be hierarchical in form. The organization will be divided into major subparts, each of these into parts, and so on, in familiar forms of departmentalization. The exact basis for drawing departmental lines may change somewhat. Product divisions may become even more important than they are today, while the sharp lines of demarcation among purchasing, manufacturing, engineering, and sales are likely to fade.[13]

We agree essentially with this picture of the future. However, we want to emphasize the notion of systems as set forth in several layers. This connotes basic horizontal organization cutting across typical departmental lines. Thus the systems that are likely to be emphasized in the future will develop from tasks, projects, or programs, and authority will be vested in managers whose influence will cut across traditional departmental lines. The focus of attention is likely to turn more and more to patterns of material, energy, and information flow throughout organizations. Identifying information-decision systems will provide a useful means of analysis and synthesis.

SYSTEMS CONCEPTS AND MANAGEMENT

Management is the primary force within organizations which coordinates the activities of the subsystems and relates them to the environment. Management as an institution is relatively new in our society, stemming primarily from the growth in size and complexity of business since the industrial revolution. As Drucker says:

[13]Herbert A. Simon, *The New Science of Management Decision,* Harper & Row, Inc., New York, 1960, pp. 49–50 (italics by authors).

The emergence of management as an essential, a distinct and a leading institution is a pivotal event in social history. Rarely, if ever, has a new basic institution, a new leading group, emerged as fast as has management since the turn of this century. Rarely in human history has a new institution proven indispensable so quickly; and even less often has a new institution arrived with so little opposition, so little disturbance, so little controversy. . . . Management, which is the organ of society specifically charged with making resources productive, that is, with the responsibility for organized economic advance, therefore reflects the basic spirit of the modern age. It is in fact indispensable—and this explains why, once begotten, it grew so fast and with so little opposition.[14]

Managers are needed to convert the disorganized resources of men, machines, and money into a useful and effective enterprise. Essentially, management is the process whereby these unrelated resources are integrated into a total *system for objective accomplishment.* A manager gets things done by working with people and other resources in order to accomplish the objectives of the system. He coordinates and integrates the activities and work of others. To accomplish this task the manager should be aware of the danger of isolating problems. He should recognize relationships and the need to synthesize. According to Herbst:

In dealing with practical problems, one cannot tease out separate psychological, economic, or technological aspects, for the problem nearly always involves working with a total, integrated organizational unit. For instance, in studying the functioning of a work group, we cannot isolate the observed structure of interaction relationships from the technological structure which determines the nature of the task to be done and the types of relationship required for task performance. Nor can we disregard the economic aspects of behaviour either from the point of view of individual group members or in relation to the conditions for group survival. There is a need for the development of interstitial disciplines, among which social psychology, sociotechnical analysis, and socioeconomic theory are of special interest, since they demonstrate different ways in which bridging or unifying disciplines can be constructed and they provide the natural growing-points for the development of a unified approach.[15]

One approach to the study of management focuses attention on the fundamental administrative processes—planning, or-

---

[14]Peter F. Drucker, *The Practice of Management,* Harper & Row, Inc., New York, 1954, pp. 3–4.
[15]P. G. Herbst, "Problems of Theory and Method in the Integration of the Behavioural Sciences," *Human Relations,* November 1965, pp. 353–354.

ganizing, and controlling—which are essential if an organization is to meet its primary goals and objectives.[16] These basic managerial processes are required for any type of organization—business, government, education, social—and other activities where human and physical resources are combined to meet certain objectives. Furthermore, these processes are necessary regardless of the specialized area of management—production, distribution, finance, and facilitating activities.

Another way to study management involves identification of basic organizational subsystems—strategic, coordinative, and operative—and the primary managerial tasks for each of them (see Figure 1–1).[17] In general, these subsystems coincide with the layers described by Simon, and the model can apply to an organization of any size. The smaller the organization the more likely that the various aspects of the managerial task will be carried out by one individual. Obviously, for a proprietorship, the owner-manager is involved in all the activities set forth in Figure 1–1. He must define his task in relation to his environment, plan his activities over both the short run and the long run, and then carry them out in order to achieve his objectives.

For large, complex organizations it is more likely that these subsystems are separable and identifiable. Top management is involved in relating the organization to its environment—identifying a niche which it must fill in order to survive and grow. Strategy formulation also involves designing comprehensive systems and plans. Systems concepts are useful in conceptualizing the long-run nature of the organization and assembling the appropriate resources for achieving desired goals. The environmental system is relatively open; general processes are typically nonprogrammable; and the viewpoint is essentially one of satisficing—finding workable solutions to complex, ill-structured, novel problems. Decision making is largely judgmental and cogitative—reasoned evaluation of all relevant inputs to the problem-solving process.

In the operating subsystem the primary task is accomplish-

---

[16]See, for example, Harold F. Smiddy and Lionel Naum, "Evolution of a 'Science of Managing' in America," *Management Science,* October, 1954, pp. 1–31, and Harold Koontz (ed.), *Toward a Unified Theory of Management,* McGraw-Hill Book Company, New York, 1964.

[17]See also Thomas A. Petit, "A Behavioral Theory of Management," *Academy of Management Journal,* December 1967, pp. 341–350; James D. Thompson, *Organizations in Action,* McGraw-Hill Book Company, New York, 1967; Talcott Parsons, *Structure and Process in Modern Societies,* The Free Press of Glencoe, New York, 1960, pp. 60–96.

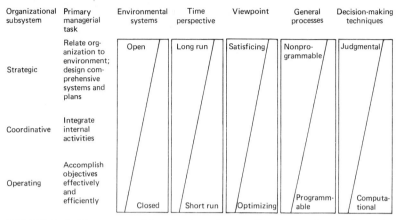

Organizational subsystem	Primary managerial task	Environmental systems	Time perspective	Viewpoint	General processes	Decision-making techniques
Strategic	Relate organization to environment; design comprehensive systems and plans	Open	Long run	Satisficing	Nonprogrammable	Judgmental
Coordinative	Integrate internal activities					
Operating	Accomplish objectives effectively and efficiently	Closed	Short run	Optimizing	Programmable	Computational

FIGURE 1-1. The managerial task: strategic, coordinative, and operating subsystems.

ing stated objectives effectively and efficiently.[18] It is here that the organization "does its thing"—producing bicycles or toothpaste, providing health care or fire protection. The environmental system is relatively closed and general processes can be programmed; e.g., standard operating procedures or computer programs. Systems concepts provide a framework for a short-run, optimizing outlook and computational decision making via quantitative techniques.

In the coordinative subsystem—ranging between the strategic and operating activities—the primary concern is integrating internal activities which have been specialized by function and/or level. Middle management is involved in translating comprehensive plans into operational plans and procedures. It is involved in interpreting the results of the operating system and in focusing existing resources in appropriate directions. Systems concepts facilitate a managerial approach which can be used to coordinate several functions, projects, or programs within an overall organization. A pragmatic point of view is essential in integrating short- and long-run considerations. Compromise is often necessary in decision making at this level in order to achieve a practical or utilitarian outcome via analysis and synthesis of problems.

The terms used in the various dimensions shown in Figure 1-1 are illustrative of general tendencies, i.e., most likely activities

---

[18]Effectiveness = degree of objective accomplishment. Efficiency = ratio of resource input to output.

or approaches. It is not to say that judgment is not important in the operating subsystem or that computational techniques are never used in developing comprehensive plans. However, the terms do provide the basic flavor for the managerial task in three relatively distinct organizational subsystems.

This approach is complementary to the process model of management. While we will refer to Figure 1–1 throughout the book, we will, in the remainder of Part 1, relate systems concepts to the managerial functions of organization, planning, and controlling. It is our view that the organization represents the system to be managed. This task is accomplished via managers planning and controlling organizational endeavor (toward objective accomplishment) by means of an information-decision system.

THE SYSTEMS APPROACH

The term *systems approach* requires clarification in order to facilitate consistency in usage. Our model is set forth in Figure 1–2. The systems approach has a broad connotation covering several fairly distinct divisions of current usage. Literally, the term *approach* means "to bring to bear" or "to deal with."

The underlying body of knowledge is general systems theory which has relevance for a wide variety of scientific endeavors and

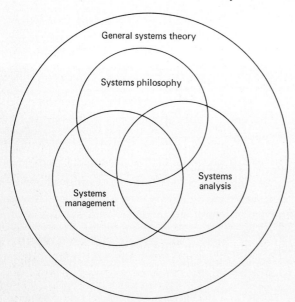

FIGURE 1–2. The systems approach.

practical applications. The systems approach involves applying relevant concepts from general systems theory in order to facilitate the understanding of organization theory and management practice.

In the broadest or most general sense we have *systems philosophy*. This refers to "a way of thinking" about phenomena in terms of wholes—including parts, components, or subsystems and with emphasis on their interrelationships. This aspect of the systems approach can be readily applied to the managerial task of strategy formulation.

Systems analysis refers to a method or technique used in problem solving or decision making. It is closely related to the scientific method. It involves awareness of a problem, identification of relevant variables, analysis and synthesis of the various factors, and determination of an optimal (at least better) solution or program of action. Although the term *systems analysis* has tended to connote quantitative techniques and computational problem solving in relatively closed systems, the general model is quite applicable to problem solving where quantification is difficult or impossible. The same "approach" can be useful in all organizational subsystems.

Systems management involves the application of systems theory to managing organizational systems or subsystems. It can refer to management of a particular function or to projects or programs within a larger organization. An important point is that systems theory is a vital ingredient in the managerial process. It involves recognizing a general model of input-transformation-output with identifiable flows of material, energy, and information. It also emphasizes the interrelationships among subsystems as well as the suprasystem to which a function, project, or organization belongs.

Thus the systems approach is at once (1) a way of thinking, (2) a method or technique of analysis, and (3) a managerial style. These distinctions will become more clear as we proceed through the several parts of the book.

What does the systems approach offer to students of management and/or to practicing executives? Is it a panacea for solving problems that will replace scientific management, human relations, management by objective, operations research, and many other approaches to, or techniques of, management? Perhaps a word of caution is needed at this stage. Anyone looking for "cookbook" techniques will be disappointed. In this book we do not develop "ten easy steps" to success in management. Such approaches, while seemingly applicable and easy to grasp, are usually short-sighted and superficial. Fundamental ideas, such as systems concepts, are more difficult to comprehend, and yet they present an opportunity for a large-scale payoff. The systems approach can help the manager cope with complex situations which include many parts and interacting subsystems. It provides a useful analytical framework. We agree with Churchman who states:

> Well, then, what is the systems approach? On the one hand, we must recognize it to be the most critical problem we face today, the understanding of the systems in which we live. On the other hand, however, we must admit that the problem—the appropriate approach to systems—is not solved, but this is a very mild way of putting the matter. This is not an unsolved problem in the sense in which certain famous mathematical problems are unsolved. It's not as though we can expect that next year or a decade from now someone will find the correct systems approach and all deception will disappear. This, in my opinion, is not in the nature of systems. What is in the nature of systems is a continuing perception and deception, a continuing re-viewing of the world, of the whole system, and of its components. The essence of the systems approach, therefore, is confusion as well as enlightenment. The two are inseparable aspects of human living.[19]

Managers should have a tolerance for ambiguity—yet not be wishy-washy. Managers should be knowledgeable about organization theory—yet not apply "laws" or "principles" regardless of specific conditions. The body of knowledge is still tentative in large measure. This suggests a contingency point of view and situational management. If certain conditions prevail, then the manager can select an appropriate action which has a reasonable probability of success. The systems approach fosters this type of managerial behavior—a coping style that recognizes complex interrelationships and adapts accordingly.

PLAN OF THE BOOK

Part 1, "Systems Theory and Concepts," is related to the primary activities of the managerial process—organizing, planning, and controlling. Also included is a chapter on communication and information flow, the means by which managers coordinate (plan and control) organizational endeavor. In this part, we show in

---

[19]C. West Churchman, *The Systems Approach,* Dell Publishing Co., Inc., New York, 1968, pp. 230–231.

detail how each of the primary managerial functions can be related to systems concepts. Moreover, we show how, in each instance, there has been an evolution within each of these activities toward systems thinking.

Another reason for developing the relationship between systems theory and the primary managerial functions in Part 1 is to emphasize that the familiar managerial process will be essentially the same in the future, even with significantly increased cognizance of systems concepts. As indicated earlier, management via systems concepts is primarily "a way of thinking." It provides a framework within which these basic managerial functions can be carried out more effectively.

After these functions are discussed separately, they will be integrated in terms of our model of the systems approach—systems philosophy, systems management, and systems analysis. The material in Chapter 6 summarizes Part 1 and sets forth a definite framework or model within which the managerial functions can be applied via "a way of thinking." It sets the stage for Parts 2 and 3 which relate to the other two parts of our model of the systems approach—systems analysis and systems management.

In Part 2, "Design and Analysis," we discuss the various means of translating concepts into operational systems. First, the fundamentals of design, evaluation, and redesign are considered. Emphasis is placed on systems design as a way of maintaining organizational viability within a dynamic environment. The potential usefulness of quantitative techniques will be examined. Topics such as model building, quantification, and simulation are important considerations in analyzing and designing systems. Network analysis and various techniques of critical-path scheduling are discussed as methods to facilitate a coordination of large-scale, complex project systems.

The impact of change resulting from analysis and design activity will be discussed, with particular reference to people involved in such systems. An important thread running through Part 2 is the evaluation of the appropriateness of various analytical techniques in implementing systems theory and concepts.

Once the theoretical concepts have been developed and we have explored the ramifications of systems analysis and design, we turn to, Part 3, "Managerial Applications." The various chapters in this part are designed to show the pervasiveness of systems concepts in current operations. For example, distribution systems are discussed in detail, emphasizing material flow from raw material sources to final consumer. Producing systems will also be considered, including discussions of automation in general and numerical control in particular. Program management will be explored in depth, as will the concept of planning-programming-budgeting systems (PPBS). Data processing systems will be discussed in terms of their relationship to the above-mentioned applications. A key idea is that information feedback provides management with the means to coordinate activities, whether they be distribution, producing, or program systems. The various examples in Part 3 should give the reader a better "feel" for systems management as carried out within the framework established in Parts 1 and 2.

Short cases at the end of each chapter in Parts 2 and 3 provide additional opportunity for the reader to apply the concepts previously developed. Descriptions of real situations illustrate both the promise and the problems involved in systems analysis and design when applied to real situations—distribution, production, program management, and data processing.

Part 4 contains a look to the future, indicating the role of systems theory and concepts in the coming decades. It summarizes to some extent the material throughout the book. Then, using this summary as a springboard, we conjecture about the future as it is related to the systems approach.

QUESTIONS

1. Define systems. Describe systems that fit each level of Boulding's hierarchy.
2. Why is the term *system* popular with scientists?
3. Are systems concepts as useful to managers as they are to scientists? Why or why not?
4. Differentiate between open and closed systems. Which model is more appropriate for business and for government organizations? Why?
5. Does utilization of systems concepts supplant the process or functional approach to management? Why or why not?
6. For an organization with which you are familiar, analyze its activities by using the framework presented in Figure 1–1. Describe how the managerial task is carried out in each of the three organizational subsystems.
7. Illustrate the application of the systems approach by referring to a specific organization and citing examples.
8. Does utilization of the systems approach simplify the managerial task? Why or why not?

CHAPTER 2

Organization and Systems Concepts

General systems theory implies an interconnected complex of functionally related components or parts. As indicated in Chapter 1, many types of purely mechanistic systems are of the structured, closed variety. However, the business organization and other institutions of human interrelationships are open social systems. Organizations are contrived or man-made systems. It is only through the process of *organizing* that the vast complex of men, machines, materials, monies, and other resources are combined into an effective, efficient, and viable enterprise. The primary cohesiveness is applied by man himself to systematize his social organizations.

In recent years the study of organization theory has drawn heavily upon systems concepts and also has contributed to a better understanding of systems theory. In modern organization theory, systems concepts provide a basis for integration of the various diverse viewpoints. The organization is an open, sociotechnical system composed of a number of subsystems and in continuing interaction with its environmental suprasystem. The systems approach discounts simplistic statements of "principles of organization" and reflects the search for patterns of relationships, configurations within and among subsystems, and a contingency view. The following topics will be discussed:

WHAT IS AN ORGANIZATION?

Since the words *organization* and *system* have similar connotations, it is important to understand what is meant by the term *organization*. One of the difficulties in definition is that organizations are not concrete, physical entities; an organization may have a number of properties both physical and abstract. United States Steel Corporation has many physical assets but it also has many relational and social aspects which cannot be seen. An additional complexity in definition is caused by the many types of organizations—ranging from families to informal work groups, to formal systems such as the Mayo Clinic, General Electric Company, the Teamsters Union, the U.S. Department of Health, Education, and Welfare, and the United Nations. It is useful to think of a continuum ranging from individual activity at one end to highly formalized organizations at the other with a wide variety of social organizations in between. There are, however, common elements. Organizations are (1) *goal-oriented,* people with a purpose; (2) *psychosocial systems,* people working in groups; (3) *technical systems,* people using knowledge and techniques; and (4) *an integration of structured activities,* people coordinating their efforts.

In this chapter we shall consider primarily the more formalized, large-scale organizations which Pfiffner and Sherwood define as follows:

> Organization is the pattern of ways in which large numbers of people, too many to have intimate face-to-face contact with all others, and engaged in a complexity of tasks, relate themselves to each other in the conscious, systematic establishment and accomplishment of mutually agreed purposes.[1]

This definition emphasizes the systematic interrelationship between people working together to accomplish certain purposes.

[1]John M. Pfiffner and Frank P. Sherwood, *Administrative Organization,* Prentice-Hall, Inc., Englewood Cliffs, N.J., 1960, p. 30.

The social psychologist E. Wight Bakke emphasizes even more strongly the importance of thinking of human organizations in their social context, with the following definition:

> A social organization is a continuing system of differentiated and coordinated human activities utilizing, transforming, and welding together a specific set of human, material, capital, ideational and natural resources into a unique, problem-solving whole whose function is to satisfy particular human needs in interaction with other systems of human activities and resources in its particular environment.[2]

The similarity between this definition of the social, or human, organization and the definition of the open system is quite evident. Organizational behavior in contrast to individual behavior is highly structured, more predictable, and stable. It is only by focusing individual behavior on the accomplishment of overall goals that the organization is able to accomplish its objectives.

As there is a biological analogy for the systems concept, so there is a similar analogy between organization and biology. In many ways the individual organization in our society can be differentiated as a sociological unit comparable to the existence of individual organisms in biology. March and Simon have drawn the comparison as follows:

> Organizations are assemblages of interacting human beings and they are the largest assemblages in our society that have anything resembling a central coordinative system. Let us grant that these coordinative systems are not developed nearly to the extent of the central nervous system in higher biological organisms—that organizations are more earthworm than ape. Nevertheless, the high specificity of structure and coordination within organizations—as contrasted with the diffuse and variable relations *among* organizations and among unorganized individuals—marks off the individual organization as a sociological unit comparable in significance to the individual organism in biology.[3]

This analogy introduces consideration of two conflicting views about the nature of organizations. One considers the organization from a *rational* or goal approach. This view is basic to the traditional literature of management and considers the or-

[2]E. Wight Bakke in Mason Haire (ed.), *Modern Organization Theory,* John Wiley & Sons, Inc., New York, 1959, p. 50.
[3]James G. March and Herbert A. Simon, *Organizations,* John Wiley & Sons, Inc., New York, 1958, p. 4.

ganization as a rational means to accomplish known goals. It is mechanistic, with each functional part of the organization perfectly integrated so as to achieve overall goals most efficiently. On the other hand, the *natural systems* approach focuses on an organization's properties, processes, and adaptive mechanisms as a dynamic, operational unit. It is basically an open model within which the organization is operating with varying degrees of uncertainty and must develop means of adapting to its changing environment. Much of the current literature on organizations utilizes the natural systems approach as a basis of analysis.[4]

We are not satisfied completely with either of these approaches but see elements in each that are useful. In our view the organization is an adaptive, social system striving for rationality in its environment. We agree with Thompson, who says, "We will conceive of complex organizations as open systems, hence indeterminate and faced with uncertainty, but at the same time as subject to criteria of rationality and hence needing determinateness and certainty."[5]

Interdisciplinary Nature of Organization Theory

Over the past several decades interest in the study of organizations and organizational behavior has become a focal point for interdisciplinary research. Increasingly, emphasis has been placed on the study of organization as a scientific field. Because this field is relatively new, there is no single well-defined community of scholars. Researchers working in such diverse fields as biology, mathematics, animal psychology, logic, and philosophy have made indirect contributions to organization theory. Other fields that have contributed more directly are sociology, anthropology, social psychology, psychology, political science, and history, as well as fields related to business administration, such as general administrative theory, human relations, operations research and management science, and industrial sociology.[6]

[4]For discussions of the natural systems approach see Amitai Etzioni, "Two Approaches to Organizational Analysis," *Administrative Science Quarterly*, September 1960, pp. 257–278; and James D. Thompson, *Organizations in Action*, McGraw-Hill Book Company, New York, 1967, pp. 3–13.
[5]*Ibid.*, p. 10.
[6]In an interesting book relating social-science research to business, Haire points out the various fields that are cooperating in developing or showing an interest in organization theory as follows: "In many ways, the interest in organization theory is a particularly apt example of the interdisciplinary focus of many of the social sciences. It broadens part of the economist's traditional theory of the firm. For the

EVOLUTION OF HUMAN SOCIAL ORGANIZATIONS

The cultural anthropologist often takes as his initial frame of reference the characteristics of family relationships within different cultures. Certainly the family represents man's earliest social organization. In every society the family is a basis for a cooperative system for the accomplishment of certain objectives.

From this earliest form of social organization, the family, evolved the tribe, village, larger political states, nations, and various other types of social integration. Each of these separate sociocultural systems has its own modes, behavioral norms, hierarchical relationships, and generally some differentiation or specialization of skills and labor.

Moving to more current consideration of social organizations, we find that a major distinction is made between the informal, small, face-to-face group and the more complex social institution, the large-scale business or political, labor, or other organization. Informal social groups have a dominant role in any culture. Moreover they have an important bearing on the study of large organizations. The importance of these small, informal groups within the larger organizational system was indicated in the famous Hawthorne-Western Electric studies. These studies suggested that worker output and performance were as strongly influenced by the norms, standards, and rewards of the informal work groups as they were of the more highly structured formal organization. The large, complex organization is built upon the foundation of a number of more informal interrelated group activities. Here again, the overall system—the business organization—is a composite resulting from the interaction of a number of subsystems.

Growth of Large, Complex Organizations

Through nearly all man's history, his social institutions were primarily on an informal face-to-face basis. Up through medieval times, the feudal system provided the primarily large-scale social

---

student of business, narrowly considered, there are customary problems of control and administration. The sociologist turns to status, roles, and the informal structure, as well as to the microcosmos itself. Political scientists join several other groups in the interest in power and authority in hierarchical structure, and in the institutional forms of governing structures. Social psychologists apply their concepts about group structures and communication nets." Mason Haire, "Psychology and the Study of Business: Joint Behavioral Sciences," in *Social Science Research on Business: Product and Potential,* Columbia University Press, New York, 1959, pp. 71–72.

system to which the individual belonged. Within the past several centuries, the growing importance of large groups or organizations has been one of the most pervasive phenomena. The industrial revolution, with its demand for concentration of resources and its greater scale, fostered large economic organizations. Modern governments are typically massive systems organized under the bureaucratic form. Man's social organizations have evolved toward larger-scale, complex, more diversified systems. Arthur Stinchcombe states:

> It is common knowledge that "modern" societies carry on much more of their life in special-purpose organizations than do "traditional" societies. . . . Any one of the numerous ways of dividing societies into "modern" and "traditional" gives the same result: wealthier societies, more literate societies, more urban societies, societies using more energy per capita, all carry on more of their life in special-purpose organizations, while poor, or illiterate, or rural, or technically backward societies use more functionally diffuse social structures.[7]

This evolution is not restricted to Western culture. As other countries pass through the phases of industrialization, they also find it necessary to evolve large, more complex organizational systems. Witness the current evolution within India from a small, family-oriented society to one of more complex, centralized systems. The breakdown of the traditional family pattern and local social structure within China and the evolution of strongly centralized organizational systems under the Communists are even more dramatic. It would appear that this trend toward larger and more complex organization is basic in all human society, one which is moving in a massive wave through many cultures.

Organization of Individual Activities

A related trend in modern societies is the increased integration of previously independent activities into organizations, particularly the professions. Many professionals have lost their traditional autonomy and independence and have had to adjust to working in large organizations. We consider the old "free" professions as *the* model of professionalism and think of the researcher as pursuing his objective of scientific discovery independently. Increasingly, however, scientists work in large organizations and

[7]Arthur L. Stinchcombe, "Social Structure and Organizations," in James G. March (ed.), *Handbook of Organizations,* Rand McNally & Company, Chicago, 1965, pp. 145–146.

must integrate their efforts with many others. Lawyers increasingly are working for corporations rather than in private practice. The medical profession appears to be undergoing a major revolution away from independent practitioners and toward many forms of group practice. University professors carry on their teaching and research in highly formalized structures. This integration of professionals into organizations has been a steady process and has resulted in many conflicts between professional and organizational norms and values.[8]

CHARACTERISTICS OF MODERN BUSINESS ORGANIZATIONS

The business organization with its primary objectives of production and distribution of physical products or services represents one of the most complex forms of man's social organization. Using the United States and Western culture as a frame of reference, we can look at some of the characteristics of these organizations.

Growing Size

The growth in size of business organizations is unparalleled. Even the small-to-medium-size business organizations of today would dwarf the largest firms of a century ago. The largest business organizations employ thousands of people and have annual sales volume well over one billion dollars. This growth in size has created many problems for the integration of the various segments or parts in the organization.

Complexity

In addition to growth, there has been a general increase in the complexity of the business organization. Whereas firms of fifty years ago concentrated on a limited line of products, most of the

[8]William Kornhauser, *Scientists in Industry: Conflict and Accommodation,* University of California Press, Berkeley, Calif., 1963, p. 12. For additional discussions of the relationships between professionals and organizations see Simon Marcson, "Organization and Authority in Industrial Research," *Social Forces,* October 1961, pp. 72–80; Ralph M. Hower and Charles D. Orth, *Managers and Scientists,* Graduate School of Business Administration, Harvard University, Boston, 1963; Talcott Parsons, "Social Change and Medical Organization in the United States: A Sociological Perspective," *The Annals of the American Academy of Political and Social Science,* March 1963, pp. 21–33; and Gloria V. Engel, "Professional Autonomy and Bureaucratic Organization," *Administrative Science Quarterly,* March 1970, pp. 12–21.

large corporations today have diverse operations. There has been a transition in the way business firms achieve growth. In the latter part of the nineteenth century and early twentieth century, most firms grew through vertical integration—by moving further back in the productive process or further forward in the distributive process for their given line of product. This was typical of the growth of U.S. Steel, Standard Oil, American Tobacco, and other large firms of the era. During the 1920s and 1930s the pattern of growth tended in the direction of horizontal integration— a movement toward the expansion of similar-type activities throughout a wide geographical area. This type of integration was typified by the chain-store movement. More recently, and particularly in the post-World War II period, the pattern of growth for most enterprises has been through heterogeneous growth and diversification into new and varied fields.[9] This approach has increased greatly the complexities of the business organization. Witness the diverse activities of many giant corporations— General Motors, General Electric, Du Pont, General Dynamics, and many others. They have become vast enterprises operating in widely different economic and political environments. The dynamic growth of conglomerate corporations in recent years is a further indication of this trend toward diversity.

Multinational Operations

In the post-World War II period, American business corporations have entered a new, important phase of boundary expansion— international operations. Increasingly, large- and medium-sized corporations are operating in other countries. The multinational corporation has significantly changed the boundaries of its activities and the diversity of its environment. It must operate in a new sociocultural system and must maintain dynamic flexibility. There is growing evidence that the corporation cannot simply transplant its domestic operations to a foreign country but must significantly change and adapt its goals, organization structure, and managerial approach to the different culture.

Specialization of Skills

There has been a growing tendency toward specialization and division of labor within the organizational structure. Specializa-

---

[9]For an excellent discussion of the evolution in structure and growth patterns of major United States corporations see Alfred D. Chandler, Jr., *Strategy and Structure,* The M.I.T. Press, Cambridge, Mass., 1962.

tion at the worker level was a result of mechanization and the scientific management movement. The trend toward specialization of managerial skills has been given less emphasis. There has been an increasing use of management specialists over the past few decades—the personnel expert, the risk manager, the quality control manager, the operations research team, public relations expert, and a number of other specialists. With this increase of specialization, the problems of integrating the people in a modern business organization into an effective operating unit have multiplied greatly.

Diversity of Objectives

Another characteristic of modern business organization is the diversity of objectives of the various people and organizational units. While it is generally accepted that the business organization operates for long-run profit maximization (recent discussions of the responsibilities of business for social well-being have questioned even this concept), there are many subsystems operating within the business organization, each having its own unique objectives. Indeed, every individual participant within the business organization brings to his work activity a multitude of personal goals and motives which influence his organizational behavior. To speak of the enterprise as having one single, unique goal does not give recognition to the organization as a social institution. The diversity of objectives of the individual participants and subsystems within the organization creates problems of goal integration. Here again, the systems concept provides a basis for integrating these various objectives into a systematic whole.

Meeting Change

A further characteristic of business enterprises is the necessity of accepting change. Increasingly, the environment within which organizations are operating makes the demands for change and evolution. It is impossible to think of the organization as static. It has to be a dynamic, adaptive system in order to meet the challenge of change. The impact of technological change upon business organizations is apparent. We are less aware of the underlying sociological, moral, and ethical changes which are influencing business organizations. The growing interest of the social scientists in the study of the business enterprise is indicative of the awakening to the importance of social and cultural norms in the organization.

External Demands

The modern business organization does not operate in a vacuum. It is an integral part of society as a whole. There have been a number of forces tending to restrict or change the role of the business organization. The growth of labor unions has placed restrictions upon business decisions, as has the increase in governmental regulations and control. The environmental influences will continually evolve and provide an important reason for maintaining the business organization as a viable system.

TRADITIONAL ORGANIZATIONAL CONCEPTS

In order to place organization theory in proper perspective in relation to systems concepts, it is desirable to look at some of the primary ideas about organizations. They have evolved over an extended period and represent a transition in the study of organizations. Some of the most important of these views come from traditional, or classical, organization theory, while others have evolved from the neoclassical, or "human relations," school, and still others have come from modern organization theory.

Traditional organization theory is based upon contributions from a number of sources, including scientific management, administrative management theorists, microeconomics, and public administration. This theory was set forth in the early part of the twentieth century and led to the development of the following concepts.

Structure

Structure is the relationship of the various functions or activities in an organization. Efficient management requires that the structure be in balance and adapted to the objectives and primary operations of the enterprise. The basic organizational structure provides the pattern around which more detailed administrative functions are interrelated. Organizational structure can be compared to the skeleton structure of animals—it provides the basic framework around which the various parts or units are related and function. Furthermore, the structure provides for known and established relationships between participants in the organization. Simon emphasized this idea as follows:

> The organization structure establishes a common set of presuppositions and expectations as to which members of the organiza-

tion are responsible for which classes of decisions; it establishes a structure of subgoals to serve as criteria of choice in various parts of the organization; and it establishes intelligence responsibilities in particular organization units for scrutinizing specific parts of the organization's environment and for communicating events requiring attention to appropriate decision points.[10]

Hierarchy

Closely related to structure in the organization is the concept of hierarchical relationships. Large organizations are almost universally hierarchical in nature. Almost any organization—the church, university, or business organization—is divided into units, which are subdivided into smaller units, which are in turn subdivided into smaller units. In classical organizational theory this concept of a hierarchical structure is the *scalar principle,* initially referred to by Mooney and Reiley.[11] The scalar principle refers primarily to the vertical division of authority and responsibility and the assignment of duties to organizational units.

Hierarchical structure has important implications for the general systems concept. Almost every system, both human and natural, has a hierarchical structure. Even the universe is made up of a complex array of subsystems—the earth with its own system is a subsystem of a galaxy, which is perhaps a subsystem of an infinite number of other supersystems. Smaller units, such as the atom, are a combination of a number of subsystems organized into a larger system unit. Hierarchy appears to be a natural order of nature. According to Simon:

> The near universality of hierarchy in the composition of complex systems suggests that there is something fundamental in this structural principal that goes beyond the peculiarities of human organization. . . . There are strong reasons for believing that almost any system of sufficient complexity would have to have the room-within-rooms structure that we observe in actual human organizations. The reasons for hierarchy go far beyond the need for unity of command or other considerations relating to authority.[12]

Again we see the similarity; one of the fundamental aspects of

[10]Herbert A. Simon, *The New Science of Management Decision,* Harper & Row, Inc., New York, 1960, p. 10.
[11]James D. Mooney and Allen C. Reiley, *Onward Industry,* Harper & Row, Inc., New York, 1931.
[12]Simon, *op. cit.,* pp. 41–42.

organization theory, the hierarchical structure, is also fundamental to any general systems theory.

Authority

In the classical view the legitimization of authority at a central source is of prime importance in that the superior "has the *right* to command someone else and that the subordinate person has the *duty* to obey the command. This is implied in the notion of official legitimacy, legal in nature rather than social and informal."[13] Authority is the capacity to invoke compliance in subordinates on the basis of formal position and of the control over rewards and sanctions that accompany the formal position. It is impersonal and goes with the position rather than with the individual. Authority is significantly different from charismatic leadership which is based upon the personal skills and traits of the leader.

This view of authority provides the framework for much of traditional organizational theory. It is the basis for legitimizing the organizational hierarchy and control system and for the establishment of many other concepts such as span of control and line and staff relationships. Authority is the means for integrating the activities of organizational participants toward the goals and provides the basis for centralized direction and control.

This traditional view has obvious limitations. Blau and Scott suggest these as follows:

> Important as formal authority is for meeting the minimum requirements of operations in a complex organization, it is not sufficient for attaining efficiency. It promotes compliance with directives and discipline, but does not encourage employees to exert effort, to accept responsibilities, or to exercise initiative.
>
> The narrow scope of formal authority induces management, in the interest of effective operations as well as in its self-interest, to seek to widen the sphere of its influence over employees beyond the controlling power that rests on the legal contract or on formal sanctions. For this reason many books on management place heavy emphasis on administrative leadership rather than sheer legal authority.[14]

The traditional view of authority remains as an essential element in much of the management literature. However, there has been a moderation of these views exemplified by Barnard's

---

[13]Pfiffner and Sherwood, *op. cit.*, p. 75.
[14]Peter M. Blau and W. Richard Scott, *Formal Organizations*, Chandler Publishing Company, San Francisco, Calif., 1962, pp. 140–141.

"acceptance view of authority." He stated that the authority relationship is determined by the willingness of the subordinate to accept the orders or directives of his superior. "Authority is the character of a communication (order) in a formal organization by virtue of which it is accepted by a contributor to or member of the organization as governing the action he contributes."[15] This acceptance view of authority has become a major element of the behavioral model.

Specialization

The principle of functional specialization is another important part of organization theory. Frequently it is encountered under the theories or concepts of departmentation, the division of the organization into specialized units which are assigned the performance of particular functions. The traditional division into production, distribution, and finance departments is an example of functional specialization. The concept of specialization is closely related to the scalar concept. However, the difference is that the scalar concepts deals with the vertical superior-subordinate relationship, whereas the functional concept is related to the differences in duties assigned to various units or people within the organization.

Span of Control

The *span-of-control*, or *span-of-supervision*, concept relates to the number of subordinates a superior can supervise effectively. It relates closely to the hierarchical structure and to the concept of departmentation. Implicit in the span-of-control concept is the necessity for the coordination of the activities of the subordinate by the superior. Span of control emphasizes the necessity for establishing a superior-subordinate relationship which allows for the systematic integration of activities. In formal organization theory the span-of-control principle recommended a narrow span in order for the executive or superior to provide adequate integration. However, this recommendation did not give sufficient recognition to the relationship between a narrow span and number of vertical levels within the organization. Thus a narrow span of control results in an elongated vertical structure and often creates

---

[15]Chester I. Barnard, *The Functions of the Executive,* Harvard University Press, Cambridge, Mass., 1938, p. 163.

problems for the systematic integration of activities on a horizontal level. Many of the modern writers have been critical of the usefulness of the span-of-control concept as a means of designing organizations.

Line and Staff

In classical organization theory, the line organization is vested with the primary source of authority and the staff functions support and advise the line. The traditional concept of the staff was an aid to the executive, an extension of his personality. Through the use of special staffs reporting directly to the executive, it was possible to increase his span of control without sacrificing his coordinating abilities. But this concept of staff has changed greatly with advancing specialization and complexities within business enterprises. Staffs have come to play a much more important role, providing service, information, and even control over other organizational units. With the expansion of the role of the staff, the clear delineation between line and staff relationships is no longer possible. This is particularly true in functional-staff operations. Functional authority refers to the authority which resides within a specialized staff and is exercised within other operational units. Quite frequently the industrial relations department has functional authority over the labor relations activities in all departments throughout the organization. The concept of functional authority represents a substantial variation from the traditional hierarchical organization, where the relationships are based upon the unity-of-command concept, with authority directed from only one superior and with each subordinate responsible to only one superior for his total activities. The enterprise with functional staffs does severe damage to the unity-of-command concept. With functional staffs, a number of specialists in each of the functional areas exercise an authoritarian relationship which results in multiple rather than unified supervision. The growth in the use of functional authority has complicated the clear-cut organizational relationship existing under traditional concepts.

The foregoing concepts of structure, hierarchy, authority, specialization, span of control, and line and staff relationships come mainly from traditional organization theory, where the primary concern was one of grouping work in the most efficient way. Given the general objectives for an organization, it sought to identify the tasks necessary to reach this goal. Then the problem was to group these jobs into administrative units, to group the units into larger units, and finally to establish the top-level departments.

BUREAUCRATIC MODEL

A view of the formal organization which is traditional with the social scientist rather than with the management-oriented student was postulated by Max Weber at the turn of the century. In Weber's view, the bureaucratic form was the most efficient type of organization in a modern society. Basically, he wanted to construct an ideal organization which would provide a maximum of rationality in human behavior. This obviously differs from the label "bureaucratic" often attached to large-scale, cumbersome government or business units. In speaking of the technical advantages of bureaucracy, Weber said:

> The decisive reason for the advance of bureaucratic organization has always been its purely technical superiority over any other form of organization. The fully developed bureaucratic mechanism compares with other organizations exactly as does the machine with the nonmechanical modes of production.
> Precision, speed, unambiguity, knowledge of the files, continuity, discretion, unity, strict subordination, reduction of friction and of material and personal costs—these are raised to the optimum point in the strictly bureaucratic administration, and especially in its monocratic form.[16]

A second aspect of Weber's theory of bureaucracy was its emphasis on universality. He suggested that this form of organization would result in the greatest efficiency for a wide variety of organizational units, ranging from the business enterprises to governmental units, to military operations, and to such associations as labor unions. The literature on Weberian bureaucracy suggests the following dimensions or key elements of the "ideal-type" bureaucracy:

1. A division of labor based upon functional specialization
2. A well-defined hierarchy of authority
3. A system of rules covering the rights and duties of positional incumbents
4. A system of procedures for dealing with work situations

[16]H. H. Gerth and C. Wright Mills, *From Max Weber: Essays in Sociology,* Oxford University Press, New York, 1946, p. 214.

5. Impersonality of interpersonal relations
6. Promotion and selection for employment based upon technical competence[17]

Basically it was Weber's contention that man was unpredictable, often emotional, not necessarily rational, and would interfere with efficient organizational performance. He therefore set forth as an ideal model of bureaucracy a depersonalized form of organization which would minimize the impact of human capriciousness. He anchored his bureaucratic mechanism in the institutionalization of authority by society, a type of power legitimized by a society that "makes a man do what he does not want to do." Weber's bureaucratic model had much in common with the traditional concepts discussed previously. It was mechanistic and impersonal, in sharp contrast to later concepts.[18]

BEHAVIORAL MODEL

Behavioral organizational concepts evolved as a reaction against the more mechanistic and impersonal bias of the classical school. This view, stemming from the well-known Hawthorne–Western Electric studies during the 1920s and 1930s, transformed the focus from the rational model of traditional theory to a behavioristic model which accepted man as he is. Basically, this school accepted the structural aspects of organization as discussed previously but modified the concepts regarding human resources and informal-group relationships within the organization.

Mayo, Roethlisberger, Whitehead, and other early human relationists developed many concepts about human behavior in organizations such as

1. The business organization is a social system as well as a technical-economic system. This social system defines individual roles and establishes norms which may be at variation with those of the formal organization.
2. The individual is not only motivated by economic incentives, but by diverse social and psychological factors as well. His behavior is affected by feelings, sentiments, and attitudes.

[17]Richard H. Hall, "The Concept of Bureaucracy: An Empirical Assessment," *American Journal of Sociology,* July 1963, p. 33.
[18]For a discussion of bureaucracy and its role in modern society see Peter M. Blau, *Bureaucracy in Modern Society,* Random House, Inc., New York, 1956, and Warren G. Bennis (ed.), *American Bureaucracy,* Aldine Publishing Company, Chicago, 1970.

3. The informal work group became a dominant unit of consideration. The group has an important role in determining the attitudes and performance of individual workers.
4. Leadership patterns based upon the formal structure and authority of position in the organization under the traditional view should be modified substantially in order to consider psychosocial factors. The human relationists emphasized "democratic" rather than "authoritarian" leadership patterns.
5. The human relations school generally associated worker satisfaction with productivity and emphasized that increasing satisfaction would lead to increased efficiency.
6. It is important to develop effective communication channels between the various levels in the hierarchy that allow the exchange of information. Thus "participation" became an important approach of the human relations movement.
7. Management requires effective social skills as well as technical skills.
8. Participants can be motivated in the organization by fulfilling certain social-psychological needs.

The human relations view brought to the forefront the concept of the organization as a total system encompassing individuals, informal groups, intergroup relationships, and formal relationships. In effect, this school put the human element back in the organization—the element which the traditional school had so carefully attempted to minimize.[19]

The concepts developed by the early human relationists have been expanded and modified by modern behavioral scientists interested in studying organizations. They use an open-systems approach and consider many variables which were excluded in the traditional views. The behavioral approach has been developed primarily by psychologists, sociologists, and anthropologists who are interested in empirical investigations to verify their concepts. Typically they have a "humanistic" view and seek

[19]An interesting play on words aptly expresses the distinction between classical organization theory and the human relations approach to organizational behavior. Bennis has called the traditional theory "organizations without people" and the human relations approach "people without organizations." Warren G. Bennis, "Leadership Theory and Administrative Behavior," *Administrative Science Quarterly*, December 1959, pp. 263–266.

to modify the organization toward greater satisfaction of human participants. Many of the ideas from behavioral science are important in understanding the human aspects of systems and will be discussed more completely in Chapter 10, "Behavioral Aspects of Systems Design."

DECISION-MAKING MODEL

Simon focused the attention of organization theorists on the decision-making processes within the organization. He rejected most of the traditional concepts and placed emphasis on the human problem-solving processes and decision mechanisms as primary forces in organizational behavior. According to his thesis, organizational participants should not be viewed as mere mechanical instrumentalities. They should be perceived as individuals with wants, motives, aspiration levels, and drives who have limited rationality and capacity for problem solving.

Simon uses the term decision making as though it were synonymous with "managing." In this sense, decision making has three principal stages: *intelligence*—searching the environment for conditions calling for decision; *design*—inventing, developing, and analyzing possible courses of action; and *choice*—selecting a particular course of action from the available alternatives.[20] In a book in collaboration with March, Simon later used the decision-making process as a frame of reference to set forth a more general theory of organization. A key concept of this book is illustrated by the following:

> The basic features of organization structure and function derive from the characteristics of human problem-solving processes and rational human choice. Because of the limits of human intellective capacities in comparison with the complexities of the problems that individuals and organizations face, rational behavior calls for simplified models that capture the main features of a problem without capturing all its complexities.[21]

Such concepts greatly augment traditional organization theory with current knowledge from social sciences about the motivational aspects, conflicts of interest, perception, and restrictions on rationality, all of which influence organizational behavior significantly.

[20]Herbert A. Simon, *The New Science of Management Decision*, pp. 1–4.
[21]March and Simon, op. cit., p. 169.

In a more recent book, Cyert and March developed an elaborate theory of business behavior with the central focus on organizational decision making. Their basic premise is that, "in order to understand contemporary economic decision making, we need to supplement the study of market factors with an examination of the internal operation of the firm—to study the effects of organizational structure and conventional practice on the development of goals, the formation of expectations, and the execution of choices."[22]

The organization is viewed as an adaptive system—with many interest groups integrated into a loose coalition—which develops mechanisms for avoiding uncertainty, engages in problemistic search, learns through experience, and seeks satisfying rather than optimal decisions. These views are associated closely with our consideration of the organization as an adaptive social system.

MODERN ORGANIZATION THEORY— A SYSTEMS CONCEPT

Traditional organization theory generally emphasized parts and segments of the organization and was concerned with the separation of activities into tasks or operational units. It did not give sufficient emphasis to the problem of interrelationships or integration of activity. Nor did the human relations view move in this direction. Its approach was aimed at interjecting human motivations, aspirations, desires, and limitations into the mechanistic traditional models. Neither of these approaches provided a basis for an integrated, systematic organization model.

Increasing attention is being given to the notion that the most useful way to study organizations is to consider them as systems. This modern view tends to treat the organization as a system of mutually dependent parts and variables, and the enterprise is thought of as a social system within the broader, more inclusive system of society. Parson's definition of the organization expresses this view:

> It seems appropriate to define an organization as a social system which is organized for the attainment of a particular type of goal; the attainment of that goal is at the same time a performance of a

---

[22]Richard M. Cyert and James G. March, *A Behavioral Theory of the Firm,* Prentice-Hall, Inc., Englewood Cliffs, N.J., 1963, p. 1.

type of function on behalf of a more inclusive system, the society.[23]

Modern organization theory and general systems theory are closely related, with organization theory a special element of general systems theory. They are both concerned with the investigation and performance of the organization as an integrated whole. However, general systems theory is concerned with all nine levels of systems as described in Chapter 1, whereas organization theory focuses primarily upon human social organizations. Nevertheless, many concepts taken from the investigation and study of other types of systems are meaningful to the study of human organizational systems.[24]

An Integrative Systems View of Organizations

We view the organization as an open, sociotechnical system composed of a number of subsystems, as illustrated in Figure 2–1. It receives inputs of energy, information, and materials from the environment, transforms these, and returns outputs to the environment.

The internal organization can be viewed as composed of several major subsystems. The organizational *goals and values* are one of the more important of these subsystems. The organization takes many of its values from the broader sociocultural environment. A basic premise is that the organization as a subsystem of the society must accomplish certain goals which are determined by the broader system. The organization performs a function for

---

[23]Talcott Parsons, "Suggestions for a Sociological Approach to the Theory of Organizations," *Administrative Science Quarterly,* September 1956, p. 238. For further elaboration of this view see Neil W. Chamberlain, *Enterprise and Environment,* McGraw-Hill Book Company, New York, 1968; Paul R. Lawrence and Jay W. Lorsch, *Organization and Environment,* Harvard Graduate School of Business Administration, Boston, 1967; Shirley Terreberry, "The Evolution of Organizational Environments," *Administrative Science Quarterly,* March 1968, pp. 590–613; and Thompson, op. cit., pp. 25–38.

[24]For an interesting discussion of the relationship between organization theory and general systems theory see William G. Scott, "Organizational Theory: An Overview and an Appraisal," *Journal of the Academy of Management,* April 1961, pp. 7–26. Scott suggests the interrelationship between general systems theory and organization theory as follows:

Modern organizational theory leads, as it has been shown, almost inevitably into a discussion of general system theory. A science of organization universals has strong advocates, particularly among biologists. Organization theorists in administrative science cannot afford to overlook the contributions of general system theory. Indeed, modern organization concepts could offer a great deal to those working with general system theory.

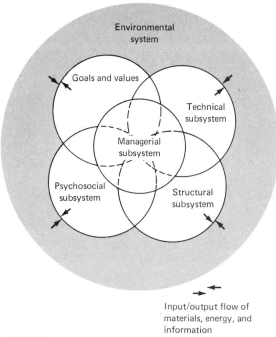

FIGURE 2-1. The organizational system.

the society and if it is to be successful in receiving inputs, it must conform to social requirements.

The *technical* system refers to the knowledge required for the performance of tasks, including the techniques used in the transformation of inputs into outputs. The technical system is determined by the task requirements of the organization and obviously will vary depending upon the particular activities. The technology frequently prescribes the type of organizational structure and psychosocial system.[25]

Every organization has a *psychosocial* system which consists of individual behavior and motivation, status and role relationships, group dynamics, and influence systems. Obviously, this psychosocial system is affected by external environmental forces

[25]For discussions of the relationships between the technical system and other organizational systems see Tom Burns and G. M. Stalker, *The Management of Innovation,* Tavistock Publications, London, 1961; Lawrence and Lorsch, op. cit., Charles Perrow, *Organizational Analysis: A Sociological View,* Wadsworth Publishing Company, Inc., Belmont, Calif., 1970; Thompson, op. cit.; and Joan Woodward, *Industrial Organization: Theory and Practice,* Oxford University Press, Fair Lawn, N.J., 1965.

as well as by the tasks, technology, and structure of the internal organization.

The organization *structure* can be considered as a third major subsystem intermeshed between the technical and the psychosocial subsystem. Structure is concerned with the ways in which the tasks of the organization are divided (differentiation) and with the coordination of these activities (integration). In the formal sense, structure is set forth by the organization charts, by position and job descriptions, and by rules and procedures. It is also concerned with the pattern of authority, communication, and work flow. The organization's structure provides for formalization of relationships between the technical and psychosocial subsystems. However, it should be emphasized that this linkage is by no means complete and that many interactions and relationships occur between the technical and the psychosocial subsystems which bypass the formal structure.

The *managerial* system spans the entire organization by relating the organization to its environment, setting the goals, and planning, organizing, and controlling the necessary activities. As indicated in Chapter 1, there are three key subsystems in the administrative hierarchy of complex organizations: operating, coordinative, and strategic. The managerial task in each of these subsystems is substantially different and requires an appropriate perspective. In the next three chapters we will look more closely at the managerial task with specific consideration of the planning, controlling, and communicating functions.

Toward a Contingency View

One of the consequences of the acceptance of the systems approach to the study of organizations and their management is a rejection of simplistic statements of "principles of organization or management." Modern organization theory reflects a search for patterns of relationships, configurations between subsystems, and a contingency view. Lorsch and Lawrence say:

> During the past few years there has been evident a new trend in the study of organizational phenomena. Underlying this new approach is the idea that the internal functioning of organizations must be consistent with the demands of the organization task, technology, or external environment, and the needs of its members if the organization is to be effective. Rather than searching for the panacea of the one best way to organize under all conditions, investigators have more and more tended to examine the functioning of or-

ganizations in relation to the needs of their particular members and the external pressures facing them. Basically, this approach seems to be leading to the development of a "contingency" theory of organization with the appropriate internal states and processes of the organization contingent upon external requirements and member needs.[26]

Numerous others have stressed a similar viewpoint. Thompson suggests that the essence of administration lies in understanding the basic configurations which exist between the various subsystems and with the environment. "The basic function of administration appears to be coalignment, not merely of people (in coalitions) but of institutionalized action—of technology and task environment into a viable domain, and of organizational design and structure appropriate to it".[27]

But, it is not enough to suggest that a "contingency view" based upon systems concepts of organizations and their management is more appropriate than the simplistic "principles approach." If organization theory is to advance and to make contributions to managerial practice, it must more explicitly define certain patterns of relationships between organizational variables. The view of the organization as an open sociotechnical system in interaction with its environment provides a framework for this development.

Fortunately there are many examples of attempts to develop concepts relating patterns of interactive relationships between various organizational subsystems. The work of Burns and Stalker provides a useful example of this approach.[28] It was their hypothesis, substantiated by research findings, that a different configuration of organizational subsystems is appropriate for concerns involved with stable vis-à-vis unstable technology and environment. Organizational systems which were adapted to a stable technology were termed *mechanistic.* Such a system is characterized as having a rigidly prescribed organization structure. There are well-defined tasks; the methods, duties, and powers attached to each functional role are determined precisely. The interactions within the managerial system tend to be vertical between superior and subordinate—a strong command hierarchy.

By contrast, *organic* managerial systems are best adapted to conditions of rapidly changing technology and environment.

[26]Jay W. Lorsch and Paul R. Lawrence, *Studies in Organization Design,* Richard D. Irwin, Inc. and the Dorsey Press, Homewood, Ill., 1970, p. 1.
[27]Thompson, op. cit., p. 157.
[28]Burns and Stalker, op. cit.

They are suitable to unstable conditions when problems and requirements for action arise which cannot be broken down and distributed among specialized roles within a clearly defined hierarchy. The organic system is characterized by a relatively flexible structure. Continual adjustment and redefinition of individual tasks through interaction with others, a network rather than hierarchical control, emphasis upon lateral rather than vertical communications, and a wide dispersal of power based upon technical expertise and knowledge rather than upon hierarchical position are characteristic of the organic system.

To summarize these and other findings it can be suggested that

> The *mechanistic* organizational form is most appropriate for routine activities where productivity is the major objective, where technology is relatively uniform and stable, where decision making is programmable, and where environmental forces are relatively stable and certain.
>
> The *organic* (or adaptive) organizational form is most appropriate for nonroutine activities where creativity and innovation are important, where heuristic decision-making processes are necessary, and where the environment is relatively uncertain and turbulent.

No one organizational system is appropriate for all circumstances. Rather, the total organization, its technology and environmental circumstances, must be considered in designing the most appropriate system. In most organizations there will be a mixture between the mechanistic and the organic forms. For example, an assembly line might well be organized along mechanistic lines whereas the research and development department would adopt the organic form.

We see the systems approach as a basis for helping organization theorists and management practitioners to better understand these patterns of relationships and to design organizational systems which will facilitate meeting the variable requirements of the internal subsystems and the external environment.

SUMMARY

General systems theory implies an interconnected complex of functionally related components, or parts. The business organization and other institutions of human interrelationships are open social systems.

A simple and easily understood definition of the business

organization is the following: *The organization is an assemblage of people, materials, machines, and other resources geared to task accomplishment through a series of interactions and integrated into a social system.*

The growth of large-scale, complex organizations has been one of the main characteristics of the evolution of modern industrial societies. Many professional activities which previously were performed independently are now integrated into large organizations.

The business organization, with the primary objectives of production and distribution of physical products or services, represents one of the most highly developed forms of man's social organizations. It generally has the characteristics of increasing size, growing complexity, specialization of skills, increasing diversity of objectives, viability to meet change, and adaptation to external demands.

Modern organization theory has developed from traditional organizational concepts which placed emphasis upon the organization structure, hierarchical relationships, authority, specialization, span of control, and line and staff relationships. This traditional theory was modified substantially by behavioral view, which placed greater emphasis upon personal and social needs of organizational participants. The behavioral model brought to the forefront the concept of the organization as a total system encompassing individuals, informal groups, intergroup relationships, and formal structures.

The modern view treats the organization as a system of mutually dependent parts and variables, and the enterprise is thought of as a social system within the broader, more inclusive system of society. Thus, the organization is a structured, sociotechnical system in interaction with its environment. It receives inputs of energy, information, and materials from the environment, transforms these, and returns outputs to the environment. The internal organization can be viewed as composed of several major subsystems: (1) goals and values, (2) technological, (3) structural, (4) psychosocial, and (5) managerial. The managerial functions span the entire organization by relating the organization to its environment, setting the goals, and planning, organizing, and controlling the necessary activities.

One of the consequences of the acceptance of the systems approach is a rejection of simplistic statements of "principles of organization or management." Modern organization theory reflects a search for patterns of relationships, configurations between subsystems, and a contingency view. In this view no one organizational system is appropriate for all circumstances. Rather, the total organization, its technology and environmental circumstances, must be considered in designing the most appropriate system.

QUESTIONS

1. Why is an organization an open system?
2. How would you use the systems approach to describe these types of organizations: (a) a business, (b) a hospital, (c) a university?
3. Discuss the differences between the *rational* or *goal* approach and the *natural systems* approach in the study of organizations.
4. What do you think the various social sciences contribute to the development of organization theory?
5. Why are more professionals working in large organizations? What are the implications of this trend?
6. What are the major differences between traditional organization concepts and the behavioral model?
7. Do all large organizations employ features of Weber's "ideal bureaucracy"? Why or why not?
8. Relate a specific organization to the subsystems in Figure 2–1.
9. What are the major differences between the mechanistic and the organic organization? Give examples of each.
10. Why might modern organization theory be considered as a special element of general systems theory?

CHAPTER 3

Planning and Systems Concepts

The recent development of comprehensive, integrative planning programs in business enterprises, governmental agencies, educational institutions, hospitals, and other organizations is a prime example of the application of the systems approach. Although the managerial functions are interrelated and the manager undoubtedly performs each at one time or another, any given phase of organizational activity must start with planning. Planning is the process by which the system adapts its resources to changing environmental and internal forces. It is a dynamic function and must be carried out effectively in order to establish a solid foundation for the remaining managerial activities. The purpose of the planning function in an organization is to provide an integrated decision system which establishes the framework for its activities. The following topics will be discussed in this chapter:

The environment of planning
Definition of the planning function
Planning: the framework for an integrated decision system
Hierarchy of planning
Planning dimensions
A conceptual model for planning

THE ENVIRONMENT OF PLANNING

The systems concept of planning has evolved as the result of many important changes both in the environment in which the organization must operate and in its internal operations. Planning for the future is becoming an increasingly important managerial activity. As the industrial, social, and political environments grow more complex, greater emphasis is placed upon planning as a means of coping with the uncertainty of the future.

Organizations operate in an environment of change. They must be prepared to accept change as the inevitable consequence of operating in a dynamic world. The general political, economic, social, ethical, and moral philosophies in our country have promoted an atmosphere of freedom of change for the enterprise. In fact, continued success generally has demanded adaptation and innovation.[1] This is in direct contradiction to many societies— both past and contemporary—in which political, religious, cultural, and other institutions placed major impediments in the path of economic progress.

Rapidly advancing technology has also emphasized the need for planning. Companies not abreast of current technology are in trouble over the short run. Moreover, companies unaware of the technical changes likely to occur in the next five to twenty years will be in a disadvantageous position.[2]

On the other hand, the organization faced with a changing environment often has found many obstacles which make planning for optimum adaptation difficult. Even technological advances, which themselves are purveyors of change, can create degrees of inflexibility. For example, automation, while requiring major changes for its establishment, results in some inherent inflexibilities and increased resistance to change. In a typical multiproduct business, for instance, automated operations are predicated on expected variations in volume, product mix, quality, and demand. Since automation establishes a relatively inflexible overall system, it is vitally important that the right decision be made at the outset, thus emphasizing the critical importance of effective long-term planning.

Other factors, such as the tendency for labor costs to become fixed, have created additional impediments to flexibility. The

[1]Neil W. Chamberlain, *Enterprise and Environment*, McGraw-Hill Book Company, New York, 1968, pp. 141–143.
[2]Peter F. Drucker, *Technology, Management and Society*, Harper and Row, Publishers, New York, 1970.

restrictions of the labor contract, growing fringe benefits, and provisions for guaranteed annual wages have tended to make even so-called direct labor costs inflexible and less subject to unilateral management discretion. Without evaluating the rationale of these trends, one of the major implications has been to create a stability of conditions—in many ways similar to those created by automation and greater mechanization. Nor are executives free from practices which restrict change and make planning difficult. Current experience with the impact of computers on integrated systems of information flow indicates reluctance on the part of white-collar workers and management personnel with vested interests to accept the required modifications in organization and status relationships. As business organizations have increased in size and complexity, they have had difficulty in ensuring that the innovations necessary to meet new conditions and evolving objectives will be accepted by each department as guidelines to action. These and many other forces tend to make it more difficult for the business organization to sustain adaptiveness in a dynamic environment.

With a stable environment and small, uncomplicated operations, the planning function can be carried out relatively easily with a short-range viewpoint. With a more dynamic environment and large, complex units operating in the face of many forces restricting flexibility, the planning function becomes critical and must be thought of on a total-systems basis. Since the consequence of any decision has such a broad and drastic impact, management, through its planning function, must try for the optimal course of action.

Planning as a Vehicle for Systems Change

In a dynamic society, the organization adapts to changing requirements through planning. *The planning process can be considered as the vehicle for accomplishment of systems change.* Without planning the organization would be slow to change and would not adapt to different environmental forces. This distinguishes the social organization from other open systems. In other types of open systems change occurs when environmental forces demand that a new equilibrium be established. In the organization these changes are dependent upon the human process of planning. For the social system the only vehicle for change, innovation, and adaptability is the human decision-making and planning process.

Increasingly, the business enterprise has adopted comprehensive planning as a means of coping with an uncertain environment. Galbraith suggests that planning has become a vital function of business, both as a method of adapting to market forces and as a means of shaping the market and the total environment. "Market behavior must be modified by some measure of planning."[3] No longer can the enterprise merely adapt to the demands of the marketplace; it must anticipate and modify the future environment in order to survive. Other institutions, such as universities and hospitals, also are actively engaged in comprehensive organizational planning. It the past these institutions have adapted primarily to forces in the society rather than engaging in comprehensive planning which would help shape the environment and the institution's responses to it. Many public universities, which have grown to tremendous size and complexity, are attempting to determine their social objectives more rationally and to plan the utilization of resources toward their accomplishment comprehensively. Hospitals, rather than merely adapting to the demands for patient services as transmitted through private physicians, are engaged in comprehensive planning to meet their future role as community health service centers.

Managerial Role in Planning

Managers on all levels of the organization are engaged in all the basic functions of the management process. As the manager moves up the organization hierarchy, however, he is likely to spend relatively more of his time planning than carrying out other managerial functions. Moreover, higher management should be engaged in long-range, strategic planning. Its function is to define the desired role of the organization in the future, to relate the organization to its various environmental systems, to perceive the needs which the organization can fulfill, and to chart the broad strategies.

This does not mean that top executives can plan in a vacuum. Rather, they should develop their long-range plans with the full participation of those organizational members who have information inputs vital to the decision process. Systems concepts emphasize that effective planning is not the exclusive domain of a few top managers but requires the integration of inputs from all levels in the organization. Furthermore, there should be an awareness

[3]John Kenneth Galbraith, *The New Industrial State,* Houghton Mifflin Company, Boston, 1967, p. 25.

of the motivational impacts of participation, not only in the actual planning process but also in the implementation of plans. With expanded requirements for innovation, creativity, and flexibility within modern organizations and with increased employment of participants with high educational levels and professional knowledge, it is imperative for management to develop effective means for integrating this knowledge into the planning function.

After receiving informational inputs from various sources, higher management has the responsibility for setting forth the long-range, strategic plans for the organization. The character of the company must be established, and its objectives and goals set forth explicitly as guidelines to decision making throughout the entire organization. Clear-cut statements of expectations, along with both external and internal premises for planning, help focus the effort of all managerial levels toward common objectives.

DEFINITION OF THE PLANNING FUNCTION

Planning has been defined as "intelligent cooperation with the inevitable." This definition emphasizes the futurity of planning but it stresses the adaptive rather than the innovative nature of planning. Therefore, the following definition is preferable: *Comprehensive planning is an integrative activity which seeks to maximize the total effectiveness of an organization as a system in accordance with its objectives.*

Planning is the managerial process of deciding in advance what is to be done and how. It involves selecting objectives and developing policies, programs, and procedures for achieving them. The results of this process are *plans*. Steiner emphasizes the distinction between planning and plans:

> Planning is a basic organic function of management. It is a mental process of thinking through what is desired and how it will be achieved. . . . Plans are commitments to specific courses of action growing out of the mental process of planning.[4]

In short, a plan is a predetermined course of action resulting from the planning process. Essentially, a plan has three characteristics. First, it must involve the future. Second, it must involve action. Third, there is an element of personal or organizational identification or causation; that is, the future course of

---

[4]George A. Steiner, *Top Management Planning,* The Macmillan Company, New York, 1969, p. 8.

action will be taken by the planner or someone designated by or for him within the organization. Futurity, action, and personal or organizational causation are necessary elements in every plan.[5]

Forecasting is not planning. Forecasting attempts to anticipate and predict future conditions affecting the organization. Forecasts are essential in providing the premises for planning activities, but they are just part of the relevant information input. Many organizations develop elaborate forecasts of future conditions, place these in very secure files, and then sit back, happy with their efforts. But forecasts are meaningless unless they are used in the development of plans.

Over the past several decades the scope and time period for managerial planning has increased. Thus, greater emphasis is placed upon strategic, comprehensive, long-range planning in contrast to short-term operational planning. This trend reinforces the importance of a systems approach to planning.

PLANNING: THE FRAMEWORK FOR AN
INTEGRATED DECISION SYSTEM

Planning is not an entity in itself—its primary purpose is to provide the guidelines necessary for the vital decision-making processes throughout the organization. Planning, therefore, should be geared to obtaining, translating, understanding, and communicating information that will help to improve the rationality of current decisions which are based upon future expectations. Expectations are developed through the process of forecasting and predicting the future. A great deal of effort has been devoted to refining predictive techniques to enable companies to forecast their ideological, political, legislative, technological, and economic environment. Companies are becoming much more interested in broad economic data such as national income and product accounts and are relating industry, company, and product data to the overall economic outlook.

While forecasting provides a basis for understanding and formulating expectations, management must go beyond this orientation state and develop programs of action designed to optimize the company's overall performance. Since these programs themselves may alter the future—not only of the company but of the total environment—forecasts, no matter how rigorously

---

[5]Preston P. LeBreton and Dale A. Henning, *Planning Theory*, Prentice-Hall, Inc., Englewood Cliffs, N.J., 1961, p. 7.

developed, are seldom completely valid. If a company programs its future to fit the forecast conditions, its behavior will be characterized as adaptive and its future success is a function of the predicted environment. On the other hand, if a company plans for aggressive action in pursuit of predetermined goals and objectives, its behavior can be characterized as innovative, that is, shaping the environment.

Planning is an *integrative* activity which should seek to maximize the total effectiveness of the system. Frequently, in a complex organization, a great deal of planning is carried on by specialized functional or staff groups without a system for the coordination of these efforts. Unless there is a clear-cut understanding of what overall objectives are paramount, some of the subgroup activities may be maximized at the expense of total organizational effectiveness. All elements in a company should be aware of the expectations and directions set forth by top management and should understand the various premises upon which a course of action is founded.

Steps in the Planning Process

A comprehensive systems approach to planning would include the following steps:

1. Appraising the future political, economic, competitive, and technological environment
2. Assessing the long-run values, interests, and aspirations of managers and other participants
3. Visualizing the desired socioeconomic role of the organization in its future environment
4. Analyzing the organization's resources and capabilities for fulfilling this desired role
5. Designing a corporate strategy which matches the future environment, values and aspirations, desired socioeconomic role, and organizational resources
6. Developing specific objectives and strategic plans which will direct the efforts of the total organization
7. Translating this broad planning into functional efforts on a more detailed basis—research, design and development, production, distribution and service
8. Developing more detailed planning and control of resource utilization within each of these functional areas—always related to the overall planning effort

9. Providing a system of communications and information flow whereby organizational members can participate in planning processes
10. Designing an information feedback and control system to determine the progress and problems in the implementation of plans

This approach, developed and understood throughout the organization, will provide an integrated decision system. Such a framework or comprehensive planning program will be used to focus the efforts of the entire organization toward a common set of objectives. Furthermore, if the underlying expectations and planning premises are set forth explicitly, all departments can carry out their planning functions within the same guidelines. Major decisions can be evaluated in light of the comprehensive plan to determine whether a particular course of action would carry the organization toward or away from its desired future position. In this way the systems approach to planning tends to facilitate the integration of all segments of the organization.

HIERARCHY OF PLANNING

Planning provides the framework for an integrated decision system. In this approach to planning it is necessary to recognize the concept of a hierarchy of plans. Under this heirarchy, comprehensive plans are established for the enterprise primarily in the form of objectives at a high organizational level. The top-management strategic planning function is really one of systems design and should give consideration to the overall goals of the enterprise and to the integration of the operation of subsystems toward these goals.[6] These broad goals and objectives are then translated into more detailed and specific plans, which are further translated throughout the organization to even more detailed and specific plans. In effect, the planning process is one of spreading out the planning functions throughout the entire organizational system.

A well-documented example of this hierarchical relationship of plans is illustrated by the Allied invasion of Europe during World War II. First the broad objective of the invasion was established, and this led to a whole series of secondary goals and objectives, for example, requirements for weather conditions,

---

[6]For a further discussion of strategic planning, see H. Igor Ansoff, *Corporate Strategy*, McGraw-Hill Book Company, New York, 1965, pp. 103–121; and Steiner, op. cit., pp. 37–41.

goals as to the number and types of military men needed, and determination of materials needed. These were translated into more detailed plans which were further translated throughout the military hierarchy, down to the most detailed planning at the lowest operating level.[7] This planning process was made more complicated by the requirements for secrecy of the entire operation.

We can see the hierarchical relationship in planning for a more current national effort, the National Aeronautics and Space Administration (NASA) program leading to man's exploration of the moon. In May 1961, President Kennedy set forth the broad national objective as follows: "I believe that this Nation should commit itself to achieving the goal, before this decade is out, of landing a man on the moon and returning him safely to earth."[8] With this broad objective as a guideline, the Office of Manned Space Flight was established within NASA with prime responsibility for the manned lunar landing.[9] Three major projects were established under the Manned Space Flight Program—Mercury, Gemini, and Apollo. They constitute a step-by-step approach to develop a broad capacity for manned exploration of space. Given the broad goal, planning for each of these projects was initiated and integrated into the complete program. Operating under the premise of this broad strategic decision, it was necessary to develop increasingly detailed plans to meet specific requirements. For example, for each launch of an orbiting, manned vehicle it was necessary to develop a myriad of detailed plans for launching, tracking, communications, and recovery: the safety of the astronauts being always a prime consideration. The landing of Apollo 11 on the moon and the safe return to earth in August 1969 was a tribute to man's scientific and technological achievements and to his ability to comprehensively plan a tremendously complex program.

The difficulties which confronted Apollo 13 in April 1970 on its ill-fated lunar voyage illustrate another aspect of planning— the need to respond to unforeseen contingencies. With the massive failure of the command/service module on the way to the

[7]Dwight D. Eisenhower, *Crusade in Europe,* Doubleday and Company, Inc., New York, 1948.

[8]*Urgent National Needs,* Address of the President of the United States, H. Doc. 174, 87th Cong., 1st Sess., 1961, p. 11.

[9]For a discussion of this organization and its responsibilities, see D. Brainerd Holmes, "NASA Programs Leading to Exploration of the Moon," in F. E. Kast and J. E. Rosenzweig (eds.), *Science, Technology, and Management,* McGraw-Hill Book Company, New York, 1963, pp. 238–247.

moon, it was necessary to abort the mission and to make major modifications in the existing plans. The lunar module whose primary mission was for the direct descent and ascent to and from the moon became the Apollo 13 crew's "lifeboat" for the emergency flight back to earth. Although preflight simulations and mission studies considered a large variety of potential malfunctions and developed "contingency" plans to take care of these, the massive breakdown of the system required the development of new emergency plans. It was impossible to prevent or foresee all contingencies in a program as complex as Apollo 13. The initiation of new procedures through "real-time flight planning" was made possible by the usage of two complete sets of Apollo mission simulators located at the Manned Spacecraft Center in Houston and the Kennedy Space Center in Florida.[10] These simulators, working with the astronauts, developed many new complex plans and procedures which resulted in the safe voyage back to earth. Without elaborate contingency planning based upon a well-established hierarchy of plans and an adaptive response to the emergency through real-time flight planning the results would have been disastrous.

Organizational Objectives

Of prime importance in the establishment of a hierarchy of plans is the setting forth and acceptance of organizational objectives. Clear-cut, well-defined organizational objectives help provide the basis for systematic planning at lower operating levels. Some of the benefits of goals as guides for further planning are that they provide

1. The basis for unified, integrated planning and for coordinating the activities between various, often diverse, functional operating units within the organization
2. The premises within which more specific planning should take place and a basis for well-defined delegation and decentralization of specific planning to lower operating levels
3. The standards of performance used in the control function
4. A primary means for human motivation—a sense of accomplishment in terms of known goals

[10]"Apollo 13 Crises Spur Massive Support," *Aviation Week and Space Technology,* April 27, 1970, pp. 22–25.

This concept of the establishment of goals as a basis for the planning hierarchy is of crucial importance. Yet it is certainly one of the most difficult functions of top management. As our industrial enterprises become larger and more complex, the determination of the goals in the organization becomes more difficult. For example, should the organization have as its primary function that of profit maximization or of consumer service? Or is the major objective one of long-run perpetuation of the enterprise, or just perpetuation of the management, or of the investment of the stockholder? Or is it to provide long-term employment for the employees, or meeting other social responsibilities? Every business organization has a multiplicity of objectives and requirements. And these objectives are generally in a dynamic state; the requirements made on the organization by both internal participants and external forces will cause most organizations to vary their short-run goals and objectives to meet these pressures. Thus, we should recognize that the objectives of an organization are dynamic and are subject to degrees of evolution and change.

The abstract nature of the highest-level goals and their value-oriented determination makes it vitally necessary for the managerial planning function to translate these broad goals into more tangible operating objectives. To say that the goal of an organization is to satisfy customers, to meet social needs, and to make a profit may sound good as public relations or as a company motto, but it does not serve effectively as a guideline to organizational decision making at operating levels. These broad, general goals must be translated into specific operating goals if there is a systematic planning hierarchy. This translation and the establishment of meaningful objectives for each function, each organizational unit, each functional specialty, and each job is one of the most complex problems in planning.

PLANNING DIMENSIONS

The systems approach to planning facilitates understanding the multidimensional nature of the planning process and the resulting plans. For example, planning might be discussed in terms of some continuum of *repetitiveness*—planning for novel, one-time projects as against development of policies and procedures to handle activities which will occur repeatedly. Another relevant dimension is the *time span*. Planning may be considered in terms of the day-to-day activities of an organization or in terms of its attempts to achieve long-term goals. Similarly, the *scope* of planning may vary from comprehensive organizational plans to functionally oriented activities. It is also desirable to discuss planning from the standpoint of the organization *subsystems involved*. Finally, consideration should be given to the dimension of *flexibility*. Some plans may be highly fixed and respond to anticipated future conditions while others may be flexible, capable of adaptation to a variety of potential circumstances. It will become apparent from the discussion that there are often patterns of relationships between these various dimensions. For example, long-range, comprehensive plans are the primary concern of top management and frequently deal with complex, multidimensional problems. The resulting plans are usually quite flexible and capable of adapting to changing circumstances. In contrast, short-term, operational plans are more limited in scope, tend to be the responsibility of lower management, and usually are more fixed.

Repetitiveness

Essentially, plans for nonrepetitive problems *(single-use plans)* set forth a course of action to fit a specific situation and may be obsolete when the goal is reached. This is in contrast to standing plans which are designed to have continuing usefulness. There is a hierarchy of single-use plans ranging from (1) major programs, (2) projects, and (3) special tasks to (4) detailed plans.

There are many examples of major programs such as the design, development, and construction of a rapid transit system. The success of a major program depends upon the establishment of more detailed single-use plans for special projects. These single-use plans should all be integrated into an overall planning hierarchy.

Plans for repetitive action are often called *standing plans.* They include policies, methods, and standard operating procedures designed to cover the variety of repetitive situations which organizations frequently face. These plans are of importance to any established organization. It can be argued that even informal organizational relationships such as social groups and bowling teams have established plans. For the more formal organization the standing plans are a primary cohesive force connecting its various subsystems. Plans for repetitive action become the habit patterns of the organization, similar to the habit patterns of individuals.

Policies are the broadest of the standing plans and are general guides to organizational behavior. Every large organization has a wide variety of policies covering its most important functions which frequently are formalized and written in organization or policy manuals.

Methods and procedures are also standing plans. Usually they are less general than policies and establish more definite steps for the performance of certain activities at the technical level.

There are many organizational advantages to the use of plans for repetitive action. Through the use of standing plans and the concept of "management by exception," top management's influence is extended to all organizational levels. Once a policy decision has been reached, the standing plan serves as a guideline for decision making throughout the organization. Another advantage of the standing plan is that it creates a uniformity of operations throughout the organization. Once established, understood, and accepted, it provides similarity of action in meeting certain situations. On the negative side, standing plans may create resistance to change when new and dynamic situations occur.

Time Span

Recently much emphasis has been placed upon long-range planning. Generally, long-range planning deals with decisions regarding the broad technological and competitive aspects of the organization, the allocation of resources (human and material) over an extended period, and the long-run integration of the organization within its environment.

It is our view that long-range plans are not a separate type of plan. Rather they are an integral part of the total planning process and establish the basic framework upon which more detailed programming and operational planning take place. There is an interdependency of plans for various time periods. Long- and medium-range plans provide a framework for short-range plans, which refer primarily to current operations. Feedback from ongoing activity is a part of the information flow which management uses in making decisions. Forward planning is based on past history, the current situation and estimates of the future.

Scope

Another useful dimension in thinking about planning is that of scope. We often hear the terms "comprehensive plans" and "strategic plans," which connote the idea of a general or overall plan for the organization. Within this framework, other more detailed plans are developed for subparts of the total endeavor. Steiner describes three types of planning—strategic planning, medium-range programming, and short-term budgets and detailed functional plans:

> *Strategic planning.* Strategic planning is the process of determining the major objectives of an organization and the policies and strategies that will govern the acquisition, use, and disposition of resources to achieve those objectives.
>
> *Medium-range programming* is the process in which detailed, coordinated, and comprehensive plans are made for selected functions of a business to deploy resources to reach objectives by following policies and strategies laid down in the strategic planning process.
>
> *Short-term budgets and detailed functional plans* include such matters as short-range targets for salesmen, budgets for material purchases, short-term advertising plans, inventory replenishment, and employment schedules.[11]

The complexity of the environment increases rapidly as the scope of the planning process increases. Comprehensive or strategic plans must, of necessity, deal with broad societal elements. Corporate planning for a large industrial firm would include sociopolitical considerations, legal aspects, and other similar variables which might not be necessary or appropriate at the branch-plant level.[12] The necessary information might be provided by headquarters and hence dealt with as "given" in managerial planning at that branch. Planning activity at the subsystem level is complex in a different way because of the increasing amount of detail that must be considered.

Subsystems Involved

There is a relationship between the scope and the organization subsystem involved in the planning effort. Generally, top management in the strategic subsystem is responsible for comprehensive planning, management in the coordinative subsystem is concerned with medium-range programming, and management in the technical or operational subsystem is concerned with more specific, short-term planning.

With the growing need for investigation, analysis, and evaluation, planning has frequently become a specialized activity.

---

[11]Steiner, op. cit., pp. 34–35.
[12]Melville C. Branch, *Planning: Aspects and Applications,* John Wiley & Sons, Inc., New York, 1966, pp. 297–314.

Increasingly, specialized corporate planning staffs have been established to aid in the planning function. This is particularly true in the area of long-range, comprehensive planning. All too frequently, this staff assumes that its role is planning rather than facilitating the planning activities of line management. Left to its own discretion, this staff frequently proceeds to set up goals and plans according to its own conception and premises, often developing elaborate research reports to substantiate its position. Unless there is considerable dialogue and mutual understanding between planning staff personnel and operating managers, a gap may develop which is dysfunctional for the organization. Line managers should participate actively and continually in the planning function. They should be encouraged to consider relatively longer time periods as they move upward in the organizational hierarchy. Similarly, they must be concerned with more comprehensive plans and begin to comprehend combinations of subsystems.

In large-scale organizations with many-leveled departmentation, diverse subobjectives, and organizational and human limits on rationality, it is improbable that the planning gap can be eliminated completely. To do so would be to assume complete knowledge, absolute predictability, perfect communication, and full agreement throughout the organization. These assumptions are too much to ask for. However, the gap can be minimized if specialized staff work is conceived of as an extension of the manager's planning function.[13] The centralized planning staff can be instrumental *in helping* management design and implement an integrated planning system.

In recent years, many organizations have adopted the concept of "management by objectives" wherein individual managers determine what specific goals they plan to achieve as a result of their efforts and then carefully plan how these results will be accomplished. These objectives and resulting plans are then reviewed by their superiors and integrated into more comprehensive plans. Although originally "management by objective" was geared primarily to improving performance appraisals and compensation systems, in many organizations this concept has expanded into a comprehensive planning system.[14] To make such a program effective it is necessary to establish a meaningful

[13]For a more complete discussion of the problems involved in the planning gap, see Fremont E. Kast and James E. Rosenzweig, "Minimizing the Planning Gap," *Advanced Management,* October 1960, pp. 20–23.
[14]Walter S. Wikstrom, *Managing by—and with—Objectives,* Studies in Personnel Policy, No. 212, National Industrial Conference Board, Inc., New York, 1968.

two-way flow of information and objectives. Information about the view of the future from the top has to be transmitted downward in the organization so that individual managers have a meaningful context within which to formulate their specific objectives and plans.

Flexibility

One of the major considerations in planning is the degree of rigidity or flexibility of plans. This dimension is particularly important for long-range planning. Many authors writing about long-range planning emphasize that it involves decision making which commits resources over the long run and that planning is necessary in dealing with the uncertainty of the future. Herein lies a major dilemma. On the one hand, there is rapidly advancing technology, changing competitive and market situations, increasingly active governmental, labor and other interests, and many other forces which make forecasting the future environment extremely difficult. Yet organizations must plan their activities over a long-run period and must commit resources in spite of future uncertainties. Witness the problems of planning for a program such as the SST aircraft in which the Boeing Company and the federal government cooperated in the design, development, and production planning. Both parties had to make commitments of resources based upon plans which were subject to drastic changes (e.g., the possibility that society, through Congress, would not tolerate sonic booms). What is the solution to this long-range planning dilemma? More thorough and complete planning at the early stages runs the risk of complete inflexibility in the face of inevitable changes. Extending the planning period runs the risk of even more uncertainty.

While we cannot provide any final solution to this dilemma, we can suggest that alternative approaches are available. One of the major mistakes in long-range planning is to assume future certainty in the face of a turbulent environment. This leads to great rigidities in plans and limits adaptiveness. This is a *Cook's-tour planning approach*[15] and assumes that the future is sufficiently certain so that we can move in an exact straight line from here to there (see Figure 3-1). Cook's-tour planning requires sub-

[15]Cook's World Travel Service is one of the oldest and largest travel agencies. It was the originator of thoroughly planned travel tours with clearly prescribed itineraries and schedules. "Cook's-tour" suggests a highly organized and thoroughly planned program of activities.

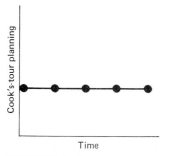
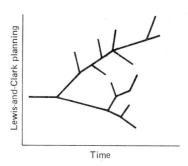

FIGURE 3-1. Two approaches to planning.

stantial precision by the planner. It is most appropriate where the planner is facing a relatively certain environment.

In contrast, the *Lewis-and-Clark planning approach* acknowledges that in the future there will be many decision points and alternative courses of action.[16] From the present viewpoint it is impossible to determine their location or timing. In this approach it is not the function of planning to chart a precise course of action. Rather, it is to prepare the organization to cope with the uncertainties of the future, to note the signs in the environment which indicate that a point of decision has been reached, and to develop a means of responding.

The Lewis-and-Clark planning approach is similar to that suggested by Colm for governmental planning:

> It is important to recognize that planning means more than merely preparing a plan—it should be understood as a system of decision-making. Government decisions, in part, are always concerned with factors which are outside government control, such as foreign markets, foreign capital, the response of people to government measures, the weather, etc. Estimates can be made concerning these factors, but they are subject to a high degree of error. Consequently, planning is decision-making under conditions of uncertainty which requires a mechanism for adapting the plan to unexpected developments. Under conditions of uncertainty a plan is always tentative and subject to revision in the course of its execution and in the preparation of a subsequent plan.[17]

For the manager it would seem that whenever uncertainties in the internal subsystems and in the environment are sub-

[16]These two approaches are discussed in detail in James R. Schlesinger, *Organizational Structure and Planning*, Rand Corporation, Santa Monica, Calif., 1966.
[17]Gerhard Colm, *Integration of National Planning and Budgeting*, National Planning Association, Washington, D.C., 1968, p. 3.

stantial, planning should shift toward the Lewis-and-Clark approach. Although it gives the appearance of ambiguity and less certainty than the Cook's-tour approach, it is most adaptable in a changing environment. However, it often goes "against the grain" of the more bureaucratic, stable organization because it substitutes flexibility for fixity and false exactness. There are many organizational pressures to establish long-range plans in a highly specific and exact fashion. This gives the appearance of planning perfection, but with the high cost of inflexibility and the likelihood of future events completely destroying the established plans.

The organization may have to compromise on the rigidity versus flexibility dimension. It will generally accomplish this by developing relatively fixed short-term operational plans under the general umbrella of more flexible, longer-range, strategic plans.

A CONCEPTUAL MODEL FOR PLANNING

The foregoing discussion suggested the importance of planning, defined the planning function as providing a framework for an integrated decision system, and set forth the multidimensional nature of the planning process and the resulting plans. In this section we will present a conceptual model for total organizational planning on a systematic basis and then will discuss the relationship between planning and the other managerial functions.

The comprehensive planning model set forth by Steiner and shown in Figure 3-2 illustrates the structure and process of an effective planning program.[18] This model suggests that planning is based upon certain premises relating to the fundamental socioeconomic purpose of the organization, the values of top management, and an evaluation of the external and internal environment. These premises are primarily developed at the strategic managerial level and are concerned with the fundamental nature of the organization, its goals and aspirations, and its relationship to its environment. The premises provide the foundation for the comprehensive planning program.

The next structural element is strategic planning, which is the process of determining the major objectives and the strategies for their accomplishment. Strategic planning is a function of the highest management level, frequently supported by specialized planning staffs. Strategic plans establish the basic missions of

[18]Steiner, op. cit., pp. 31-37.

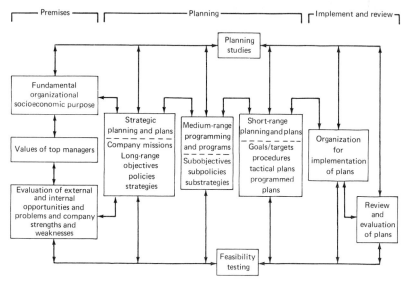

FIGURE 3-2. Structure and process of planning. (Source: George A. Steiner, *Top Management Planning,* **The Macmillan Company, New York, 1969, p. 33.)**

the organization and the broad policies and programs for their accomplishment. Generally strategic plans are long-run, broad in scope, established at the highest organizational level, and tend to be relatively flexible.

Strategic plans provide the framework for the next step, medium-range programming. These medium-range plans are usually developed for the major fundamental areas of the organization. In business these might be production, sales, personnel utilization, capital expenditures, and research and development. These plans are developed by the coordinative level of management for a medium time period (usually three to five years). The scope is generally limited to a specific functional area, with more emphasis upon details and relatively fixed as compared to strategic plans.

Short-range planning is based upon the medium-range plans and includes short-term budgets and detailed functional plans which provide detailed guides for all organizational activities over the short run, usually one year. In the business organization these might include short-term plans for sales activities, production schedules, purchasing budgets, and plans for employee utilization. These plans are generally developed at the operating or technical level in the organization, are short-term, limited in scope to specific activities but extensive in detail, and fixed.

This comprehensive planning model also recognizes the

importance of adapting the organization to ensure the proper implementation of the plans. For example, if the business has adopted a strategic plan for diversification into new market areas, it must develop the organizational structure for the implementation of this plan. Similarly, if the company plans to engage in a major new activity, such as a program to construct new plant facilities, it will need to modify its organizational arrangements.

The final stage in a comprehensive planning program is the establishment of procedures for review and evaluation of plans. Continuous surveillance to assure that plans are carried out and that new plans are devised as circumstances require is a vital step.

Figure 3–2 further suggests the needs for special planning studies in all phases of a comprehensive planning program. These planning studies are often associated with the analysis of the broad premises and the establishment of strategic plans. Quite frequently these planning studies are undertaken by a corporate planning staff which provide information to line executives. More detailed planning studies may be involved for medium-range and short-range plans, for example, studies on machinery replacement policies, routing of salesmen, procurement procedures, and inventory policies. Again, many of these studies are performed by lower-level staff specialists, such as industrial engineers, operations researchers, and market analysts.

There should be a continuous process of testing to determine the feasibility of the various objectives and the plans for their accomplishment. Quite frequently the more detailed plans, emanating from a functional area, have to be modified to mesh with comprehensive organizational plans.

This planning model also provides for numerous feedback loops which tie the various components of the process together. It should be emphasized that no organization operating in a complex and turbulent environment is able to plan in an exact step-by-step fashion. Comprehensive planning is a continual, adaptive process in which new information inputs and feedback provide the basis for appraisal, evaluation, and review of existing plans.

Relationship of Planning and Control

Planning, action, and control are closely related managerial functions. Although they may be separated for discussion purposes, these phases of the managerial task are not completely separable in practice. Therefore, it is important to consider how these functions are related.

A complete operating cycle for any individual or organization would include the following phases:

1. Objective setting
2. Planning
3. Action
4. Accomplishment
5. Feedback
6. Control

This is a generalized model which can be applied at any level. It does not specify the technology employed in carrying out the designated activities. Feedback may be relatively automatic and computer based, or it may depend on the subjective appraisal of human beings. Control is the process of ensuring that accomplishments are in conformance with plans. Planning and control are intergral phases of the overall cycle; in a sequential process their interdependence is evident. They can only be separated conceptually.

Anthony presents a meaningful approach which identifies two different types of control activity—management control and operational control. He distinguishes these from strategic planning and uses all three as a framework for planning and control systems. He defines the concepts as follows:

> *Strategic planning* is the process of deciding on objectives of the organization, on changes in these objectives, on the resources used to attain these objectives, and on the policies that are to govern the acquisition, use and disposition of these resources. . . .
>
> *Management control* is the process by which managers assure that resources are obtained and used effectively and efficiently in the accomplishment of the organization's objectives. . . .
>
> *Operational control* is the process of assuring that specific tasks are carried out effectively and efficiently.[19]

In general, these categories coincide with the three subsystems—strategic, coordinative, and operating—which have been cited previously as parts of the organization. They are also closely related to the three types of planning processes and plans set forth in Figure 3–2.

[19]Robert N. Anthony, *Planning and Control Systems: A Framework for Analysis,* Division of Research, Harvard Graduate School of Business Administration, Boston, 1965, pp. 16, 17, 18.

TABLE 3-1 Examples of Activities in a Business Organization
Included in Major Framework Headings

Strategic planning	Management control	Operational control
Choosing company objectives	Formulating budgets	
Planning the organization	Planning staff levels	Controlling hiring
Setting personnel policies	Formulating personnel practices	Implementing policies
Setting financial policies	Working capital planning	Controlling credit extension
Setting marketing policies	Formulating advertising programs	Controlling placement of advertisements
Setting research policies	Deciding on research projects	
Choosing new product lines	Choosing product improvements	
Acquiring a new division	Deciding on plant rearrangement	Scheduling production
Deciding on nonroutine capital expenditures	Deciding on routine capital expenditures	
	Formulating decision rules for operational control	Controlling inventory
	Measuring, appraising, and improving management performance	Measuring, appraising, and improving workers' efficiency

SOURCE: Robert N. Anthony, *Planning and Control Systems: A Framework for Analysis,* Division of Research, Harvard Graduate School of Business Administration, Boston, 1965, p. 19.

In the *strategic subsystem* managers engage primarily in *strategic planning*—operating at the boundary to relate the organization to its environment. There is a relatively long-run outlook, and forecasting is used to reduce uncertainty. The *coordinative subsystem* is concerned primarily with what Anthony calls *management control* and the *operating subsystem* is involved with *operational control.*

As a means of illustrating the main categories in his framework, Anthony sets forth examples of activities in a business organization which might be included under the headings described above. These activities are shown in Table 3-1. The difficulty in separating planning and controlling is evidenced in the listing. Most of the activities under strategic planning are in fact planning activities. Management control, on the other hand, involves a mixture of both planning and control activities, and those listed under operational control are almost entirely control activities.

The systems approach emphasizes the integrative nature of planning, action, and control. Although we may treat them separately for convenience purposes, they are all part of a total cycle. In the following chapter, we will consider the control function in more detail.

SUMMARY

Planning is the managerial process of deciding in advance what is to be done and how. It involves selecting objectives and developing action programs for achieving them. The results of this process are plans which are predetermined courses of action.

Managerial planning provides a framework for integrated decision making across a spectrum of diverse activities and over a relatively long time period. It is a means of coping with the uncertainty of the future; it facilitates adaptation and innovation. Under the systems approach the planning process can be considered as the vehicle for accomplishing system change.

There is a hierarchy of plans which starts with the formation of overall objectives, moves to the development of strategic plans, then medium-range plans, and finally to detailed operational plans. Clear-cut, well-defined organizational goals and strategic plans help provide the basis for systematic planning at lower operating levels.

It is necessary to understand the multidimensional nature of the planning process and the resulting plans. Several of the most important dimensions are repetitiveness, time span, scope, subsystems involved, and flexibility.

Strategic planning is a function of higher management, is long-run, broad in scope, and tends to be relatively flexible. Medium-range plans are developed by the coordinative subsystem, are for a medium time period, are functional in scope, and are relatively more fixed than strategic plans. Short-run plans are developed in the operating subsystem, and are short-term, limited in scope to specific activities but extensive in detail, and fixed.

Planning, action, and control are closely related managerial functions. Although they may be separated for discussion purposes, these phases of the managerial task are not completely separable in practice. The systems approach emphasizes the integrative nature of these activities.

QUESTIONS

1. Define planning. What are the forces which have increased the importance of planning in (a) a large business organization? (b) a large general hospital?
2. What is the relationship between planning and (a) forecasting, and (b) decision making?
3. How has advancing technology affected the problems of planning?
4. Describe ways in which higher management can ensure adequate participation in the planning process.
5. How can the systems approach provide the basis for integrated planning?
6. Discuss the various dimensions of planning and relate them to the plans in an organization with which you are familiar.
7. Select any new program or activity of which you have knowledge and indicate the hierarchy of planning.
8. Why is the establishment of goals and objectives particularly important in the systems concept of planning?
9. Discuss the distinction between fixed and flexible planning. Provide examples to illustrate this distinction.
10. What recommendations do you have for minimizing the planning gap?
11. Using the model presented in Figure 3-2, select a major problem and establish a model for systematically planning to meet this problem.
12. How are planning and control related in the overall operational cycle of an organization?

CHAPTER 4

Control
and Systems Concepts

In the previous chapter we reviewed the function of planning and pointed out how it relates to control. The illustration used in showing this relationship can be categorized as "organizational control." In this chapter we illustrate how the concept of control applies to many situations at different levels of decision making and various kinds of systems. For example, the theory of control applies to man, to man-machine, and to machine systems. It applies to biological, social, political, economic, and technical systems; it is the application and not the nature of control that changes. Control is not an end in itself; rather it is a means to an end, a way to improve the operation of a system. Our discussion of control and systems concepts will cover the following topics:

> Definitions of control
> Elements of control
> Relationship between the elements of control and information
> Kinds of control
> Problems of control

DEFINITIONS OF CONTROL

The concept of control is not new or difficult to understand; however, it has been used in different ways and with varying degrees of sophistication. One of the first definitions of management control was offered by Henri Fayol in 1916: "Control consists of verifying whether everything occurs in conformity with the plan adopted, the instructions issued and principles established. It has for object to point out weaknesses and errors in order to rectify and prevent recurrence."[1] A recent and more comprehensive definition of management control is given by Robert J. Mockler:

> Management control can be defined as a systematic effort by business management to compare performance to predetermined standards, plans, or objectives in order to determine whether performance is in line with these standards and presumably in order to take any remedial action required to see that human and other corporate resources are being used in the most effective and efficient way possible in achieving corporate objectives.[2]

Definitions of control have been suggested that have application beyond the business firm. For example, Norbert Wiener, a mathematician, defined control to mean *to direct.* "Control . . . is nothing but the sending of messages which effectively change the behavior of the recipient. . . ."[3] Earlier he provided a foundation for control theory in a treatise on the science of control over complex systems, information, and communication.[4] Much of his writing concerned systems and communication processes amenable to mathematical formulation. However, the concepts extend to processes involving groups of people and the activities of man and machines in systems.

We shall define control as *that function of the system which provides adjustments in conformance to the plan; the maintenance of variations from system objectives within allowable limits.*

Control is maintained through a network of information flow which serves as the medium of control. When relevant information is not fed back, it is of little value to a control system.

[1]Henri Fayol, *General and Industrial Management,* trans. Constance Storrs, Pitman Publishing Corp., New York, 1949, p. 107.
[2]Robert J. Mockler, *Readings in Management Control,* Appleton-Century-Crofts, New York, 1970, p. 14.
[3]Norbert Wiener, *The Human Use of Human Beings,* Houghton Mifflin Company, Boston, 1950, p. 124.
[4]Norbert Wiener, *Cybernetics or Control and Communication in the Animal and the Machine,* Technology Press, Boston, 1948.

On the other hand, information in motion is the vital flow of intelligence which establishes the basis for controlling a system.

An election can be used to illustrate the concept of control and the importance of feedback. A political party organizes a campaign to get its members elected and outlines a plan to communicate both the candidate's credentials and the platform to the public. As the election nears, the various opinion polls furnish feedback about the effectiveness of the campaign and the probability that the candidate will win. Depending on the nature of this feedback, certain adjustments in strategy and/or tactics can be made.

The "sensitivity" of a system refers to the degree of variation from the norm which occurs before an adjusting response is invoked. "Stability" concerns the ability of a system to maintain a predictable behavior pattern over time. "Rapidity of response" pertains to the speed with which a system can correct variations from stated objectives.

ELEMENTS OF CONTROL

The four basic elements in a control system, as shown in Figure 4-1, occur in the same sequence and maintain a consistent relationship to each other.

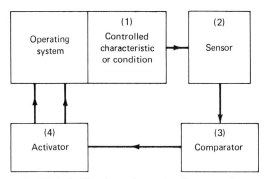

FIGURE 4-1. The four elements of a control system:
1. A characteristic or condition to be controlled
2. A sensor—a way to sense or measure the characteristic or condition
3. A comparator—an individual, unit, or device that compares measurements with the plan or standard
4. An activator—an individual, unit, or mechanism that directs action to bring about a change in the operating system

The first element is the characteristic or condition of the operating system which is to be measured. This element may be the output of the system during any stage of processing, or it may be a condition which has resulted from the output of the system. For example, it may be the heat energy produced by the furnace, or the temperature in the room which has changed because of the furnace output. In an elementary school system, characteristics that may be used include the hours a teacher is at school or the gain in knowledge demonstrated by the students in a national examination.

The second element of control (sensor) involves the measurement of performance. The system should be designed to provide a sensory device or method for measuring the controlled characteristic or condition. In a home heating system this would be the temperature gauge, and in a quality control system this may represent the visual inspection performed on a product.

The third element of control determines the need for correc-

FIGURE 4-2 Examples of the elements of control.

	Measurable characteristic	Sensor	Comparator	Activator
Driving to visit a friend	Geographic location	Perception of location (mental)	Driver with aid of various landmarks	Driver
Coaching a football team	Number of games won and lost	Published records: conference standings	Coach ("aided" by alumni, sports writers, faculty, students, and others)	Coach
Managing an advertising campaign	Sales and/or market share	Company records and industry reports	Advertising manager and/ or superior(s) in organization who are aware of goals	Advertising manager and/ or superior(s) in organization
Administering Medicare	Health care for people 62 and over	Agency statistics and qualitative societal "feelings" (as reported in various media)	Director, Secretary of HEW, President, Congress, and society	Director, Secretary of HEW, President, Congress, and society

tion. Some deviation from plan is usual and expected, but when variations are beyond those considered acceptable, action is required. Often, it is possible to identify trends in performance and to take action before an unacceptable variation from the norm occurs. This sort of preventive action indicates a good control system in operation.

The fourth element of control is the corrective action. The actual person, device, or method used to direct corrective inputs into the operating system takes on a wide variety of forms. It may be a hydraulic controller positioned by a solenoid or electric motor in response to an electronic error signal from the comparator, an employee directed to rework the parts which failed to pass quality inspection, or a school principal who decides to replace an ineffective teacher. As long as a plan is performed perfectly, corrective action is not necessary, but theoretical perfection seldom occurs in practice.

Four examples of control are illustrated in Figure 4–2, with the elements listed in each instance. When a person wishes to drive to another part of the city to visit a friend, he checks the address and then uses the street signs and house numbers (characteristic) as a guide. He notes (sensor) the various streets as he drives, and compares his progress against various landmarks or perhaps a map. If he makes a wrong turn, he activates a correction by steering the automobile to make the proper adjustment.

RELATIONSHIP BETWEEN THE ELEMENTS OF CONTROL AND INFORMATION

Information is the medium of control, because it is the flow of sensory data and later the flow of corrective information which allows a characteristic or condition of the system to be controlled. In order to illustrate how information flow facilitates control, it is helpful to review the elements of control in this context.

Controlled Characteristic or Condition

As noted earlier, the primary requirement of a control system is that it maintain the level and kind of output necessary to achieve the objectives of the system. Usually it is not practical to control every feature and condition associated with the system's output. Therefore, the choice of the controlled item (and appropriate information about it) is of extreme importance. There should be a direct correlation between the controlled item and the operation of the system. In other words, control of the selected characteristic should have a direct relationship with goal or objective achievement.

Sensor

After the characteristic is sensed or measured, pertinent information pertaining to control is fed back. It is important to determine what information needs to be transmitted and also to consider the language which will both facilitate the communication process and reduce the possibility of distortion in transmission.

Information that is to be compared with the standard should be expressed in the same terms or language so as to facilitate decision making. If machine methods are used, and sometimes even if they are not, extensive translation may be required. Optimum languages for computation and for human review are not always the same. This should not be overlooked, since the relative ease of translation may be a significant factor in selecting the units of measurement, or the language unit in the sensing element.

In many instances the measurement may be sampled rather than providing a complete and continuous feedback of information about the operation. A sampling procedure suggests that some segment or portion of the operation can be measured which will represent the total. It also suggests that when a system can be controlled with less feedback, the cost of control can be reduced.

Comparison with Standard

In a social system the "norms" of acceptable behavior become the standard against which deviant behavior may be judged. Regulations and laws provide a more formal collection of information for the society. Social norms change, but very slowly. In contrast, the standards outlined by a law can be changed from one day to the next when a law is revised, discontinued, or replaced by another.

Information about deviant behavior becomes the basis for controlling social activity. Output information is compared with the standard or norm and significant deviations are noted. In another example, a frequency distribution (a tabulation of the number of times a given quality characteristic occurs within the sample of products being checked) may be used to show the average quality, the spread, and the comparison of output with standard.

If there is a significant and uncorrectable difference between output and plan, a system is "out of control." This means that the objectives of the system are not feasible in terms of the capabilities of the present system. Either reevaluation of the objectives must be considered, or the system must be redesigned to add new capacity or capability. For example, the crime rate has been increasing in some cities at an alarming rate. People are afraid to walk in the streets at night or to leave their homes unguarded. The citizens of a city in this category must decide whether to change the system of protection so as to regain control, or whether to modify the law to reflect a more realistic norm of acceptable behavior.

Activator

The activator unit responds to the information received from the comparator and initiates corrective action. If the system is a machine-to-machine system, the corrective inputs (decision rules) are designed into the network. When the control relates to a man-to-machine or man-to-man system, however, the individual(s) in charge must evaluate (1) the accuracy of the feedback information, (2) the significance of the variation, and (3) what corrective inputs will restore the system to a reasonable degree of stability. A small amount of energy can transmit information to control jet airplanes, automatic steel mills, and hydroelectric power plants. The pilot presses a button, and the landing gear of the airplane goes up or down. The steel-mill operator pushes a lever and a ribbon of white-hot steel starts racing through the plant. A worker at a control board directs the flow of electrical energy throughout a regional network of stations and substations. It takes only a small amount of control energy to release or discontinue large quantities of input.

The comparator may be located far from the operating system, although some of the elements must be in close proximity to operations. For example, the measurement (the sensory element) is usually at the point of operations.[5] The measurement information can be transmitted to a distant point for comparison with the standard (comparator), and when deviations occur, the correcting input can be released from the distant point. However, the input (activator) will be located with the operating system. This ability to control from afar means that aircraft can be flown by remote

[5]Remote detection and measuring devices (like radar) are fundamental to some control systems, however.

control, dangerous manufacturing processes can be operated from a safe distance, and national organizations can be directed from centralized headquarters.

KINDS OF CONTROL

Control may be classified in three general categories: (1) by the nature of the information flow designed into the system (i.e., open- or closed-loop control), (2) by the kind of components included in the design (i.e., man or machine control systems), and (3) by the relationship of control to the decision process (i.e., organizational or operational control).

Open- and Closed-loop Control[6]

The difference between these two types of control is determined by whether all of the control elements are an integral part of the system being regulated, and whether allowable variations from standard have been predetermined. In an open-loop system, not all the elements will be designed into the system, and/or allowable variations will not be predetermined.

A street-lighting system controlled by a timing device would be an example of an open-loop system. At a certain time each evening, a mechanical device would close the circuit and energy would flow through the electric lines to light the lamps. It should be noted, however, that the timing mechanism is an independent unit and is not measuring the objective function of the lighting system. If on a dark, stormy day the lights should be needed, the timing device would not measure this variation in need and would not activate new energy inputs. Corrective properties may sometimes be built into the controller (e.g., to modify the time the lights are turned on as the days grow shorter or longer), but this would not close the loop. In another instance, the sensing, comparison, or adjustment may be made by action taken by a component not regarded as a part of the system. For example, the lights may be turned on by someone who happens to pass by and recognizes the need for additional light.

If control is exerted in terms of the operation rather than because of outside or predetermined arrangements, it is a closed-loop system. The home thermostat is the classic example of a

[6]It is easy to confuse the idea of open- and closed-loop control with open and closed systems. The latter concept pertains to design and not to operations and is discussed in Chapters 1 and 6.

control device in this kind of system. When the room temperature drops below the desired point, the control mechanism closes the circuit to start the furnace and the temperature rises. The furnace operating circuit is turned off as the temperature reaches the selected level. The significant difference is that the control device is an element of the system it serves and measures the performance of the system. In other words, all four control elements belong to the same system.

An essential part of a closed-loop system is feedback; that is, the output of the system is measured continually in terms of the item controlled, and the input is modified to reduce any divergence or error toward zero.

Many of the patterns of information flow in organizations are found to have the nature of closed loops. The reason for such a condition is apparent when one recognizes that any system, if it is to achieve a predetermined goal, must have available to it at all times an indication of its degree of attainment. In general, every goal-seeking system employs circuits, or feedback.

Man and Machine Control

The elements of control are easy to identify in machine systems; the characteristic to be controlled might be, for example, some variable like speed or temperature while the sensing device could be a speedometer or a thermometer. An expectation of preciseness exists because the characteristic is quantifiable and the standard and the normal variation to be expected can be described in exact terms. In automatic machine systems, inputs of information are used in a process of continual adjustment to achieve output specifications. When even a small variation from the standard occurs, the correction process begins. The automatic system is highly structured, designed to accept certain kinds of input and produce specific output, and programmed to regulate the transformation of inputs within a narrow range of variation.

As the load on a steam engine increases and the engine starts to slow down, the regulator reacts by opening a valve and additional inputs of steam energy are added. This new input returns the engine to the desired revolutions per minute. This is a mechanical illustration and crude in comparison to the more sophisticated electronic control systems in everyday use. However, it does illustrate the basic process of control for a machine system.

When people are grouped in some organized arrangement, the process of control is quite different. The relationship between objectives and possible characteristics is often vague, the measurement of the characteristic may be extremely subjective, the expected standard is difficult to define, and the amount of new inputs required are impossible to quantify. To illustrate, let us refer once more to a formalized social system where deviant behavior is controlled through a process of observed violation of the existing law (sensing), court hearings and trials (comparison with standard), incarceration when the accused is found guilty (correction), and the release from custody after the rehabilitation of the prisoner has occurred.

The speed limit established for freeway driving is one standard of performance that is quantifiable, but even in this instance the degree of variation to permit and the amount of the actual variation, if any, are often a subject of disagreement between the patrolman and the suspected violator. The complexity of our society is reflected in many of our laws and regulations which established the general standard for economic, political, and social operations. The typical citizen may not understand the law and would not know whether or not he was guilty of a violation.

The reader will recognize that most organized systems are some combination of man and machine. Some of the elements may be performed by machine while others are accomplished by man. Some standards may be precise in structure while others may be a little more than a general guide with wide variations of output expected. Man must act as the controller when measurement is subjective and judgment is required. Machines (e.g., the programmed computer) cannot be expected to make exceptions from the stated control criteria regardless of how much a particular case might warrant special consideration.

Organizational and Operational Control

The concept of organizational control was inherent in the bureaucratic theory of Max Weber. This theory holds that control in an organization depends on the supervision of all levels which exist below it. Associated with this theory are such concepts as "span of control," "closeness of supervision," and "hierarchical authority." There has been much investigation of the effect of close supervision on employee perceptions of freedom, morale, job satisfaction, and performance. The number of employees that could be supervised effectively by one person has also been the subject of many studies.

Weber's view tends to include all levels or types of control of organization under one category. More recently, writers have tended to classify the control process between that which emphasizes the nature of the organizational or systems design and that which deals with daily operations. To illustrate the difference, we "evaluate" the performance of a system to see how effective and efficient the design proved to be, or why it failed. In contrast, we operate and "control" the system with respect to the daily regulation of material, information, and energy. In both instances, the function of control is present; whereas organizational control tends to review and evaluate the nature and arrangement of components in the system, operational control tends to adjust daily inputs.

The direction for organizational control comes from the goals and strategic plans of the organization. General plans are translated into specific performance measures such as share of the market, earnings, return on investment, or budgets. The process is to review and evaluate the performance of the system against these established norms. Rewards for meeting or exceeding standards may range from special recognition to salary increases or promotions. On the other hand, a failure to meet expectations may signal the need to reorganize or redesign.

The approach used in the program of review and evaluation (organizational control) will depend on the reason for the evaluation; i.e., is it because the system is not effective (accomplishing its objectives)? Is the system failing to achieve an expected standard of efficiency? Is the evaluation being conducted because of a breakdown or failure in operations? Is it merely a periodic audit and review process?

Let us assume that the reason for the review is to determine if system objectives are being met. In this instance the review and evaluation might be organized in the following sequence:

1. Determine the objectives of the system, or the mission the system is designed to achieve
2. Translate the objectives by describing in some detail those specific goals which are to be accomplished
3. Identify those key characteristics which correlate with goal achievement
4. Choose the appropriate measuring techniques
5. Gather and sort performance information
6. Analyze the information that is collected
7. Compare the analyzed information with the selected characteristics to determine the extent to which objectives have been achieved

8. Reward outstanding performance, or proceed to the design phase if the need for redesign is indicated by the study

The need to declare clear-cut objectives for a system should be reemphasized. When the precise purposes for which the system exists are not understood, it is difficult, if not impossible, to establish criteria for evaluation. There is an increasing tendency for business institutions to highlight certain objectives which are not related directly to the profit motive, although most decisions and actions still tend to be evaluated on the basis of the profit ethic (i.e., the idea that the alternative which will maximize long-run profits is selected). In contrast to business, public institutions may have objectives concerning specific kinds and levels of service to be performed in comparison to specific cost constraints, e.g., police protection related to a budget (cost benefit).

Within the general statement of objectives, the broad policies which are to be stressed in achieving the overall purposes of the system should be described. Such policies as the quality and reliability of the product, the level and nature of customer service, the kinds of social service performed in the community, and the stability and nature of the employment opportunity to be provided are examples of significant policies of business organizations.

Major goals for a distribution system might be to sell a specified family of products and, of course, to make a profit. Policies which are significant in achieving these goals could include the selection of a specific clientele to serve, or a liberal credit policy along with complete freedom to return merchandise. In this instance the credit and return policies become the strategy by which the organization plans to achieve its objectives.

Characteristics of operations are selected which provide specific evidence about the performance of the system. It is important to select characteristics that correlate closely with major policy achievement, but also to select those that can be isolated and measured in a practical way. There is an inherent danger that characteristics which lend themselves to measurement in arithmetic units may be selected, even when their association to systems performance may be insignificant. For example, would the number of traffic citations made by a police department indicate whether or not the community was receiving adequate police protection at a reasonable cost?

It should be noted that only in rare instances is it possible to plot the performance of a system by measuring a single characteristic, or even two or three. It usually is necessary to select many characteristics, all of which have relationships with each other and to total performance.

An indication of the nature and quality of service that a distribution system is providing can be measured, in part, by the characteristic of on-time deliveries. The number of orders which were available to the customer as scheduled would be a characteristic of significance. This would not in itself be sufficient evidence to determine whether or not the system was fulfilling its objectives, however. The goods delivered may not meet specifications, may be of inferior quality, or may be made in a manner which increased cost unreasonably.

It should be noted that the same difficulties of measurement which pertain to operational control also apply to the general evaluation and, in addition, that identical characteristics often are measured in both the control of operations and the review and evaluation of systems design.

A system may be performing effectively but using an unreasonable amount of resources in the process. An evaluation of system efficiency would be appropriate whenever an inordinate amount of inputs is being allocated in order to accomplish the desired mission. Of course, how much input should be used, or what ratio should exist between input and output is a difficult question to answer. The goal is to optimize this ratio or to achieve the maximum output with the minimum input.

In reviewing the efficiency of a system, an approach similar to that outlined to evaluate effectiveness may be followed. The standard of expected performance can be established by internal and/or external bench marks. For example, historical ratios serve as a guide to measure present performance, and industry figures provide some indication of how efficient the system is operating relative to competition.

When a system has failed or is in great difficulty, a different approach may be appropriate. Special diagnostic techniques are used to isolate the trouble area(s) and to identify the cause(s) of the difficulty. It is appropriate to investigate those areas that have been troublesome before, or to look where some measure of performance can be identified quickly. For example, if an organization's output backlog builds rapidly, it is logical to check first to see if it is due to such readily obtainable measures as increased demand, or to a drop in available man-hours. When a more detailed analysis is necessary, a systematic procedure should be followed.

In contrast to the review and evaluation process (organizational control) that often results in design changes, *operational control* serves to regulate the day-to-day output relative to schedules, specifications, and costs. Is the output of product or service of the right quality and is it available as scheduled? Are inventories of raw materials, goods-in-process, and finished products being purchased and produced in the proper quantities? Are the costs associated with the transformation process in line with cost estimates? Is the information needed in the transformation process available in the right form and at the proper time? Is the energy resource being utilized properly?

Perhaps the most difficult task of management concerns the task of monitoring the behavior of individuals, comparing performance to some standard, and providing rewards or punishment as indicated. Sometimes this control over people relates entirely to their output. For example, a manager might not be concerned with the behavior of a salesman as long as sales were as high as expected. In other instances, surveillance of the salesman might be appropriate if the achievement of customer satisfaction were an important objective of the sales organization.

The larger the unit, the more likely that the control characteristic will be in terms of some output goal. It also follows that if it is difficult or impossible to identify the actual output of individuals, it is better to measure the performance of the entire group. This means that the motivation of individuals and the measurement of their performance becomes a subjective judgment performed by the supervisor. This also suggests the difficulty in controlling the performance of individuals and relating this to the objectives of the total system. Some of these difficulties will be discussed in more detail in the following section on problems of control.

PROBLEMS OF CONTROL

The perfect plan could be outlined if every possible variation of input could be anticipated and the system would operate as predicted. This kind of planning would not be economical or feasible for most business systems. In fact, planning requirements (if feasible) would be so complex that the system would be out of date before it could be installed. Therefore, we design control into systems. This requires more thought in the systems design, but allows more flexibility of operations and makes it possible to operate a system of unpredictable components and undetermined input with meaningful results. Nevertheless, the design and effective operation of control are not without problems.

The objective of the system is to perform some specified function, the purpose of organizational control is to see that the specified function is achieved, and the objective of operational

control is to maintain variations in daily output within prescribed limits. It is one thing to design a system that contains all
the elements of control, and quite another to make it operate
true to the best objectives of design. "In control" or "with plan"
does not guarantee optimum performance. The plan may not make
the most effective use of the inputs of materials, energy, or information, or the system may not be designed to operate efficiently. Some of the more typical problems relating to control include
the difficulty of measurement, the problem of information flow,
and the setting of proper standards.

Measurement of Output

The measurement of system effectiveness, when the objectives
are not limited to quantitative output, is difficult to determine and
subsequently perplexing to evaluate. Many of the characteristics
pertaining to output do not lend themselves to quantitative
measurement. This is true particularly whenever inputs of human
energy cannot be related directly to output. The same situation
applies to machines and/or other equipment associated with
human involvement when output is not discrete. In the evaluation
of man-machine or man-oriented systems, the difficult of measuring the psychological and sociological factors should be evident.
For example, how does mental fatigue affect the quality or quantity of output; and, if it does, is it a function of the lack of a challenging assignment, the danger of a potential injury, or what?

Subjective inputs may be transferred into numerical data,
but there is always the danger that an incorrect appraisal and
transfer may be made, and that the analyst may assume undue
confidence in such data after it has been quantified. Let us suppose, for example, that the decisions made by an executive are
rated from 1 to 10, 10 being the perfect decision. After determining
the ranking for each decision, adding these, and dividing by the
total number of decisions made, the average ranking would
indicate the score of a particular executive in his decision-making
role. On the basis of this score, judgments might be made about
an executive's decision-making effectiveness which could be
quite erroneous. One executive with a ranking of 6.75 might be
considered more effective than another who had a ranking of
6.25, and yet the two managers may have made decisions under
different circumstances and conditions. External factors, over
which neither person had any control, also may have influenced
the difference in effectiveness.

Quantifying human behavior is extremely difficult and subjective and lacks the precise qualities of physical measurement; however, in most large systems it is the most prevalent and important measurement to be made. The behavior of individuals ultimately dictates the success or failure of every man-made system.

Information Flow

Another problem of control relates to the improper timing of information introduced into the feedback channel. This can occur in both computerized and human control systems, either erroneously or through mistakes in judgment. Acknowledging that much of the data introduced into the feedback channel may be added as improper or erroneous data, there also may be a problem because the data are not introduced or processed in a timely manner (rapidity of response). The more rapid the response of a system to an error signal, the more likely it is that the system could overadjust; yet, the need for prompt action is important because any delay in providing corrective input also can be crucial. A system generating feedback inconsistent with current need will tend to fluctuate and will not adjust in the desired manner.

The most critical problem arises when the delay in the information feedback is exactly one-half a cycle, for then the corrective action is superimposed upon a deviation which at that moment is the same direction as that of the correction. This causes the system to overcorrect, then if the reverse adjustment is made out of cycle, to correct too much in the other direction, and so on, until the system fluctuates out of control. This phenomenon is illustrated in Figure 4–3. If at point A the trend below standard is recognized, and new inputs are added but not until point B, the system will overact and go beyond the allowable limits. Again, if this is recognized at point C, but inputs are not withdrawn until point D, it will cause the system to drop below the lower limit of allowable variation.

One solution to this problem rests on anticipation, which involves measurement not only of the change, but on the rate of change as well. The correction is outlined as a factor of the type and rate of the error. The difficulty also might be overcome by reducing the time lag between the measurement of the output and the adjustment to input. If a trend can be indicated, a time lead can be introduced to compensate for the time lag, bringing about consistency between the need for correction and the type and magnitude of the indicated action. It usually is more effective

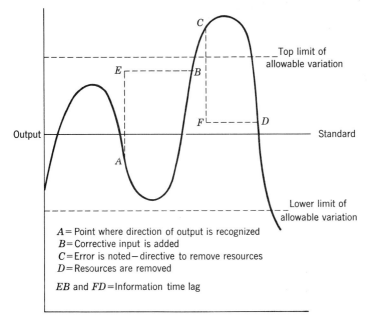

FIGURE 4-3. Oscillation and feedback.

for an organization to maintain continuous measurement of its performance, and to make small adjustments in operations constantly (a highly sensitive control system). Information feedback, therefore, should be timely and correct in order to be effective. That is, the information should provide an accurate indication of the status of the system.

Standards

Setting the right standards or control limits is a problem in many systems. Parents are confronted with this dilemma in outlining what is expected of their children, and business managers face the same issue in establishing standards which will be acceptable to employees. It has been proposed that workers be allowed to set their own standards on the assumption that when employees establish their own goals, they are more apt to achieve them.

Standards should be as precise as possible and communicated to all persons concerned. Moreover, communication alone is not sufficient; understanding is necessary. In people systems standards tend to be poorly defined, with the allowable range from standard also indefinite. For example, how many hours each day should a professor be expected to be available for student consultation, or what kind of behavior should be expected of students in the classroom? An element of discretion and personal judgment is necessary in such systems to determine whether action or new inputs are required.

Perhaps the most difficult problem in human systems is the unresponsiveness of individuals to indicated correction. This may take the form of opposition and subversion to control, or it may pertain to the lack of defined responsibility to take action. Leadership and positive motivation then become vital ingredients in human systems so as to get the proper response to input requirements.

Most control problems relate to design and the solution to these problems must start at that point. Automatic control systems, provided that human intervention is possible to handle exceptions, offers the greatest promise. There is a danger, however, that we measure characteristics that do not represent effective performance, or that improper information may be communicated—like the speaker who suggested that all people in the back row raise their hands if they could not hear what he was saying.

Systems breakdowns are another cause of ineffective operation. Designers have attempted to solve this problem by designing simplicity into systems, adding redundant components, and building systems with greater potential than required. Machine systems may be designed to repair themselves, or at least to indicate the need for repair.

SUMMARY

Control is that function of the system which provides adjustments in conformance to the plan, or the maintenance of varations from system objectives within allowable limits. The theory applies to man, man-machine, and machine systems. There are four elements in every control system: (1) the control characteristic, (2) the sensor or sensing device, (3) the controller or comparison between standard and actual, and (4) the activator or the unit adjusting input to change operations.

Information is the medium of control because it is the flow of measurement data and later the flow of corrective information which allows a characteristic or condition of a system to be controlled. Keeping in mind that information flow is the connecting link of any control cycle, the control characteristic, the means of measurement, the standard, and the corrective unit should be designed in consideration of the total system.

Control may be classified in three general categories: (1) as open- or closed-loop control, (2) as man or machine control, and (3) as organization or operational control. In an open-loop system, not all the elements are designed into the system, and/or allowable variations are not predetermined. In a closed-loop system all the elements are an integral part of the system being regulated. The elements in a machine control system are easy to identify whereas in a man system, they are somewhat more obscure. Nevertheless, they occur and follow the same sequence in both kinds of systems and also in the most common man-machine combinations.

A meaningful classification of a control process is to separate that control which emphasizes the nature of the organizational or systems design from that which deals with daily operations. We evaluate the performance of a system to see how effective and efficient the design has been (organizational control), and we measure the daily output of a system to see whether or not there are unacceptable variations from plan (operational control).

Problems occur in control systems when we fail to design the proper values or relationships among the four elements. Problems are most frequent in man systems because the values of expectations and output are more difficult to associate with the objectives of the system.

QUESTIONS

1. Define control. What are its objectives? Illustrate several connotations of control with organizational examples.
2. Define the following terms: rapidity of response; stability; sensitivity.
3. Relate the four basic elements of control to the control cycle. Give an example of a control system and illustrate the elements.
4. What relation does information flow have in a control system? In what way would this information flow differ in machine and/or people systems?
5. What is the difference between open- and closed-loop control?
6. Describe the difference between organizational and operational control. How do these terms relate to the effectiveness and the efficiency of the system?
7. What kind of control problems do you believe would be the most typical in machine systems? In human systems?
8. Why is information timing so important in the effectiveness of control systems?

9. How can standards be established in people systems so that they will be meaningful to both workers and management?
10. Describe a control system for a department store with the objectives to (*a*) regulate inventory levels, and (*b*) protect the inventory from pilferage.

CHAPTER 5

Information and Systems Concepts

Information plays an essential role in implementing the managerial functions of planning, organizing, and controlling. The flow of external information allows organizations to function as open systems, interacting with their environments. Internal control includes the communication of feedback messages, a vital ingredient in managerial decision making. The primary concern in this chapter will be the broad aspects of information flow in organizations. While we will refer to interpersonal communication processes, we will emphasize the concept of an overall management information-decision system. The following topics will be covered:

> Information defined
> Information transmission
> Information flow and organization
> Management information systems

INFORMATION DEFINED

The concept of information is related to facts, data, and knowledge. A fact is something that has happened in the real world and that can be verified. Data are facts obtained through empirical research or observation. Knowledge represents facts or data gathered in any way and stored for future reference. It may be thought of as a body of "well-confirmed law-like generalizations which relate data to their environment."[1]

Information represents data or knowledge evaluated for a specific use.[2] We like the proviso or connotation that information alters intelligence, that it changes the degree of uncertainty about a given situation from the point of view of a decision maker.[3] Thus, information is evaluated in terms of its pertinence for decision making. Facts or data are processed to provide meaningful information—an increment of knowledge. For example, miscellaneous accounting data provide information when arrayed in balance sheets and income statements. Ratio analysis and graphic displays of pertinent relationships provide even more meaningful information.

But if the problem is one of evaluating the effectiveness of a new advertising campaign, traditional accounting data, however elaborately processed, may be meaningless. Thus what constitutes "information" depends on the problem at hand and the decision maker's frame of reference.

The phrase "74 with one out of bounds" would mean more to a golfer than a nongolfer and its impact would depend on the source. For Arnold Palmer it would depict a bad day; for any of the authors it would suggest cheating, an inordinate amount of luck, or a nine-hole course.

Information can be conveyed in many ways, both formally and informally. Periodic reports with a standard format provide formal feedback on the operating system. The "grapevine" illustrates how informal interpersonal relationships provide channels of information flow.

Information—data or facts which are processed so that they are relevant (alter the degree of uncertainty or knowledge) to the recipient—can be the substance of communication systems. In its various forms—electronic impulses, written or spoken words, informal or formal reports—information provides a basic ingredient for decision making.

[1]John A. Caspari, "Fundamental Concepts of Information Theory," *Management Accounting*, June 1968, p. 8.
[2]It has also been defined as "a statement that describes an event (or an object, or a concept) in a way that helps us distinguish it from others." Samuel Eilon, "Some Notes on Information Processing," *The Journal of Management Studies*, May 1968, p. 139.
[3]Robert H. Hayes, "Qualitative Insights from Quantitative Methods," *Harvard Business Review*, July–August 1969, p. 114.

Information Theory

Information theory, or the mathematical theory of communications, has been described as a powerful tool for studying various systems. The foundations of information theory are generally attributed to Claude Shannon.[4]

By invoking certain basic assumptions (ignoring semantics or meaning), a simplified set of mathematical relationships was developed which is useful primarily in the technical aspects of information transmission.

Information theory is used as a tool in determining the rate at which information can be transmitted under certain specified circumstances. Some of the factors affecting transmission might be the nature of the signal source, whether the signal is discrete or continuous; the nature of the channel and, in particular, its capacity for transmitting information; the nature of the noise, if any, which disturbs the transmission; and the fidelity criterion by which the adequacy of the transmission is judged.[5]

Information theory in the sense employed by Shannon, Weaver, and others has a much narrower meaning than might be connoted by the term. A wide range of applications is claimed for information theory, but most of these are in the technical aspects of transmission. Some of the subdisciplines are filtering theory, detection theory, and the analysis of signal statistics. Information theory is cited as an integral part of such areas as the theory of communication, the theory of automata, the theory of automatic control systems, the analysis of languages, and informational aspects of physics. There are fields where information theory is cited as operative and unifying, e.g., thermodynamics, statistical mechanics, photography, language, models, gambling, cryptology, pattern recognition, and computer technology.

One author divides information theory into three principal areas: communication systems, mathematical theory (a branch of probability theory and statistics), and various considerations of entropy and uncertainty applied to physical and biological systems. He goes on to say:

> The one thing information theory does not pertain to is "information"! The sense in which the term is used in the theory is quite

[4]Claude Shannon and Warren Weaver, *The Mathematical Theory of Communication,* University of Illinois Press, Urbana, Ill., 1949.
[5]Harry H. Goode and Robert E. Machol, *System Engineering,* McGraw-Hill Book Company, New York, 1957, p. 428.

arbitrary in that it has almost no relation to the term as popularly understood.[6]

For our purpose the concept of information flow must be broader than that represented by information theory in its technical sense. Therefore we shall try to go beyond the terminology used in information theory, or at least broaden the connotation if appropriate.

Information Technology

Another concept that has received considerable attention is information technology. Technology is defined as the application of knowledge to the accomplishment of tasks. Within organizations technology is used in the process of transforming inputs into outputs. When applied to the broad connotation of information, it would seem to cover a wide spectrum. An even broader connotation for this phrase is indicated by several authors. For example, Whisler and Shultz state:

> Within the last decade we have seen rapid and extensive progress in the application of quantitative techniques to the analysis of management problems. Three areas of activity are involved: (1) the use of mathematical and statistical methods, with or without the aid of electronic computers; (2) the use of computers for mass integrated data processing; and (3) the direct application of computers to decision-making through simulation techniques. These areas are clearly interdependent, although the nature and the degree of interdependence are still undergoing exploration. We will lump these areas together here under the heading "information technology."[7]

Without question, problems of information flow or communication are of vital concern in each of these three areas. If management decision making is viewed as the focal point in the application of quantitative techniques of analysis, then information flow becomes an integral part of the total system. However, many additional factors are involved in the question of management decision making; therefore the use of the phrase "information technology" to encompass the entire field is misleading.

[6]Robert C. Hopkins, "Possible Applications of Information Theory to Management Control," *IRE Transactions on Engineering Management,* March 1961, p. 41.
[7]George P. Shultz and Thomas L. Whisler (eds.), *Management Organization and the Computer,* The Free Press of Glencoe, New York, 1960, p. 3.

INFORMATION TRANSMISSION

Information is transmitted by means of a communication process. Therefore it is important to understand the concept of communication and its relationship to organization and management.

Communication Defined

Numerous definitions (or connotations) of the term *communication* have been set forth according to the purpose of various writers or researchers. For example:

> *Communication* comes from the Latin *communis,* common. When we communicate we are trying to establish a "commonness" with someone. That is, we are trying to share information, an idea, or an attitude. . . . The essence of communication is getting the receiver and the sender "tuned" together for a particular message.[8]

This definition covers face-to-face interpersonal relationships (micro) as well as communication in organizations and communities (macro). Both aspects are considered in this chapter, but emphasis will be given to macro concepts because of their direct relationship to the managerial planning and control functions in organizations.

Communication is intercourse by words, letters, or similar means, and it involves the interchange of thoughts or opinions. It also presents the concept of communication systems, for example, telephone, telegraph, or television. Regardless of the sophistication of the transmission system involved, there is a basic communication process which can be identified.

Communication Process

Shannon and Weaver presented a basic symbolic representation of the communication process as shown in Figure 5–1. This basic model has been adapted by other writers since that time by changing some of the terminology or by making the model more elaborate. In all cases there is an information source which provides the raw material for a message which is to be transmitted to a destination. The general model includes a transmitter and a receiver, with the receiver connected directly to the destination.

[8]Wilbur Schramm, *The Process and Effects of Mass Communication,* University of Illinois Press, Urbana, Ill., 1954, p. 3.

Also involved is the concept of a noise source which theoretically interferes (to some degree) with information flow between the transmitter and receiver. With a large system, noise or interference obviously could come at numerous junctures within the subsystems. Regardless of the size or sophistication of the system, communication always requires three basic elements—the source, the message, and the destination. Some writers substitute the words *encoder* and *decoder* for *transmitter* and *receiver* in order to depict a more general process.

Examples of the communication process can be abstracted in terms of the model shown in Figure 5–1. The usefulness of such an approach is explained by Schramm as follows:

> Now it is perfectly possible by looking at those diagrams to predict how such a system will work. For one thing, such a system can be no stronger than its weakest link. In engineering terms, there may be filtering or distortion at any stage. In human terms, if the source does not have adequate or clear information; if the message is not encoded fully, accurately, effectively in transmittible signs; if these are not transmitted fast enough and accurately enough, despite interference and competition, to the desired receiver; if the message is not decoded in a pattern that corresponds to the encoding; and finally, if the destination is unable to handle the decoded message so as to produce the desired response—then, obviously, the system is working at less than top efficiency. When we realize that *all* these steps must be accomplished with relatively high efficiency if any communication is to be successful, the everyday act of explaining something to a stranger or writing a letter seems a minor miracle.[9]

[9]Schramm, op. cit., pp. 4–5.

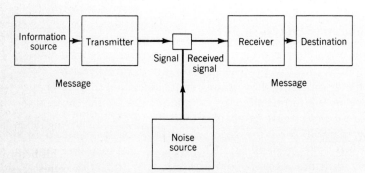

FIGURE 5–1. Symbolic representation of the communication process. (Source: Claude E. Shannon and Warren Weaver, *The Mathematical Theory of Communication.* **University of Illinois Press, Urbana, Ill., 1949, p. 98.)**

By checking day-to-day experiences in either face-to-face or organizational communication it is easy to find instances where *all* the steps indicated above are not in effect, and hence where a communication system is not working optimally. Visualizing the complexities involved in modern organizations, ideal conditions cannot be expected for all communication processes. However, such conditions can provide goals which can be used as a frame of reference in designing and implementing systems of information flow.

Types of Communication

Three types of communication have been set forth which involve human beings: (1) intrapersonal, (2) interpersonal, and (3) mass communication. In addition, there are examples of man-machine or even machine-machine communication systems. Ruesch and Bateson describe the communication apparatus of man as follows:

(*a*)   His sense organs, the receivers
(*b*)   His effector organs, the senders
(*c*)   His communication center, the place or origin and destination of all messages
(*d*)   The remaining parts of the body, the shelter of the communication machinery.[10]

This model can be integrated with the general symbolic representation of a communication system by physically locating information source and destination in contiguous positions. Furthermore, phase *d* of the above listing could be broadened to include organizations and institutions of varying size and complexity, or it could involve an entire society in the case of mass communication. Thus the various types of communication can be depicted by the basic model set forth above.

Man uses his communication system:

(*a*)   To receive and transmit messages and retain information.
(*b*)   To perform operations with the existing information for the purpose of deriving new conclusions which were not directly perceived and for reconstructing past and anticipating future events
(*c*)   To initiate and modify physiological processes within his body
(*d*)   To influence and direct other people and external events[11]

[10]Jurgen Ruesch and Gregory Bateson, *Communication*, W. W. Norton & Co., New York, 1951, pp. 16–17.
[11]Ibid., pp. 17–18.

Human beings are involved in communication systems of various sizes and degrees of complexity. They are involved in their intrapersonal communication system, which is a part of their own physiological and mental processes. They are involved in interpersonal systems when communicating to one or more people. In the area of mass communication the individual can participate to varying degrees, depending on the particular issues and his involvement.

The same hierarchy can be established for one machine communicating with itself in the sense of automation or feedback control; a machine controlling a group of machines (numerical control applications); or more complex man-machine systems of communication and control. All the various levels and types of communication indicated can be analyzed or developed in their own context, and yet each must be considered in terms of its relationship to a whole. Thus an overall framework should be recognized when analyzing communication in general, and the same principles apply when considering detailed aspects of systems or subsystems.

Communication Problems

Breakdowns in interpersonal relationships and organizational behavior often are attributed to faulty communication. While separation of specific causal factors is difficult in practice, it is useful to categorize problems for analysis. For example, Shannon and Weaver identify three levels of communication problems:

> Level A. How accurately can the symbols of communication be transmitted? (The technical problem.)
> Level B. How precisely do the transmitted symbols convey the desired meaning? (The semantic problem.)
> Level C. How effectively does the perceived meaning effect the conduct in the desired way? (The effectiveness problem.)[12]

Guetzkow develops two foci of attention, "communications as message *flows* and communications as message *contents*."[13] These two schemata can be integrated if "message flows" refers to technical and structural problems of accurate transmission and if "message contents" refers to semantic problems. The effectiveness of communications depends on performance in both categories.

[12]Shannon and Weaver, op. cit., p. 96.
[13]Harold Guetzkow, "Communication in Organizations," in James G. March (ed.), *Handbook of Organizations,* Rand McNally & Co., Chicago, 1965, p. 534.

The narrow applicability of information theory (to technical aspects of transmission) was mentioned previously in the discussion of terminology. But progress in technology makes it feasible to consider problems at other levels. Semantics and effectiveness certainly would be affected if technical aspects could not be solved. Communication systems should consider the mechanical and structural aspects of transmitting symbols accurately. In human interpersonal relationships, however, other communications problems seem paramount.

The question of semantics in communication is one which has received considerable attention from researchers and writers,[14] since variation in word connotation can alter significantly the meaning or information content of a message.

The goal is *understanding*—getting the sender and receiver "tuned" together for a particular message. Although repetition (redundancy) can be helpful, there is no direct correlation between the amount of communication or information transmission and the degree of understanding. Several basic problems are apparent according to Guetzkow.

> When the symbols fail to carry the full contents of the messages, their semantic properties are transformed as they are handled within a communication flow—either by omission of aspects of the contents, or by the introduction of distortions.[15]

Some of the sender's meaning is lost in the process of encoding and transmitting a message. A memo may not reflect accurately the manager's feeling about a situation. Direct conversation with his staff may help clarify the issue, but even in this case his tone of voice or facial expression can alter the message significantly. The use of graphic display adds another dimension—"a picture is worth a thousand words."

Another basic problem in achieving understanding in communication systems is that of decoding. Even if a message were coded and transmitted accurately, it is unlikely that it would be decoded in the same way by everyone receiving it. People read, see, and hear what they want to read, see, and hear. Memos, statistics, and diagrams are interpreted in terms of value systems which are as unique to individuals as fingerprints. A person's perception or "image" of the environment depends on his sum total of past experience; messages are distorted as receivers "read in" meanings not intended by the sender. A report from head-

[14]S. I. Hayakawa, *Language in Thought and Action,* Harcourt, Brace & Co., Inc., New York, 1949.
[15]Guetzkow, op. cit., p. 551.

quarters to several branches might be interpreted several ways with each receiver quite satisfied that he "got *the* message." Zalkind and Costello summarize their findings on the problem of managerial perception as follows:

> Without vigilance to perceive accurately and to minimize as far as possible the subjective approach in perceiving others, effective administration is handicapped. . . . Research would not support the conclusion that perceptual distortions will not occur simply because the administrator says he will try to be objective. The administrator or manager will have to work hard to avoid seeing only what he wants to see and to guard against fitting everything into what he is set to see.[16]

Understanding is facilitated if there are means and time for feedback and verification. If the issue can be "talked out" there is a chance that people can empathize and understand. However, time pressure works against this process. If information flows on complex issues must be accelerated, the probability of complete understanding decreases. Distance and medium of communication also affect the process significantly.

Understanding on the part of organization members is critical in implementing plans appropriately, and it is central to the control function as well. For example, the central theme in the whole field of cybernetics is that of communication and control.

> In giving the definition of Cybernetics in the original book, I class communication and control together. Why did I do this? When I communicate with another person, I impart a message to him, and when he communicates back with me he returns a related message which contains information primarily accessible to him and not to me. When I control the actions of another person, I communicate a message to him, and although this message is in the imperative mood, the technique of communication does not differ from that of a message of fact. Furthermore, if my control is to be effective I must take cognizance of any messages from him which may indicate that the order is understood and has been obeyed.[17]

In this sense, unless there is effective control the communication process has not been complete.

[16]Sheldon S. Zalkind and Timothy W. Costello, "Perception: Some Recent Research and Implications for Administration," *Administrative Science Quarterly*, September 1962, p. 235.

[17]Norbert Wiener, *The Human Use of Human Beings*, Houghton Mifflin Company, Boston, 1954, p. 16.

INFORMATION FLOW AND ORGANIZATION

Information flow has been receiving more and more attention in organizational contexts. Management has long been concerned with "getting its message across" to the workers, that is, communicating downward throughout the organization. In terms of the problem areas cited previously, management often is concerned with its lack of effectiveness in the communication process and may not be entirely familiar with the semantic problems involved. In other cases, administrators encourage good upward communications, that is, soliciting feedback concerning the attitudes and feelings of the lower echelons and encouraging their transmission upward through the hierarchical structure. In addition, management is interested in communicating its message outward to other institutions in the form of public relations efforts directed at customers, stockholders, and the general public. Emphasis is being focused on "tuning" all parts of the system to the same frequency.

Organization structure is definitely tied to communication systems. The relationship is apparent when formal structures, channels, and media are involved; for informal alignments and irregular information flow the relationship is not as evident. Communication does not necessarily follow stated organizational arrangements, or vice versa. Numerous overlaps and gaps are evident in most organizations, phenomena which cause problems. Deutsch explains these relationships in the following manner:

> Communication and control are the decisive processes in organizations. Communication is what makes organizations cohere; control is what regulates their behavior. If we can map the pathways by which communication is communicated between different parts of an organization and by which it is applied to the behavior of the organization in relation to the outside world, we will have gone far toward understanding that organization. . . .
>
> Generally speaking, the communications approach suggests lines of attack in the study of organizations. First, instead of concentrating on the ostensible purpose of the organization, it will concentrate on two questions: how are the formal and informal communications channels of the organization connected, and how are they maintained?[18]

These suggestions for research indicate that organization structures might follow the development of communication

[18]Karl W. Deutsch, "On Communication Models in the Social Sciences," *Public Opinion Quarterly,* Fall 1952, pp. 367–368.

systems rather than vice versa. For many organizations, communication systems have been designed to follow organizational lines without recognition of the fact that this may not provide for optimal flows of information for decision making.

Some of the problems in communication systems for decision making have resulted from changes in organizational relationships in recent years. Companies have been faced with dynamic world conditions, rapidly changing technology, changing markets, and other similar phenomena which have required adaptation on their part. Adjustments have been made, but without recognition, in many cases, of the impact of the organizational changes on communication systems. Thus much information that was appropriate under older arrangements now has become obsolete. Furthermore, additional types of information are urgently needed in order to plan and control current operations. According to Daniel:

> Unfortunately, management often loses sight of the seemingly obvious and simple relationship between organization structure and information needs. Companies very seldom follow up on reorganizations with penetrating reappraisals of their information systems, and managers given new responsibilities and decision-making authority often do not receive all the information they require.[19]

Granting that organization structure and communication systems are inextricably intertwined, there remains the problem of which comes first. Although this problem does not seem important from the standpoint of research or analysis, it becomes increasingly significant as one attempts to design either an organization or a communication system. Focusing attention on decision making is one way to approach this problem. Information flow should be related to decision making and the resultant communication system should be an indicator of the way the organization actually functions.

Pfiffner and Sherwood describe the relationship between decision making and communication systems as follows:

> The relationship between the communications system and decision-making is extremely important. If decision-making and communication processes are not identical, they are so interdependent they become inseparable in practice. As a result all studies of communication inevitably involve decision-making.[20]

[19]D. Ronald Daniel, "Management Information Crisis," *Harvard Business Review*, September–October 1961, pp. 112–113.
[20]John M. Pfiffner and Frank P. Sherwood, *Administrative Organization*, Prentice-Hall, Inc., Englewood Cliffs, N.J., 1960, p. 308.

The decision-making system of organizations includes information about objectives, strategies, alternatives, probabilities, and consequences. The function of the organization is to facilitate the flow of information and the making of appropriate decisions. In this view, the communication system appears paramount, with organization structured around it as a frame of reference. In turn, the communication system is considered primarily as a supplier of information for decisions. More and more attention has been devoted to organizations as decision-making units. In a pioneering work in this area Simon states:

> The anatomy of the organization is to be found in the distribution and allocation of decision-making functions. The physiology of the organization is to be found in the processes whereby the organization influences the decisions of each of its members—supplying these decisions with their premises.[21]

Organizations are complex networks of decision processes, and there are decision points throughout, ranging from individuals at the lowest operating levels to policy-making groups at the top. The primary aspect of the physiology of the organization is the communication system, which supplies information for decisions at various points in the organization; that is, each decision point can be considered an information-processing unit with input, processing, and output. The connection between decisions and communications is stressed by Dorsey as follows:

> Thus decision may be conceived of as a communication process, or a series of interrelated communication events. A decision occurs upon the receipt of some kind of communication, it consists of a complicated process of combining communications from various sources, and it results in the transmission of further communication.[22]

This analogy to the intrapersonal communication or decision process can be expanded to the interpersonal decision-making situation.

A manager decides issues based on the current information received in conjunction with previously developed strategies, procedures, or rules. Depending on the level in the organization and/or the type of decision (programmed or nonprogrammed), the decision maker has several alternatives. If the matter is fairly commonplace and routine, he can dismiss it quickly, particularly

---

[21]Herbert A. Simon, *Administrative Behavior,* The Macmillan Company, New York, 1959, p. 220.
[22]John T. Dorsey, Jr., "A Communication Model for Administration," *Administrative Science Quarterly,* December 1957, p. 309.

if there are rules or procedures covering the situation. If the matter at issue is more complex, more of a nonprogrammed nature, the decision maker may require additional inputs and may request some consultation on the part of subordinates, superiors, or peers. In any case, the communication process is obviously important and the flow of proper information to the decision points throughout the organization is vital.

For our purposes, concepts of communication patterns and information flow are particularly important. The patterns relate communication to organization, and the information-flow concept relates to decision making. Thus the several concepts—decision making, information, communication and organization—are inexorably interwoven.

A simplified system is represented by Figure 5-2, a skeletal model of an organization showing the basic flow of information necessary for objective accomplishment. Management considers internal capabilities in light of environmental information in the process of establishing goals or objectives. Premises with regard

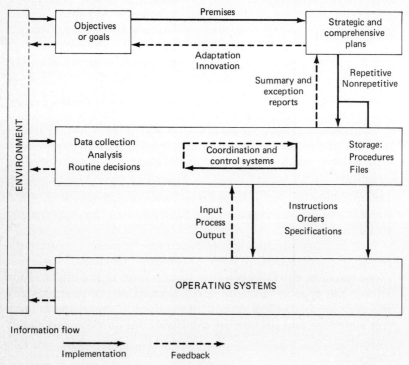

FIGURE 5-2. Information flow in an organization.

to governmental relations, political conditions, the competitive situation, customer needs and desires, and many other factors, evolve over a period of time and form a frame of reference for strategic and comprehensive planning. Plans for repetitive and nonrepetitive activities are transmitted to the operating system and to storage in the coordination and comparison with operating results. Detailed orders, instructions, and specifications flow to the operating system.

Feedback is obtained on the output of the system in terms of factors such as quality, quantity, and cost. The operating system is monitored in order to maintain process control, and input inspection provides feedback at the earliest stage in the operating system. Information flow is an integral part of the control system because it provides the means of comparing results with plans. Feedback data from various phases of the operating system are collected and analyzed. The analysis consists in processing data, developing information, and comparing the results with plans. Decisions also are made within the control system itself because routine adjustments can be preprogrammed in the set of pro-cedures or instructions. Within the control system itself there is a flow of information to implement changes to the program based on feedback from the operating system. Thus, procedures are changed and files updated simultaneously with routine de-cision making and adjustments to the operating system.

Summary and exception reports are generated by the control system and become a part of a higher-level process of review and evaluation which may lead to adaptation or innovation of goals or objectives. Subsequent planning activity reflects such feedback and the entire process is repeated. Over time, an organization "learns" through the process of planning, implementation, and feedback.[23] Approaches to decision making and the propensity to select certain ends and means change as organizational value systems evolve. This basic or simplified model of information flow can be applied to any organization; it shows the necessary flow of information regardless of the sophistication of the tech-nology or equipment involved.

The term *management information-decision system* is used to emphasize that information developed should be requested in light of the decisions to be made by managers throughout the organization. Thus an information-decision system should be designed as a communication process relating the necessary in-

[23]Richard M. Cyert and James G. March, *A Behavioral Theory of the Firm,* Prentice-Hall, Inc., Englewood Cliffs, N.J., 1963, p. 123.

puts to the stored information and the desired decisional outputs. It is likely that decisions at a given stage in the organization represent output from one communication process and information for a subsequent decision at the same level, a lower level, or a higher level. The overall information flow must be regarded as a system with many interdependent elements and subsystems.

Information-decision systems should be considered in conjunction with the fundamental managerial functions: planning, organizing, and controlling. If organization is to implement planning and control, if organization is tied to communication, and if communication is represented by an information-decision system, then the key to success in planning and controlling any operation lies in the information-decision system.

In his discussion of the management information crisis caused by too rapid organizational change, Daniel states:

> The key to the development of a dynamic and usable system of management information is to move beyond the limits of classical accounting reports and to conceive of information as it relates to two vital elements of the management process—planning and control. . . . We hear more and more these days about new techniques for inventory, cost, and other types of control, but information systems for business planning still represent a relatively unexplored horizon.[24]

He goes on to describe several kinds of information required for planning: environmental information, competitive information, and internal information. While most companies have some systematic approach to development of internal information for planning purposes, few have formal systems for developing information concerning competitors' plans, programs, and past performance. Nor do they deal in a systematic fashion with the social, political, and economic environment of the industry or industries within which they operate. Formal recognition of the decisions which must be made at various points and of the type of information required to do an optimal job in that decision process should point the way toward development of information flows which will be helpful.

Differences in the type of information needed for planning, on the one hand, and control, on the other, should be recognized. The contrast can be seen in terms of the following attributes of information:

[24]Daniel, op. cit., p. 113.

1. *Coverage*—good planning information is not compartment-alized by functions. Indeed, it seeks to transcend the divisions that exist in a company and to provide the basis on which *integrated* plans can be made. In contrast, control information hews closely to organizational lines so that it can be used to measure performance and help in holding specific managers more accountable.
2. *Length of time*—planning information covers fairly long periods of time—months and years rather than days and weeks—and deals with trends. Thus, although it should be regularly pre-pared, it is not developed as frequently as control information.
3. *Degree of detail*—excessive detail is the quicksand of intelligent planning. Unlike control, where precision and minute care do have a place, planning (and particularly long-range planning) focuses on the major outlines of the situation ahead.
4. *Orientation*—planning information should provide insights into the future. Control information shows past results and the reasons for them.[25]

This emphasis on the differences between information appropriate for planning purposes and that appropriate for control purposes indicates the importance of carefully designing informa-tion-decision systems. Blind adherence to organizational patterns for the flow of information often will hamper the development of an optimal system. Particularly where there have been organiza-tional adjustments and there is a mixture of functional organiza-tion and program or product organization, the development of an appropriate information-decision system becomes critical. Key decision points should be identified and the concept of flows of material and information should be kept paramount when de-signing overall systems of information flow. In such systems, the planning function can be carried out with the necessary informa-tion and premises, the organization can be adjusted to reflect the decision-making activities involved, and control information can be readily developed along appropriate lines.

MANAGEMENT INFORMATION SYSTEMS (MIS)

Unfortunately, the term *MIS* has often implied "computer based."[26] In reality, such an approach is not entirely appropriate.

[25]Ibid., pp. 117–118.
[26]"Management Information System: The combination of human and computer-based resources that results in the collection, storage, retrieval, communication, and use of data for the purpose of efficient management of operations and for business planning." Joseph F. Kelly, *Computerized Management Information Sys-tems*, The Macmillan Company, New York, 1970, p. 5.

The information system should be related to the managerial task. Figure 1–1 (page 17) shows several dimensions of the managerial task as seen in three organizational subsystems—operating, coordinative, and strategic. In the strategic subsystem, management is concerned primarily with comprehensive planning and control—defining the organization's niche in its environment. In the operating subsystem, management is concerned primarily with tactical planning and control—maintaining the organization's basic operations within allowable limits. Intermediate managers— coordinative subsystem—are concerned with integrating differentiated and specialized functional units as well as interrelating the activities of the operating and strategic subsystems.

Computer-based information systems may be appropriate at some levels and for some functions. However, it is obvious that, alone, they are inappropriate at the top level for strategic planning and control. For example, Keegan reports the findings of a study concerning the sources used by executives to gather external information as follows:

1. Human sources—about 67% of all important information acquired by the executives surveyed was obtained from individuals and 75% of that was gained in face-to-face conversations.
2. Documentary sources—27% of the information came from documentary sources, 60% of which were publication and information service reports from external sources.
3. Physical sources—6% of the information was obtained through observation or sensory perception by the executive. In some cases the information gained this way was not available elsewhere. In other instances it was available but required observation to make an impact on the individual.[27]

It seems obvious, then, that the term *management information system* must have a broad connotation if it is to relate to the overall managerial task. If we look at the decisions managers make at all levels, and then determine the information necessary, we will have defined the management information system.

Data Processing

It is important to relate data processing and management information systems. Data may be generated and transferred or communicated from point-to-point without processing. However, if we

[27]Warren J. Keegan, "The Acquisition of Global Information," *Management Review*, June 1968, pp. 54–56.

use the term *information* as defined previously, we mean that an increment of knowledge has been provided (or the degree of uncertainty altered). Data processing systems have been developed to facilitate many organizational functions—payroll, inventory control, accounting (accounts payable or accounts receivable, for example), and others. Such data processing systems (to be discussed in more detail in Chapter 15) are useful in their own right, and they provide some of the raw material for management information systems. Figure 5-3 indicates the relationship between these various elements of an overall system.

While all data could be considered part of an organizational information base, it is obvious that for any fairly large and complex organization such an approach would be impossible. Therefore, most systems include exception reporting wherein pertinent information from the various internal data processing activities becomes part of the overall information base when it is brought to the attention of appropriate decision makers. As indicated in Figure 5-3, a considerable amount of such information is used in planning and controlling in the operating subsystem of the organization. Some of the internal information is useful for strategic planning and controlling. Such information is coupled with that gathered from external sources in order to provide appropriate information for decision making at the top level. Most of the rele-

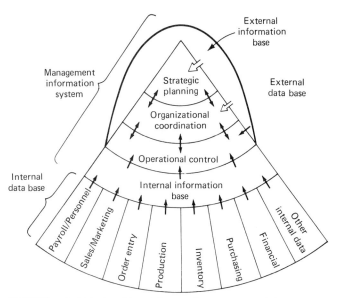

FIGURE 5-3. Relationship of data and management information systems.

vant external information flows into the organization through the strategic subsystem. However, some of it comes in via the coordinative and operating subsystems as well. Information used in the coordinative subsystem comes from both operations and strategic planning activities.

In an age of increasingly sophisticated computerization, it may be possible to include all data from all subsystems in a management information system. But, even if it were possible, it is not clear that it would be an efficient use of resources. The data processing system should be designed to provide relevant information for managerial decision making at all levels. However, the system should be evaluated on the basis of cost/benefit analysis. A balance should be maintained between the cost of the system and the value of the information generated.

SUMMARY

Throughout history the transmission of information—data or knowledge evaluated for a specific use—has been a key to progress. Efficient communication is important in all fields of human endeavor. However, as society has become more complex, as technology has increased at an accelerating rate, and in spite of improvements in communication media, it is becoming more and more difficult to communicate effectively. The growth of organizations and increased specialization and functionalization have developed barriers to communication in many spheres of activity. Scientists and researchers find it more and more difficult to communicate on a broad scope. Managers of business and other organizations also find that understanding is increasingly difficult to achieve in their day-to-day operations.

On the other hand, technical breakthroughs in data processing equipment have provided an opportunity for development of integrated systems of information flow. In spite of this opportunity, however, few organizations have really capitalized on it. In order to do so, management must be cognizant of the role of information flow in the primary managerial activities: planning, organizing, and controlling.

Information-decision systems can be developed which provide the proper flow of information among decision points in the organization. The organization then can be structured around such systems of information flow. Both formal and informal communication must be recognized. Management might well analyze informal communication patterns in some detail because the information-decision system may follow "natural" patterns of systems, even though they are not recognized in the formal organization structure. Once the overall information-decision system has been established, the functions of planning and control are greatly facilitated.

Systems concepts are vital to the establishment of appropriate information flow. Overall systems consist of subsystems of communication processes; these are represented as flows of information through a decision process. A hierarchy of such processes can be established and fitted to the framework of an integrated, management information-decision system.

Much attention has been focused on computerized management information systems (MIS). However, it is important to recognize that managerial decision making typically requires the input of much information—opinions for example—that cannot be computerized. Thus overall management information-decision systems should be designed to include explicit attention to nonquantifiable inputs as well as those which result from computerized data processing applications.

QUESTIONS

1. Define information and relate it to data and knowledge.
2. What is the focus of information theory?
3. How do Shultz and Whisler use the term *information technology?*
4. Define communication. Describe several communication systems.
5. Using the communication process model shown in Figure 5-1, give examples of how messages can be distorted between source and destination.
6. Give samples of communication problems at the following levels: (*a*) technical, (*b*) semantic, (*c*) effectiveness.
7. Is the *degree of understanding* directly correlated with the *amount of communication* in the system? Why or why not?
8. Relate information flow to: (*a*) planning, (*b*) organization, (*c*) control, (*d*) decision making.
9. Discuss the concept of information-decision systems.
10. Does development of a management information system (MIS) involve computerization? Why or why not?
11. Relate data, information, and data processing systems. Explain the concept of a data base.
12. Using an organization with which you are familiar, outline a general management information-decision system.

CHAPTER **6**

The Systems Approach and Management

In the preceding chapters we have related organization, planning, control, and information flow to systems concepts. In this chapter we integrate these functions of management into the general framework of the systems approach. This approach augments an organization's flexibility to make changes, isolates responsibility of individuals, and promotes gains in effectiveness and efficiency by optimizing the total system rather than its parts. The materials in this chapter will be organized under the following topic areas:

> The systems approach
> Systems philosophy
> Systems management
> Systems analysis

THE SYSTEMS APPROACH

The term *systems* has been used in many different ways. Most people accept this term as an everyday expression and use it to describe what they do and how they live. Managers consider phrases like systems philosophy, systems management, and sys-

Systems Theory		
Systems philosophy	**Systems management**	**Systems analysis**
Viewpoint Conceptual	Pragmatic	Optimizing
Method Cogitative	Synthesis	Modeling
Organization subsystem Strategic	Coordinative	Operating
Task Integration of the organization with the environment	Integration of operations through design and emphasis of interrelationships	Achievement of goals and efficient utilization of resources

FIGURE 6-1. The systems approach.

tems analysis as synonymous terms. We have found it most meaningful to include all aspects of systems under the general classifications of the *systems approach,* and to include in this framework the various uses of systems as appropriate, e.g., systems theory, as the set of related concepts or the body of knowledge which underlies the applications of systems philosophy (a way of thinking), systems management (the design and operation of organizations as systems), and systems analysis (techniques of problem solving). The relationships among these terms are described in Figure 6-1.

In systems philosophy, the viewpoint is conceptual; the method is cogitative (thinking or reflection); the organizational subsystem is strategic;[1] and the task is to integrate the organization with its environment. In systems management, the viewpoint is pragmatic; the method is synthesis (the art of building an organization as a system through the assemblage or combination of parts); the organizational subsystem is coordinative; and the task is to integrate operations and achieve objectives through design. In systems analysis, the viewpoint is optimizing or problem solving; the method is through modeling (the identification and abstraction of factors of the real world, manipulation of the variables, interpretation of analytical conclusions, and the relation of those conclusions to the real world); the organizational

[1]Refer to Figure 1-1, page 17.

subsystem is concerned with operations, and the task is the achievement of objectives and the efficient utilization of resources.

Notice that the items in Figure 6–1 flow from theory to practice, from conceptual to the techniques of analysis, and from science to day-to-day operations. Throughout this model of the systems approach, the idea of systematic (i.e., logical, thorough, and regular) thinking is emphasized.

SYSTEMS PHILOSOPHY

General systems theory has been described as the development of a systematic, theoretical framework for describing relationships of the empirical world. Models have been developed that are applicable to many systems, whether physical, biological, behavioral, or social. The many similarities in the theoretical construction of various disciplines become apparent upon examination.

One school of thought relates systems to science, which can be described as a systematic body of knowledge; an array of essential principles or facts arranged in a rational dependence or connection; a complex of ideas, principles, laws, forming a coherent whole.

The "vitalist" theory of deduction or philosophical reasoning outlines some principles for the general theory:

1. The whole is primary and the parts are secondary.
2. Integration is the condition of the interrelatedness of the many parts within one.
3. The parts so constitute an indissoluble whole that no part can be affected without affecting all other parts.
4. Parts play their role in light of the purpose for which the whole exists.
5. The nature of the part and its function is derived from its position in the whole and its behavior is regulated by the whole to part relationship.
6. The whole is any system or complex or configuration of energy and behaves like a single piece no matter how complex.
7. Everything should start with the whole as a premise and the parts and their relationships should evolve.[2]

The whole renews itself constantly through a transposition process: the identity of the whole and its unity is preserved, but

[2]L. Thomas Hopkins, *Integration: Its Meaning and Application,* Appleton-Century-Crofts, Inc., New York, 1937, pp. 36–49.

the parts change. This process continues endlessly; sometimes it is planned and observed, or it may occur without notice.

Within the context of the general theory, we stated in Chapter 1 that *a system is an organized or complex whole; an assemblage or combination of things or parts forming a complex or unitary whole.* In this usage it covers an extremely broad spectrum of concepts —in the world around us, there are mountain systems, river systems, and the solar system. The human body is a complex organism made up of a skeletal system, a circulatory system, a nervous system, and other systems. We come into daily contact with such phenomena as transportation systems, communication systems, and economic systems.

When relating systems to organizations it may be more meaningful to say that a system is *an array of components designed to accomplish a particular objective according to plan.* This definition contains three significant parts. First, there must be a purpose or objective which the system is to perform. Second, there is design (and sometimes construction) of components in a meaningful arrangement. Finally, inputs of information, energy, and materials are allocated according to an operating plan. This definition can be related to Figure 6–2, a model of a basic system. Planned resource inputs of information, energy, and materials are transformed by men and/or machines to produce output of products or services. The output, if the system is effective, accomplishes the objective of the system.

Leaver has classified the basic ingredients of a process (information, energy, and materials) as they relate to the operation or to the output (product):

1. "Information" is used in the broad sense to mean shape, pattern, or arrangement (static) or instructions (dynamic). It cannot exist in the practical sense unless it is associated with either energy or materials. Information associated with differences between product and raw material in form, structure, or state may be called "product" information in contrast to that associated with the structure or state of the manufacturing equipment used to make the product or with instructions to the

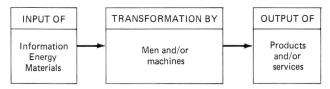

FIGURE 6–2. Model of a basic system.

manufacturing elements, which may be called "operational" information in that it determines the actual operations on the product. If the product reacts to this information in a linear way, the product information can be a linear function of the operational information.

2. Energy is used for the movement of the workpiece, tool, and assembly devices; heat, etc., used in the fabricational process. In most factories, energy is generally all "operational." The product rarely contains stored useful energy (product energy) as a result of the manufacturing process. An interesting exception is compressed-gas plants, where such substances as carbon dioxide may contain a considerable amount of stored energy.

3. Materials are both "operational" and "product." Operational materials are those embodied in the machines and plant, while product materials are those converted into useful output by the action of the operational information, energy, and material on the raw-material input.[3]

All inputs or outputs in the design or operation of a system can be classified as information, energy, or materials. Leaver's examples are rather mechanistic; however, the same classification can be made for all systems—e.g., the energy input exerted by a bricklayer in building a new structure for a bank (energy used in creating a system), or the electric power used in running the accounting machines (energy used in operating the system). While the output of a system may be in the form of materials (a product), it also can be information (legal advice) or energy (the output from a hydroelectric plant).

Types of Systems

Systems may be classified in different ways. One categorization would be a grouping of *natural systems* (e.g., the solar system) as compared to *man-made systems* (e.g., a transportation system). Natural systems are those relations between objects and sequences of events observed in their natural setting to which we identify some meaning. We say that such systems behave according to the laws of nature and their input-output relationships are predictable in a scientific sense. In contrast, man-made systems are those designed and operated by man. They utilize inputs from natural systems, but retain little of the scientific predictability found in

[3]Eric W. Leaver, "How Automatic Can We Get?" in *Keeping Pace with Automation,* American Management Association, Special Report 7, 1956, pp. 1–2.

nature, largely because man is somewhat unpredictable. Our discussion is limited to man-made systems.

A distinction may be made between *flexible* and *rigid systems.*[4] A flexible system is one where the structure or design of the system is continually adjusting to maintain a useful capability in the midst of changing environmental inputs. A balance or equilibrium between the system and its environment is maintained. In contrast, a rigid system is not a self-maintaining unit and its structure does not adjust, at least not in the short run. Examples of flexible systems would include most life forms, as well as economic, political, and social systems. An automated paper plant would be an example of a rigid system. Once constructed, there is little that could be done to adjust to a change in demand.

Man tries to build some flexibility into every system he constructs. For example, a building might be designed so that it could be convertible to some other use if the primary need for the structure changes.

Another classification of systems pertains to the degree of human involvement, man or machine systems. At one end of the spectrum we can visualize a system utilizing few, if any, machines or tools. For example, a group of natives weaving straw hats would be illustrative of a manual system of production. At the other extreme, an automated refinery programmed to produce petroleum products without human involvement during the transformation process is an example of an automatic machine system. The man-machine relationship in most systems falls somewhere between the extremes represented by these two examples. Some industries have a high capital investment in machines (e.g., the steel industry), whereas in others the human factor is more significant (e.g., a law firm).

The classifications natural versus man-made, flexible versus rigid, and man versus machine all pertain to the design or structure of systems. Another grouping can be made concerning the nature of output: (1) *systems that produce things,* and (2) *systems that serve clients.* The manufacturing department of the Chevrolet Division of the General Motors Corporation is a subsystem of that corporation that is designed to produce automobiles. Men and machines follow informational inputs to achieve the operating goals outlined by the company. The essence of a producing or-

---

[4]Most authors use the terms *open* and *closed systems.* We have substituted *flexible* and *rigid* in an attempt to reduce the confusion which may arise with the idea of open- and closed-loop control systems discussed in Chapter 4.

ganization or system rests in the processes by which resources are converted or transformed into output.

The fundamental purpose of other systems is to serve clients. Service may be performed by distributing products, ideas, or providing utility for people in general. For example, a retail store does not produce a product per se, but makes goods available to customers and therefore produces a service. Similarly, a doctor or lawyer produces a service by providing medical or legal assistance for the client.

The classifications which have been presented illustrate some of the different types of systems, but also reveal the difficulty of distinct and meaningful groupings. The various categories are used chiefly to help the reader gain some "feel" for systems, and to see the relationship between this "way of thinking" and the world in which we live.

Segments of Systems

Authors have used the "black-box" idea to illustrate that the inputs and outputs of a system may be of most significance in many kinds of analysis, while what occurs during transformation may be of lesser importance. We can use this black-box approach to demonstrate the relationship between components and systems. A component is that segment of a system which performs, or provides the facility for performing, some part of the defined transformation process. A component is a basic unit (black box) in a system where there is limited or no value to subdivide or describe it in further detail. For example, a classroom building can be considered a component in an education system when it is of limited value to detail the analysis of the building according to its heating system, lighting system, etc. Further, a teacher may be classified as a component in a university system, even though for a medical illustration the same individual may be described as a system with several subsystems. A component cannot satisfy the total requirements of a system as the system is defined, although it may qualify as a system in another situation or context. Moreover, a component may be a part of more than one system; e.g., we are components in our economic system, and also in parallel social and political systems.

It is really a matter of description, or stated boundaries, therefore, and the determination of what is a system, subsystem, or component occurs when the objectives of that system are determined. The ability to define the system and outline the exact boundaries turns out to be a significant advantage of the systems approach. The system definition determines the "total system" for the purpose of operation and analysis. Every system includes components, some of which may qualify as systems under different circumstances, and each system in turn is a subsystem of the next higher level of abstraction. The boundaries, as defined, are a function of the scope of the organization or system, the extent to which control can be exercised, and/or the nature of the problem requiring analysis. Figure 6-3 shows the relationship of systems, subsystems, and components in a network hierarchy. A is defined as the total system in this illustration with two subsystems, A_1 and A_2. Subsystem A_2 has four subsystems, A_{01}, A_{02},

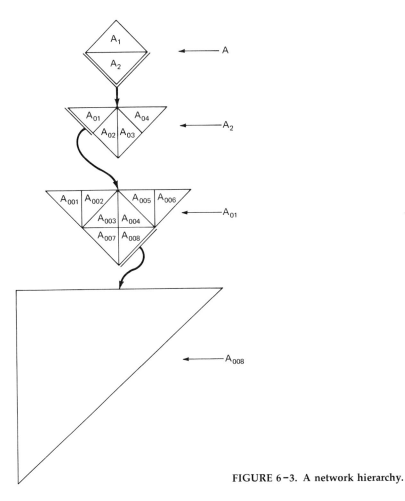

FIGURE 6-3. A network hierarchy.

A_{03}, and A_{04}. Sub-subsystem A_{01} has eight subsystems, A_{001}, A_{002}, etc. The segments of A_{01}, A_{008}, ect., may be regarded as components of the system if it is not meaningful to establish an additional level of analysis.

To illustrate, A might represent the education system in the United States, with two main subsystems, i.e., private A_1 and public A_2. As subsystems of A_2 there are colleges A_{01}, technical schools A_{02}, secondary schools A_{03}, and elementary schools A_{04}. Public colleges A_{01} could be grouped in eight regions of the country and, if warranted, each region could be subdivided by state.

In many instances the analysis may concern only a lower-level system and this segment would then, by definition, be regarded as the total system. For example, the public institutions of higher learning in California could be considered as the total system.

SYSTEMS MANAGEMENT

We can apply systems concepts in the management of resources. When organizational units are arranged and operated as systems, we refer to this as *systems management* or *management by system.* Each segment of the total, or each subsystem, is viewed as a distinct entity and its relationship or contribution to the next level in the hierarchical structure is programmed and measured, but always in consideration of the total system.

There are four characteristics which apply to systems management: (1) it is goal-oriented, with continual emphasis on objective achievement (effectiveness); (2) it is total-system oriented, as the decision strategy stresses the optimization of the total system (as described) rather than the subsystems; (3) it is responsibility-oriented, because each manager should be given a specific assignment where inputs and outputs can be measured; and (4) it is people-oriented, because workers are given challenging assignments and identified with output (achievement is recognized and rewarded). Although work assignments may be more specific in systems management, the ability of systems to adjust to changing demand should encourage the intellectual growth and development of employees.

There are four decision stages in the management of systems; each is distinct but closely related to the others:

1. Systems determination
2. Design and creation

3.   Operation and control
4.   Review and evaluation

First, a decision is made to create a system. This is the decision an entrepreneur makes when he decides to open a corner grocery store, the decision a large aerospace organization makes in establishing a missile division, or the decision made to create an agency to help solve the problems of the cities.

Next, a system must be designed; that is, components must be arranged in some combination to produce a desired goal. For example, a system designed to prepare invoices for mailing might include billing machines and operators. These components would be arranged in a planned order to provide optimum utilization. Notice that it requires information to determine the exact and proper way to organize so as to accomplish the objectives (design and procedures), and to utilize materials (machines) and energy (time spent designing the system) efficiently.

After the system has been designed it is ready to operate. There will be inputs of information (e.g., customer data, quantities, prices, discounts, and delivery dates), inputs of materials (e.g., invoice forms and machine ribbons), and inputs of energy (energy exerted by the workers and the electrical energy supplied for the machines).

The operating inputs are allocated according to a plan. For example, a supervisor may determine which kind of invoice to use, when various customers should be billed, when the operators should work overtime, and when the machines should be repaired.

It is possible to eliminate parts of the planning required during operations by designing systems with predetermined input allocations, structuring the system to operate in a specified fashion and with more predictable results. The more the operation of the system is preplanned, the more automatic it becomes. There are always two stages of planning; first in planning strategy and design, and then in operating the system.

Basic to the theory of systems is the premise that given certain inputs, the processor will give certain outputs or operate within established limits. However, an organization is not a structured or predictable system. Its equilibrium cannot be determined by equation, and it will change, within limits, as the components of the system are rearranged or as the inputs are reallocated.

In more advanced form, a system will include some means of control, i.e., a sensor for measuring output or related characteristics, a means of comparing the measurement with a standard, and an activating unit to adjust inputs to correct the indicated deficiencies. The objective is to control all variables so that the system will tend to stabilize near its ideal equilibrium point. This objective is possible only if that standard can be determined and if the operating values can be measured.

The fourth stage pertains to how well the system has operated. Has it been effective and/or efficient? A system is *effective* if it accomplishes its objectives, while *efficiency* is the relation of resource input to output. A system can be effective while wasting resources (inefficient), and conversely, may transform inputs efficiently without achieving the objectives as outlined (e.g., more shoes per man-hour of input, but all for the left foot; or a product few people wish to buy). The answer is to determine a balance between effectiveness and efficiency whenever the two are opposing each other. This becomes the appropriate course of action and we say the system is optimized. To the extent this balance does not occur, there is a nonoptimal condition. To illustrate, there is always a question pertaining to the quality of the product and the cost of production. We would attempt to achieve the greatest quality (effectiveness) and still keep costs (efficiency) acceptable to the competitive environment.

Review and evaluation occur at periodic times during the life cycle of a system and may lead to design changes in the present system, or recommendations for change which may be incorporated in future systems. Information for the review and evaluation process is often gathered as control data for operations. The feedback of operating information furnishes evidence of how the system is doing, and whether or not design changes are required. A review or audit analysis may bring changes in design, whereas action pertaining to control causes changes to occur in operating input.

Inputs of information, energy, and materials are basic to all four stages. For example, note that *information* is needed during the design and creation stage to determine how the stated objectives can be accomplished (determination of the transformation process); *energy* (effort spent designing and creating the system) is exerted by people; and *materials* in the form of equipment and machines become part of the system. In operation and control, all inputs are either inputs of *information* (for example, customer data, quantities, prices, discounts, and delivery dates), inputs of *energy* (energy exerted by the workers or the energy used to operate machines), or inputs of *materials* (raw materials, invoice forms, and machine ribbons, for example).

It should be noted that planning or decision making takes place at all four stages. The kind and extent at each stage, however, will vary with the nature or kind of system. For example, an automated oil refinery (rigid system) must be carefully preplanned. Most operating decisions are programmed into the system. A department store (flexible system) establishes more general objectives and plans, and uses human decision making in the operating subsystem to adjust the organization to various environmental influences.

Figure 6–4 illustrates the flow of planning information when decisions are made to release resources of materials, energy, and processing information. A record of the plan is stored where it can be used as a standard for control purposes. The resources are released by an activating unit. For example, detailed schedules are

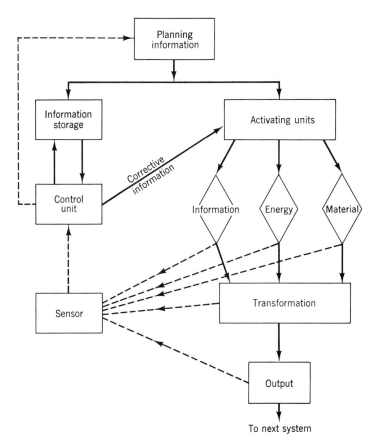

FIGURE 6–4. Flow of planning and controlling information.

planned (processing information), workers are assigned to specific tasks (energy), and the necessary raw materials or purchased parts are provided (materials). The combination of these inputs according to the plan results in the performance of a task (processing), and output occurs.

Sensory devices are placed at strategic points in the system flow to measure performance or output. These measurements are fed back to a control unit or group, and this information is compared with the standard. As significant deviations from plan are recognized, information to correct the situation is released to the activating unit, which adjusts the release of resources of information, energy, or materials.

If this diagram represented a system used by an insurance company to pay accident claims, the process could be outlined as follows:

1. The system may be designed to make certain that valid claims are paid promptly and accurately (objective).
2. The action to be followed in settling various kinds of claims and determining the payment schedule would be planned (planning information).
3. Claims would be received (processing information).
4. Workers would be assigned to process the claims. Heat, light, and power would be used in the office area (energy).
5. Claims blanks, typewriter ribbons, etc., would be used (materials).
6. The claims would be reviewed and paid (processing).
7. Claim payments would be measured against the time in process and against the standards or criteria for judging correct payment (control).

This illustration represents a structured system and yet there are times when it is not feasible or desirable to structure a system so precisely. Nevertheless, the systems approach does imply the tendency to systematize—and to allocate resources so as to provide the maximum utility to the organization. In any process where actions taken in one area relate to and depend upon actions taken in another area, it is likely that a smoother and more efficient operation can be provided when these actions are repetitive. Activities can be routinized to the extent that the choice can be simplified or eliminated. As the degree of repetition decreases, the less likely or the more difficult it becomes to have an efficient operation. The activities which are not repetitive will vary in relation to their frequency of occurrence. The more infrequent they become, the less possibility there is that they can be controlled in the finite limits of the operation.

The greatest amount of variation among components is likely to be found in the behavior pattern of individuals:

> Complex man-machine systems are designed and developed to meet the ever-expanding tasks that technology and organization make possible, on the one hand, and that the aspirations of man to describe, predict, and control nature and other men demand, on the other. System development is characterized by continuous compromise between the desire and the possible; each new system stretches physical science and technology and our capacity to the limit.[5]

If managers remember that systems are created *by* people and *for* people, the human problems associated with precise structuring can be minimized.

Illustrative Models

It is obvious that a single model cannot describe the detailed activities of every organization; each one is unique. However, Figure 6–5 does show the major activities of an organization that applies the systems approach. How these activities would be grouped and detailed in a specific situation depends entirely on the pertinent objectives and conditions associated with each case.

The master planning committee would consider inputs relating to the demand or need for the product or service, the present state of research and development technology, the resource capability of the organization, and other influences generated by the environment. At this level, decisions would be made concerning the selection of new programs and the expansion or discontinuation of existing programs.

Once such decisions are made the actual design and creation of the system are delegated to a resource-allocation group. Specific inputs of manpower (energy), facilities (materials), and technology (information) are combined as required to plan and assemble new systems, or to make major revisions in existing systems.

Two types of operating systems can be created—project systems and facilitating systems. Project systems are the major pro-

---

[5] J. L. Kennedy, "Psychology and System Development," in Robert M. Gagné (ed.), *Psychological Principles in System Development*, Holt, Rinehart, and Winston, New York, 1962, p. 15.

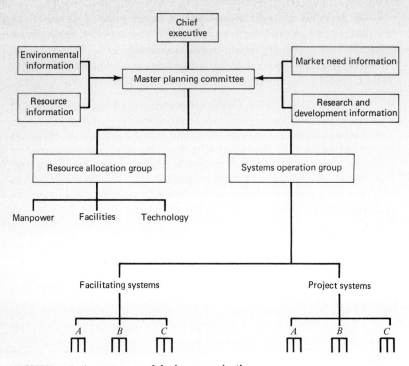

FIGURE 6-5. A systems model of an organization.

grams of an organization and their output is referenced directly to organizational objectives. In contrast, facilitating systems are created to service project systems. Some may classify facilitating systems as subsystems of the major projects, but it is more meaningful to consider them as distinct systems inasmuch as they usually serve more than one project. To illustrate, a hospital organization may include major programs for maternity, heart, and elderly patients, and also have a facilitating system to provide drugs or medicines for all three programs. (It should be noted that the objective of a hospital is not to dispense drugs.)

Generally, it is better to provide each program with all the subsystems and components it needs to accomplish its goals. Such a strategy maintains closer responsibility; reduces problems of communication, transportation, and scheduling; and simplifies the process of administration. There are times, however, when the service may be unique or specialized, or when the cost of operating a facility cannot be justified for each project system. In such instances, it is proper to create a facilitating system, but even in such cases the goals of the service system should be specified and the inputs and outputs measured.

A detailed model of an operating system is illustrated in Figure 6–6. The planning of operations may be of two types, i.e., specifications planning or transformation planning. On the basis of the information released, material and energy inputs are introduced into the system and transformation occurs. The close relationship between planning and control is symbolized in the model by the union between the two. The feedback from input, transformation, and output is measured and compared with the plan, and new information is released to introduce corrective inputs as required.

Each project or program is responsible for meeting its objectives in the most efficient manner possible. Consequently, a periodic review and evaluation of operations is a common practice in many organizations.

The Relation to Functions

Managers are needed to convert the disorganized resources of men and machines into a useful and effective enterprise. Essentially, management is the process whereby these unrelated resources are integrated into a total system for objective accomplish-

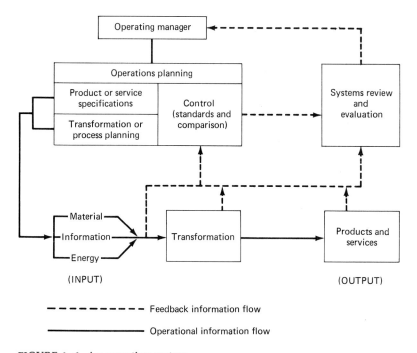

FIGURE 6–6. An operating system.

ment. A manager gets things done by working with people and physical resources in order to accomplish the objectives of the system. He coordinates and integrates the activities and work of others rather than performing operations himself.

Designing an organization according to the systems approach does not eliminate the need for the basic functions of planning, organization, control, and information flow. However, there is a definite change of emphasis, for the functions are performed in conjunction with the operation of the system and not as separate entities. In other words, everything revolves around the system and its objective, and each function is carried out only as a service to this end.

SYSTEMS ANALYSIS

The analysis of systems is a significant input to strategic planning. Questions pertaining to the exact mission of the system, the kind or nature of facilities to use, and the arrangement of the facilities and the people who use them all involve detailed study. The effectiveness of the analysis will be indicated by the responsiveness of the system to the demands of its environment. The nature of the analysis will set a pattern for the more routine study of operations.

During the operation of a system, it is important to analyze the various units of input and to decide on the combination which will provide the most effective and efficient output. During this process, an analysis is made of the timing of inputs relative to outputs (scheduling); and material staging at input, processing, or output (inventory management). During operations, an analysis of the operation relative to the plan (control) also is an important part of the operation. Finally, an analysis may be made of the operation to find out why the system is not working properly (trouble shooting), or in evaluating the design of a system relative to its effectiveness and efficiency. During every stage of the process a study should be made about the nature and kind of information which should be provided to accomplish the kind of analysis required.

Decision Making

Systems analysis results in a decision-making process. As a part of this process, it is necessary to outline the possible alternatives, determine the factors which pertain to each alternative, and establish value coefficients for the variables.

The hierarchies of decisions have been illustrated in systems management by pointing out that some decisions involve organizational strategy, others involve design and construction of systems, others relate to the operation and control, and, finally, some relate to the review and evaluation process whereby changes in design may be indicated. Decision making will be reviewed in more detail in Chapter 8.

Model Building

Model building, an abstract representation of a system, is one important way to understand complex relationships and improve the quality of decision making. It is used to capture the essence, but not necessarily the detail of the system. It permits experimentation among various decision strategies to test the results of assigning different values to the variables involved. To the extent that models are appropriate representations, they can be extremely valuable in analysis.

Figure 6–7 illustrates how problems from the real world can be abstracted in a form suitable for analysis, testing, and evaluation. Starting with the real world, the model builder abstracts those factors which represent the behavior of the system. The abstractions, to begin with, are of the major variables, with little or no attempt being made to detail or to refine the model. Once the general model has been developed, it is much easier to expand the details to make the model a more realistic representation.

The model should be an accurate representation of the system, an outline of the various parts in relationship to each other. Building appropriate models is probably the key to good decision making, for a problem well defined is half solved. Examples of the questions which should be asked include:

1. What is the general nature of the relationships among the variables in the system. If certain action is taken, how will this affect other variables?

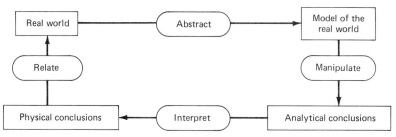

FIGURE 6–7. Modeling and the decision process.

2. How sensitive is an alternative solution to errors of mea-
    surement or changes in the general parameters which
    have been outlined?
3. If one does not or cannot adopt the optimal solution,
    how much will this change the effectiveness or efficiency
    of the system?
4. Does the analysis permit consideration of more variables
    than one could handle in an unstructured model?

Whether model building can extend beyond the theoretical
and to the practical depends upon the analyst's ability to recognize
that theoretical problems are vast simplifications, generally, of
practical problems. Most practical problems are extremely complex, unique to a particular situation, and with consequences that
are far reaching.

The model can be manipulated by solving for unknowns
based on known values, or hypothetical values can be given to the
unknowns to test the reaction of different values on the total system (simulation). As a result of these kinds of exercises, certain
analytical conclusions are drawn.

There are many instances when analytical solutions are developed that may not be realistic. This means that such conclusions must be interpreted by managers who can add the dimension of experience, common sense, and good judgment to the
analysis. All this points to the inevitable fact that the model cannot capture the full complexity of reality. When the analyst realizes
this, and is cautioned to respect the role that experienced managers can play in the total decision process, everyone benefits.

The decision, once it has been made and implemented, is related to the real world in a follow-up exercise to judge whether
or not it was an appropriate solution.

A Model for Systems Analysis

A general framework or model can be a valuable vehicle of analysis—a systematic method for problem solving. As such, it becomes
an orderly method by which to review and appraise alternative
ways of using scarce resources to accomplish a particular objective. Considering the integrative nature of a problem (i.e., the
cause and effect relationships among the elements), the constantly
changing environment in which planning must be formulated,
and the limited resources and time available to complete a study,
it becomes apparent why the logic of a systematic approach can
assist and refine the decision-making process.

The analyst should (1) determine, first of all, the boundaries of the defined system; (2) describe the system in detail; and (3) be completely objective, i.e., not make judgments or hazard solutions at the beginning of the study.

The logic of the model we use to illustrate the value of a systematic approach follows the deductive-inductive sequence.[6] In other words, the process starts with the objectives or general statement of the problem, and then develops those details or data relevant to solving the problem or in outlining a plan of action. This pattern of thinking produces a cycle to create, as nearly as possible, a closed loop for continuous feedback with periodic inputs. The process illustrated in Figure 6-8 goes through several stages of development, starting with a cluster which includes general objectives, translation of objectives, constraints, and analysis; and then proceeds through a second cluster which includes alternatives, criteria for selection, trade-off analysis, and synthesis. Figure 6-8 illustrates the close relationship between objectives and selection criteria, and also the need to relate the plan or decision back to the objectives in an evaluation procedure.

The broad objectives establish the initial format, but it is necessary to translate these objectives into more specific terms. The more specific the objectives can be, the easier it becomes to direct the systems analysis. It is not always possible to have a

[6]P. G. Thome and R. G. Willard, "The Systems Approach—A Unified Concept of Planning," *Aerospace Management,* General Electric Company, Missile and Space Division, Fall–Winter 1966, pp. 25–44.

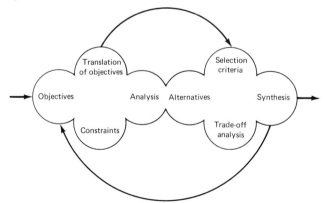

FIGURE 6–8. A model of systems analysis. (Source: Adapted from P. G. Thome and R. G. Willard, "The Systems Approach—A Unified Concept of Planning," *Aerospace Management,* General Electric Company, Missile and Space Division, Fall–Winter 1966, p. 31.)

clear and precise definition of these objectives early in the study. Therefore, it is necessary to iterate and to refine the general definitions as more information becomes available. Often, for example, an analysis of the various factors will clarify the mission and permit the analyst to refine the objective in more precise terms.

The constraints represent those factors which limit the number of feasible solutions or alternative plans of action. They establish the boundary within which a solution must be found. Constraints may be technical, a limitation on the state-of-the-art knowledge; economical, the money available or the cost restrictions to a particular solution; political, legal restrictions resulting from laws or from a political subdivision; educational, the ability of the population to understand and/or initiate certain action; social, involving restrictions imposed by religious, work, or informal organizations; and time, the need to find a solution within a predetermined time which would obviously eliminate from consideration some long-range solutions.

Whereas the first cluster of the model is an organization and study cluster, the second grouping involves action. First a list of alternatives is prepared. It should be noted that each alternative must be a feasible plan or solution to the problem. In other words, it must meet the objectives and not violate the constraints which have been outlined. Once the alternatives are developed they are tested against the selection criteria. The selection criteria provide a list of priorities. It is an admission that each of the various alternatives will have certain characteristics which satisfy the original objectives better than others. It is necessary to decide which characteristics are the most important, assuming that it is not possible to satisfy all characteristics to the same degree. The listing and ranking of the selection criteria will determine the best solution. It will also establish for all parties the basis upon which the decision was made. If a manager disagrees with the selection criteria as listed, it is obvious that a different solution will be reached. On the other hand, if there is agreement at this point, and the logic and analysis are sound, most researchers should reach the same decision.

The tradeoff is the process of evaluating each alternative in terms of the selection criteria and, as the process occurs, of trying to develop additional alternatives which may be either new or combinations of those already suggested. The creation of new alternatives is a logical development after the pros and cons of the first list of alternatives are evaluated.

The best alternative is synthesized into an action plan or decision. One of the significant features of this model is the feature of iteration, the process of continually refining the objectives, investigating the restrictiveness of certain constraints, developing the analytical process, investigating other alternatives, and refining and synthesizing the actual plan or decision.

FIGURE 6-9   An illustration of systems analysis—paper recycling.

The following hypothetical example is presented to illustrate the "systems analysis model." Obviously, a real example would be more comprehensive.

Objective

Initiate and implement a paper recycling program for a university.

Translation of Objectives

Design and create for a university a system of paper recycling that is capable of:

1. Efficiently collecting 75 to 90 percent of all paper products used by the university that are now considered waste.
2. Effectively channeling collected waste to facilities capable of sorting paper into biodegradable and nonbiodegradable categories for recycling waste into products that can be utilized by the community at large.

Constraints

1. Present technology—recycling facilities cost approximately $20 million to build.
2. Availability of water—adequate facilities use 10 million gallons of water daily and produce 2 million gallons of effluent, plus solid wastes from deinking and other operations.
3. Only certain grades of paper can be recycled.
4. Paper can only be recycled a maximum of five or six times before fibers become too short for processing.
5. Legal constraint—the university is limited by law in the type of operations it can undertake.
6. Public support—it may be necessary to receive the support of the users before a feasible system can be outlined.

Analysis

1. Investigation of various collection schemes
   (a.) wastepaper containers
   (b.) central disposal locations
   (c.) conveyors
   (d.) incinerators
   (e.) compressor/processors
2. Various removal schemes
   (a.) trucks
   (b.) conveyors
   (c.) incinerators
   d.) compressor/processor

FIGURE 6-9   An illustration of systems analysis—paper recycling (*cont'd*)

3. Investigation of future requirements and opportunities
   (*a.*) Growth in paper consumption
   (*b.*) Pending disposal legislation
   (*c.*) Attitudes of paper suppliers, users, disposers, public
   (*d.*) Techniques of disposal and recovery
   (*e.*) List of agencies, organizations dealing with disposal and recovery
4. Investigate costs of various kinds of collection, sorting, and processing schemes

Alternative Courses of Action

1. Collect, sort, and recycle the paper at a university plant.
2. Collect and sort, but sell the paper to an outside contractor for recycling.
3. Contract the collection, sorting, and processing of paper for recycling with outside organizations.
4. Same as points 1, 2, 3, but purchasing for use only that paper which has been recycled.

Criteria for Selection

1. How effective is the program in utilizing the greatest percentage of wastepaper for recycling?
2. What are the costs of the various alternatives to the university?
3. How acceptable is the system to the students, faculty, staff, and public?
4. How difficult will the program be to implement relative to time and degree of change from present systems?

Tradeoffs

The alternatives which have been suggested are all feasible in that they will achieve the objectives within the constraints which have been outlined. Now they need to be tested with regard to which of the alternatives rates highest relative to the selection criteria. That is, which will recycle the greatest amount of paper, at the lowest cost, with the least objection, and with the least difficulty of implementation? Each alternative may have certain advantages.

Synthesis

At the synthesis stage it is necessary to develop a composite or program alternative which may include features of all alternatives or, as the alternatives are reviewed in the trade-off/synthesis process, it may be possible to generate new alternatives or to refine some of those which have been suggested.

SUMMARY

The systems approach is the most general term in classifying systems concepts. Included under this classification are systems philosophy, systems management, and systems analysis.

General systems theory has been described as the development of a systematic, theoretical framework for describing relationships of the empirical world. The many similarities in the theoretical construction of various disciplines become apparent upon examination. One school of thought relates systems to science, which can be described as a systematic body of knowledge; an array of essential principles or facts arranged in a rational dependence or connection; a complex of ideas, principles, laws, forming a coherent whole. The strategy used in developing an overall framework (general systems theory) is to identify phenomena common to many different disciplines and to develop general models that include such phenomena.

Within the context of the general theory, a system is described as *an organized or complex whole; an assemblage or combination of things or parts forming a complex or unitary whole.* More specifically, we define a system as *an array of components designed to accomplish a particular objective according to plan.* Planned resource inputs of information, energy, and materials are transformed by men and/or machines to produce output of products, ideas, or service.

Systems may be classified in different ways pertaining to the nature of the input, transformation, or output. Each system has subsystems and components. How these groupings are determined is a matter of description, or stated boundaries.

When organizational units are designed and operated as systems, we refer to this as systems management or management by systems. There are four decision stages which occur in the management process: (1) systems determination, (2) design and creation, (3) operation and control, and (4) review and evaluation.

Managers are needed to convert the disorganized resources of men, machines, and money into a useful and effective enterprise. Structuring an organization according to the systems approach does not eliminate the need for the basic functions of organization, planning, control, and information control. However, there is a definite change of emphasis, because the functions are performed in conjunction with the operation of the system and not as separate entities.

During any stage of systems management where decisions occur, systems analysis is important. The kind of decisions to be made, and the impact of these decisions on the effectiveness and efficiency of the system, should be determined in a systematic and orderly way. Model building helps to identify the important factors and determine the coefficients so that all variables will receive proper consideration. A model of analysis illustrates the value of using an orderly systematic approach.

QUESTIONS

1. Define the terms *systems approach, systems theory, systems philosophy, systems management,* and *systems analysis* as used in this text.
2. In what way does the vitalist theory of deduction or philosophical reasoning differ from the scientific method?
3. Give three examples of systems and classify the inputs of the system according to information, energy, and materials.
4. Distinguish between flexible and rigid systems. Give an example of each.
5. What is the difference between systems, subsystems, and components? Give an example of this hierarchical relationship and indicate which segments would be grouped under each classification.
6. What are the four decision stages of systems management? Would these four decision stages occur in all systems? Explain.
7. What is the difference between a major operating system and a facilitating system? Under what conditions would management add a facilitating system?
8. Does management by system make functional organizations obsolete? Explain.
9. What role can modeling play in the decision-making process?
10. Using the model of systems analysis described in this chapter, develop an illustration considering the question of zero population growth.

PART 2

Each day a hundred thousand rout
Followed this zigzag calf about
And o'er his crooked journey went
The traffic of a continent.
A hundred thousand men were led
By one calf near three centuries dead.
They followed still his crooked way,
And lost one hundred years a day;
For thus such reverence is lent
To well-established precedent.

A moral lesson this might teach
Were I ordained and called to preach.
For men are prone to go it blind
Along the calf-path of the mind,
And work away from sun to sun
To do what other men have done.
They follow in the beaten track,
And out and in, and forth and back,
And still their devious course pursue,
To keep the path that others do.
They keep the path a sacred groove,
Along which all their lives they move;
But how the wise old wood-gods laugh,
Who saw the first primeval calf.
Ah, many things this tale might teach—
But I am not ordained to preach.

Sam Walter Foss, *The Calf Path*

Design and Analysis

INTRODUCTION The conceptual foundations of management via the systems approach were set forth in Part 1. The general usefulness of the systems approach for practitioners was demonstrated by its integration with traditional managerial functions. Now the reader asks, and logically, "How do I use these concepts?" Therefore, Part 2 is concerned with the implementation of the systems approach in the management process.

Chapter 7 covers systems design, an activity which we contend is one of management's most vital functions. It involves strategic considerations—relating the organization to its environment and developing comprehensive systems and plans. The design activity also includes identification of the critical decision and processing points involved in a proposed operation. It requires connection of these points via meaningful flows of materials and/or information. The design phase involves planning and organizing both the job-task system and the information-decision system as an integrated whole. The question of primary responsibility for systems-design activity is considered in some detail.

Chapter 8 considers the present and potential contributions of quantitative techniques to the implementation of the systems approach. A number of general concepts are discussed, such as problem solving, scientific method, models, mathematical analysis, and computers. Several specific techniques of analysis are described, with particular emphasis on symbolic system simulation as an aid in systems-design endeavors. The relationship between management scientists and managers is discussed in detail, focusing on problems of implementing the results of research and analysis.

One type of simulation, network analysis, is the subject of Chapter 9. Timing the integration of parts, components, minor subsystems, and major subsystems for projects is a key management responsibility. Network analysis is a tool which helps managers to design better systems, and to plan and control operations effectively and efficiently. Although there are many varieties of network analysis, Performance Evaluation and Review Technique (PERT) is the most common. It, along with PERT/Cost, is reviewed and evaluated as a specific example of implementing the systems approach through network analysis.

The impact of the systems approach on people is covered in Chapter 10. The discussion includes such points as the human need for systematic relationships, the need for systems change, and how people resist change. Major areas of impact resulting from the implementation of the systems approach are also delineated. Finally, some steps are outlined for management to consider in meeting the human and social problems which may arise.

CHAPTER 7

Systems Design

Systems design provides the overall framework for implementing systems concepts. It includes strategic and comprehensive planning for the entire organizational system, as well as the development of operating and facilitating subsystems. Specific techniques of quantitative analysis are applicable in certain aspects of the implementation process, but it is vital to provide broad guidelines within which they can be employed advantageously. In this chapter we shall create such a framework by relating the systems-design function to the systems approach as set forth in Chapter 6. Once the conceptual foundation for systems design is established, we shall proceed to outline various approaches for carrying out this function. The discussion will focus on the following topics:

> Scope of the design function
> Characteristics of effective systems
> Flow concepts
> Designing organizations
> Master planning
> Resource allocation
> Systems review and evaluation
> Constraints on the design function
> Responsibility for systems design

SCOPE OF THE DESIGN FUNCTION

Design means to "mark out, designate, or indicate." It includes combining features or details and often calls for the preparation of preliminary sketches or plans. A system is an array of components designed to accomplish a planned objective. Figure 6-2 (page 117) depicted a basic system combining input, processor, and output, designed to operate according to a plan. The design function is important in establishing a relationship between the various stages or phases of a system, linking them together, and outlining the composite whole. For business systems the design function includes the arrangement of physical facilities for production and auxiliary activities. It also covers the arrangement of people and communication networks established to provide information concerning the process.

As the systems approach is accepted and as its various ramifications are applied throughout business and other organizations, the function of systems design will become increasingly crucial. For example:

> As automated subsystems take over minute-by-minute and day-by-day operation of the factory and office, the humans in the system will become increasingly occupied with preventive maintenance, with system breakdowns and malfunctions, and—perhaps most important of all—with the design and modification of systems.[1]

When establishing a new business operation, the design function seems fairly straightforward. However, the scope of systems design also covers the function of "redesign," assessing existing systems with an eye toward change. This activity has received considerable attention over the years under headings such as systems and procedures, work simplification, systems analysis, or systems engineering. Of these terms, *work simplification* seems to have the narrowest connotation in that it applies primarily to simple man-machine operations or clerical activity. However, as with most techniques, its practitioners have proclaimed its applicability to a wide range of problems. In any case, it applies to existing systems rather than to the establishment of new systems.

Systems and procedures work also has been described as an

---

[1] Herbert A. Simon, "The Corporation: Will It Be Managed by Machines?" in Melvin Anshen and G. L. Bach (eds.), *Management and Corporations 1985,* McGraw-Hill Book Company, New York, 1960, p. 50.

all-encompassing activity, covering many facets of any operation. However, implicitly it seems limited to office work, the flow of paper work, and the design of forms. Since the advent of electro-mechanical equipment, systems and procedures activity has included the designing and programming of data processing systems. Unfortunately, EDP has been emphasized in recent years to the exclusion of broader concepts of systems design. The specific aspects of programming, form design, and routing of paper work—as a part of the information-decision system—should be fitted into the overall systems design.

Another term used in describing this general sphere of activity is *systems analysis.* Originally, it also focused on existing systems rather than new designs. It seemed to apply primarily to information flow in the office rather than to production or processing. In military and space environments, however, the term *systems analysis* has taken on a different and more specific connotation. For example, in the Department of Defense it represents a framework for the overall decision-making process, including determination of objectives and allocation of resources for mission accomplishment. (This is consistent with the approach described in Chapter 6.) Cost effectiveness analysis and a planning-programming-budgeting system are related aspects in the process.

Systems engineering implies the creation of systems as well as the analysis of existing systems. Systems engineering sometimes is assumed to deal only with physical components; that is, it deals with the integration of components and subcomponents into a total product such as a computer or missile. It can also be defined as "making useful an array of components designed to accomplish a particular objective according to plan." This approach implies the interaction of more than equipment. It suggests the development of a man-machine system which could function as a task-oriented assemblage. However, systems engineering still seems to emphasize technical aspects.

The term *systems "designer"* may need some clarification. It is our view that operating managers are systems designers. They make decisions concerning the overall scope of an organization's activities—its strategy, organizational relationships, and operational processes. In modern medium- and large-scale organizations managers may receive design help from staff personnel—systems analysts, planners, operations researchers, computer programmers, and others. However, even though suggestions for design changes emanate from such staff groups, the ultimate responsibility for implementation lies with the manager. This fundamental relationship should be kept in mind as we discuss the various dimensions of the systems-design function.

Both systems design and redesign will be discussed in the remainder of the chapter. For the first half of the chapter we shall be concerned primarily with initial design based on implementing systems concepts. Even here, however, some attention will be devoted to the function of *systems review and evaluation*, which is primarily a redesign process. In the latter part of the chapter both design and redesign will be discussed but the emphasis will be on working with existing systems.

CHARACTERISTICS OF EFFECTIVE SYSTEMS

Why is one system effective and another ineffective? In general, it is a function of design and operation; the system should be designed with certain characteristics and, hopefully, accepted by the people who will be operating it. Characteristics associated with effective system operation include simplicity, flexibility, reliability, economy, and acceptability.

Simplicity

A system does not have to be complex to be effective. On the contrary, a simple system can be understood and followed better than a complex system. Learning will take place faster, and the operation will be more efficient. In addition, there is usually a positive correlation between simplicity and reliability—there are fewer things to go wrong.

A system becomes complex when the boundaries between systems and/or subsystems are not defined. It is important, therefore, to make the limits or boundaries of operations definite.

Flexibility

Conditions change and managers should be prepared to adjust their operation accordingly. There are two ways to meet the evolution in operating environment: new systems can be designed, or operating systems can be modified. An existing system should not be converted to meet a basic change in objectives; however, it should be flexible enough to absorb changes in certain environmental conditions or input factors. For example, an organization should not use the same system for building missiles as for building airplanes, or the same system for selling appliances as the one designed for selling groceries. However, it should be possible to modify an existing system to produce different sizes, varieties, or types of the same product or service.

To be effective and simple, the system must be well defined, but to be practical, it cannot be rigid. There will always be minor variations, and the system should be able to accept these changes without breaking down.

Reliability

System reliability is an important factor in organizations and refers to consistency of operation. This can vary from zero output (a complete breakdown or work stoppage) to a constant and predictable output. The typical business system would operate somewhere between these two extremes. A greater degree of reliability can be designed into the system by a careful selection and arrangement of the operating components. Where the requirements of a particular element, e.g. an operator, are critical, it may be necessary to design redundant or standby operators. In all situations provision should be made for repair and recovery, to overcome failure. One valid approach toward solving the reliability-maintenance problem is the use of the modular construction to permit maintenance by substitution of submodules. This should be considered when the system is designed.

Economy

A system may be effective without being economical. For example, an operating service system can control output by using a large task force of expeditors. However, achieving this kind of performance would be costly. In another example, inventories can be controlled by a comprehensive system of storekeeping; however, if the cost of the storekeeping is more than the potential savings from this degree of control, the system would not be economical. Often it is dysfunctional and expensive to develop one segment of the system with much greater capacity than some other part. Also, building in great redundancy or providing for every contingency usually destroys the operating economy of the system.

Acceptability

Any system, no matter how well designed, is worthless unless accepted by the people who operate it. If they do not believe it will benefit them, are opposed to it, are pressured into using it, or think it is not a good system, it will not work. Two things can happen: the system will be altered by the people who are using it, or the system will be used ineffectively and ultimately fail. Unplanned alteration of an elaborate system might result in a situation which is worse than the "presystem" era. This is why it is so important for operating managers to help in designing the system. Decentralization of responsibility also tends to foster acceptance of the system.

FLOW CONCEPTS

A general approach to systems design involves identification of material, energy, and information flow. These three elements are part of every system and subsystem. Consideration of flow concepts facilitates thinking about fundamental divisions of operating systems.

Material

The material aspects of any system include both the facilities involved and the raw material, if any, which flows through the process. A system should be designed to ensure the *acquisition* of raw materials and/or components necessary for processing into finished products. The systems design would include identification of transportation media required to move the material to the processing location.

The *processing* operation should be designed in terms of constructing new facilities or realigning existing facilities. Questions of plant layout and materials-handling equipment would be a vital part of the systems-design function for in-plant processing and material flows. Industrial engineers have considered problems of this nature for many years and have developed detailed methods and techniques for optimizing layout and materials handling. The trend toward automation has been evident in many material-processing operations. We shall not consider techniques in detail in this chapter. Rather, we shall emphasize the conceptual problems in systems design and point up the areas where specific tools and techniques can be useful.

Much attention also has been focused on *distribution* of finished goods. Where items become raw material or components in subsequent processing operations, the distribution problem is often straightforward. In such cases the material flow would be considered part of the flow of raw materials for the next processing operation. Physical-distribution management, for items moving from producer to ultimate consumer, can be a more difficult problem. In this case, channels of distribution vary from direct producer to consumer to numerous combinations of middlemen. Inventory management, at various points along the distribution channel, must be considered, as well as modes of transportation. In many cases transportation costs have been isolated for analysis without reference to the impact of such decisions on stocks of material in the pipeline. Systems design, in this sphere, would concern itself with identifying the flow of materials and with the development of an explicit network of distribution, recognizing *all* the costs involved—handling, inventory, and transportation costs. Increasing effort is being devoted to the design of explicit material-flow systems from a raw-material stage through the production process and to the final consumer.

Whenever the operation in question involves the flow and processing of material, appropriate systems can be designed. For business operations such as insurance companies or other commercial institutions, there may be no flow of material per se. Rather, the material in these systems is represented by the facilities and equipment involved.

Energy

Some source of energy is present in any operating system. It may be electricity obtained from available sources or generated by a firm's own power plant. The process may require natural gas, petroleum, coal, or other fuel for production. A business usually requires electrical energy for operating facilitating systems, if not for the main processing operation itself.

Another obvious source of energy is people. Both physical and mental energy are required to operate business systems and people represent a renewable source, at least for the short run. People are quite variable as individuals. However, in toto, the group represents a reasonably stable source of energy for the system.

Electricity, natural gas, or petroleum can be described in terms of flow concepts, which are under continual inspection by systems designers. However, they are concerned primarily with the energy or power system itself, not the integration of the energy system with other subsystems and the whole. It is somewhat more difficult to visualize people, or the work force, in terms of flow concepts. However, in a very real sense, this is entirely appropriate. There may be a continual flow of workers in terms of shifts where 24-hour, 7-day weeks are scheduled. Even for 5-day, 40-hour weeks there is a systematic flow of worker energy into the operation. In a larger sense, organizations maintain a flow of worker energy throughout their life—from the recruiting, hiring, and orientation stages, all the way to retirement. Thus all energy can be considered as a flow process both in and of itself and as a part of other systems.

Information

Another basic element in any system is information. It facilitates interrelationships among subsystems and provides the linkage necessary to develop systems of systems. Information flow may be developed to flow along with the routing of material. Requisitions, orders, bills of lading, packing slips, receiving information, inspection reports, accounts payable, and checks might represent the information flow connected with the acquisition of raw material requirements, processing information, inspection requirements, routing, and scheduling would be developed from engineering drawings and/or other specifications. The information would flow through the system along with the material necessary to accomplish the planned objectives.

The accounting system requires a flow of information toward the development of income statements and balance sheets for tax purposes or stockholder reports or both. While many data processing systems have developed on the basis of periodic batch processing, more and more systems are being developed which call for flow concepts approximating real-time activity; that is, the action or activity to be considered is recorded at the time it happens and action is taken at that time.

Information flow is the primary focus of attention for systems designers in many cases. If manufacturing facilities are fixed and if layout requirements are rigid, then the only variables remaining are raw materials (which may be uniform), energy (in the form of power and/or people), and information (in the form of plans and instructions). Systems design in such cases must concentrate on the arrangement of people and the use of information flow to optimize decision making within the system under observation. For many other systems where manufacturing and material flow are not present—service, commercial, and many governmental organizations—the flow of information is the critical element. Information must flow to key decision points where action is taken with regard to a service to be performed by the organization in question. In such cases the system can be defined primarily on the basis of the flow of information to appropriate decision points. Subsystems can be identified on this basis, and they in turn can be interrelated to define the total system.

DESIGNING ORGANIZATIONS

As indicated in Part 1, there are many ways to view organizations. One approach involves identification of five major subsystems: (1) goals and values, (2) technology, (3) structure, (4) psychosocial, and (5) managerial. In terms of organizational design, structure has received the most attention because it is easy to represent explicitly in the form of a chart—usually a model of hierarchical relationships.

Early examples of organization design were rather simplistic because they were based on experience in relatively stable organizations such as the church, the military, or mass production industries. As the external environment became more turbulent and as internal relationships became more complex, the hierarchical model needed amplification in order to depict the organization with any degree of realism. For example, dotted lines were introduced to identify staff (advisory) rather than line (command) relationships, or to specify lateral relationships. Also, it is impossible to show the various informal systems on a typical organization chart.

Moreover, it has become increasingly important to consider additional subsystems—goals and values, technology, psychosocial, and managerial—when describing organizations. Structure cannot be considered in isolation; it should be designed with various combinations of factors in mind. As summarized in Chapter 2:

The *mechanistic* organizational form is most appropriate for routine activities where productivity is the major objective, where technology is relatively uniform and stable, where decision making is programmable, and where environmental forces are relatively stable and certain.

The *organic* (or adaptive) organizational form is most appropriate for nonroutine activities where creativity and innovation are important, where heuristic decision-making processes are necessary, and where the environment is relatively uncertain and turbulent.

These conclusions emphasize a contingency view of organization design; each situation should be analyzed in order to determine the most appropriate form. What is the most useful way to divide the work—product, function, or geographic? Will a narrow or wide span of control be most appropriate?

In addition, attention should be given to designing other aspects of organizational systems, e.g., planning processes, control processes, reward systems, and information-decision systems. Managers should devote explicit attention to the design of both structure and process in organizational systems.

Differentiation and Integration

A basic consideration in the design of organizations is the differentiation and integration of activities. The findings from several research projects on this dimension can be useful in designing organizations.[2] Although the concept of differentiation and integration, as described by Lawrence and Lorsch, is somewhat more complex, the basic idea involves differentiating the necessary activities of an organization both horizontally and vertically— dividing up the work into doable tasks. At the same time attention must be given to coordinating these activities and integrating the results into a meaningful composite result. The fundamental purpose is objective accomplishment.

The degree of differentiation can vary from relatively homogeneous (a number of Sears and Roebuck stores under a regional manager) to extremely diverse (a variety of consumer and industrial products with common research, engineering, and marketing functions). The amount and sophistication of integrative activity must increase with the degree of differentiation, in order to ensure overall effectiveness and efficiency. The means of integration include the formal hierarchy, plans and procedures, role specifications, committees, project teams, or other special integrating mechanisms. Examples of integrating units must be applied research (between fundamental research and production), production planning (between engineering and production), or market research (between fundamental research and sales). Differentiation and diversity often lead to conflict in situations where integration is necessary.[3] The most effective organizations (among

[2]P. R. Lawrence and J. W. Lorsch, *Organization and Environment: Managing Differentiation and Integration,* Division of Research, Harvard Graduate School of Business Administration, Boston, 1967.
[3]Another approach is autonomous units and very little integration, except for financial aspects. Conglomerates are examples of this approach.

those investigated) seemed to emphasize creative conflict management as a way to facilitate the integration of activities.

> In high-performing organizations in all environments, it was found
> that conflict was managed by involved individuals who dealt
> openly with the conflict and worked a problem until a resolution
> was reached which best met total organizational goals. In effective
> organizations, there was more of a tendency to *confront* conflict
> instead of using raw power to *force* one party's compliance or in-
> stead of *smoothing* over the conflict by agreeing to disagree.[4]

How can the concepts of differentiation and integration be
applied to organizational design? Several suggestions stem from
the research referred to above. With respect to grouping activities:

1. Units which have similar orientations and tasks should
    be grouped together. (They can reinforce each other's
    common concern and the arrangement will simplify the
    coordinating task of a common manager.)
2. Units required to integrate the activities closely should
    be grouped together. (The common manager can co-
    ordinate them through the formal hierarchy.)

These two examples are relatively straightforward. The task becomes more complex when we have units which are similar in
nature and function but relatively independent, or conversely,
when we have units which are diverse and differentiated but also
highly interdependent. In these cases, a manager must use judgment and his knowledge of the specific situation to determine the
most appropriate way to group activities.

The second step is designing a means of integration for the
basic structure. As indicated above, the decision concerning
grouping is, in itself, a means of integration through the management hierarchy. If the situation requires more differentiation and
hence more sophisticated integration, it is necessary to build supplemental mechanisms such as coordinating departments, cross-
functional teams, or other similar approaches. Research results
suggest that special means should be "built into the organization
in such a way that they facilitate the interaction of integrators
with functional specialists who have the relevant knowledge to
contribute to joint decisions. Alternatively, they may also need to
facilitate the direct interaction among functional specialists who
have the necessary knowledge to contribute to these joint de-

---

[4]Gene W. Dalton, Paul R. Lawrence, and Jay W. Lorsch (eds.), *Organizational
Structure and Design,* Richard D. Irwin, Inc. and the Dorsey Press, Homewood,
Ill., 1970, p. 11.

cisions."[5] A specific example of an integrating mechanism, program management, is discussed in detail in Chapter 13.

MASTER PLANNING

The systems can be implemented by means of design activity at the various planning levels throughout the organization. Referring to Figure 6-5, a master planning committee engages in high-level design activity and establishes guidelines for the entire organization. Within that framework design activity is carried on by the resource-allocation group in order to put together combinations of manpower, facilities, and technology to form a working system organized to accomplish given objectives. The system so designed may be one of several integral parts of the total operation. Within either facilitating systems or major project systems, additional design activity—systems review and evaluation—is necessary to maintain working systems on a current basis.

The master planning committee should have a definite approach to developing premises which serve as the basis for systems design. Meaningful information should be translated from environmental data on such questions as economic activity, political developments, and social trends. It is important that top management develop clear-cut systems of such information flow, providing inputs for planning and decision making. In most organizations such systems are left to chance or, at best, periodic review.

Another part of the environment that should be monitored continually is the competitive situation. Industry intelligence, or other similar approaches, should be set up to provide more meaningful data than are readily available from secondary sources. Again, this system of data collection and screening should be established explicitly to complement other sources, thus augmenting top management's information-decision system.

Another aspect of this system is internal feedback. In order to establish broad guidelines for future activity and to make specific decisions on new projects or programs, top management should be appraised of skills and resources available.

Product Missions

A useful approach to outlining the role of the master planning committee in systems design is the product-missions concept.

---

[5]Ibid., p. 14

Rather than concentrate on the particular product, whether it be a piece of hardware or a service, it is often more beneficial to consider the role of such a product in a larger system. For example, automobile manufacturers should be cognizant of the role of their product in a larger system—vehicular transportation. Even this system, including automobiles, trucks, buses, highway networks, the petroleum industry, service stations, and others, is a part of a still larger system—the overall transportation system, including water, rail, and air systems. The automobile manufacturer ought to recognize possible missions for his product. It might be transportation; it might be prestige; or it might be various combinations of the two. In any case, it is important to define exactly what mission is to be accomplished in order to design products to fit the need.

Several petroleum companies have advertised their recognition of a changing product mission. Instead of emphasizing the production of gasoline, these companies have described themselves as producers of energy. In this way they have broadened the scope of their mission and have included a number of things other than gasoline. This broader scope will allow such companies to maintain a position in a dynamic environment because of their ability to adjust to changing markets and breakthroughs in research. For example, in perceiving its role as a producer of energy rather than gasoline for automobile consumption, a company could maintain an active interest in the evolution of the automobile as a means of transportation and in research and development on sources of power. A company with such an outlook would be able to participate in the development of atomic-powered automobiles, adjusting its niche in the market as changes occurred.

This function of perception of need is of vital concern in master planning. It should appraise continually the future potential for the corporate system as a whole and be cognizant of where its output fits into larger systems. The ultimate utilization of products or services must be understood. For producers of component parts or semifinished goods, the manufacturer should be aware of the use of the components and the ultimate end-product mission. Even raw-material producers can benefit from this broad-gauged view and thereby be prepared to adjust to a dynamic environment.

By being cognizant of product missions and the role of the company's product or products in such missions, the master planning committee can establish broad guidelines for systems design. Understanding the overall system, which may involve several industries and multiple channels of distribution, provides premises for deciding on new ventures or adaptations of existing programs. Once the desirability and feasibility of projects or programs have been established, the matter is referred to the resource-allocation planning group for more specific action.

Designing the Top Level

Identifying top-level organizational relationships is a key step in the designing process. Particular titles are less important than the concepts involved. The master planning committee might be the executive committee or an active board of directors. For example, many organizations have emphasized operating groups and product divisions rather than functional departments and included one central staff group covering finance, marketing, and other areas of interest. The executive committee or the board of directors, both of which include the group executives, is analogous to the master planning committee.

There seems to be growing concern for the complexity of the typical chief executive's task, and steps have been taken to combat the problems. One approach involves increasing the capacity of the president's "office" so that "it" rather than "he" can cope with the full range of responsibilities and pressures. The growth in the White House staff is a good example of such an approach, designed to augment the capabilities of the President of the United States in coping with a broad range of complex problems and numerous agencies reporting "directly" to him. Daniel cites several examples of the same approach in industry:

> In April 1963 the Ford Motor Company set up a three-man Chief Executive Office composed of the chairman, president, and executive vice president, with the company's seven operating groups reporting to the office as a unit.
>
> Six months later the National Biscuit Company announced a "most important change in executive alignment"—the creation of an executive department comprising the president, executive vice president, and four senior vice presidents. The group's collective responsibility is "directing overall planning and policy making" for foreign and domestic operations.
>
> Still another company—beset by the challenge of "going international"—has evolved an arrangement in the last two years whereby five executives share chief-executive responsibilities. In this instance it began with the chairman and president splitting the work load; in time three senior vice presidents were appointed;

and now this five-man group collectively exercises the authority of the chief executive.[6]

There may be variations in the way the "team at the top" operates, depending on the environment and the resources at hand. In any event, it will concern itself primarily with long-range planning, strategic decisions, and policy formulation—leaving day-to-day operating decisions to other echelons. The impact of this approach on staff groups is outlined by Daniel as follows:

> But whether or not a trend toward team top management stimulates the development of a new staff structure or vice versa, I believe we shall see some significant new organizational arrangements at the top. If my reasoning is correct, functional staffs will diminish in importance, while staffs capable of integrating and coordinating functional viewpoints will flourish. These staffs will have personnel with functional training and experience, but they will be obliged to subordinate functional interests to the welfare of the company, shaping their analyses and recommendations in the same frame of reference as the team they serve.[7]

The team-at-the-top concept fits the design criteria in the systems model for top management and illustrates the notion that implementation may take numerous forms, depending on the specifics of the situation.

RESOURCE ALLOCATION

Systems design is an important function or activity of the resource-allocation group. It is set up specifically to develop integrated arrangements of facilities, manpower, and technology in order to accomplish given objectives. This function involves providing the elements necessary for mission accomplishment. It may include the acquisition of new facilities and/or manpower or reallocation of those elements that have reverted back to the overall system because of the "phasing out" of a major project system. The system to be designed may be quite elaborate, or it may be fairly routine, depending on corporate experience in the planned area of endeavor. The resource-allocation group is also involved in designing facilitating systems (see Figure 6-5). Several examples will help to explain the process of implementation.

[6]D. Ronald Daniel, "Team at the Top," *Harvard Business Review,* March–April 1965, pp. 75–76.
[7]Ibid., pp. 81–82.

A Space System

A company in the aerospace industry might decide to pursue actively the acquisition of contracts for an advanced space system. Questions of facilities would need to be considered; existing buildings might be available, or entirely new housing might be required. Similarly, equipment for research and development and prototype construction might exist in present company stocks, or all or part of the needed equipment might have to be purchased. Working relationships would have to be established with raw-material and subcomponent suppliers in order to integrate the development of the entire space system.

Similarly, the work force necessary to man the new system might be available internally, or it might be necessary to obtain all or part outside. Another basic element in any system, technology, also would be defined explicitly in order to develop a complete picture of needed and available resources.

The systems design would take into account the relationship of the company with the customer (NASA), with major subsystem suppliers, with component suppliers, and with raw-material sources. Physical facilities would be designed, a plant layout would be set forth explicitly, and organizational relationships would be established among the people involved in the project. Flow concepts could be introduced by the use of network analysis which would identify the critical points over a period of time and relate the accomplishment of various tasks to the overall system. The decision points within the man-machine system could be identified, and the necessary data processing system could be designed to provide meaningful information at such points. The result would be a systems design establishing a number of subsystems making up a total project system, which in turn might be one of a number for the organization as a whole. The design would recognize the basic elements of material, energy, and information which are part of every system and would tie them together in meaningful relationships on the basis of flow concepts, particularly the information-decision system.

Other Project Systems

The introduction of small cars by United States automobile manufacturers in the late 1960s represents another example of a project system. Manufacturers had to design a system which was significantly different from existing systems. This decision by top management represented more than a mere model change: objectives were set forth; facilities were acquired and adjusted; manpower was realigned; and advertising and promotion were directed toward a "new" market.

The entertainment industry provides good examples of project systems. For a movie production company, each new film represents a new project to which resources must be allocated. Existing facilities might be appropriate, or new sets or locations might be required. People must be acquired for both acting roles and all the behind-the-scenes activity. Publicity and distribution must be arranged. These tasks can be relatively routine, yet variations may be desirable. The entertainment industry in general—movies, television, radio, and the theater—provides good examples of the application of the systems approach.

Another example of the need for systems design in the allocation of resources would be the decision of a large casualty-insurance company to enter the life insurance field. Again, the basic elements must be assembled in the form of facilities, manpower, and technology. Decisions must be reached with regard to a distribution system (advertising, promotion, and salesmen). The system must be designed to achieve its own mission, yet it must also fit into the existing corporate system in order to complement the casualty and/or accident and health business.

These examples illustrate the need for systems design in terms of resource allocation once a decision is reached to embark upon a particular project or program. The decision is made on the basis of external environmental conditions in relation to top management's perception of existing or readily obtainable skills and resources. The systems-design function should implement this decision by specifically aligning the available resources into a meaningful and integrated system for objective accomplishment.

However, the systems created at this level are not static; they too must evolve over time as the project progresses through its life cycle. This life cycle might be a few months, as in the case of some movie-making projects, or it might involve many years, as in the case of a space program which runs from preliminary research and development efforts through operational status and eventual obsolescence.

SYSTEMS REVIEW AND EVALUATION

As indicated in Figure 6-6, a systems-review function is an integral part of each operating system. The system as a whole should be reviewed periodically by means of a thoroughgoing analysis and synthesis of the system and its components. The system should be broken down into its individual subsystems, and each of these should be evaluated in terms of the likelihood of continuing efficiency. Adjustments can be made on the basis of the results of such analysis. Then a process of synthesis takes place in order to restructure an integrated whole.

Why is it that subsystems and/or project systems should be reviewed and adjusted continually? One obvious reason is that requirements change over a period of time, hence the system needs to be redesigned in the light of evolutionary trends. Static systems design goes out of date almost immediately. In fact, the battle cry of some systems analysts and designers is, "If it works, it must be obsolete!" As a particular project progresses through its life cycle, the product mission may change, as may other environmental or competitive conditions. Organizational adjustments may be required, or technological advancements may allow improvements in the handling of either material or information flow.

Some systems are built around individuals within an organization. If identification of decision points is based on strong or dominant personalities, the information-decision system may be disrupted completely whenever key-personnel changes are made. Hence systems must be redesigned in order to accommodate the changes in managerial personnel.

The original allocation of resources may have been temporary in the sense of availability of necessary elements either internally or externally. Makeshift systems have a way of perpetuating themselves regardless of inefficiencies. It is important to reappraise the situation often enough to make sure that such temporary arrangements are revised when conditions allow.

Another typical problem is the tendency toward empire building, the accumulation of more than enough material, manpower, and facilities to accomplish given objectives. The project manager must resist the tendency toward bigness for the sake of prestige or status. A semidetached, hopefully objective systems-review group can help nurture such a point of view.

CONSTRAINTS ON THE DESIGN FUNCTION

In order to place the systems-design function in proper perspective it is important to consider the various constraints on this activity. Policy decisions on the part of the master planning committee not only provide guidelines for systems design at lower levels; they also provide boundaries. If top management does not embrace the systems approach as a managerial philosophy, systems design, as set forth in this chapter, cannot be implemented. The proper atmosphere must be created at all levels in order for this approach to be utilized.

Other limiting factors include the amounts and kinds of facilities available as well as the work force and its skill mix. Elaborate and sophisticated systems designs might be forthcoming which could not be implemented because of lack of facilities and/or manpower. However, we suggest that the systems-design group start with designs for systems that are needed rather than those which obviously can be implemented. The organization will progress if it is encouraged to strain toward ideals. If the design proves too much of a "cloud nine" approach, the system can always be scaled back to meet existing capabilities.

The resource-allocation group places constraints on the system-review function in terms of policy decisions with regard to allocation of the resources between major project systems and facilitating systems. It may be that systems analysts within major project systems have designed optimal arrangements for their own operation without regard to other project systems. The resource-allocation group may decide that certain facilitating systems common to several or all project systems should be set up to serve the entire organization. Thus policy decisions throughout the total system provide constraints within which systems designers must operate.

Along with policy decisions and equipment and facility limitations, another constraint which must be taken into consideration by systems designers is people. The remark "It would be a great system if it weren't for the people involved" is appropriate here. Problems of resistance to change or of out-and-out antagonism are evident throughout the literature describing the impacts of automation and electronic data processing. Similar reaction is often evident when designing information-decision systems which call for realignment of people and equipment. A typical point of view is the assertion that systems fail because they are misused. An alternative view is set forth by Myers:

> The system designer is correct in diagnosing systems failures as human failures. But he usually fails to recognize that his responsibility embraces the human factor—that the system designer's role is one of facilitating human processes, and that helpful systems function as extensions of man, not man as an appendage of systems. Furthermore, the system designer often overlooks his

responsibility for seeing to it that the system user is adequately trained to administer the system. Systems failures sometimes result from designer permissiveness in allowing the user to divest himself of the responsibility for helping design the system. Because of sheer job pressure, the user sometimes welcomes the staff man's takeover.[8]

The problems are evident; the solutions are not so evident. Because this is such a critical issue, we shall devote an entire chapter to the subject.

External forces are ever-present constraints for systems designers. Unions may affect the planning for systems involving members' compensation and working conditions. Government rules and regulations often dictate at least part of the information-decision system for suppliers in order that comparability of data is assured. Systems designers should recognize the role of their organization in suprasystems involving intercompany and/or government-industry relationships.

Continuing attention should be devoted to systems review and the implementation of proposed changes. Follow-up is necessary because of the seemingly inherent resistance to change on the part of people involved in the system. Unless such resistance can be overcome, poor systems may be prolonged. Once the atmosphere is established for continual evaluation and review, implementation of change becomes progressively easier.

So far, we have talked primarily about management's responsibility for systems design and the design activities appropriate at various levels. While it is important to establish this general conceptual framework for the systems-design function, it is also important to spend some time on the question of how this function should be carried out. Who should be responsible for systems design?

RESPONSIBILITY FOR SYSTEMS DESIGN

Implementation is implicit in the connotation of systems design; otherwise it would be an empty exercise. Therefore, the interface between managers and systems designers is critical, and mutual understanding should be fostered in order to maximize returns from design efforts. The system should be tailored to the needs of the organization and adapted continually as circum-

[8]M. Scott Myers, "The Human Factor in Management Systems," *California Management Review*, Fall 1971, p. 9.

stances change. Since managers are ultimately responsible for organizational endeavor, they should play a large and active role in design projects in order to ensure the development of useful systems.

In a general sense managers engage in systems-design work on a day-to-day basis. They plan activities and organize systems to accomplish objectives. However, staff groups have evolved for tasks such as long-range planning, organization studies, and systems design. Special effort should be made to make such activities an extension of the manager's role rather than a separate function.

In discussing the design of information systems Thurston cites four factors which play a major role in determining success in systems work:

1. Understanding of the objectives of an operation and knowledge of the existing operating patterns, coupled with ability to relate the information system to operating needs.
2. Ability and organizational position to work with operating people to effect change.
3. Competence in the designing of information systems.
4. Motivation to make systems changes.[9]

Operating managers fulfill the requirements in points 1 and 2; they understand the organizational decision-making requirements and the information needed to support the system. Probability of success in implementation is enhanced considerably if management is vitally interested in the project. On the other hand, technical expertise and motivation for change are more likely to be found in staff groups.

The answer would seem to be a team approach, with specialists supporting operating managers who would be responsible for the project's success. A manager might devote part time to such an effort or full time on a temporary basis if the task requires it. Thurston says, "I want to emphasize, however, that where I have seen operating men who, being motivated to do the job, did take control, the record of successful completion of projects was better than where staff men directed operations."[10]

If the project involves an integrated system for the entire company it may well require years to complete. If operating people are delegated responsibility and authority for the project,

[9]Philip H. Thurston, "Who Should Control Information Systems?", *Harvard Business Review*, November–December 1962, p. 138.
[10]Ibid.

particularly systems specification, they should maintain enough contact with day-to-day operations to retain their expertise on decision making and attendant information flow. If the environment is dynamic and/or internal capabilities undergo changes, it might be wise to rotate people from operations to systems-design work periodically so that operating expertise is updated continually. Similarly, programmers and data processing specialists should maintain their expertise so that an optimal skill mix can be brought to bear on systems design problems at all times.

Centralization-Decentralization

In assessing the appropriate degree of centralization-decentralization for the systems-design function, it is useful to identify several subcategories of activity. For example, Dearden suggests three phases in a continuous process of information system design and implementation:

> *Systems Specification* . . . includes the design of all of the aspects of a management information system that are important *to the users.* It includes principally the basic decisions as to what information should be provided by the system.
> *Data-Processing Implementation* . . . is concerned with those things that are important *to the processing of the data.* The purpose in this stage is to design a data-processing system that will most efficiently implement the systems specified.
> *Programming* . . . starts with the systems flow charts and ends when the program is running on the computer.[11]

Specification work should be delegated to operating people who will use the system. If decisions and information flow form the basis for the system, decision makers will be in a better position to identify current and future needs. Specialists can "get in the act" in the second phase when the feasibility of implementing the specified system is investigated.

The data processing implementation can and should be centralized because knowledge of equipment and techniques is essential to sound selection decisions. If a companywide data base is to be established, compatibility throughout the system is an important consideration. Integration of information systems provides economies, and staff specialists can contribute their expertise to the various subsystems without detailed understanding of the specifications.

---

[11]John Dearden, "How to Organize Information Systems," *Harvard Business Review,* March–April 1965, pp. 66–67.

Programming also can and should be centralized for reasons of economy and because it requires special knowledge of equipment and programming languages. These skills can be applied effectively to various subsystems with significantly different specifications.

Problem Orientation

An important concept in ensuring managerial involvement in systems design is that of focusing on the problem. Using the scientific method (or general approach to problem solving) involves defining the problem initially in terms of the objectives of the overall system and its various subsystems. Even though the specific system under analysis may be a minor subpart, it is important for the manager/designer to be cognizant of the composite system and the interrelationship between it and its parts. Changes and adjustments in a subsystem could be disruptive unless the impact on interrelationships is considered.

Once a problem has been defined and placed in proper perspective with regard to an overall system, various techniques of analysis can be employed. It is important for analysts to keep in mind the necessity of focusing on the problem rather than on the techniques of analysis. Sometimes attention on the part of researchers or analysts is devoted to the improvement of a specific technique regardless of its applicability to a particular problem. In such cases, "the tail begins to wag the dog," thus hampering the analysis.

Staff groups with equipment and programming expertise can be considered facilitating systems because resources are allocated to various systems-design projects as needed to implement the specifications. In actual practice the phases overlap somewhat because operating managers, as designers, will want to enlist the advice and counsel of staff specialists. Moreover, if the systems-design and implementation project is a major one, it is likely to last for months and even years. In such cases there will be redesigning and reprogramming work along the way because of changes in the environment and/or internal capabilities of the organization. This requires the integration of managers and specialists to achieve the best possible systems design.

Implementation

In order to install a new system or to adjust the existing system in some manner, it is necessary to specify the changes explicitly. Haphazard or loose instructions with regard to implementation often negate excellent work on the part of the analyst/designer. He should be able to specify the required changes and communicate them to the organization in a manner that enhances acceptance, at least initially.

Upon installation, the system should be debugged and modified in order to fit the situation. Revised systems do not resemble interchangeable parts. The approach is more like fine watchmaking, where individual parts often must be filed and fitted in order to complement the other parts of the system. This process is vital and requires great skill. Once installed, debugged, and modified, the subsystem under study has become a part of the total system. The analyst can then look toward other aspects of the overall system, possibly those systems which are interconnected with the one most recently under scrutiny. Moreover, the systems-review and evaluation function requires periodic checking of all the systems in order to ensure that they maintain their complementary nature and are integrated toward effective and efficient accomplishment of the objectives of the organization as a whole.

SUMMARY

Systems design is a key managerial activity in implementing the systems approach. This function provides an overall framework by establishing subsystems, larger systems, and a composite, integrated whole. Within this framework and within the philosophical setting of systems concepts, other techniques of management science can be employed, e.g., linear programming, queuing theory, network analysis, and simulation.

Simplicity, flexibility, reliability, economy, and acceptability are all characteristics associated with effective and efficient system operation.

Systems design considers three basic elements in every system: material, energy, and information. In addition, each of these elements can be structured on the basis of flow concepts as systems in and of themselves. The flow concept facilitates the consideration of systems of systems by emphasizing the interconnections between subparts.

The design of an organization should be tailored to its specific situation—reflecting environmental conditions, goals, technology, and other related factors. Key dimensions to consider are differentiation and integration of activities; both structure and process can be designed around them.

In terms of the suggested organization for implementing the

systems approach, the master planning committee utilizes a top-management information-decision system to facilitate strategic planning. On the basis of inputs from research and development, market research, environmental analysis, and an assessment of internal resources and capabilities, it establishes the programs or projects upon which the organization will devote its time. It is charged with the responsibility for recognition of the niche which the company occupies in a larger system or systems. In this way, top management establishes broad guidelines and parameters for the systems-design function.

Given a policy decision on which projects or programs are to be undertaken, the resource-allocation group designs systems which can accomplish the objectives established. The design effort, at this level, involves putting together systems of manpower, technology, and facilities and coordinating such systems on the basis of information-decision systems. The important task at this level is allocation of appropriate resources among project and facilitating systems. All these subsystems should complement each other and should be integrated into the total organizational system.

Within project systems a review function should be established. At this level systems analysts should continually appraise the appropriateness of the major project system and its various subsystems as the program moves through its life cycle. Analysis and synthesis must be carried out to ensure up-to-date approaches at all times.

Management should play a large and active role in design projects to ensure the development of useful systems and enhance their implementation. Operating people should be delegated the responsibility for determining specifications, particularly when information-decision systems are at stake. Staff specialists can be used to add technical expertise.

It is important to recognize constraints on the systems-design function. Policy decisions at various levels in the organization represent constraints on systems analysts at lower levels. Also, the facilities and equipment available, as well as the work force and its skill mix, represent limitations. The impact of systems design and change on people is critical—a point important enough to be deferred to a later chapter.

QUESTIONS

1. What is meant by design? How is it important in implementing the systems approach?

2. Compare and contrast systems design, systems analysis, systems and procedures, and systems engineering.
3. Briefly describe the general characteristics of effective systems.
4. How can flow concepts be used in systems design?
5. Using an organization with which you are familiar, illustrate vertical and horizontal differentiation of activities. Point out several existing and/or potential means of coordinating and integrating the various activities.
6. How is master planning related to systems design? For industrial concerns? For the Department of Defense? For a college or university?
7. What part does resource allocation play in the system-design function?
8. Why should systems be reviewed and adjusted periodically?
9. Describe several constraints on the systems-design function. Will designers have *more,* or *less,* freedom to innovate in the future?
10. Who should be responsible for systems-design activities in an organization? Why?

Weyerhaeuser Company (A)

The Setting

The Weyerhaeuser Company is a large-scale, complex organization. Incorporated as the Weyerhaeuser Timber Company on January 18, 1900, the company was organized to cut and process timber from 900,000 acres of land purchased from the Northern Pacific Railroad. A number of individuals and companies joined together with Frederick Weyerhaeuser to take this initial step. Growth and diversification since 1900 have been spectacular and the Weyerhaeuser Company is certainly a leader in the forest products industry today.

The company's products can be classified under general categories, such as lumber, softwood plywood, laminated products, hardwood products, manufactured panels, paper products, pulp and paperboard, containers and cartons, and others. Exhibit 7–1 shows domestic production facilities for all of the company products plus an indication of the rapidly expanding foreign operations as they existed in 1964. Coordination of such widespread domestic and international production facilities is a challenge.

Exhibit 7–1 also shows the Weyerhaeuser Company distribution system with general and regional sales offices plus distribution centers. The complexity involved in managing the flow of raw material through production processes and through distribution centers to ultimate consumers is evident. Without a well-designed, integrated system chaos could reign.

In its annual reports the Weyerhaeuser Company is described as "a materials-flow company." Exhibit 7–2 illustrates the concept involved. Raw materials, primarily timber, flow into the various stages of the production process; they flow through the process, taking on new shapes, forms, or chemical composition, until they become finished

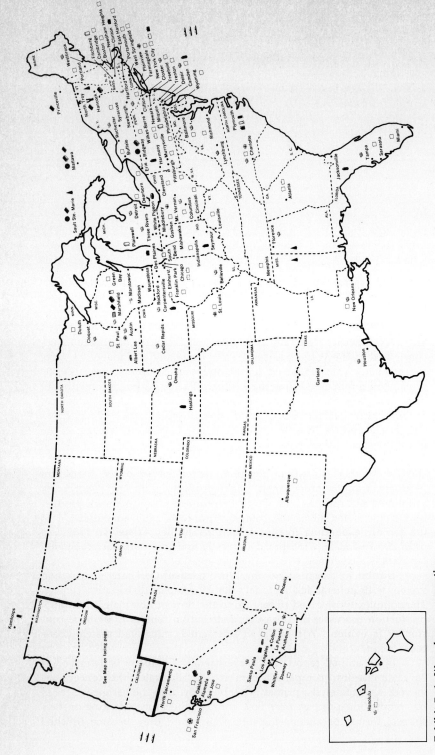

Exhibit 7-1. Weyerhaeuser operations.

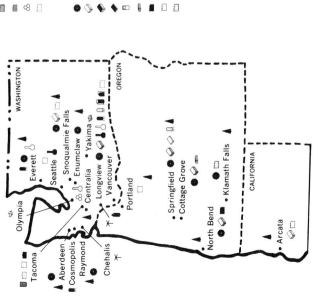

NEW PRODUCTS

- Molded fiber plant
- Bark fractions plant
- Honeycomb plant
- Wood fiber plant

WOOD PRODUCTS

- Lumber mill
- Plywood mill–softwood
- Plywood mill–hardwood
- Veneer plant–hardwood
- Door plant–hardwood
- Laminated products plant
- Fabrication plant
- Flakeboard plant
- Hardboard plant

PULP, PAPER, PAPERBOARD

- Pulp mill
- Board mill
- Boxboard mill
- Jute containerboard mill
- Paper mill
- Paper mill–RW
- Chemical plant
- Paperboard distribution center
- General sales office
- Region sales office

CONTAINERS AND CARTONS

- Shipping container plant
- Folding carton plant
- Milk carton plant
- General sales office

OTHER

- Executive offices
- General office – Weyerhaeuser line
- Research–general
- Research–pulp
- Research–forestry
- Steamships
- Railroad
- Timber holdings

Particleboard plant
Ply-veneer plant
Distribution center
General sales office
Region sales office

FOREIGN OPERATIONS–1964

BELGIUM–Shipping containers
FRANCE–Shipping containers
GERMANY–Folding cartons and specialty papers
GUATEMALA–Shipping containers
SCOTLAND–Specialty papers
VENEZUELA–Milk cartons, Flexible packaging, Pulp and paper

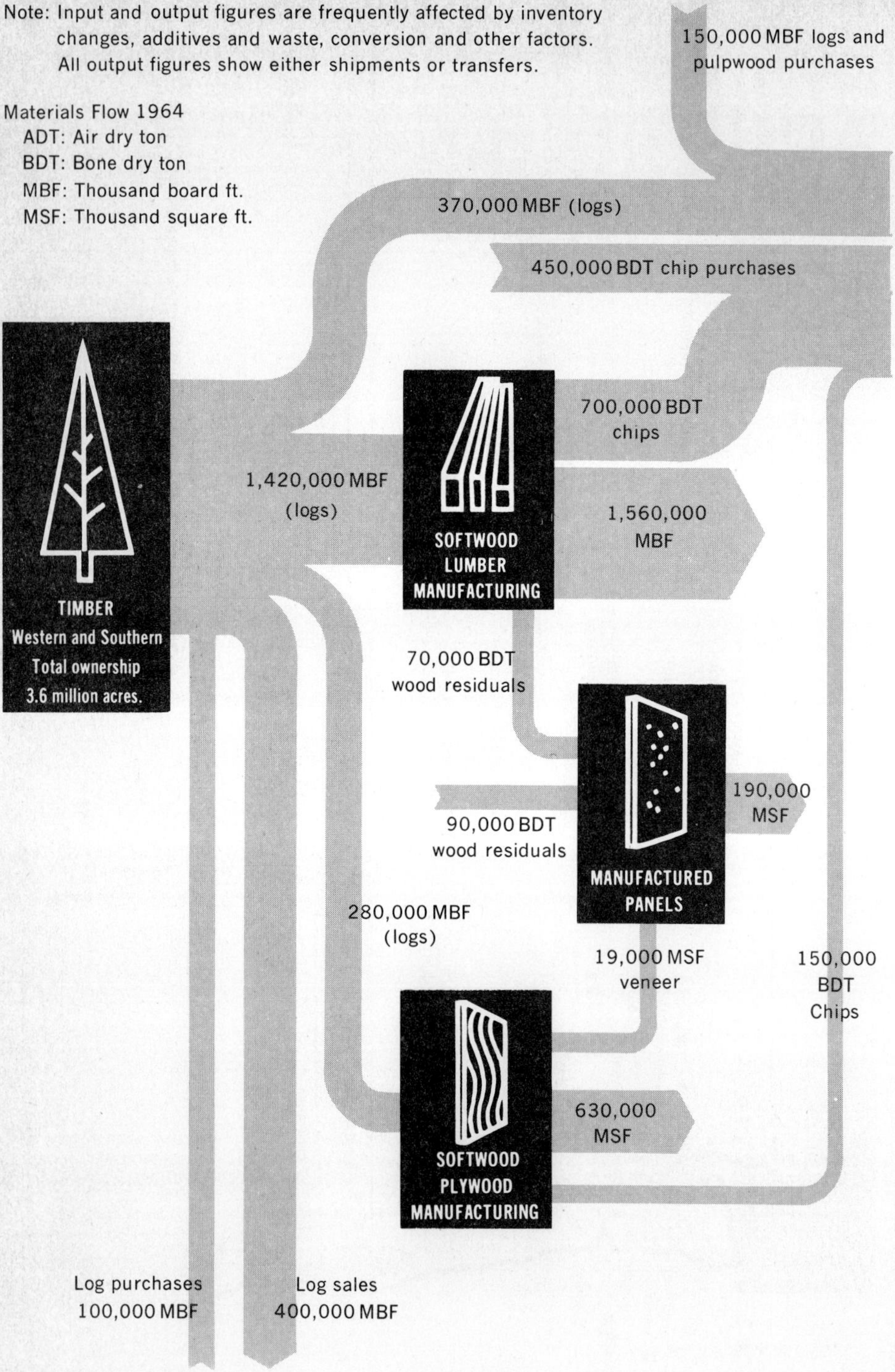

Note: Input and output figures are frequently affected by inventory changes, additives and waste, conversion and other factors. All output figures show either shipments or transfers.

150,000 MBF logs and pulpwood purchases

Materials Flow 1964
  ADT: Air dry ton
  BDT: Bone dry ton
  MBF: Thousand board ft.
  MSF: Thousand square ft.

370,000 MBF (logs)

450,000 BDT chip purchases

700,000 BDT chips

1,420,000 MBF (logs)

SOFTWOOD LUMBER MANUFACTURING

1,560,000 MBF

TIMBER
Western and Southern
Total ownership
3.6 million acres.

70,000 BDT wood residuals

90,000 BDT wood residuals

MANUFACTURED PANELS

190,000 MSF

280,000 MBF (logs)

19,000 MSF veneer

150,000 BDT Chips

630,000 MSF

SOFTWOOD PLYWOOD MANUFACTURING

Log purchases
100,000 MBF

Log sales
400,000 MBF

Exhibit 7-2. Weyerhaeuser . . . a materials flow company.

58,000 tons of
waste board

94,000 tons container-
board purchases

**PULP
MANUFACTURING**

780,000
ADT

**PAPERBOARD
MANUFACTURING**

420,000
tons

460,000
tons

**SHIPPING
CONTAINER
MANUFACTURING**

54,000
ADT

210,000 tons

110,000 tons

540,000
ADT

185,000
tons

**PAPER
MANUFACTURING**

92,000
tons

**MILK
CARTON
MANUFACTURING**

115,000 ADT
pulp purchases

36,000
tons

47,000
tons

**FOLDING
CARTON
MANUFACTURING**

8,000 MBF
log sales

360,000
doors

26,000 MBF
logs

230,000 MSF
veneer

43,000 MSF
plywood

28,000 MBF
lumber

22,000 tons
board purchases

**TIMBER
HARDWOOD**

**HARDWOOD
MANUFACTURING**

17,000 MBF
log purchases

18,000 MBF lumber purchases

110,000 MSF veneer purchases

goods; and then flow through distribution systems until they reach the ultimate consumer.

Coupled with the material flow are energy and information flow. Electrical and other forms of energy facilitate production processes throughout the system. Human energy also flows through the process on a continuing basis. The organization itself has evolved over time to correlate with the natural breakdown emanating from the material flow and natural product breakdown. Exhibit 7–3 shows the organization as it relates to the "materials-flow" operation.

Information is the most important factor in coordinating a dispersed and diversified operation such as the Weyerhaeuser Company According to a company spokesman:

> At Weyerhaeuser the computer is symbolic of the speed, change, complexity, and co-ordination. It provides us the heart of the most complete management-information system in the forest products industry. This system is one part of a comprehensive program that enables our management to guide a large and complex group of operations in swift and effective response to the changes in the business environment.

Development of a management information-decision system was an extremely difficult, time-consuming, and expensive project. The balance of this case describes the efforts of the Weyerhaeuser Company to develop an information-decision system which would provide the means of coordinating the large-scale, complex organization described above.

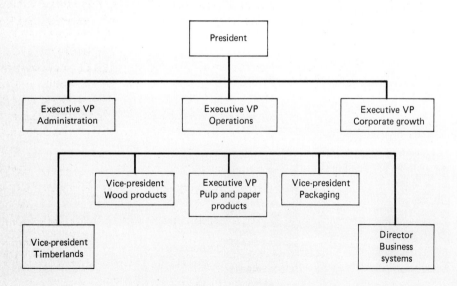

Exhibit 7–3. Weyerhaeuser Company Organization, Feb. 1, 1966.

Objectives

The status of the Weyerhaeuser Company was described by the president as follows:

> . . . Only a few years ago we were known as a lumber company with some pulp manufacturing facilities. We were a Northwest commodity-oriented concern. Today we make and distribute a broad and highly sophisticated line of forest products. Today the nation and the world are our markets. We are a major factor in world pulp and paperboard production and distribution. We are rapidly becoming an important force in both national and international packaging. We are moving effectively into the fine paper field on a national basis.
>
> These efforts are supported by widely dispersed forests containing various species of trees. Our timber holdings have spread to western and eastern Canada, Mississippi, Alabama and North Carolina.
>
> Since 1956, our employees have more than doubled to 32,913, our shareholders have more than tripled to 24,000 and our operations have expanded until today we have more than 100 manufacturing plants in 27 states, Puerto Rico and Canada, and plant investments in 10 countries overseas.
>
> Today Weyerhaeuser is a company committed to a healthy and prosperous rate of growth. We are in business to generate earnings in ever-increasing amounts for our owners. Continued growth in earnings will result from good plans, competently executed, and the wise use of our human and material resources.
>
> . . . Our future as a company looks bright.

Evolution of Data Processing

The Weyerhaeuser Company, like many others, has progressed through a series of data processing systems geared primarily to the capabilities of available equipment. Manual systems were augmented by adding machines and calculators. Punched cards and tabulating machines provided new capabilities and expanded systems. As electronic computers became available, systems were adapted to the new machines. The job of data processing, translating data into information, could then be done much faster and new applications could be developed.

Data processing was carried out on a decentralized basis at various branch plants with a piecemeal approach to information systems. Marketing, manufacturing, and financial applications were developed in order to use the "weird and wonderful" machines that had arrived.

In most cases the approach involved batch processing whereby data were collected for a period of time, then processed and summarized into reports for use by management. However, the reports provided did not always facilitate the day-to-day decision making, which had to be practiced by operating management. Exhibits 7–1 and 7–2 indicate the complexity of the production and distribution system which had to be coordinated.

Thus, it became apparent that a new companywide information system would have to be designed and implemented in order to do a better job of decision making on a day-to-day basis. The initial phase of this approach is outlined in a company memo:

Subject: INFORMATION PROCESSING STUDY

To: Corporate Management

> Region Managers
> Assistant Region Managers
> Area Managers
> Distribution Center Managers
> Branch Managers
> Stock and Price Managers
> Mill Sales Managers

To achieve success in the marketing of our products, it's essential that our communications process on such important matters as order entry and inquiry handling meet the needs of the market. Our present systems in many ways are not adequate to meet the requirements of our customers or our mills. For this reason, we believe we should take a fresh look at all of our present systems and bring them up-to-date.

Accordingly, we have started a study of our Wood Products information processing systems and procedures. Initially, the study will concentrate on our inquiry and sales order entry systems. The study is under the general direction of _____, manager of marketing services. _____, supervisor of machine accounting systems, is the project leader and _____ will be working with him. As required, additional help will be assigned to the study team. Because of their familiarity with our marketing service requirements, ABC Consultants will provide counsel and guidance to the over-all project. In addition to _____, whom most of you know, the ABC men working on the study will be _____, _____, and _____.

It is anticipated that the initial phases of the project will take about six months to complete. During this time, members of the study team will be in touch with many of you and others in your organization to obtain factual data, explore alternative approaches, and test tentative solutions. There appears to be opportunity to improve our inquiry and order handling, and, accordingly, I am sure that you will understand my interest in making this a successful endeavor.

If you have any questions about the project, your immediate super-visor can find the answers for you.

Will you please give the team your wholehearted cooperation.

(signed)

_____

Executive Vice-President

Original IDP Study

In the early stages of this project it was termed the "communications study" but it dealt primarily with the marketing function. The project director sought advice and counsel from people both inside and outside the company with regard to what a communications or integrated data processing system should be like and how the company should proceed to develop whatever system was proposed.

A national consulting firm was engaged in these initial stages to help identify the problem and chart a preliminary course of action. The results of one of the initial sessions is indicated in the following excerpt from a memo written by a member of the consulting firm's staff:

> At the beginning of a communications or integrated data processing study it is important to go through the rigor of developing both short and long term plans for a large nationwide information system. Such questions as these must be answered:
>
> > What are present information needs?
> > How do present information needs overlap between Marketing, Production, and other organizational functions within the division?
> > What will the information needs be five or ten years from now?
>
> Another phase of planning should be directed to the principals and organization for carrying out the activities that are necessary to maintain a continuing, successful integrated data processing system. Such questions as these should be answered:
>
> > How should we organize to meet the need?
> > What technical skills are needed to staff this function?
> > What responsibilities will this function assume on a continuing basis? And should they be centered within the division or elsewhere?
>
> The significant point to remember is that long range plans though necessarily broad and general should be made first. The specific

communication or information systems should then be designed to fit an overall system that is "open-ended." The overall integrated data processing system must be conceived so that individual parts can be fitted together with other parts as they are developed at minimum cost and effort.

Within a week or two the director of machine accounting systems sent a memo to top management outlining his appraisal of the situation at that time:

I have discussed our general concept of the communications study with a number of people within the company as well as ———.

The purpose of this memo is to report to you my findings and to propose a program for carrying out the study. Actually, the term "communications" does not cover the whole subject for we are, in fact, looking for a system of integrated data processing that will satisfy all of the information needs of the Wood Products Division, both marketing and production, and that should also give consideration to the needs of the corporation.

This memo is divided into the following sections:

Objective
Scope
Approach
Responsibility

Objective

Our basic objective in this study is to determine the best over-all system for processing order information from initial development by the salesmen to receipt at the mill and at the same time capitalize on obtaining all possible by-product information for use in such functions as invoicing, statistics, sales and production control, etc.

Scope

The scope of the study should provide for complete evaluation of the company's over-all long-range data processing and communications requirements and to develop against this background an order entry system embracing the necessary functions.

Approach

The sequence of the steps necessary to set this study in motion would be as follows:

1. Appraise long range company data processing and communications requirements. This would be a brief, general appraisal that would nevertheless force those who will design the order entry system to think through the long

range implications of the system with the total corporation's needs.

2. Identify the specific information requirements for the
   entire Wood Products Division. Due to the work that has
   and is being done in connection with the reorganization,
   this information is pretty well known but nevertheless an
   organized approach to this subject is essential.

3. Identify all functions of the division to which a systems
   network can be applied plus the various time span requirements of all important elements in data-processing
   transmission.

4. Develop a specific communications and information
   system that meets the division's over-all requirements.
   At this point, it is recommended that the Wood Products
   Division's order entry problems and tentative objectives
   be submitted to three or four systems equipment manufacturers with a request for their proposals for a complete
   integrated data-processing program. We should select
   those companies who can demonstrate proven performance rather than speculating with new equipment or
   custom designed systems.

5. Review, analyze and appraise the equipment manufacturers' proposals considering the following points:

   (a.) Completeness of the proposed system in terms of
        providing all of our requirements.

   (b.) A comparison of costs in relation to what will be
        gained.

   (c.) The timing at which a new system can be made
        available to us.

   (d.) Evaluation of previous installations of the recom-
        mended system as to its effectiveness in doing a job
        at reasonable costs.

6. Select the equipment that best meets the points listed in 5
   above and get rolling.

Responsibility

If it should be decided that a study at this time must encompass the
needs of the total corporation, then I believe the help of outside
specialists would be mandatory. On the other hand, if the objective
as stated is accepted, then I believe a satisfactory order entry system that meets the needs of the Wood Products Division can be
developed in a reasonable time by your own people, provided
adequate talent can be made available. To this end, I strongly
recommend that an experienced systems manager be furnished by
the controller's department to assume the complete responsibility
for carrying out this assignment. I understand consideration has

already been given to the hiring of such an individual and certainly the results we are looking for require special skills and background in systems work.

The only alternate would be to pick the best outside specialist we can find to carry this project through. In addition, other people within the company with needed skills must be made available as required to work on various phases of the study.

Assuming these recommendations are acceptable, responsibilities for conducting the study would line up as follows:

1. The responsibility for carrying out the complete study would fall basically in the controller's department under the direction of the systems manager.
2. Marketing Services will coordinate the work as required and make decisions as necessary to maintain progress and bring the study to a conclusion.
3. The final recommendations as developed under 1 and 2 above will be submitted to marketing management for concurrence and final approval.

GE: IAO: MSO

General Electric requested an opportunity to present some of their ideas on communication systems to top-level Weyerhaeuser executives. It was described as an on-line, real-time system capable of handling the volume of data transmission necessary to implement Weyerhaeuser's nationwide network of information flow among production and distribution centers.

At the same time, GE's Internal Automation Operation (IAO) was presented as a consulting organization which could provide valuable assistance to Weyerhaeuser in this phase of their study. The IAO group had been developed originally to provide internal consulting for General Electric with special emphasis on information systems. The organization was staffed by General Electric computer users; two-thirds were operating people and one-third were technically oriented personnel. According to the IAO staff, there had been a concerted effort to develop a customer rather than a hardware orientation. Indeed, at times they apparently had recommended equipment other than that manufactured by General Electric in order to implement systems designed specifically for departments or branches of General Electric.

Ultimately it was decided that this group could bring valuable experience to a Weyerhaeuser management information study effort. The review was carried out and a report made which included a recommendation for a large-scale feasibility study, the primary purpose of which would be to design, in skeleton form, a management information system to meet the basic operating needs of the Wood Products Division.

Emphasis was directed toward identifying a "data base" which would be the backbone of a total information-decision system. The philosophy expressed was one of a comprehensive management information system rather than a piecemeal approach.

This next stage could require considerably more time and effort than had been focused thus far on the management information system study. The Executive Vice President for Operations was convinced that the company would have to staff a feasibility study and systems design team with top-caliber managers. A Vice President was made a member of the study team which included operating executives who had been tabbed as "most likely to succeed" within the company over the next ten years. They were people who had an intimate knowledge of the operating organization and the information needs of management.

For the most part they were not technically trained in the details of systems analysis nor computer programming. On the other hand, they were described as people with open minds and logical approaches to problem solving. It was hoped that innovation and creativity would be forthcoming from the group assembled. Nine Weyerhaeuser employees and four from GE's Internal Automation Operation carried out the feasibility study. Their report included the following highlights:

> Emphasis was placed on a basic system designed to provide all levels of management better and more accurate information from which to make business decisions. Communications and data-processing hardware was considered only to the extent necessary to determine its capabilities and to develop estimated costs.

> To obtain the benefits of an integrated management information system, certain basic requirements must be met:

> 1. Rapid communications of data between all division locations.
> 2. Get information into the system early—preferably at point of origin.
> 3. Create one integrated master file for all transactions.
> 4. Preserve details on master files for later analysis as required.
> 5. Perform all data processing.
> 6. Provide information necessary for management of the business.
> 7. Use computers only in areas where they can do jobs faster or more economically than people.
> 8. Generate operating reports as a primary product of the system not as a by-product of financial data processing.

> The proposed system appears feasible from a financial point of view. After full implementation the total system will produce annual savings of approximately $450,000 net, after taxes. It will take

four to five years to complete implementation, which will cost approximately $1.6 million gross, before taxes. The break-even point, on a conservative basis, will be reached after 6.3 years.

The intangible benefits appear to be sufficiently compelling reasons to install the system, even if there were no potential savings. These benefits are summarized as follows:

1. Provides the ability for improved management control reporting.
2. Better over-all control of the business.
3. Better opportunity to match demand and production.
4. Provides the opportunity for improved selling efficiency which should result in lower selling costs and better customer service.
5. Provides means for developing and maintaining raw data base for management analysis of the business.
6. Provides the means for forecasting key elements of the business resulting in better production and market planning.
7. Routine functions performed mechanically—cheaper, faster, more accurately—which frees up management to perform its functions more effectively.

The systems design team should be established as quickly as possible so that early implementation steps can be initiated. For the system to succeed it is not merely important but vital that a competent manager be selected and placed in a position reporting directly to the Vice-President of the Division.

It must be recognized that a commitment to implement the proposed system will have far-reaching impact on our way of doing business. Top management must be prepared to accept the responsibility and support the system effort totally including systems operation, as well as implementation.

If the Wood Products Division is to derive full benefit from the Management Information System proposed in this report, it will be necessary that implementation be firmly and carefully controlled. This necessitates the establishment of an organization that will be held together for the full four year period, be full-time on the job (have no other responsibilities), and be wholly accountable for the success of all systems (see Exhibit 7–4).

The team will have a Project Manager. He should understand systems design and computer capabilities, understand the business of the Wood Products Division, have administrative skill, and be capable of earning cooperation from all levels of the Wood Products Division.

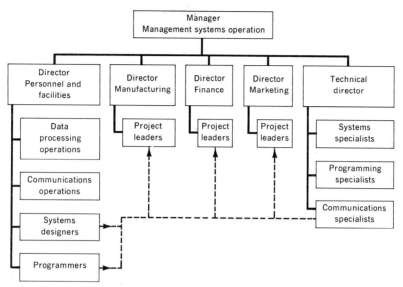

Exhibit 7-4. Organization of management systems operation.

Under the Project Manager we recommend there be five Team Managers. Each Team Manager should bring to his job either considerable systems design skill, or thorough understanding of the operation effected by his particular subsystems. Whichever knowledge the man does not have, he must be willing to recognize the lack, and to work with people whose skills are complementary to his own.

Consideration should be given to selecting people from an outside consulting firm either on a per diem basis or by direct hire. It's estimated that the services will be required for two years.

The recommendations were implemented by the appointment of a manager of Management Systems Operation (MSO). Experienced operating personnel were selected to staff the three functional units—manufacturing, marketing, and finance. Two facilitating functions were identified—personnel and facilities and technical support. Primary responsibility for design and implementation was vested in the experienced management people with the technical specialists playing a supporting role. During the early phases some of the operating people found themselves being frustrated at the discipline and extreme detail required to define the management information system for programming. All in all, the general approach seemed to work quite well with what appeared to be an appropriate combination of technical know-how and ability to improvise within the constraints of operating management views.

Reaction of a Branch Manager

When a companywide management information system was first proposed, the manager of the Snoqualmie Falls branch of the Wood Products Division was apprehensive and skeptical. He wondered whether or not the new comprehensive system of information flow would lead to centralized decision making or to a better way to manage the branch and hence help improve the overall operation. He indicated that he was in complete agreement with the objective of such a system as he understood it—"increased profits from better use of raw material correlated with consumer demand."

However, his initial contacts with technical personnel and outside consultants did not reduce his apprehensiveness appreciably. He remembers saying to himself, "our business is unique, at least enough so to cause consternation for outside analysts." An orientation seminar put on by the equipment manufacturer provided additional information concerning the hardware and the technical aspects of the system being designed. However, familiarity with the "black box" or "giant brain" did not alleviate his concern for the future role of the branch manager in the decision-making process.

He was somewhat relieved when the branch manager at Longview was appointed to head the study team. He felt that here was someone he could trust to understand the environment and the information needs for decision makers at the branch level. He recalls that the head of the study team was somewhat apprehensive and skeptical in the initial stages, also. But as he grew to understand the goals and objectives of the management information system, his confidence began to permeate the organization. As he became more positive, it became easier and easier for branch personnel to cooperate in the study. They could communicate readily with a former colleague and hence grow to understand the goals and objectives of the study and the ultimate management information system proposed.

Field Trip Meetings

In the early phases of the management information-system study, it was decided that contact with field personnel would be desirable throughout the design and implementation stages. Teams of top-level executives involved in the study met with employees throughout the nationwide production-distribution system. The purposes of these meetings were outlined as follows:

1. To present a proposed system.
2. To "try on for size," not to sell.
3. To provide an informal work session.
4. To solicit comments and suggestions for improvement.
5. To emphasize that the system was not fixed, had not been ap-

proved by management, and could be adjusted according to the needs of those who would be using it.

The basic objective of providing information for management decision making and, hopefully, more profitable operations was stressed. The secondary benefits of handling clerical operations faster, more accurately, and less expensively also were emphasized. The scope and timing of the study were outlined and the task force organization assigned responsibility for completing the study was identified. The approach to be used by the systems-design team was outlined as follows:

1. Define basic work of the business.
2. Identify the information necessary to conduct the work—more information is needed to make decisions.
3. Determine how to gather and process data.
4. Determine how to provide feedback to management.

The general outlines of the system were set forth and some of the details of hardware and software considerations were discussed. The key elements of the proposed system were identified as follows:

1. Designed to do the basic work of business independently of organization.
2. Create one integrated master file.
3. Get information into system early—preferably at the point of origin.
4. To preserve details on master files for later analysis as required.
5. To use computers only in areas where they can do the job faster or more economically than people.

An important consideration at meetings with field personnel was that of implementation. Tentative schedules for implementing various phases of the systems were outlined.

Response to this phase of the overall management information-system study is indicated in the following memo:

Location: Newark—Region VII

Subject: Management Information Systems Study

To: Vice President, Assistant to Executive Vice President

The presentation of the proposed Management Information Systems Study, put on at Newark by your team, was most interesting and informative. I would like to take this opportunity to congratulate you, and the others on the team, for the excellent job done to date in the development of such a truly advanced and sophisticated system. I will be very surprised if you don't get full approval to proceed with detailed development and implementation.

The opportunity for field personnel to participate in development and eventual implementation is much appreciated. Although this enlightened approach may be more costly at the outset in terms of man hours and system development time, it will unquestionably lead to a more usable, meaningful and effective system. And, implementation will be faster and easier because of better understanding on the part of everyone who will be concerned with its use.

From conversations I had with the others present at the meeting from the eastern Regions, it is safe to say that everyone is willing and eager to help in any way possible, for as long as it takes to get the system into operation. Do not hesitate to call on us at any time.

(signed)

———————————————

Manager Atlantic Region

Designing the Total System

Network analysis and CPM (critical path method) were used to visualize the sequencing of activities in the various subsystems of the overall design. The master chart covered an entire wall and showed in general terms what has to be done in designing subsystems and indicated sequencing of the parts to be developed and integrated into the total management information system. As is appropriate in systems design and data processing work, an acronym had to be developed for this particular chart. It was dubbed the "Whole Cotton Pickin' Mess" (Whole CPM).

The Only Thing Constant Is Change

Investigation indicated that eventually 2,500 orders would be received during any three-week period, time enough for a normal order-delivery cycle. Enough capacity was designed into the system to allow for contingencies and some expansion of the system. This seemed to provide for considerable flexibility.

However, subsequent to the design of the order-entry system, sales people engaged in serious negotiations with customers for arrangements which would call for orders on a yearly basis. For example, a customer could estimate his needs for the coming year and the Weyerhaeuser Company would use that information in scheduling production and delivery over an extended period of time. This represents the management of material flow on an intercompany basis rather than intracompany. If many customers could be programmed accordingly, the planning for production and distribution could be done on a much longer time cycle, certainly longer than six weeks.

In order to have such information in a data base, however, it would be necessary to provide for storing over 20,000 orders—more than five times the maximum provided for in the order-entry design. One reported reaction was: "You can't do that; this system has already been designed!"

D: PROBLEMS AND PROMISE IN IMPLEMENTATION

How to Win Friends and Influence People

Although the philosophy of using operating people in the design and implementation of the management information system seemed to be accepted by most everyone in the organization, there were conflicts from time to time. Certainly the use of operating personnel in the design and implementation effort can cause temporary inconvenience in the day-to-day affairs of the company. One example of this type of problem is represented by the following sequence of memos.

Subject: Region VII Personnel on MSO Implementation Team

To: _____—Tacoma

We have made the services of key people available for use on his MSO implementation team. This has been done at some considerable inconvenience to both the New York and Baltimore Areas. We have had to shuffle a number of people in each Area to take up the work normally performed by them.

We have been informed that the dates when he will need these men are to be changed. He further apparently cannot give us any definite period of time, beginning or ending dates, as to when he will require their services. The result is a rather untenable position.

We want to cooperate with MSO in its implementation and we certainly want some first class people in the Region to be fully acquainted with it so they can train others in the Region as needed. At the same time, we must have a little more definite information concerning when these people are going to be needed and for how long. They are too important to our operations for us to have them on an in and out basis without any forewarning. People have to be trained to replace them on a temporary and/or a permanent basis, depending upon how long they are going to be gone.

In addition to the problem of replacing our people while they are working for MSO, we apparently are expected to continue to pay their salaries while we also pay salaries of their replacement personnel. Are there any plans to alleviate this extra load from the Areas?

Your advice and suggestions will be appreciated.

(signed)

_____

Eastern Region Manager

P.S. "How to win friends and influence people."

Subject: Communications
To: _____,

Your progress bulletin dated April 1 is excellent. This is the kind of thing that will bring our field people aboard and keep them informed. While I hate to do this all in the same letter, I have to pat you on the back and also kick you in the pants. I suppose it would be more diplomatic to edit the attached letter (above) and give it to you in more palatable doses, but since I honestly believe we're both just trying to get the job done, I will let you have it right off the cuff. After you have read his letter, will you please discuss this with me. I believe we can come up with a reasonable solution to his problem.

(signed)

_____

Subject: MSO Order-entry Implementation
Dear _____,

The reaction to our temporary withdrawal from implementation training was not unexpected and only points up one of several problems of coordination which will be with us for quite a period from now on. It will require sincere, strong support from your management level and a little better understanding on the part of field people to see us through our most difficult time.

We are confident that we have a practical, workable order-entry system which will form the data base for our Company's very much required (and costly) management information system. Too many dedicated people have worked too hard and too long to achieve our present position to risk losing it because we haven't "won friends and influenced people."

There isn't any use to stop and explain why it is that we miss date estimates. We apologize, but we don't intend to be defensive.

Right now I am not going to try to name a date when we will need help from your group for field training. By its very nature, systems work of our type mitigates dealing in closely fixed dates even though the rest of the world seems to demand them. Some time in the next few weeks we may have a better line on implementation requirements but if we are going to face castigation for not meeting a firm date perhaps it would be best to say that we will need help, when we do need it, on a quick-warning basis.

Again, we need the support of the National Sales Office in making the levels of field management, over which it has the most direct influence, aware of the need for understanding and sacrifice. It is hoped, then, that mature field management will transmit its support to the lower levels. The picture is much larger than the temporary displacement of some people or similar inconveniences.

(signed)

_____

Organizational Adjustments

During the period which the management information system was under study, a number of organizational adjustments were made. In December, 1963, a Vice President—Marketing was named to supervise the activities of the product-line managers for softwood lumber, softwood plywood, hardwood plywood and doors, manufactured panels, and laminated products. The market planning functions and the Management Systems Operation (MSO) also were under his jurisdiction.

With regard to the structure, the Executive Vice President of Operations said:

These organizational alignments have been set up in recognition of the fact that each of these product lines is really a separate and distinct business operating within the overall sales and production framework of the Wood Products group. As such, they require strong business management and identification. This new organization is designed to provide such business direction through our product line managers and to insure full product management impact on our operations.

Also in 1965 the manager of the Weyerhaeuser Company's Softwood and Lumber Division and MSO was appointed to a new post entitled Director of Business Systems. The announcement said: "In the new position, he will direct the planning and control of business systems and supervise Operations Research activities." (See Exhibit 7-5.)

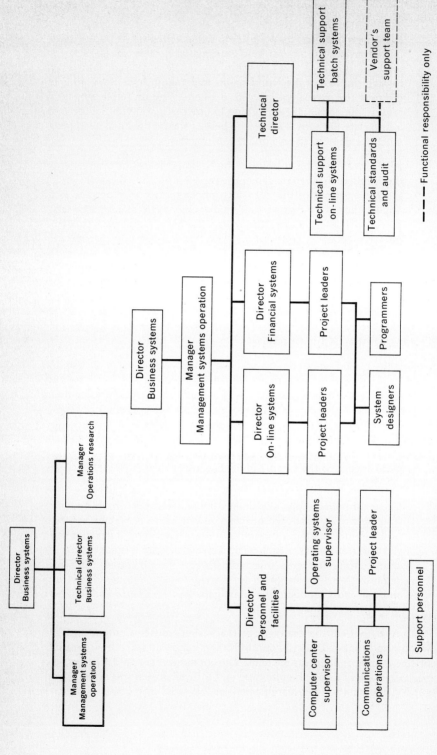

Exhibit 7–5. Weyerhaeuser Company, Wood Products Management Systems Operation organization chart, Apr. 1, 1966.

An Interview with the Director of Business Systems

The new director, a mechanical engineer by training, had worked for General Electric for several years, and then joined the Weyerhaeuser Company. He was chief electrician at the Everett Branch and later manager of the Snoqualmie Falls Branch. In 1958, he was involved in product-line planning at Headquarters in Tacoma. He was manager of the Softwood Lumber Division and, simultaneously, manager of the Management Systems Operation (MSO). He then became Corporate Director of Business Systems.

He felt that he was appointed to head the design and implementation of the management information system because someone was needed who could "carry the ball" through the corporate jungle and not get lost. Also, there was a need for someone with an overall point of view who could integrate the systems-design work with the operation of the company.

Because he could not devote full time to the MSO job (he was also manager of the Softwood Lumber Division), he felt a need to pick "better" managers to staff the MSO organization. That is, he needed experienced mature people to make it feasible to decentralize much of the decision making in the design and implementation phases of the project. It would be necessary for many decisions to be "hammered out" on a group basis and a consensus developed among the functional and technical directors in the MSO organization. In addition, there is the critical problem of maintaining relations and soliciting cooperation from operating management throughout the Weyerhaeuser Company. This later process seemed to occupy 30 to 40 percent of the time of the top-level echelon in MSO.

The Director of Business Systems stressed this later point over and over again—"operating managers will not accept anything that they don't understand." They could frustrate implementation even if top-level support is obvious and vigorous. Sometimes the operating people are not even aware they need help, "the job seems to be going all right." But systems designers need to communicate with and understand the operating people in order to evaluate realistically the decision making at all levels and the necessary information flow for that process.

He described the changing role of the branch manager over the years from a primarily production manager to emphasis on public relations. He suggested that the management information system will define the branch manager's task more definitely and pinpoint crucial decisions for an exception reporting system. He stressed the idea that the decision-making process was the focal point of the study and that it might even be considered synonymous with management. He stressed the importance of *designing a system for the business—rather than designing a business for the system.* He felt they had been able to get equipment people to design or at least adjust the equipment to implement the management information system designed by the study team.

Once implemented, the on-line, real-time information system should help management make the decisions concerning material and energy flow which will balance demand and supply; that is, equate the best markets with resources available.

In a subsequent interview, the Director of Business Systems reflected on the development of the management information system as it has evolved. It is quite comprehensive and integrates decision making throughout the entire material-flow process—from raw material to ultimate consumer. In the initial stages, however, the system was conceived primarily as a marketing system which would allow better order entry. Systems designers implied that improvements in the order-entry system would "automatically" improve scheduling and material flow in the production process. However, improvements did not turn out to be "automatic" at all. There seemed to be no necessary reason why an improved order process would lead to an improved production operation.

As a result, the information-system study had to be enlarged to deal explicitly with the production phase as well. Thus, it became apparent that an integrated system would be necesary to provide the desired capabilities. Later, financial systems were included in the information-decision system which was geared primarily to the logistics problem for the Weyerhaeuser Company.

Early efforts in data processing were segmented systems. As it became apparent that they had an impact on each other, it appeared necessary to think of integration. As the overall system of information flow was designed, a philosophy gradually evolved which emphasized centralization of planning for decentralized decision making.

Systems work cannot be delegated to specialists who are asked to come up with "the answer." Management must work close enough with systems designers and operations research people to make them aware of value systems and premises used in planning and decision making. Often, however, systems analysts can think through the process from a fresh perspective and define the "real" problem which may not have been identified by management.

While total information systems may be a utopian concept, we are getting closer and closer to achieving such an objective in the future. Hardware and software improvements continue to provide opportunity for more sophisticated systems design. For example, we are considering several possible applications of real-time problem solving as part of the overall information-decision system.

An Interview with the Executive Vice President—Operations

By 1965, the Executive Vice President—Operations felt that the Wood Products Division had come quite a way toward developing an integrated system. The organization had been realigned around product managers who were concerned with the flow of material from its source to the ultimate consumer. "In order to facilitate the most efficient system there is a compelling need for information flow. The demands of consumers must be matched with the production of the system on a timely basis. This can be done only if information is available for decisions and if the system is flexible and responsive to the demands placed upon it."

The management information system under design should provide the means for achieving the objectives outlined above. The system was designed by a combination of top-grade operating personnel and a staff of technical people to provide complementary skills. The people assigned to the feasibility study and systems-design project were considered to be aggressive with regard to change.

The Executive Vice President described the problems of implementation as primarily people-oriented. "The organization itself very likely would inhibit the change to some degree. Therefore, considerable emphasis would have to be placed upon orientation, education, and training. Continuing attention would have to be devoted to restructuring the organization in order that the formal management alignment might more closely describe the system as it operates around the flow of management information."

The problem of centralization versus decentralization of decision making is one that the company must evaluate. An on-line, real-time management information system undoubtedly would allow the collection of pertinent data concerning far-flung operations. The data could be processed and information developed for centralized decision making. On the other hand, the information could be transmitted back to field offices where additional inputs from the local scene might be significant factors.

The question of centralization-decentralization involves more than availability of information; it involves a philosophy of administration. The Executive Vice President stressed the need for decentralization of decision making as a means of developing managers for the future. This strong stand by top management should ease the apprehensions of those in the field who are concerned for their role in decision making in the future.

The large-scale effort toward a management information system for the Wood Products Division was described as a "leapfrog" approach. Three basic steps are involved: (1) deciding where we should be, (2) deciding where we are now, and (3) deciding how to get there. The experience obtained in the current effort should be valuable as the company looks toward similar systems for other divisions.

QUESTIONS

1. What part does information flow play in the coordination of Weyerhaeuser Company operations? Why is it important?
2. Compare the evolution of data processing in the Weyerhaeuser

Company with your understanding of developments in the field in general. Did it appear that management's outlook at the beginning of the case was a long-run view? Short-run? Piecemeal? Comprehensive?

3. When, if at all, would you use outside consultants in systems-design work? How would you select them?

4. How did the scope of the "communications study" change over time? Why did the change take place?

5. Do you agree with the approach suggested in the initial phases of the study by the outside consulting firm? Why or why not?

6. Compare the approach to responsibility for overall systems design recommended by the director of machine accounting systems (page 176) to that taken in establishing the joint Weyerhaeuser–General Electric (IAO) feasibility study team.

7. What are the advantages of using high-caliber operating people to lead the systems-design effort? The disadvantages?

8. Compare the organization of MSO (Management Systems Operation) as shown in Exhibit 7–4 to that shown in Exhibit 7–5. What changes are reflected in the adjustments made?

9. What actions were taken at various stages to facilitate implementation of the overall management information system?

10. What do you think of the reaction "You can't do that; the system has already been designed!" to a suggested change in the scope of the order-entry subsystem?

11. How did the development of the Wood Products MIS affect other aspects of systems design, such as organization structure?

12. How important is top management's view concerning concepts such as centralization versus decentralization (of decision making) in the implementation of a companywide information-decision system?

13. Assume that you are Director of Business Systems. Develop a long-range strategy for extending the Wood Products MIS to other parts of the company.

CHAPTER **8**

Quantitative Techniques of Analysis

The systems approach provides a framework for integrated decision making. Within the framework a number of tools of analysis have been developed over the years, including the latest, most sophisticated techniques used in operations research. One of the objectives of this chapter will be to place these techniques in perspective as they relate to the science and art of managing. In order to do this we shall trace the common elements of problem solving, decision making, and management, with particular emphasis on the scientific method.

In surveying the field of quantitative methods, no attempt will be made to cover the techniques exhaustively; each warrants book-length treatment to ensure some degree of expertise or even understanding. Rather, we shall describe the techniques from the manager's point of view, emphasizing those aspects which are important in assessing applicability. In particular, we are interested in their usefulness in implementing the systems approach—either in analysis and decision making or in systems design. The following topics will be considered:

Systems analysis
Problem solving
Scientific method
Mathematical analysis
Models
Computers
Techniques of analysis
Simulation
Managers and scientists/technicians

SYSTEMS ANALYSIS

As indicated in Chapters 6 and 7, the analysis of systems is an extremely pervasive activity. Indeed, system analysis has special connotations in systems engineering, systems and procedures work, and operations research or management science. In recent years, however, the term has taken on special meaning because of its use in large-scale, complex decision problems. For example, its use in national security planning, pollution control, and designing urban transportation systems has received much publicity.

In these cases the term applies to the process of evaluating alternative courses of action in allocating resources to meet system-wide objectives. Within the constraints of accepted (at least temporarily) objectives, various programs are proposed to accomplish designated tasks. Systems analysis is used in the process of setting objectives as well as in evaluating alternative proposals. Technical feasibility may be of prime importance in this latter stage; the immediate goal is to develop means of achieving the objective(s). As more alternatives become feasible the systems-analysis process may involve choosing the most appropriate solution or mix of solutions in terms of technical superiority in meeting specified requirements. Both quantity and quality are considered.

Given unlimited resources, the task would be accomplished at this stage. In the real world, however, resources are scarce and cost becomes an important consideration. Systems analysis involves thorough scrutiny of cost effectiveness tradeoffs. At what point does cost become prohibitive (economic objective) regardless of the increasing effectiveness of alternative solutions (pollution control objective)? The answer is to balance these factors within an overall systems-analysis approach to goal setting and resource allocation.

The planning-programming-budgeting philosophy requires the identification of system missions and all associated costs from perception of need through design, production, delivery, and utilization. In national security planning, budgets developed by functions and services are of little value in assessing the cost effectiveness of a particular weapon system over its projected life span. Each mission fits into the overall scheme for national security and can be evaluated in terms of its contribution in light of attendant costs.

More detailed quantitative techniques can be used to carry out the computational steps in systems analysis. Computers facilitate the use of detailed, comprehensive calculations to ensure a thorough consideration of all the relevant variables. Qualitative approaches are important also; "analysis cannot supplant decision making. . . . Policy decisions cannot be calculated."[1]

Systems analysis stresses the importance of developing a balanced approach to decision making—quantifying where appropriate and mixing in value judgments at the proper time.

> All of this is to suggest that although analysis in support of decision makers at the national policy level must be honest, in the sense that the quantitative factors are selected without bias, that the calculations are accurate, that alternatives are not arbitrarily suppressed, it cannot be objective in the sense of being independent of values. Value judgments are an integral part of analysis; and it is the role of the analyst to bring to light for the policymaker exactly how and where value judgments enter so that the latter can make his own value judgments in the light of as much relevant information as possible.[2]

Systems analysis is primarily a managerial approach to decision making wherein overall system effectiveness is related to resource allocation in a process of careful, searching evaluation. Planning-programming-budgeting and cost effectiveness analysis are two useful approaches to the task; other, more specific techniques can be applied where appropriate.

PROBLEM SOLVING

Throughout history man has approached problem solving in a number of ways. At least six reasonably distinct methods can be identified:

1. Appeal to the supernatural
2. Appeal to worldly authority—the older the better

[1]Alain C. Enthoven, "Systems Analysis and Decision Making," *Military Review,* January 1963, p. 15.
[2]Ibid., p. 14.

3. Intuition
4. Common sense
5. Pure logic
6. The scientific method[3]

No chronology is implied by the list because all the approaches are being employed currently in problem-solving situations throughout the world. The list does imply, however, a gradation leading toward more careful, searching, and systematic approaches. Combinations of several of these are involved in many problem-solving efforts. Intuition can be helpful in the laboratory, as can common sense and logic. Disciplined imagination, a vital ingredient for researchers, may depend on both intuition and common sense.

In business organizations the problem-solving activity often is termed decision making. In this context decision making sometimes is considered synonymous with managing. The process of managing or decision making has been described as follows:

> The first phase of the decision making process—searching the environment for conditions calling for decision—I shall call *intelligence* activity (borrowing the military meaning of intelligence).
> The second phase—inventing, developing, and analysing possible courses of action—I shall call *design* activity
> The third phase—selecting a particular course of action from those available—I shall call *choice* activity.[4]

These phases of the decision-making process coincide closely with the related stages of problem-solving activity described by Dewey:

> What is the problem?
> What are the alternatives?
> Which alternative is best?[5]

In a sense, these listings are simplifications of the problem-solving or decision process; yet it is useful to spell out the process explicitly in order to understand it better. Obviously, the stages overlap in any particular case. And there are normally a number of problems "in the wind." Thus the manager is involved simultaneously in intelligence, design, and choice activity. Attempts at designing

[3]Stuart Chase, *The Proper Study of Mankind,* Harper & Row, Publishers, Incorporated, New York, 1956, p. 3.
[4]Herbert A. Simon, *The New Science of Management Decision,* Harper & Row, Publishers, Incorporated, New York, 1960, p. 2.
[5]John Dewey, *How We Think,* D. C. Heath and Company, Boston, 1910, pp. 101–115.

alternative courses of action may turn up additional problems, thus setting off new intelligence activities. An overall problem-solving cycle or decision process might contain a series of sub-cycles.

Such a description brings us back to systems concepts and emphasizes the view of an organization as an integrated decision system. As the system becomes more complex it is obvious that refined tools of analysis must be developed in order to facilitate the decision process. The fundamental framework of management science, as for any science, is the scientific method.

SCIENTIFIC METHOD

The term *scientific method* means many things to many people. Quite often, however, it involves taking the following steps:

1. Define the problem
2. State objectives
3. Formulate tentative solutions
4. Collect data and information
5. Classify, analyze, and interpret
6. Draw conclusions, generalize (restate the problem or define new problems)

The specific steps involved in the scientific method are not particularly important for our purposes. We are interested, however, in certain fundamentals implied by the term *scientific method.* It suggests the use of generally recognized procedures and techniques. Another important ingredient of the scientific method is the attitude of the researcher or decision maker. A relatively formal, systematic, and thorough approach to problem solving implies objectivity and reasoning rather than emotion. It applies logical solutions to problems with as little bias as possible. Using the scientific method, either explicitly or implicitly, one reserves judgment until all the pertinent information is available. For many centuries man sought final, definitive answers to problems; more recent approaches have pointed toward a spectrum of possibilities and show a tendency to express knowledge in terms of probability rather than certainty. The scientific method suggests a mind which constantly is challenging, weighing, and explaining—one which continually asks "why?" The scientific method implies objectivity rather than subjectivity; it implies selectivity and discrimination; and it implies creativity. According to Brown:

> The scientist is primarily creative in his efforts. The thrill of discovery is his great reward. After he has taken things apart, he sees new ways to put them together, new arrangements to make. This is the mark of creative thinking. Without the creative thinking, which carries analysis into the synthesis which produces an integrated result, there can be no true scientific method.[6]

This comment points up the similarity in typical descriptions of the scientific method, problem-solving or decision-making processes, and creativity. Emphasis in all cases is on both the methods and techniques used and the attitude of the researcher, decision maker, or innovator.

In organizations managers are confronted with complex situations involving men, machines, money, and time. When problems arise which deal with only the inanimate factors, methods of analysis can be relatively straightforward. When dealing with the human aspects, such a task becomes more difficult. And when the analysis must include large-scale, man-machine systems, the problem becomes even more complex. If social science involves the use of the scientific method to answer questions about human behavior, then management science can be defined as *the use of the scientific method to answer questions of concern to managers.* Scientific management represents one approach to the development of a science of managing.

Scientific Management

Frederick Taylor in his book *The Principles of Scientific Management* had the following purpose:

1. To point out, through a series of simple illustrations, the great loss which the whole country suffers through inefficiency in most all of our daily acts.
2. To try to convince the reader that the remedy for this inefficiency lies in systematic management, rather than in searching for some unusual or extraordinary man.
3. To prove that the best management is a true science, resting upon clearly defined laws, rules, and principles as a foundation.[7]

He wanted to show that the fundamental principles of scientific management are applicable to all kinds of human activities, from

---

[6]Lyndon O. Brown, *Marketing and Distribution Research,* The Ronald Press Company, New York, 1949, p. 275.

[7]Frederick W. Taylor, *The Principles of Scientific Management,* Harper & Row, Publishers, Incorporated, New York, 1947, p. 7.

our simplest individual acts to the work of great corporations which call for the most elaborate cooperation. A prime goal in scientific management was the substitution of science for rule-of-thumb approaches to problem solving. Taylor's efforts were focused on relatively simple tasks, as indicated by the "science of shoveling" and the "pig-iron-handling experiment." He concentrated on the operating level and the physical-physiological aspects of the job.

The term *scientific* in the phrase *scientific management* is justified primarily in terms of the approach used in problem solving. The scientific method was employed to provide a logical, systematic, thorough analysis of shop-level problems. Efforts toward increased efficiency which would result in both increased profits and higher wages fostered the development of specific procedures within individual companies. In some cases, the findings could be generalized to similar operations. However, Taylor himself emphasized the fact that each situation must be analyzed separately in order to ensure success. He continually stressed that the findings in any specific study were only narrowly applicable and that the important factor was the approach used, the scientific method. He was convinced that the greatest problem involved in the change to scientific management was the need for a complete revolution in the mental attitudes and habits of all those engaged in management. He called attention to the interrelationship of the following four points:

1. Science, not rule of thumb
2. Harmony, not discord
3. Cooperation, not individualism
4. Maximum output, in place of restricted output; the development of each man to his greatest efficiency and prosperity[8]

Out of the early beginnings of scientific management a number of tools of analysis and groups of practitioners have developed. The field of industrial engineering stemmed from the early scientific management movement. The field of statistical quality control has grown substantially over the past decades. As the problems have become more complex, additional techniques have been developed. In many cases they represent fairly straightforward approaches which can be related directly to the scientific method. However, other more sophisticated techniques (fostered by the development of electronic computers) have evolved, almost

[8]Ibid., pp. 36–37.

as fields in themselves—mathematical programming, for example. The term *operations research,* developed during World War II, encompasses a large number of specific techniques for use in problem solving. As we explore some of these more sophisticated techniques in greater detail, let us bear in mind that the overall umbrella for these tools of analysis is still the scientific method.

MATHEMATICAL ANALYSIS

The general heading "management science" is related to several other terms: scientific management, operations research, and mathematical analysis. It might be helpful to attempt some reconciliation of terminology before proceeding with the more detailed discussion of specific mathematical techniques.

In terms of its philosophy, operations research fundamentally is *not* different from general approaches to problem solving, particularly the scientific method. From the standpoint of methodology, there is nothing that differentiates operations research from many other types of business or economic analysis. The method involved is still the scientific method: the analyst must examine a problem and pick out the dominant variables, then hypothesize specific relationships between these chosen variables, and finally test his model in the real world. The acid test is the ability to predict future behavior.

The scientific management practitioners and/or the industrial engineers would insist that they have been using this approach for years. The interdisciplinary-team approach distinguished operations research in its early days. In many cases, however, the research team now includes industrial engineers. Thus "no meaningful line can be drawn any more to demarcate operations research from scientific management or scientific management from management science."[9]

Although there is no clear-cut line of demarcation between operations research and other applications of the scientific method to management decision making, the term mathematics is stressed somewhat more in its definitions. For example:

O.R. [operations research] is the application of scientific methods, techniques, and tools to problems involving the operations of a system so as to provide those in control of the system with optimum solutions to the problems. . . . Its procedures can be broken into the following steps:

[9]Simon, op. cit., p. 15.

1. Formulating the problem
2. Constructing a mathematical model to represent the system under study
3. Deriving a solution from the model
4. Testing the model and the solution derived from it
5. Establishing controls over the solution
6. Putting the solution to work[10]

The use of mathematical models is stressed in operations research problems, and the definition implies treatment of larger-scale problems—the operation of a system—than was practicable with earlier techniques. The team approach which draws members from various disciplines has been an integral part of many operations research studies. Again, the team concept implies the ability to handle larger-scale problems than was feasible with other approaches.

The systems concepts embodied in the definitions of operations research are particularly important. As stated previously, the systems approach provides no cookbook recipe for problem solving; rather, it involves a frame of mind which can serve to orient the application of specific techniques.

> Along with some mathematical tools, . . . operations research brought into management decision making a point of view called the systems approach. The systems approach is no easier to define than operations research for it is a set of attitudes and a frame of mind rather than a definite and explicit theory. At its vaguest, it means looking at the whole problem—again, hardly a novel idea, and not always a very helpful one. Somewhat more concretely, it means designing the components of a system and making individual decisions within it in light of the implication of these decisions for the system as a whole.[11]

The reader should evaluate the various techniques described throughout the remainder of this chapter in terms of their contribution to implementation of a systems approach. Before discussing specific techniques, it will be helpful to set the stage by describing another aspect of mathematical analysis—models.

MODELS

Construction of a model is a common technique of abstraction and simplification for studying the characteristics or behavioral aspects

---

[10]C. West Churchman, Russel L. Ackoff, and E. Leonard Arnoff, *Introduction to Operations Research,* John Wiley & Sons, Inc., New York, 1957, p. 18.
[11]Simon, op. cit., p. 15.

of objects or systems under varying conditions. The model itself is usually a representation of objects, events, processes, or systems and is used for prediction and control. Models may be descriptive or explanatory. Manipulation of the model is used to test the impact of changes in one or more components of the model on the entity as a whole. In this way tests can be carried out without disturbing the subject of the model. The various types of models have been classified into three general groups.

> We shall distinguish three types of model: iconic, analogue, and symbolic. Roughly, we can say that (1) an iconic model pictorially or visually represents certain aspects of a system (as does a photograph or model airplane); (2) an analogue model employs one set of properties to represent some other set of properties which the system being studied possesses (e.g., for certain purposes, the flow of water through pipes may be taken as an analogue of the "flow" of electricity in wires); and (3) a symbolic model is one which employs symbols to *designate* properties of the system under study (by means of a mathematical equation or set of such equations).[12]

Scale models and wind tunnels represent an iconic model used to simulate actual flight conditions. In operations research, the word model is used to mean a mathematical description of an activity which expresses the relationships among various elements with sufficient accuracy so that it can be used to predict the actual outcome under any expected set of circumstances. Mathematical models are of many types, depending upon the real-life situations they are designed to represent. They have both advantages and disadvantages as analytical tools. The model, rather than the system it represents, can be manipulated in a variety of ways until a relatively good solution is found. On the basis of such experimentation, the actual system can be adjusted with a minimum of disruption. An obvious disadvantage of model building is the difficulty in duplicating reality completely. Also the process, while extremely beneficial, can be time-consuming and costly.

Model building provides a tool for extending the researcher's judgment in handling large-scale, complex systems.

> In a sense, the use of a model frees the intuition and permits it to concentrate on those problems to which it is particularly suited. It permits the creative manager to test rigorously the implications of new plans, new schemes, and new ideas.[13]

[12]Churchman, Ackoff, and Arnoff, op. cit., p. 158.
[13]Franklin A. Lindsay, *New Techniques for Management Decision Making*, McGraw-Hill Book Company, New York, 1958, p. 6.

Although the model often is thought of as simulating a large organization or process, any set of equations designed to represent a particular problem area, no matter how narrow, can be thought of as a model. Various assumptions are made about the number of factors which must be included in order to represent the situation accurately. Then numerical values can be assigned to the variables in the problem in order to develop a workable model. Once the system has been described and numerical values have been assigned, the problem can be solved with whatever technique seems appropriate. Implementation of mathematical models to represent complex systems has been facilitated by the use of electronic computers.

COMPUTERS

Electronic computers have fostered much of the advance in quantitative analysis over the past several decades. Trivial problems, often used as textbook examples, can be solved quite readily with hand calculations or, at most, the use of a desk calculator. However, real-life problems in complex organizational settings often are not amenable to such approaches. Numerical solutions to such problems may require thousands of individual steps, involving endless hours of clerical work. A computer allows the solution of typical problems in a matter of minutes rather than weeks or months. In fact, real-time problem solving is possible whereby the system performs computations immediately upon receipt of a query from an input station. The result can be displayed graphically or communicated in any one of several standard media. Moreover, the computer is not subject to fatigue and hence is more likely to provide error-free solutions than the typical statistical clerk. While the programming of solutions to typical problems can be both challenging and time-consuming, the results of such effort can be applied over and over again to similar problems as they arise. The trend toward modular programs, which can be put together in a variety of forms, facilitates the solution of new problems with existing computer programs.

It is dangerous to assume that all quantitative analysis must be done via electronic computers. The problems in question must be analyzed in light of the most likely techniques and the most efficient processing of data required for solution. As techniques are developed for automating management decisions in areas such as inventory, quality, and production control, the mathematical analysis involved can be integrated into the general data processing systems. In such cases the mathematical analysis required for automatic decisions is embedded in an overall information-decision system programmed to handle all but the exceptional situations involved in day-to-day operations. Larger-scale mathematical analysis may be required for management decisions in areas such as long-range planning. In this case a computer serves primarily as a calculator in the solution phase rather than as a data processor in the information-decision system.

The symbol processing and logic (compare and transfer) capabilities of computers have led to much research in artificial intelligence. While they have been called "giant brains," computers have not been considered "thinking" machines. The term often is used facetiously because "everyone knows that thinking is a *human* activity." Nevertheless research has progressed on simulating "thinking-like behavior" where the goal is, ". . . to construct computer programs which exhibit behavior that we call 'intelligent behavior' when we observe it in human beings."[14]

The general approach is one of replicating human problem-solving behavior with heuristic programs—sophisticated trial and error. Problem-solving behavior typically involves identifying alternatives, assessing their possible consequences, and making a choice. Theoretically the number of alternatives is infinite, but for "all practical purposes" only a few are relevant. Given constraints and sets of criteria the computer program can screen the alternatives and pick one. However, there is no guarantee of optimality. If the problem is complex and requires a sequence of decisions (as in most modern organizations), heuristic approaches are even more desirable. Both special-purpose and general-purpose programs have been developed in the research on artificial intelligence.

Computers also may be useful in algorithmic or "cookbook" approaches to problem solving. For well-structured problems the solution may be obtainable with a precise set of computational steps. For more complex problems an algorithmic approach may suffice by considering a large but finite number of steps. However, computer capacity limitations plus time and cost considerations rule out this approach to solving some problems.

The development of programming languages, translators, and compilers has facilitated the researcher's use of computer capabilities. The various specialized techniques can be applied more readily if managers and/or scientists can describe problems

[14]Edward A. Feigenbaum and Julian Feldman (eds.), *Computers and Thought*, McGraw-Hill Book Company, New York, 1963, p. 3.

in understandable terms. For example, simulation languages such as GPSS, SIMSCRIPT, SIMPAC, DYNAMO, and SIMTRAN have been designed to facilitate description and analysis of complex systems.

The importance of electronic computers to quantitative analysis will become evident as we explore the various techniques in the following pages.

TECHNIQUES OF ANALYSIS

For purposes of discussion various techniques of analysis will be covered separately. However, the reader should not assume that problems fall into neat categories which lend themselves to solution via straightforward, cookbook approaches. Combinations of several techniques may be appropriate in given instances. The analyst must define the problem carefully and then fit the most appropriate technique into the problem-solving process. Tailoring the techniques to the problems, plus the use of good judgment, will lead to the best possible solution.

Some of the techniques to be described have proved worthwhile in management decision making over a period of years. Some have not been applied fruitfully in real situations as yet. Still others fall in between these extremes, having had limited application in practical situations. It will be important to ascertain the usefulness of particular techniques in implementing the systems approach.

Linear Programming

One of the most useful of the operations research techniques is linear programming. It is both an approach to the formulation and statement of the problems for which it is suited and a set of mathematical procedures for making the calculations leading to selection of the best course of action. It has been defined as:

> . . . a technique for specifying how to use limited resources or capacities of a business to obtain a particular objective, such as least cost, highest margin, or least time, when those resources have alternate uses. It is a technique that systematizes for certain conditions the process of selecting the most desirable course of action from a number of available courses of action, thereby giving management information for making a more effective decision about the resources under its control.[15]

[15]Robert O. Ferguson and Lauren F. Sargent, *Linear Programming*, McGraw-Hill Book Company, New York, 1958, p. 3.

Linear programming has been applied with good results in the determination of:

1. The most profitable manufacturing program
2. The best inventory strategy
3. The effect of changes in purchasing and selling price
4. Whether to make or buy certain components
5. The best location of plants
6. The lowest-cost manufacturing schedule
7. The best location of warehouses and distribution outlets
8. The most profitable product mix

This is only a partial list of applications, but it does point out the type of problem for which linear programming is most useful. There are some common characteristics in each one of these problems. First, various processes are in competition for the allocation of a given and fixed number of units of resources. Next, the cost of allocating a given number of units of a resource to a given process is proportional to the number of units allocated. Such a situation will have a solution in which the total cost of the overall process is a minimum, or conversely, the profit is a maximum. In addition to these similarities, in each instance the manager must consider a large number of factors which may affect his decision. Also these factors are interdependent, so that the manager must consider them individually and in relation to each other. Finally, the choice must be made of one solution or course of action from among many obvious alternatives and, perhaps, some others which are not so obvious. Without linear programming techniques, these decisions must be based on experience, feel, intuition, and hope.

Application of linear programming techniques forces a clear-cut statement of the aims of the system involved in the analysis. To the extent that the system under analysis involves one or more areas of managerial responsibility, it will allow a closer approach to the stated goal by forcing on all participants an awareness of the basic purpose and structure of the system. As stated earlier, different departments often pursue divergent purposes because each follows its own objectives—reduced costs, higher production, greater utilization of capacity, or greater profit. Within the linear programming framework, such diversity will not work. The analytical procedure makes it painfully clear that to push for one goal is to do so at the expense of another. From the viewpoint of the larger system, only one of these purposes can be the correct one for the system under the set of conditions which exist. Thus linear programming provides a rationale for the homogeneous operation of those systems to which it can be, and is, applied.

Once a linear programming problem has been set up, slight modifications can be made with little additional work. Thus, once large-scale, complex problems have been defined and variables specified, relationships can be developed which allow reasonably quick assessment of the impact of changes in pertinent variables.

> In all likelihood, the most important thing to be derived from the linear programming calculation is not the optimal product mix itself, but rather the implicit values of the individual bottlenecks. This seems typical of problems of economic choice. We are interested in finding optimal solutions to a problem under carefully defined given conditions—precisely so that we can find out what it would be worth to us if those conditions could themselves be altered. . . . If linear programming provided nothing but a more reliable framework for estimating incremental costs and values, this alone would justify its importance to management.[16]

"Slack" and "artificial" variables can be used to identify unused capacity and to balance out the system of equations. Alternative allocations of resources can be tested for their effect on the system. Implicit values serve to measure the increase in the amount of pay-off obtained per unit increase in the availability of a constraining factor.

One of the limitations of linear programming is apparent in the name itself. The fact that it treats all relationships as linear limits the realism of the analysis. In many cases linear approximations are entirely appropriate. In others, they may be less appropriate, to the point of making the application of results to a real system meaningless. Linear programming cannot deal effectively with more than one set of conditions at a time. Optimal solutions to real problems involving simultaneous changes in several variables are extremely difficult to compute. Even with large-scale equipment, computational constraints for real situations do develop. Thus problems often must be simplified in order to reduce them to a form that can be handled by analytical techniques and available computational facilities. When this is done the application of the results to the overall system may not be appropriate.

Two techniques have been developed in order to offset some of the disadvantages inherent in linear programming. For example, quadratic programming is designed to handle problems with nonlinear relationships. This allows development of a mathematical model yielding a more complete description of the system under study. Dynamic programming facilitates solution of sequential

---

[16]Alan S. Manne, *Economic Analysis for Business Decisions,* McGraw-Hill Book Company, New York, 1961, pp. 19–20, 43.

problems. It is a method of solving multistage problems in which the decisions at one stage become the conditions governing the succeeding stages.[17] Quadratic and dynamic programming are still in a state of development and have not been applied widely to real problems. However, they do have considerable potential and may allow implementation of systems concepts which are vital in providing a frame of reference for analysis of large-scale, complex operations.[18]

Input-Output Analysis

Input-output analysis, originally developed by Wassily Leontief as a means of studying an overall economy, provides an approach to analyzing interrelationships in large, complex systems. To date input-output analysis has been used to relate production and distribution of products throughout the economy. The output of each industry is traced in detail through intermediate stages to final destinations. Similarly, the source of raw materials and components as inputs to a given industry also is traced in considerable detail. When arrayed in a large matrix format and given the coefficients which relate the industries directly and indirectly, a change of demand for finished goods of a particular industry can be traced throughout the system. The technique has been described as follows:

> Mathematically, it is a variation of linear programming and provides a quantitative framework for the description of an entire economy. Basic to input-output analysis is a unique set of input-output ratios for each production and distribution process. For example, the inputs of coal, ore, limestone, electrical power, etc., all enter in the production of pig iron in fixed ratios. Thus, if the ratios of inputs per unit of output are known for all production processes, and if the total production of each end product of the economy— or of that section being studied—is known, it is possible to compute precisely the production levels required at every intermediate stage to supply the total sum of end products. Further, it is possible to determine the effect at every point in the production process of a specified change in the volume and mix of end products.[19]

Given the input-output matrix, detailed analysis could be made of such changes as an increase in residential construction or

[17]Richard Bellman, *Dynamic Programming*, Princeton University Press, Princeton, N.J., 1957, pp. vii–viii.
[18]Lindsay, op. cit., pp. 42–43.
[19]Ibid., p. 43.

increases (or decreases) in space-system procurement programs. Tracing the impact of such changes throughout the economy by hand would be impossible. The input-output matrix and the computer make such analysis feasible.

Even the largest of the input-output matrices involves aggregation in order to make computation feasible. Such aggregation may limit the usefulness of this type of analysis for particular industries or products. The development of useful matrices is necessarily a laborious, time-consuming task. However, as is often the case in developing models of large, complex systems, the process itself can be valuable in understanding the overall system and the interrelationships among its parts.

Statistics and Probability

One of the most firmly established analytical techniques for management revolves around the use of statistical inference. Quite often the term *statistics* is considered primarily in terms of data, or at most in terms of descriptive statistics. However, modern statistical techniques provide a useful tool for the decision-making process, primarily in the realms of estimation and hypothesis testing. This connotation is represented in the following:

> It is the purpose of statistical analysis to provide methods of treating data so that the maximum information can be obtained with a predetermined risk of drawing false conclusions. No method of analysis can extract more information from a set of data than is contained therein, and no method, statistical or otherwise, can draw conclusions from experimental data with zero risk of error. The use of statistical methods is based on a reasonable assumption that accepted principles of logic and probability should produce correct answers more often than guessing.[20]

The use of sampling is widespread; in some cases it is the only approach to obtaining data for decision making, and in other cases it is the only feasible approach in terms of time and/or money. Many managerial decisions involve assumptions concerning the probability of future events, particularly those which are not controllable. Therefore it is important to understand the nature of probability theory and its application in decision making. For example, the probability of certain outcomes must be related to the importance of those outcomes in order to provide meaningful in-

[20]E. Bright Wilson, Jr., *An Introduction to Scientific Research*, McGraw-Hill Book Company, New York, 1952, p. 57.

formation. The probabilities which must be attached to particular events may be obtained from past experience (a probability distribution is available), and/or it may require informed judgment on the part of the decision maker. When a sequence of events is involved, each with a probability distribution for various outcomes, the problem becomes extremely complex. In such cases it is imperative that a systematic approach be employed which takes into account every pertinent facet of the problem.

A subcategory in the area of statistics is that of factorial analysis, a technique designed to study complex interactions of many variables. It provides a means of relating a number of variables and assessing the relative impact of independent variables on a dependent variable. Factorial analysis provides a maximum amount of information for minimum effort. It is an efficient way of isolating the effects of individual variables, even though numerous variables are interacting with one another and also acting simultaneously on a given outcome.

Statistics and probability provide valuable techniques for decision making. However, statisticians and managers must be constantly on the alert for sample error. Raw answers sometimes can be misleading, as in the case of spurious correlation. Results of statistical analysis which are to be used for estimation or prediction must be scrutinized for reasonableness.

Queuing Theory

Queuing theory, sometimes referred to as waiting-line theory, applies to those decisions which arise when service must be provided to meet some demand which is in any way irregular (neither controllable nor precisely predictable by management). Queuing theory is not a single set of mathematical formulas, but an expanding collection of methods and techniques based on a variety of assumptions. Some of the basic characteristics which may vary from problem to problem include:

1. The size of the group being serviced, i.e., whether it is finite or infinite
2. Whether the elements requiring service are "patient" or not
3. The distribution of holding or servicing times (the two most common assumptions being the constant and exponential servicing-time assumptions)
4. The characteristics of arrival, i.e., their time pattern
5. The number of servicing units

The general approach involved in this type of analysis can be described as follows:

> There are costs connected with the length of the waiting line and the time lost in waiting. There are also costs associated with increasing the capacity of the servicing unit, both capital costs and labor costs. Since arrivals are random, there may be times when there are waiting lines and other times when there is idle servicing capacity. As the mean arrival rate approaches capacity, it can be shown that, if that rate is maintained, the waiting line will tend to approach infinity as an ultimate limit. Clearly, then, capacity must be at least a little greater than the mean arrival rate. The optimum solution to this class of problems will provide a processing capacity just sufficiently in excess of the mean arrival rate to minimize the total of the cost of the added processing capacity plus the costs of waiting. It is also possible to determine the probable waiting time to be expected for each arrival for any given mean arrival rate and processing capacity.[21]

The optimal balance between excess capacity and time lost in waiting is an important consideration in many types of problems. The appropriate number of toll booths, bank tellers, and maintenance men can be determined with these techniques. The amount of airport facilities or the capacity of job shops can be approached in similar fashion.

Even in the simpler cases, the computations tend to get quite lengthy. In most cases practical results come from (1) the use of tables which give general solutions to various waiting-line situations or (2) the use of Monte Carlo techniques.

Monte Carlo Techniques

When problems facing management involve uncertainty, an analytical solution may be difficult or impossible to obtain. Some expressions within a model, because of mathematical or practical considerations, may not be susceptible to a satisfactorily accurate numerical evaluation. Also, the problem may involve events which can be stated only in terms of probabilities. If probabilities can be represented by standard statistical distributions, a solution may be possible. On the other hand, most problems involve variables which cannot be represented by standard probability-distribution curves. Moreover, many problems involve the interactions

[21]Lindsay, op. cit., p. 20.

of a number of probabilistic events, and some representation must be made of the combinations.

In cases such as those outlined above, a particular application of random sampling called the Monte Carlo technique can serve to obtain a satisfactory solution. Basically, the technique is a process for developing data through the use of some random-number generator. For variables which are difficult to evaluate, the Monte Carlo technique can be used to generate their respective values from the proper distribution. In other words, a sample of values can be generated and used to represent observations in the real world.

Examples of such approaches might include the generation of arrival times at some servicing station. Actual data from operations might not provide enough information unless collected over a long period of time. In order to facilitate analysis, the real world is simulated in the form of arrivals. Other problem areas such as transportation, production, inventory, and distribution usually have random factors which are too complicated for mathematical treatment. In such cases Monte Carlo techniques can be used to simulate activity, and hence develop approximations which suffice in the decision-making process. The use of Monte Carlo techniques to simulate certain aspects of problems which cannot be approached via rigorous mathematical analysis points up the need for techniques which allow more flexibility in the analytical process.

SIMULATION

Simulation means "to obtain the essence of, without reality." In the narrow sense, simulation can be used in the application of operations research techniques to specific problems. When applying Monte Carlo techniques, the method involves setting up a stochastic[22] model of a real situation and then performing sampling experiments upon the model. The stochastic model is the feature that distinguishes a simulation from a mere sampling experiment in the classical sense.[23] This approach allows the generation of a large amounts of data which otherwise might take years or months to accumulate. Following the generation of data via simulation,

[22]Variable quantities with a definite range of values, each one of which, depending on chance, can be attained with a definite probability. A stochastic variable is defined (1) if the set of its possible values is given and (2) if the probability of attaining each particular value is also given.
[23]John Harling, "Simulation Techniques in Operations Research: A Review," *Operations Research*, May–June 1958, pp. 307–319.

analytical computations can be made and the problem solved in a straightforward manner. While simulation of a single event or narrow process is beneficial from the standpoint of applying operations research techniques to problem solving, by far the greatest potential benefit lies in simulation of larger-scale systems.

Two basic types of large-scale-system simulation have been developed. In one case, the decision-making process is programmed into the simulation in order that the entire system may be run automatically without involvement of human decision makers. A second type requires recurrent decisions on the part of outside decision makers, the results of those decisions being generated by a simulated system which ordinarily is programmed for an electronic computer. The former approach is called system simulation; it will be discussed in a later section. The latter approach has been described as competitive simulation, or simply gaming.

Gaming

In business, many of the most significant problems are those where managers must not only contend with a complex environment but where they must also make decisions in competition with other managers seeking the same or similar goals. Simulation of these competitive situations has been called business gaming. This approach evolved from the traditional war games practiced by the armed forces.

The American Management Association wondered if a similar approach could be used to give businessmen the same practice in decision making. A top-management-decision game was designed as a mathematical model of business. It consists of a large number of cause and effect formulas which determine the results of each move made by the decision makers. In effect, the gaming model is a simulation of an entire industry. In most cases, play is designed for two to six teams representing a group of companies in a particular industry. While some games have been developed which can be scored by hand, the typical approach utilizes a computer in order to accommodate a large number of equations and hence provide the realism which stimulates those "playing" the game.

In the TOP MAN game the participants are presented with a sequence of over fifteen phases, each one of which adds increasing complexity and requires additional decisions.[24] The model

---

[24]Developed by Albert N. Schrieber in 1956 at the University of Washington. The game has been expanded and refined several times since then.

provides considerable flexibility regarding environmental conditions, the size and type of companies, and parameters for the basic equations in the computer program. Currencies of different countries may be used, and the wording of the output statements can be changed easily and printed in any foreign language whose characters are available on the computer printing system.

So far, simulations of the gaming variety where an entire industry is involved have been used primarily as training devices, with little effort focused on research and analysis. Some research has been done with regard to the decision process itself, and attention also has been focused on the human relations aspects of forming small groups (in this case, the top executive committee of a company). The subsequent interaction of these team members and their attempts to organize for playing the game is a fruitful area for research.

Other gaming-type simulations have been developed which deal with only a part of the business enterprise. In most of these, however, there is not the same competitive atmosphere that develops in the industry-simulation setting. When simulating a part of the company operation such as the production scheduling or the distribution of finished goods, the interaction involves only the decision maker and the environment as modeled. For example, a job shop might be simulated—given machine capacities and labor availability—the problem being one of scheduling a certain number of orders through the plant in the most efficient manner.

Other functional simulation exercises have been established in areas such as physical distribution, finance, and sales management. For example, a sales-management game could include an exercise in attaining the optimal routing for salesmen, or a more complex simulation could be developed which would include routing, scheduling, compensation plans, and other pertinent factors in the sales-management environment.

While operational gaming, or competitive simulation, is an interesting and worthwhile exercise, it does not describe a concrete, particular situation with the realism necessary for research work. Symbolic system simulation, on the other hand, appears to be a powerful tool for both training and research.

System Simulation

Computer simulation can be used as a problem-solving technique and is valuable as a part of research methods directed toward obtaining a better understanding and improved control of operations. Large-scale computers have facilitated integrated-system simulation, which has in turn allowed problem-solving efforts in the areas of designing better systems, understanding the workings of operative systems, and studying decision-making processes in man-machine operations.[25]

We quote a summary report on the Eighth Annual American Institute of Industrial Engineering symposium on system simulation.

> Now, we may well ask the crucial question. "Why should business men, management scientists, or anyone as far as that is concerned, be interested in simulating a system?" Well, there are some pretty important reasons, and they are as follows:
>
> 1. *For purpose of experimentation or evaluation;* in other words, to try and predict the consequences of changes in policy, conditions, methods, etc., without having to spend the money or taking the risk to actually make the change in real life.
> 2. *To learn more about the system* in order to redesign or refine it. The very complexity of most of our business and industrial systems makes necessary a means to provide understanding of both the system as a whole and of its parts.
> 3. *To familiarize personnel* with a system or a situation, which may not exist as yet in real life.
> 4. *To verify or demonstrate* a new idea, a new system or approach; in other words, quantify the risks and benefits, and demonstrate the chances of success.[26]

Any reference to optimal results or best solutions is noticeably lacking in the foregoing summary. In contrast to the application of operations research techniques, the application of system simulation is not undertaken with the idea of optimizing the total system or even a segment of it.[27] In any reasonably large system or subsystem, conditions such as interdependence, immeasurability, incompleteness, ineffectiveness of practical working rules, and

---

[25]For details on simulation techniques see Robert C. Meier, William T. Newell, and Harold L. Pazer, *Simulation in Business and Economics,* Prentice-Hall, Inc., Englewood Cliffs, N.J., 1969, and/or Forrest P. Wyman, *Simulation Modeling: A Guide to Using SIMSCRIPT,* John Wiley & Sons, Inc., New York, 1970.

[26]Warren E. Alberts, "Report to the Eighth AIIE National Conference on the System Simulation Symposium," *Journal of Industrial Engineering,* November–December 1957, pp. 368–369.

[27]However, heuristic programs can be developed for simulating the system repetitively in order to search for successively better alternatives. Theoretically enough runs could be made so that "for all practical purposes" an optimal solution could be found.

imperfect coordination make it impossible to derive and set forth an organization and set of decision rules which will optimize the operation of the system. Simulation of operations allows one to analyze the dynamic behavior of the system as it exists and also allows for testing new and different organizational arrangements or policies. In order to get a clearer view of the application and benefits of system simulation, it will be useful to look at some specific examples.

United Air Lines set up and operated a simulation of the activities involved in operating a large airport. This simulation is referred to as the station model. Using a large-scale computer, months of actual operation at an air terminal can be simulated in a matter of minutes. Essential elements in the model include (1) time of day, year, week, (2) weather conditions, (3) need for maintenance for type and length of repair job, (4) availability of spare aircraft, (5) delays in landing or takeoffs, (6) absenteeism of personnel, and (7) required number of maintenance personnel.

All these uncertainties, as well as company policies and practices, are built into the station model. Policy changes can be programmed and their effect tested by simulating operations under the new conditions. According to those involved in the exercise, perhaps the greatest gain from the simulation has been to instill the *concept of systems thinking* in management and to provide a format for reasoning and decision making in the broader problems of system performance.

A distribution and inventory control model was used by Imperial Oil Limited of Canada in attempting to develop the best system of warehousing their products. The problem involved determining requirements and meeting difficulties arising from severe overcrowding at many field plants. Those involved in the analysis worked with management in the manufacturing operation to develop a detailed flow diagram which represented the system and the decisions which would have to be made. A program was devised for instructing the computer to provide all basic information, control points, and other pertinent data, including various practical constraints. With this basic information in the machine, the computer could be given an initial set of inventory levels for the many hundreds of items being stocked, and a detailed daily recapitulation of orders from field plants could also be fed into the process. Data for a number of critical months were particularly useful in testing this system for possible shortages. The computer was programmed to put out periodic stock reports to indicate the inventory levels in addition to providing information on all unusual conditions such as shortages or waiting lines for facilities. These were then analyzed so that refinements could be introduced into the actual operation.

Maffei and Shycon have described their work in simulating the distribution system for the H. J. Heinz Company.[28] In this case, a large number of products are involved with complex problems of assembling raw materials, producing the products, and then marketing them through a pipeline that includes accumulation at certain points, with distribution fanning out from such central points. The complexity of a distribution system for stable items such as Heinz products can easily be imagined. Deriving an optimum solution for the number and location of warehouses throughout the continental United States would be an utterly impossible task. On the other hand, simulation of this distribution system could be accomplished, and on the basis of various "runs," better arrangements and numbers of warehouses could be programmed.

Establishing flow diagrams and programming the operation of the system for a large-scale computer involved nearly three years of calendar time and many man-years of effort. Once accomplished, however, the simulation model allowed researchers to vary parameters involved and hence to make decisions concerning the appropriateness of policy changes and possible benefits to be derived from them.

An extremely important by-product of an exercise such as programming the description of an entire system is the benefit that occurs from merely tracing explicitly the system itself. Most decision makers are not fully aware of all the factors involved in the operations under their control. When these operations have to be described quantitatively and explicitly, it forces those persons involved to describe the process in complete detail and thereby gain new insight into what they might have considered an entirely familiar operation. While the Heinz study and other simulation exercises are extremely large scale and complex, they deal primarily with only one or a few functions. In this case, the simulation dealt with the distribution problem and did not treat the accumulation of raw materials or the production function.[29]

[28]Harvey N. Shycon and Richard B. Maffei, "Simulation: Tool for Better Distribution," Harvard Business Review, November–December 1960, pp. 65–75.
[29]For additional examples of the application of simulation techniques see Albert N. Schrieber (ed.), Corporate Simulation Models, Graduate School of Business Administration, University of Washington, Seattle, 1970, and John M. Dutton and William H. Starbuck (eds.), Computer Simulation of Human Behavior, John Wiley & Sons, Inc., New York, 1971.

Another application of the system-simulation approach can be found in critical-path scheduling, or network analysis. The use of this technique has become increasingly widespread, particularly for planning and controlling large-scale projects. We shall devote the next chapter to this topic.

Some work is being done in isolated instances on simulation of an entire firm. An example of this approach is the work of a research group at MIT under the direction of Jay W. Forrester.

Industrial Dynamics

In a series of memoranda, and later in a book, Forrester and his colleagues in the School of Industrial Management at MIT have presented the philosophy, nature, structure, and use of industrial dynamics.[30] The following material on industrial dynamics has been taken from these sources.

The tool of analysis is a dynamic model of the behavior of an industrial organization. A typical industrial-dynamics model is a mathematical model for analyzing stability and fluctuation of an industrial system. It has closed-loop, information feedback characteristics and also incorporates decision-making procedures. Five interacting subsystems are developed—material flow, order flow, money flow, capital-equipment generation and usage, and manpower employment and mobility—all interconnected by information flow or a decision-making network. Preliminary studies have dealt primarily with material and information flow. Although these studies in themselves have been extremely complex, continuing efforts are being devoted toward incorporation of all the subsystems into one all-encompassing system. Since the situations to be studied can be represented realistically only by nonlinear mathematical systems, they are so formulated. Likewise, if the real-life situation is unstable, then the system-simulation program must accommodate this phenomenon. To describe accurately a total system, it is often necessary to incorporate hundreds or even thousands of variables in order to be sufficiently realistic and useful. The immediate goal is to find *improved* but *not optimum* system design; there is no meaningful definition of an optimum system nor any method of proving that the designated system behavior is the best achievable.

[30]Jay W. Forrester et al., various memoranda concerning industrial-dynamics research (unpublished materials), MIT, School of Industrial Management, Cambridge, Mass. Also included in Jay W. Forrester, *Industrial Dynamics,* John Wiley & Sons, Inc., New York, and The M.I.T. Press, Cambridge, Mass., 1961.

The industrial-dynamics philosophy claims that there is a general misunderstanding to the effect that a mathematical model cannot be undertaken until every constant and functional relationship is known precisely. This often leads to the omission of admittedly highly significant factors (most of the "intangible" influences on decisions) because they are unmeasured or unmeasurable.

A model must start with a "structure," meaning the general nature of the interrelationships within it. Assumptions about structure must be made before one can collect data from the real system. The structure is developed by obtaining a verbal account of the decision-making process at each critical point in the system. This verbalization and structuring can be accomplished only through the tedious task of asking questions and probing for answers on the part of decision makers. Having a reasonable structure that fits descriptive knowledge of the system, one can take the next step and assign plausible numerical values to coefficients, which should represent identifiable and describable characteristics of the real system. The analyst then can proceed to alter the model and the real system to eliminate disagreement and move both toward a more desirable level of performance. Mathematical models for representing industrial and economic activity adequately for top-management purposes are probably no larger (in terms of hundreds of variables) than some which already have been simulated in military operations. But they will be more subtle and more complex (higher degrees of interdependence between the variables).

The general concepts of information feedback systems are essential in industrial-dynamics model building, because such systems exhibit behavior as a whole which is not evident from examination of the parts separately. The pattern of systems interconnection, the amplification caused by decision and policy, the delays in actions, and the distortion of information flows combine to determine stability and growth. The interconnection of entirely ordinary corporate action can lead to production fluctuations, unemployment, and excess plant capacity. As one action feeds into another and eventually back to the first, it causes instability, which is the counterpart of "hunting" in mechanical servomechanisms. Careful attention must be given to representing properly time delays and information distortion.

Decision making in an information feedback system couples the information and the action channels. In the model structure the decision functions receive information and thereby control the rates of flow that interconnect the various levels (inventories, stocks, reservoirs) of the system. Representing dynamic system behavior requires formal expressions to indicate how decisions are made. The flow of information is converted continuously into decisions and thence into action.

Figure 8–1 illustrates the role of decision making in a goal-striving (not necessarily goal-achieving) system. There is a continuous feedback path of decision-results-measurement-evaluation-decision, and the difference between "real" and "apparent" achievements is a key concept. The industrial-dynamics model of an organization might include numerous subsystems of the type shown. No plea about inadequacy of understanding of the decision-making process can excuse the analyst from estimating the decision-making criteria. To omit decision making is to deny its presence, a mistake of far greater magnitude than any errors in the best estimate of the process.

The decision functions are statements of *policy*. One of the principal uses of the dynamic models is to study the influences of policy on system behavior. In formulating a model, one must extend the concept of policy beyond its usual meaning. All decisions in the system come under the complete control of policy; in this sense a policy is a statement of the basis for reaching decisions at a point in the system. *Decision functions* are therefore the statements

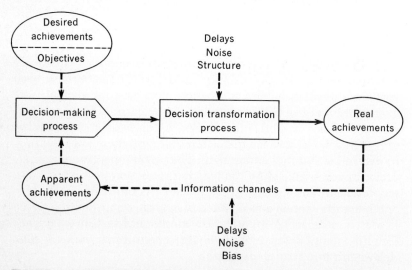

FIGURE 8–1. Control system structure of organizations. (Source: Edward B. Roberts, "Industrial Dynamics and the Design of Management Control Systems," *Management Technology*, December 1963, p. 101.)

of policy that control flows in all points in the system. These decision functions (or policy) may be complex and nonlinear; they may incorporate "superpolicy" that tells us how the decision functions themselves evolve with time and how they change in accordance with the history of system variables. The decision function can incorporate a random event variable of specified statistical characteristics to simulate some of the residual uncertainties that will remain after the principal direct variables have been incorporated.

In general, the industrial-dynamics approach seeks to develop a very simple system in terms of the fundamental nature of its equations. Simple algebraic difference equations are utilized to describe the entire system. The only complexity that does arise stems from the sheer size of the model; that is, it may take many hundreds of variables and equations in order to describe adequately the system under analysis.

Extensions of this general approach have been made to even larger, more complex systems.[31] A model has been developed to represent fundamental urban processes—showing how industry, housing, and people interact with each other as a city grows and decays. Similarly, a dynamic model has been developed to reflect the interactions among world population, industrialization, depletion of natural resources, agriculture, and pollution.

The objective which is sought when designing a simulation model should fulfill the following requirements: (1) it should allow any statement of cause-effect relationships that we may wish to include; (2) it should be simple in mathematical nature; (3) it should be closely synonymous in nomenclature to industrial, economic, and social terminology; (4) it should be extendible to large numbers of variables (thousands) without exceeding the practical limits of available digital computers; (5) it should be able to handle continuous interaction in the sense that any artificial discontinuity introduced by solution time intervals will not affect the results; and (6) it should include the effects of intangibles, particularly the role of the decision makers who are part of the man-machine system.

If simulation models of the entire system can be developed with the above characteristics, it seems obvious that this approach would be useful as an analytical tool in the application of the systems approach.

---

[31]Jay W. Forrester, *Urban Dynamics*, The M.I.T. Press, Cambridge, Mass., 1969, and *World Dynamics*, Wright-Allen Press, Inc., Cambridge, Mass., 1971.

MANAGERS AND SCIENTISTS/TECHNICIANS

Politely, the problem is one of communications. More bluntly, it's one of jargon. I can understand why medicine has its jargon. It goes back to Aristotle and Hippocrates. And I can understand why law has its jargon. It goes back to Solon. And both fields have incongruities and anachronisms about them which, I suppose, will always baffle the layman. But why sciences born in the middle of this century should need words like "algorithm," "heuristic," and "stochastic" in communications with management perplexes me. They can be translated, because they almost always are—even in technical papers. So why use foreign languages when the message alone may be complex enough in English. You may not agree with my view, but I assure you that language is a roadblock to progress and you gentlemen (scientists/technicians) are continually putting these communication boulders in the path of even sympathetic management.[32]

The problem of implementing scientific findings has been uppermost in the minds of many researchers. It is a perennial topic for discussion at professional meetings, and better communication usually is cited as an important step in attaining mutuality of interests. The Institute of Management Sciences (TIMS) has maintained a running debate since its inception on its objectives in this area.[33] Although the integration of science and management has been emphasized, divergent opinions eventually resulted in a split which is reflected in the publication of a two-part journal (Series A—Sciences, and Series B—Managerial).[34] This move illustrates Boulding's lament, referred to in Chapter 1.

Hence physicists only talk to physicists, economists to economists —worse still, nuclear physicists talk only to nuclear physicists and econometricians to econometricians. One wonders sometimes if science will not grind to a stop in an assemblage of walled-in hermits, each mumbling to himself words in a private language that only he can understand.[35]

While many causal factors could be identified, a basic controversy revolves around the question of problem versus technique orientation. In the extreme, managers are interested in problem

[32]Louis T. Rader, "Roadblocks to Progress in the Management Sciences and Operations Research," *Management Science,* February 1965, p. C–2.
[33]The journal cover states: "An international society to identify, extend and unify scientific knowledge pertaining to management."
[34]Since 1967 the division has been Theory and Application.
[35]Kenneth Boulding, "General Systems Theory: The Skeleton of Science," *Management Science,* April 1956, p. 198.

solving regardless of technique, and scientists are interested in sophistication of method regardless of applicability. Yet the question of pure and applied research is one of degree rather than kind; the designation is related to long- and short-term considerations. However, overemphasis on pure research and technique development rather than problem solving has resulted in low yield from investments in management science. In fact the "batting average" has been miserable in terms of the percentage of recommendations that eventually affect operations.

> Some of my graduate students undertook to write to the authors of cases reported in *Operations Research* over the first six years of its publication to determine to what extent the recommendations of the studies had been carried out by management. In no case was there sufficient evidence that the recommendations had been accepted.[36]

Often it is assumed that pertinent information is available, within such constraints as time and cost, and that analysis could lead to appropriate knowledge and action if communication were to bring about understanding. But effective communication requires listening, a rare skill. The manager would have to pay attention to the "correct" signals in order to ensure implementation of suggested changes. According to Churchman, such a task is formidable; "we argued in the end that none of these ingredients matters at all unless the manager pays attention to the problem, and that paying attention is an obscure process of the managerial mind, little understood by management scientists."[37]

Developing mutual understanding is necessary before progress can be made in identifying appropriate problems for analysis and in implementing the results of research in the designated areas. The standard techniques may be applicable to problems in which the manager is not interested. Or the manager may have inputs which completely restructure the situation as against the researcher's assumptions.

Four possible approaches to the interface dilemma have been identified as (1) separate function, (2) communication, (3) persuasion, and (4) mutual understanding.[38] The first approach implies

[36]C. West Churchman, "Managerial Acceptance of Scientific Recommendations," *California Management Review*, Fall 1964, p. 33.
[37]Ibid., p. 37.
[38]C. W. Churchman and A. H. Schainblatt, "The Researcher and the Manager: A Dialectic of Implementation," *Management Science*, February 1965, pp. B-69 – B-87. See also *Management Science*, October 1965, for extensive commentary by various authors concerning this article.

that the activities of managers and management scientists are mutually exclusive, that research can be carried out more or less in a vacuum and *then* implemented. The second approach emphasizes the scientist "getting the message across" and relies on the *amount* of communication. The persuader, on the other hand, is interested in the personality of the manager so that he can ascertain the *best* strategy for offsetting resistance and implementing change. Mutual understanding requires empathy on the part of all concerned; scientists should understand the whole world of the manager and vice versa.

One of the difficulties in the manager-scientist relationship is the type and level of problems that seem to interest each party. Although the well-developed techniques are quite effective on routine, easily quantified problems, top management cannot ignore novel, ill-structured problems. "The temptation for us (scientists/technicians) to 'play it safe' and apply ourselves only to limited problems that do not involve the skills on which managers most pride themselves continues strong today."[39] While some management problems involve stable, predictable relationships, most of them include values and variables which change over time. Uncertainty reigns in many situations. Hertz suggests that:

> We must bridge the gap between two types of problems: (1) the enterprise problems, in which influential variables are largely external, nonmanipulable, often nonstable, and difficult to estimate; in which the possible outcomes vary widely and the possible penalties are costly and irreversible; and in which the expected value of the outcome rarely is significant, even when calculable; and (2) the repetitive, operations, or process problems, in which the incremental penalties are low, there are many internal variables, and the environment can be made structurally stable through feedback control processes.[40]

Type 2 problems seem amenable to routine, straightforward quantitative techniques. A "separate-functions" approach may even be workable in such an environment. A more sophisticated approach involving adaptations and combinations of techniques is necessary for type 1 problems, as is mutual understanding on the part of managers and scientists. Which direction shall we take? Heany poses the question as follows:

[39]David B. Hertz, "Mobilizing Management Science Resources," *Management Science,* January 1965, p. 364.
[40]Ibid., p. 366.

Is "management science" merely a synonym for "applied mathematics"? A set of techniques and nothing more?

Is the scope of our interest restricted to well-structured problems, those amenable to quantitative tools of analysis?

Can one aspire to enterprise models embracing work going on at the top echelons of business organizations as long as managers and scientists are miles apart in terminology, interests and perspective?[41]

The answers to these questions are crucial for management science. If it continues to be narrowly construed as applied mathematics for dealing with routine, well-structured problems, implementation will continue to lag. Suggestions for improvement are summarized in Figure 8–2 with special reference to top-level nonroutine problems.[42]

The scientist and manager come together to define the prob-

[41]Donald F. Heany, "Is TIMS Talking to Itself?", *Management Science,* December 1965, p. B-155.
[42]See also Rudolph C. Reinitz, "What Is Appropriate Training for Developing a Management Scientist?" *Interfaces,* November 1971, pp. 25–27, and Martin K. Starr, "The Politics of Management Science," *Interfaces,* June 1971, pp. 31–37.

FIGURE 8–2. A Contrast in Methodology: Alternate Views of Management Science

Initial version	Proposed revision
Inputs	
Voluminous, multifunctional data in existing information systems	1. Existing, quantitative data *if relevant* 2. New quantitative *and qualitative data*
Process	
Search & Discovery via tools of —classifying —characterizing and —structuring/modeling such data	Search & Invent via same tools as in initial version *plus* purposefully formed tailored concepts, seen and manipulated as a set
Expected output	
1. Conversion of implicit theory of that business into explicit form 2. Senior managers use as their own	1. Explicit, *new or old* theory (or theories) of that business 2. Senior managers *and staff* use as their own

Source: Donald F. Heany, "Is TIMS Talking to Itself?", *Management Science,* December 1965, p. B-154.

lem and designate the information and analysis which would be pertinent. New quantitative and qualitative data should be sought, as should new concepts in processing to obtain relevant information. If there is participation by top or senior management, the process of internalizing explicit new theories for a particular situation becomes easier. The goal is for managers to become imbued with the scientific approach and for scientists to become more aware of top-management value systems. Only then will management science be capable of achieving its potential.

Systems concepts, by emphasizing wholeness and integration of the various elements to be analyzed, provide a framework for achieving mutual understanding. Relationships rather than parts are stressed in order to ascertain how the elements fit together. The penetrating analysis of scientists should be carried out in the proper context so that the probability of implementing findings is increased. Management's involvement in defining the problem and suggesting alternatives ensures the inclusion of important insights which a researcher may or may not discern. A problem well stated is half solved.

SUMMARY

Systems analysis is primarily a managerial approach to problem solving or decision making wherein overall system effectiveness is related to resource allocation in a process of careful, searching evaluation. Similarly, the scientific method can be described as a systematic, orderly approach to problem solving which includes defining the problem, formulating hypotheses, collecting relevant information, analyzing the information, and drawing conclusions.

Scientific management was described as the application of the scientific method to management problems. Stressing science, rather than rule of thumb, the early scientific management practitioners applied the scientific method to the planning of activities at the operational level.

The terms *operations research* and *management science* have followed in the wake in the term *scientific management*. While these more current approaches stress quantification, model building, and mathematical analysis, they still fit under the overall umbrella of the application of scientific method to management problems. Thus our definition of management science must be broad—the application of scientific method to managerial decision making. Within this broad framework are many techniques of analysis. One of the most important of these is the concept of a model used to represent the operational system under study. The development of models requires the explicit treatment of system variables and forces an integrated approach. The introduction of electronic computers to quantitative analysis has allowed the use of approaches heretofore considered unfeasible.

Techniques such as linear programming and input-output analysis afford management scientists an opportunity to deal with large-scale, complex problems. Some problems can be well defined and a state of certainty assumed. Other problems involving uncertainty require somewhat different techniques of analysis. Statistics and probability are appropriate tools in many cases. One large class of problems is that of queuing, or waiting-line, theory; much work has been done in this area, and many applications are evident. Monte Carlo techniques can be useful in problems of uncertainty to simulate stochastic processes that are a part of the system model under study.

Because applications of typical mathematical analysis require explicit determination of all relevant variables in the system, simplifying assumptions often must be made in order to carry out analytical solutions. Such simplifications cut down the usefulness of the techniques since the results may not be applicable in real life. To offset this problem, simulation techniques have been developed with the goal of describing systems and developing workable solutions on the basis of trial-and-error methods. Rather than striving for an optimal solution which may not be applicable because of simplifying assumptions made in structuring the problem, simulation focuses on describing the system as it exists in order to model it realistically. Policy changes can be evaluated in terms of their impact on the simulated system, thus allowing a laboratory for testing managerial decision making without committing the resources of the organization.

Quantitative techniques in general, and simulation in particular, can be useful in implementing the systems approach. Model building forces decision makers to structure the operation under analysis as an integrated system tied together by a series of equations. The use of computers in symbolic system simulation allows treatment of large-scale, complex systems. Thus the analyst can develop a model of a group of subsystems, their interrelationships, and the total system. Such an approach provides a framework for more detailed analytical examination of various segments of the system.

Managers and scientists/technicians have not achieved an effective working relationship. Problem rather than technique orientation will foster progress in the future; the identification of top-management value systems and concerns plus the use of qualitative as well as quantitative data should facilitate communication. Systems concepts, by emphasizing the wholeness and integration of the various elements to be analyzed, provide a framework for achieving mutual understanding.

QUESTIONS

1. What is the focal point of systems analysis as it has been used in national security planning? How are qualitative aspects included in the process?
2. Compare and contrast problem solving, decision making, creativity, and scientific method.
3. Define management science. How does it relate to (a) scientific management and (b) operations research?
4. What is the role of model building in management science? Describe several models that you find useful in your day-to-day existence.
5. What role has the computer played in the development of quantitative techniques?
6. Do computers think? What is the essence of artificial intelligence and heuristic problem solving?
7. Briefly define and describe the use and limitations of the following methods: (a) linear programming, (b) input-output analysis, (c) queuing theory, and (d) Monte Carlo techniques.
8. Compare and contrast "gaming" and system simulation.
9. How does simulation differ from analytical techniques used in management science? How can simulation aid in planning and policy formulation?
10. What advantages are cited for industrial dynamics as a special kind of simulation? Are *total*-system simulations feasible? Are they practical?
11. What are the stumbling blocks to more effective implementation of management science findings? What would you suggest to remedy the situation?

Weyerhaeuser Company (B)

In late 1971, the Manager of Operations Research was considering the future role of OR activity in the Weyerhaeuser Company.[1] During the process of developing the 1972 budget the question of centralization-decentralization for OR had again become an issue. The group vice presidents seemed to favor decentralization while the president leaned toward maintaining a sizable unit in the corporate headquarters organization. As indicated in Appendix A, the Operations Research Department was organized in the early 1960s "to act as an internal management consulting group that will increase the company's ability to take full advantage of the new scientific management techniques, and thereby increase profits." During the 1960s the department had grown in size to a peak of thirty-three professionals plus a clerical support staff of ten people. In 1966 a formal charter was developed to emphasize "decision systems analysis." Five organizational sections were identified as follows (see Appendix B for a description of the functions):

> Management Science–Operations Research Development
> Corporate Decision Systems
> Timberlands/Wood Products Decision Systems
> Pulp Based Products Decision Systems
> Scientific Computing Services

In 1971, the Manager reiterated that the "OR Department's role ever since its inception in 1962 has been to help improve decision making in the company." It has achieved this through the following key activities:

[1]Approximately eighteen professionals plus supporting staff reporting to the Vice President for Finance and Planning (see Exhibit 8–1).

1. Performing specific project analysis
2. Training and development in management science
3. Insertion of OR-trained personnel in non-OR jobs
4. Introduction of OR techniques and computers to the RD&E function in the corporation
5. Design and implementation of decision systems

The activities under items 1 to 4 seem to be relatively straightforward and there seemed to be consensus that reasonable progress had been made in these areas. However, the objective of becoming the "decision systems architect" for the company had not been achieved. Responsibility on this dimension seemed to be diffused in a number of directions; namely, more formalized planning activities, an investment evaluation department, management information systems endeavors, and others. In each of these cases, there was emphasis on the development of a flow of appropriate information for planning and decision making—both strategic (including mergers and acquisitions) and operational.

Internal Organizational Changes

In 1966 the OR Department changed its organization from a homogeneous corporate project–type organization to a decentralized section format with manpower dedicated to the service of particular operating groups. This was done with the explicit purpose of creating a close identification of professionals with operating managers—a key factor in the successful application of OR in a decision systems framework. The following sections were identified: (1) Timberland/Wood Products Decision Systems, (2) Pulp Based Products Decision Systems, (3) Corporate Decision Systems, (4) MS/OR Development Section, and (5) math analysis and programming group (Scientific Computing Services).

Over a period of time, OR-trained professionals were absorbed in operating groups, often in planning positions which called for direct and continuing contact with an operating manager. These developments usually followed the successful implementation of an OR research project's findings. In some cases the "consultants" worked themselves into a job by demonstrating the usefulness of a particular application in managerial decision making. More often, however, the individual analysts were hired into such jobs because of their personal skills. According to the manager of OR, the most effective analysts seemed to be able to "blend into the woodwork." Since the inception of the Operations Research Department, approximately twenty-four professionals had been "spun out" into the operating organization.

Place of OR in the Company Organization

Initially the OR function was part of the Controller's Department. Then, after several years, it became a part of Business Systems which reported to the Executive Vice President of Operations [see Weyerhaeuser Company (A)]. In 1969 Business Systems (including OR) was shifted under the Vice President of Administration. Meanwhile, corporate planning activities were located in the office of the Senior Vice President for Corporate Growth, in the form of an Investment Evaluation Department. IED was responsible for financial planning, evaluation of capital appropriation requests, and coordination of corporate planning. In early 1970, a new Vice President of Finance and Planning was appointed with responsibility for Market and Economic Research, IED, and OR, in addition to the Tax, Treasurer, and Controller functions.

Before the change the manager of Business Systems had expressed the following views:

> My current position is that I can see some valid arguments for raising the issue about where OR's home should be, but I continue to feel strongly that the best home is in the Business Systems function.
>
> My reasons:
>
> 1. Because we are a process corporation, the types of questions and problems that OR can be used to solve are of a recurring nature. (Log allocation, plant expansion, forecasting, etc.) Thus, there is great advantage for us to develop systems that allow us to use OR techniques and models on a continuing basis. Also because of a need for compatibility and a use of common data, the OR-oriented systems must be integrated with other systems in the businesses.
> 2. Once the MIS functions have essentially completed the basic data acquisition systems, such as order entry, inventory, etc., then the next level of systems is OR oriented (decision strategies, planning, forecasting, etc.). So in general, the system designer of the future is going to look more and more like the current OR practitioner, in my opinion.
> 3. The current Business Systems manager used to manage the Weyerhaeuser OR function.
> 4. I firmly believe that the future direction of the systems effort must be business decision and management science oriented, rather than accounting, computer, or any other orientation. (I would classify the orientation of our systems effort to date as being computer oriented—in other companies it is typically either computer oriented or accounting oriented.) With top-management prodding, we have started moving in the direction of making ours business decision and management science oriented, and I think this should continue.
> 5. The general trend in a number of advanced corporations with large systems efforts is to integrate operations research with its system effort.

I recognize that OR has some very high interaction and some possible overlap with the planning functions, with Market and Economic Research, and with Financial or Operations Analysis. Working relationships with all these functions are maturing, and the orientation of the OR function has been to transfer capability into these groups as they are ready and willing to handle it. I think these functions need to be closely coordinated throughout the corporation with both the OR and the systems effort.

Another comment that has been made about our OR function is that it has exceeded the *traditional* "critical mass" for OR functions. I think it is a valid question to ask whether or not our OR function is too large. I doubt it, for the type of thing we are trying to do. Typically, small traditional OR groups tend either to become the pet project team of whoever is managing them or to become technically oriented, and there tends to be proliferation of these groups throughout a corporation. In addition they tend to be in conflict with the systems function. In our OR organization we have attempted to maintain some of the advantages of small units by breaking the department into sections where each section has an applications orientation such as, Wood Products, Pulp Based Products, Corporate Projects, and Engineering and Research. Because these units have been together, we have been able to use common staff for programming, technical research, training, and recruiting.

In addition, we have managed the scientific systems development and programming for the rest of the company within the OR Department. How long this should continue is a valid question.

I think we are getting good results out of our OR Department, and we have a good corporate visibility and control of its direction. I think we should carefully examine what we think would be achieved by changing the makeup of the organization, or its home.

The impetus for relocating the operations research function had stemmed from several considerations. Progress in OR had slacked off in 1969 after some solid successes in 1968. High-powered technical people had been hired during the peak success years, and they had trouble in relating to actual company problems. Some top managers seemed to feel that the OR Department was spinning its wheels and "talking to itself" rather than working on relevant issues.

Also, it was evident that OR endeavors had become more oriented toward planning than operating and data systems development (the function of Business Systems). Therefore, a closer relationship among OR, IED, and M&ER seemed to be appropriate.

The change was made; OR was shifted to Corporate Growth, reporting to the Vice President for Finance and Planning. At that time the manager of OR assumed the task of significantly reducing the Department's size and budget. One change involved shifting Scientific Computing Services to Research, Development, and Engineering.

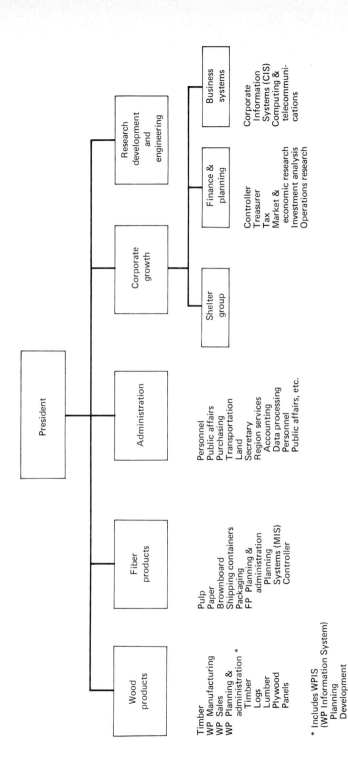

Exhibit 8–1. Weyerhaeuser company organization—1972.

In 1971 the Business Systems Department was shifted from Administration to Corporate Growth (see Exhibit 8-1).

An Interview with a Senior Vice President

Initially it was important to centralize OR activities at the corporate level in order to ensure its survival and growth. Managers and OR technicians did not seem to talk the same language. There was a period of mutual adjustment while managers grew to appreciate the contribution which could be made via powerful new techniques of analysis. At the same time operations researchers grew to appreciate the problems from the manager's point of view. In many cases, mutual understanding grew as analysts became less technique oriented and more problem oriented.

According to top management there were cases where elegant solutions were developed to solve the wrong problems, hence precluding implementation. Thus, in the early stages, management lost confidence in OR as a potential aid in managerial decision making. If the department had not been protected in the early stages, it might not have survived.

In the long run, however, decentralization will be a better approach. It can help the analysts focus on problems rather than techniques and ensure managerial involvement in problem definition and the evaluation of alternatives. It helps implement the concept that the OR function can be an extension of the manager and become an integral part of his decision-making process in both strategic and operational matters.

Major Contributions

Both top-level executives and the manager of Operations Research agreed that major contributions had been made in several key areas. Exhibit 8-2 shows the overall material-flow process for the company from timber to ultimate consumer with many key decision points identified. Allocation

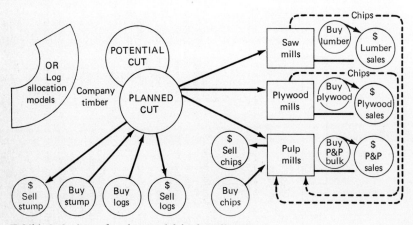

Exhibit 8-2. Area planning model for log allocation.

decisions are vital at many junctures. The manager of Operations Research described the contributions of operations research in this regard as follows:

> Of the many activities that the department engaged in, two of them had the greatest long-term impact on the company. They were the models and concepts that were developed for allocating logs and, second, the concept of using a business model to look at the business as a system whose logistics and marginal economics are an important factor in the commitment of long-term capital. Let me briefly illustrate examples of what was done in these two areas.

The Concept of an Area Model

Our raw material business and major manufacturing facilities for primary products are concentrated in geographic locations called areas. The material flow and options in a typical area for raw materials are shown in Exhibit 8-2.

This is a typical mathematical programming problem. Basically, our area models are LPs (linear programs) which deal with the following kinds of information:

Buy and sell opportunities for stumpage
Log availability in the company
Buy and sell opportunities for logs
Buy and sell opportunities for chips
Log transportation costs
Product yields
Production rate
Production capacity
Capacity cost

When the model is solved, we get suggested plans for raw material sources, raw material disposal, production capacity plans, and product-line plans for the sawmills, plywood mills, and wood rooms (chips).

The log allocation models were used by the business, although *under great protest.* The biggest problems were data inaccuracy and the handling of incredibly large volumes of information as we attempted to use these models for practical decision making. During our next phase of development we corrected these problems and today there is in the company a specially organized staff called the Log Allocation Analysis Group which monitors the data, operates the LPs, and analyzes the actual results against plans for log and primary product flows. This return-to-log (RTL) system helps us allocate $400 million worth of raw material every year.

Business Planning Models

The next example I have is the concept of a business model for our Brownboard business. Exhibit 8-3 shows the major compo-

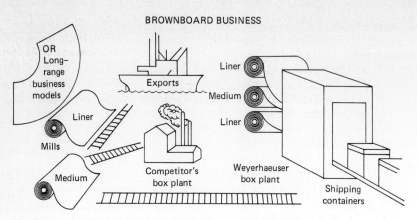

Exhibit 8-3. Business planning model for brownboard business.

nents of this business. As you can see, the primary mill produces liner and medium which are then sold in the export or domestic board market or are shipped to our own shipping container plants which make corrugated containers.

The model allocates products to markets considering manufacturing costs, labor costs, price ranges, demand and capacity bounds, trade possibilities with competitors, etc. The model solution recommends a balanced product flow and produces the associated financial statements.

Models similar to Brownboard were built for several of the businesses, and just as in the log allocation area, our biggest problem was the lack of a good system for data handling and turnaround.

Personnel Requirements

The general guidelines for hiring OR personnel were set forth in the following way. The OR Department will consist primarily of highly skilled and experienced professionals who draw the respect of the management and staff personnel in the operating groups. In addition to being technically competent, they should have a strong business orientation, either by interest or by training, and have the people skills to bring about successful change.

The growth opportunities for professional staff and the environment should be such as to attract the highest quality of staff. In particular, the department will maintain a totally open policy as far as the proportion of senior people that the staff can contain. The department's internal organization will be as flat as possible in an administrative/reporting sense. The size of the department should be small and definitely have a maximum of twenty-five (including professional and support staff). A group of six to ten OR professionals and three to six math and scientific programming professionals is likely to be most effective.

Movement of personnel from this group to other staff and operating roles should be encouraged where possible. Similarly over time, the salary structure and reward system should permit reentry of topnotch professionals who have been in other responsible jobs in the company and have the desire to be part of the professional group again. Such a policy in the department would be most cost effective for the company even though individual professionals would have high salaries.

In order to encourage breadth and total professional competence, salary policies should correspond to internal consultant scales, rather than to those of OR technicians.

Technique Development

In late 1971 the manager of Operations Research was reflecting on the appropriate balance of activities within the OR Department. A major issue was whether or not the company should continue its efforts in the more pure aspects of operations research technique development. Over the years it had devoted a part of its resources to this endeavor. However, alternative approaches had been considered, namely, the use of outside consultants from time to time or waiting until the results of such efforts elsewhere were documented and published. According to the manager of OR most of the interesting projects were located in the operating groups. It was becoming more difficult to maintain interest in the "pure" research and technique development work which remained in the central OR department.

APPENDIX A

Weyerhaeuser

NEWS

Number 60 · November 1965

OPERATIONS RESEARCH: LEVER FOR CHANGE

There is nothing more difficult to take in hand, more perilous to conduct, or more uncertain in its success, than to take the lead in introduction of a new order of things, because the innovator has for enemies all those who have done well under the old conditions, and lukewarm defenders in those who may do well under the new.

Machiavelli: The Prince
1469–1527

Machiavelli was speaking of politics but he stated a great truth that applies to all human relations when he wrote his advice to rulers more than 400 years ago.

He stopped short when he didn't say that although an innovator may lose all, the rewards for the successful innovator are as great as the risks.

Then too, he never dreamed of today's world of business and industry where innovation is the order of the day and the company that doesn't seek out innovation through research will slip behind the competition, losing customers and money.

With knowledge of the risks, but at the same time with anticipation of success bringing a big payoff, Weyerhaeuser Company is continually investing in research, looking for innovations.

The common idea of research is of men in laboratories with intricate and delicate equipment. Weyerhaeuser has these, but one of the newest of the disciplines in our world today is Operations Research, which is not much more than 25 years old.

Operations Research deals with systems, applying the same scientific techniques which have unlocked the atom, discovered DNA and sent astronauts soaring out into space to business and manufacturing systems.

Operations Research got its start during World War II when the Royal Air Force of Britain was vastly outnumbered by the Luftwaffe of Nazi Germany. Through the techniques of Operations Research, or Operational Research as the British call it, coupled with the new and secret radar, the effectiveness of each Spitfire was increased by a factor of 30.

In other words, each British plane became as effective as if it were 30 planes. Thus Operations Research played a big part in victory in the Battle of Britain.

Today, Weyerhaeuser has an Operations Research department, which is using these new techniques to study our company systems.

The results of these studies have brought and will bring still more innovations to Weyerhaeuser. The discipline of Operations Research is an innovation in itself. As Machiavelli said, the risks are great. And as he didn't say, the rewards to the company can be equally as great.

For more on Weyerhaeuser's Operations Research, see the following pages.

If you had your life to live over again would you do some things differently?

It's impossible, of course, to bring back the past, but it certainly would be nice to have more than intuition to test how key decisions today will affect the future. And in the field of business and industry a new scientific discipline has been developed which allows a manager to test the effects of his decisions on a model before he decides in the "real world."

It sounds like science fiction, but it really is the application of the same scientific approach to business systems that has been used for hundreds of years in physics, biology, chemistry and other sciences.

Models Used

It's called operations research and deals with business systems. Just as in the physical sciences, where experiments are carried on in a laboratory, with operations research, managers can set up "models" of a system and experiment with this model and not the system itself.

We can turn on an electric light with a good degree of probability that the bulb will light up. But the typical manager has not always been as certain that his administrative or production system would work as well, or for that matter that the system in use was the best possible.

For example, if a factory has nine products—say of plywood—being made in one process, there are more than 360,000 ways in which the order of manufacture can be arranged. Costs and machine-time requirements depend upon this order of manufacture, thus when one looks at the many hundreds of products being made by Weyerhaeuser at a single plant, the number of choices is overwhelming.

So operations researchers take all these possibilities, state them in the shorthand of mathematical equations or inequalities and use a computer to work out the time-consuming math. Then, if the information fed in is correct, the outcome will be the best of all the choices, according to management's criteria.

The "model" is the heart of operations research. It can help the company know such things as how much inventory to keep on hand; where we should buy chips from outside sources; which grades of pulp to sell overseas; whether a log should go into decking or 2×4's or be sold or made into plywood; how a distribution setup should be changed; or whether a change is even desirable.

Intriguing Terms

Some of the techniques of operations research sound just as exotic as the very idea of being able to take a look at the future. Linear programming, critical path method, Monte Carlo technique, queuing theory, game theory, the black-box concept, probability theory, and simulation are some of them.

Even the models have names which are strange-sounding to the layman, such as probabalistic, deterministic, qualitative and quantitative models.

Managers for years have been making the decisions that operations research helps make, but because there are so many possibilities, there has always been uncertainty. "Operations Research doesn't take the decision away from a manager, it helps relieve him of trivialities and provides him with criteria of measure for the true management-level decisions," says Bye Wynne, manager, Operations Research.

The Weyerhaeuser Operations Research Department was organized under Wynne in 1962. The purpose of the department is to act as an internal management consulting group that will increase the company's ability to take full advantage of the new scientific management techniques, and thereby increase profits.

Plans for Liaison

The department is now made up of some thirty operations researchers and computer analysts with a clerical support staff of eight. All the technical people have at least one scientific degree, many have a second. In addition, the people have brought in experience from well-known organizations including IBM, Booz-Allen Hamilton, Boeing, Douglas, and Arthur Anderson.

"This couples accounting, industrial engineering, manufacturing, marketing—the whole spectrum of management activity—with computers and mathematics to help executives deal more effectively with uncertainty," Wynne says.

Wynne commented that "the OR department as such probably will not grow much larger. Instead, senior operations research practitioners will be established in each operating division to provide a closer liaison with the managers." This step has already been taken for some divisions.

"Our activities," Wynne continued, "fall into four categories: training courses, consulting, projects, and scientific computing.

"Right now we are teaching courses in statistical applications, and the critical path method of project scheduling. We plan to start a course in linear programming soon."

Wynne points out that the group's consulting efforts bring it into contact with a wide range of management problems. Many requests are handled over the phone; most take less than a day to complete. The bulk of the inquiries are related to projects already engaged in.

Investment Picture

"Evaluation of potential investments is a very active area for us," Wynne explains. "We've developed a computer system called ARISTOTLE to assist management to evaluate the potential return and risks in medium to large investments. This system allows a manager to put a range on his estimates, and the answer is an expected range of returns rather than one answer. Typical of OR projects, continued improvement and evolution is expected here."

All current projects deal in one way or another with managing the flow of raw material to products and the flow of products to customers. Material flow charts like the one published in last year's annual report can be seen on many office walls in the department. They help show how each project fits into the company's overall material flow pattern. Planning and controlling this material flow to meet customer needs is a necessary step in converting Weyerhaeuser to a marketing-oriented company.

"The real solvers of the company's problems are the operating people," Wynne stresses. "In all our projects we have teamed up with the operating people, both to utilize their experience and so that they will implement and use the results of the analysis. The staff organizations provide tools—it's up to the operating people to use them."

"Corporate Customers"

"Most problems are too complex to be calculated by hand," Wynne continues. "The Scientific Computer Center under Harry Renick provides computing support for the operations research side of the department."

The Scientific Computer Center also provides computing service for the company on a service bureau basis. Renick lists the Longview technical center, the Seattle research center, Centralia research center, the engineering department, the timberlands department and many of the branches among his corporate "customers."

The Operations Research Department is involved in projects in every operating division. The breadth of these projects gives some idea of the diversity of the new scientific management techniques. Decisions to which OR is being applied today within Weyerhaeuser include the following:

Wood allocation among products for maximum profit. Production and sales planning in plywood to carve out a better set of markets for Weyerhaeuser. Management of chip supply as a business—and to reduce our own cost of chips as a pulp raw material. Continuing analysis of both pulp and paperboard production and distribution to improve profits. And, economic determination of size and capacity of selected new company facilities to ensure that, if built, major new investments will produce long-term operating economies.

Aiding Managers

Operations research people are not production experts; they are scientists. Their value lies in their questioning attitudes and the ability to translate uncertain alternatives into expected differences in costs or profits. They bring the methods of the laboratory out into the world of manufacturing, production, profit and loss.

So, far from competing with managers or taking their place, operations research is most successful where the managers are the most capable.

The most valuable thing a manager has is his own judgment. Operations research frees managers of details so they can work at higher levels of judgment.

Hence, the payoff for operations research study can be very high indeed to Weyerhaeuser Company.

APPENDIX B

August 29, 1966

OPERATIONS RESEARCH
OR
DECISION SYSTEMS ANALYSIS

Description of department organization and functions

The *organization* consists of five sections:

Management Science–Operations Research Development
Corporate Decision Systems
Timberlands/Wood Products Decision Systems
Pulp Based Products Decision Systems
Scientific Computing Services

The *functions* of the department and of each section are

Department	To contribute to improved operating and planning decision processes throughout the firm by providing for widespread and useful application of the management sciences.
MS/OR Development Section	To continually identify, evaluate, and develop advanced MS/OR techniques for application within Weyerhaeuser.
Corporate Section	To lead development and participate in implementation of a family of interlocking decision systems for centralized planning and decentralized operation of the firm.
Group Application Sections	To develop and assist in the implementation of decision systems for assigned groups, ensuring compatibility with corporate requirements. To contribute to and improve the group's analysis capability.
Computing Section	To enable and support the productive use of computers for research and engineering purposes in the company.

QUESTIONS

1. If you were the president of a large company, such as Weyerhaeuser, and were thinking of establishing an Operations Research Department for the first time, how would you go about it?

2. If you were asked to update the 1966 charter (see Appendix B) for OR, what changes would you make, if any?

3. Was the objective of becoming the "decision systems architect" a realistic one in the mid-1960s? In the early 1970s? Why or why not?

4. How do you interpret the statement by the manager of OR that "log allocation models were used by the business, although *under great protest*"?

5. What is the significance of the various intraorganizational changes in the OR Department?

6. How did the role for OR in the company change over time?

7. If you were the manager of OR, what would be your recommendation concerning its role in the future? Why? If your suggestion was accepted, what would be your plan for implementing it?

CHAPTER 9

Network Analysis

Network analysis is a managerial technique which is useful in systems design, planning, and control. It is as old as scientific management and as new as the Polaris missile. Actually, the Gantt chart developed many years ago bears little resemblance to its modern, sophisticated counterpart even though both are based on the same model building and evaluation philosophy. Although there are many variations of the new generation of network analysis techniques which have been developed, the two basic and most common types are critical path method (CPM) and program evaluation and review technique (PERT).

The material in this chapter is intended to familiarize the reader with the network analysis technique as it relates to systems design, operation, and control. The following topics will be discussed:

> Network analysis
> A review of network techniques
> A PERT network
> PERT/Cost
> Application of network analysis
> Evaluation of network analysis

NETWORK ANALYSIS

A network may be defined as a system, with subsystems, where the various segments interconnect and interact at one or more points. The performance of a companywide system will depend upon how effectively each subsystem is operated *and* integrated into the activities of the whole.

Network analysis is a useful technique in systems design because it assists the analyst in recognizing and identifying the relationships which exist among the subsystems. First, each separate segment, or link, of the system is described in terms of other components or activities of the system. This makes explicit the total system and the interrelationships among the parts. The network may be illustrated by a flow chart or diagram. The flow of materials and/or information is measured in terms of volume, specifications, or time. The visual representation of the system achieves a comprehensive description and therefore outlines the task to be accomplished. This technique allows the manager to reappraise existing systems and identify examples of duplication and overlapping which may detract from the efficiency of the systems operation. Further, it helps management to evaluate the subsystems and their interconnecting networks continuously, consistent with the overall objectives of the system.

Regular reevaluation of the system is necessary and feasible through network analysis. Objectives of a system are modified; different outputs are specified, and different inputs are required. It is important that subsystems are adjusted to these changes and that the total system is revised accordingly. Network analysis fosters this type of approach by representing the system visually. It also allows an evaluation of the impact of various subsystem changes on other subsystems and/or the total system. A change in type of output or a change in scheduling in a particular subsystem can affect operations in other areas. The effect can be determined in units of time, money, facilities, or other resources.

Network analysis is a valuable technique because it encourages introspection of an existing system or provides the framework for visualizing the makeup of a proposed system. Predesign auditing may identify variations in performance which could occur. However, network analysis provides no guarantee of effective systems design. There is always the danger of assuming relationships among segments which do not exist, ignoring important relationships which should be considered, or weighing existing relationships improperly. Moreover, a system is dynamic, and every analysis needs to be monitored as the system continues to function, because the relationships among the segments may change.

The Computer and Network Analysis

Network analysis is a technique where the charting and computation can be accomplished by hand. Several ingenious manual methods applying the concept have been developed by industrial firms. These manual methods range from simple inspection of small networks to clerical routines for the determination of critical areas in networks ranging from fifty to several hundred events. If the number of steps to be performed in the project is extensive, however, the value of network analysis cannot be achieved without utilizing a computer. A programmed computer can maintain and update large numbers of networks accurately, rapidly, and efficiently. It also can simulate the impact of changes before they occur and alert management to potential critical situations.

How many activities are necessary to justify using a computer? There is no answer to this question because it will depend upon the complexity of the network, the likelihood that activities will exceed the time estimates, and the value of having current information available for the decision maker. Some writers have used 1,000 activities as a rough guide, while pointing out that a hand system may still be used in such instances.[1]

Developments in computer system technology may make network analysis even more effective. Recent innovations include a high-speed photographic process which produces a microfilm output, a mechanical graph plotting process to produce a network chart as computer output, and a console display unit which provides a picture of the network via a cathode-ray tube.

The network program can be contained in disk memory storage units in a central computer, while remote consoles and teletypes are located in strategic positions throughout the company. The remote terminal would include a small computer with a display panel containing the cathode-ray tube. Instructions could be communicated to the central computer to transfer any segment of the network to the remote computer for review and updating. While the network was pictured on the cathode tube, changes could be made in the network by using an electronic pen which could alter the values or change the relationship between various events and activities. The computer can digest these changes and display the new network on the tube.

There would be several advantages to this computer routine: (1) managers could receive network information at remote sta-

[1]Richard I. Levin and Charles A. Kirkpatrick, *Planning and Control with PERT/CPM*, McGraw-Hill Book Company, New York, 1966, p. 114.

tions instantly, (2) the information could be restricted to the particular area of interest, and (3) the program could be updated from remote stations as new inputs occurred. Obviously, a program would need to be large and very involved to justify this kind of computer application.

There are many forms of network analysis. Some are simple, and others are complex; some are generalized, and others have been designed for specific types of projects. Variations of the network analysis techniques are reviewed in the following paragraphs.

A REVIEW OF NETWORK TECHNIQUES

Critical path scheduling is common to all network techniques. Networks are developed to represent a total project and to identify the specific tasks necessary to complete the program requirements. One path of the sequential work flow (out of the many possible paths) has the longest lead time and is, therefore, critical to the completion of the project.

Critical Path Method

One example of critical-path scheduling has been called *critical path method,* a technique which has been used by construction management for planning, scheduling, estimating, and controlling engineering or construction projects. CPM was used by Du Pont in 1959 to schedule plant-maintenance shutdowns during changeovers. Subsequently, it was used to plan building construction and other large construction projects.

The key tool in this technique of planning, scheduling, and controlling complex construction jobs is a diagram using arrows to represent specific jobs (Figure 9–1). The diagram may be complex, as is evident from the example which illustrates the construction requirements for building one floor of a multistory building. Therefore, it requires a comprehensive illustration to show all the required relationships of the project.

The important contribution of a line diagram showing all the key events or activities is that it clarifies the relationships of every task to every other task—something that the bar chart cannot do. In this way it also can show which jobs on a project are critical, those which can affect the completion of the project.

The diagram is the model which illustrates the jobs to be performed to finish a project. The simplest form of diagram identifies

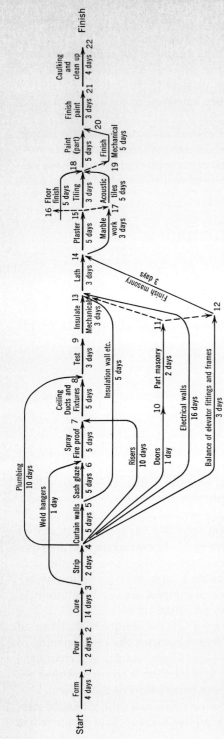

FIGURE 9–1. A CPM network to construct a building. (Source: "New Tool for Job Management," *Engineering News-Record*, Jan. 26, 1962, p. 26.)

the sequencing required; other additional requirements may involve timing and costs. Once these elements are specified, both the total time and total cost of the project can be determined by adding the different subelements.

In CPM the primary analytical emphasis is to determine the programming strategy which will satisfy schedule requirements at minimum cost.[2] Or, in other words, the approach is to reduce the time taken by the projects as much as costs will permit. The procedure is to analyze the network which depicts the task, listing the time each operation takes and its cost in labor and/or machine use. Since the objective is to reduce the time, the present time for each step is called the *maximum time.* It is assumed that a speedup could be accomplished only by additional outlays of labor or machines; therefore, the current costs are called the *minimum cost.*

Once again the analyst will trace through the paths of the diagram. In this instance the shortest time in which each job can be accomplished is estimated (minimum time) and what it would cost under this condition (maximum cost). With ranges of time and cost established, the critical path and the cost of reducing the time can be determined.

The consequence of various managerial decisions can be predicted by simulating their impact. It is obvious that total project time can be reduced only if the time required to perform the tasks on the critical path is reduced. It would be important to determine the cost involved in reducing the flow time in the critical path and whether additional efforts or resources are warranted.

The critical path method has been used in the construction industry with great success, and in other industries as well. Figure 9-2 illustrates how CPM can be used as an aid in the introduction of new products. The network shows that the product will be available in the warehouse twenty-one weeks after the process starts. It also describes the sequential relationship among the activities and the earliest and latest time that each activity can start.

Similar developments have taken place in still other industries, particularly in those areas relating to the planning, scheduling, and control of research and development activities. Here activities tend to be more intellectual and less physical (i.e., more engineering creation and less manufacturing), although the

[2]Arch R. Dooley, "Interpretations of PERT," *Harvard Business Review,* March—April 1964, p. 161.

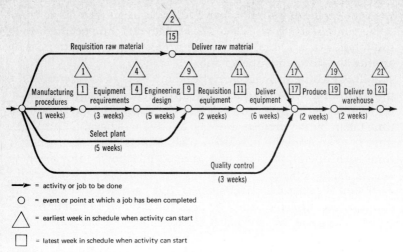

FIGURE 9-2. Portion of a critical-path diagram for the introduction of a new product. (Source: Warren Dusenbury, "CPM for New Product Introductions," *Harvard Business Review*, July–August 1967, p. 127.)

complexity of each tends to increase. Often the task is divided among several companies, which magnifies the problem of coordinating the total program. The network analysis technique developed particularly for these situations was called Program Evaluation and Review Technique.

Program Evaluation and Review Technique

Since planning and control are for all practical purposes inseparable activities, planning must be viewed as part of the research-development system. This is particularly true when the feedback control system reports that progress does not, or apparently will not, meet the requirements of the plan. When this occurs, replanning to meet objectives is necessary. In anything as complex as research and development, replanning must be reviewed thoroughly. In most cases, revised plans will provide alternative methods of schedule recovery, and here management decision should determine what feasible trades can be made between time, resources, and the performance specification.

To overcome the inherent disadvantages of existing management planning and control techniques, the Special Project Office of the Navy, charged with the responsibility for system management of the Polaris design and production program, developed—

in conjunction with the management consultant firm of Booz, Allen, and Hamilton and the Lockheed Aircraft Corporation— a new management planning and control technique. It was designed to determine and integrate all activity required to accomplish program objectives on time. This technique was defined as follows:

> PERT is a statistical technique—diagnostic and prognostic—for quantifying knowledge about the uncertainties faced in completing intellectual and physical activities essential for timely achievement of program deadlines. It is a technique for focusing management attention on danger signals that require remedial decisions, and on areas of effort for which trade-offs in time, resources, or technical performance might improve capability to meet major deadlines.[3]

The PERT technique is based on the concept that in any program there are three significant variables:

Time
Resources (personnel, facilities, funds)
Performance specifications

Any one of these may vary within certain limits established for each program while the other two are held constant. For example, holding time and performance constant, the requirements for resources may be determined. In its specific application to the Polaris program, the system held resources and performance specifications fixed while allowing the most critical element— time—to vary. However, time has a habit of becoming critical (reaching the maximum allowed by the customer), and at this point trades between resources or performance specifications are developed.

One facet of the PERT technique is that research and development work can be scheduled within a more or less predictable time frame. The procedure for accomplishing this is to break down a large complex research or development project into smaller, more easily accomplished subprojects. The second facet, that of scheduling and defining goals to be achieved and making the interrelationships and interdependencies of these goals explicit, will produce a gain in managerial control.

The PERT technique is based on critical-path scheduling. However, there is a fundamental difference between the two.

[3]Willard Fazar, "Progress Reporting in the Special Projects Office," *Navy Management Review*, April 1959, p. 2.

The PERT technique is applicable where there is no established system for doing the task and therefore no exact basis for estimating the required time to complete each task. Critical-path scheduling, on the other hand, usually is applied to jobs which are established or have been done before and where it is possible to predict performance accurately. Consequently, more sophisticated mathematical models must be used in the PERT technique.

Other Network Techniques

During the past few years the techniques of CPM and PERT have been refined, and other variations have been added. The first developments were concerned principally with a description of a total task, the relationships among various elements, and the cost of performing various segments of the operation. During the 1960s, many variations of CPM and PERT were developed which used features of "minimax" theory in determining the optimum way to complete the job.

One such variation of CPM and PERT is Least Cost Estimating and Scheduling (LESS) which resolves the problem at what time and how fast each and every job should be done so as to complete the project at a minimum cost or in a specified time. This particular technique has developed through three phases of increasing sophistication.

Another technique is called Production Analysis Control Technique (PACT)—"the basic concept is to forecast production slippages in ample time to take corrective action. It is designed as a decision-making tool to permit management to make the necessary decisions to keep deliveries on schedule, rather than as a diagnostic tool to aid in determining why schedules have slipped after the fact."[4]

SPECTRO is a computerized network-type management control system, using a milestone concept for control points. The system provides the normal information required by management for schedule planning, evaluation, cost, and control. In addition it provides the means for modifying plans and observing the results of this modification before implementation.[5]

SCANS is an acronym derived from Scheduling, Control,

---

[4]*Production and Analysis Control Technique,* Special Projects Office, Program Evaluation Branch, Department of the Navy, Washington, Feb. 8, 1961, p. 1.
[5]Thomas V. Sobczak, "A Look at Network Planning," *IRE Transactions,* September 1962, p. 115.

and Automation by Network System. The SCANS system was designed to provide a management control system which would integrate scheduling, costing, and manpower loading in a meaningful manner, one that provided for tradeoffs between functions.[6]

Resource Allocation and Multi-Project Scheduling (RAMPS) considers restrictions such as quantity of resources available, priorities, and "resource team" composition required for an individual task. Penalties for delayed completion, overtime labor, subcontracting, inefficient utilization rates, and related factors are incorporated in the procedure. Considering these restrictions and requirements, RAMPS seeks the schedule which satisfies various criteria including minimum cost.[7]

These examples of network techniques are typical of many approaches which have been used in military and industrial applications. It is safe to say that most examples are basically the same and only the acronyms differ. Inasmuch as the PERT technique was one of the first, and also the most widely accepted, we will use it to illustrate networking.

A PERT NETWORK

The Pert network is the working model of the technique. It illustrates, by diagram, the sequential relationships among the tasks which must be completed to accomplish the project. PERT treats planning and scheduling separately. First the plan is developed, and then the limitations are added to the problem.

Gathering Preliminary Data

The first step in developing the PERT network is to gather a list of all the activities needed to complete the project. The people associated with the project activities have the best knowledge about the detailed tasks which need to be performed. Other activities will be added to this list as the total task is defined more comprehensively and the entire network develops. The activities listed should include every factor pertinent to the completion of the project. For example, customer approval and available resources would be considered and listed.

[6]B. L. Fry, "SCANS-System Description and Comparison with PERT," *IRE Transactions,* September 1962, pp. 122–129.
[7]*Resource Allocation and Multi-Project Scheduling,* C-E-I-R Inc., Arlington, Va., December 1961, p. 1.

Mechanics of Network Building

Next, the network is constructed to show the sequential relationships among the activities. There are two elements shown on the network diagrams: activities and events.

Activities are defined as the time-consuming effort which is required to complete a specific segment of the total project. For example, activities might include the preparation of engineering drawings, the production of a specific forging, or the testing of the finished product. The activities in the graphic illustration of the network are shown as a solid line, with an arrow to depict the direction of sequential activities ($\longrightarrow$).

All activities begin and end with an *event*. This is a "milestone" which indicates the completion of a distinct portion of a program and the signal for dependent succeeding activities to begin. An event is illustrated in the network as a circle, square, or other convenient geometric figure. Descriptions and symbols are written in the circle to identify each event.

Figure 9–3 is an example of a simplified PERT network. Each event is numbered for the purpose of identification. Thus activity 1/2 is the activity which takes place between events numbered 1 and 2. It is possible to start the diagram from the completion of the project and work backward, or from the beginning and work toward completion.

The length of the arrow (the activity) is not indicative of the time it takes to complete the activity or to get from one event to the next. However, it does represent the logical sequence of activities and events. It illustrates, for example, which activities must be completed prior to the start of a particular activity, which activities can be worked in parallel, and which activities cannot start until a previous activity is completed. In Figure 9–3,

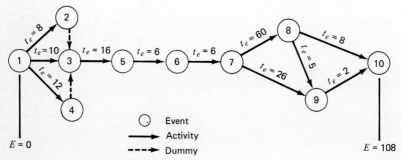

FIGURE 9–3. Network example.

activities 1/2, 1/3, and 1/4 must be completed before activity 3/5 can begin. Event 7 signifies the completion of activity 6/7 and the starting point for the remaining activities.

Dummy Constraints

A *dummy* constraint is a "dashed" arrow (— — — —→) in the network which shows a relationship but does not require a time-consuming activity. The principal use for this symbol occurs when two separate activities both begin and end with the same event. In this instance the numbering system would not distinguish between the two events. In Figure 9–3, activities 1/2, 1/3, and 1/4 all begin at 1 and end at event 3. However, dummy events 2 and 4 are added and the relation between these two and event 3 indicates zero time. Now it is possible to keep the three activities separate in graphing and in the computations.

Developing the Critical Path

Once the flow network has been determined for the system, the next step is to obtain an estimate of the elapsed time required to accomplish each activity from the individual responsible for accomplishment of that element of work. This time forecast consists of three individual estimates:

> The most likely estimate (m)
> The optimistic estimate (a)
> The pessimistic estimate (b)

The difference in these time estimates provides a measure of the relative uncertainty involved in accomplishing the activity in question, as shown in Figure 9–4. From these estimates the *expected time* t_e for each *activity* may be computed by applying appropriate statistical techniques developed for this purpose, as shown in Figure 9–5. The expected time is the average, or mean, time for the activity and may or may not be the most probable time (the estimator's most likely forecast). This discrepancy arises when the differences between the most likely estimate, the optimistic estimate, and the pessimistic estimate are not equal, thus tending to some degree to discredit the probability of the most likely estimate. The estimates (as well as the definitions of the events and activities) are outputs of the PERT planning technique, which have been based on a stipulated input of resources for the processing system. The estimate may change, however, if

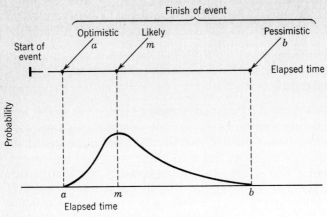

FIGURE 9–4. Estimating the time distribution.

there is a change in resource allocation and/or a change in the task or product specifications.

The flow network, with its coded events, can be programmed for a computer. The elapsed-time estimates can likewise be used as input to the computer processing. The computer solves the mathe-

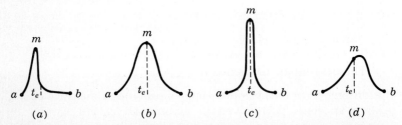

Problem: Given three estimates of elapsed time, find t_e, the expected value (mean) and σ_{te}^2 (variance) of distribution when distribution form varies as shown above

a–Optimistic estimate of interval
m–Most likely time of interval $\Big\}$ Obtained for each interval
b–Pessimistic estimate of interval

Solution: An estimating equation was developed which gives estimate of mean and variance for range of distributions to be encountered

$$t_e = \left[\frac{a + 4m + b}{6} \right]$$

Apply to each interval

$$\sigma_{te}^2 = \left(\frac{b - a}{6} \right)^2$$

FIGURE 9–5. Determining "expected" value and variance of time intervals.

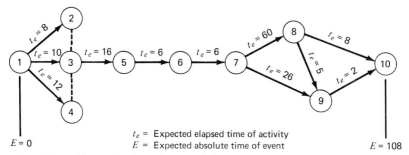

FIGURE 9-6. Determination of expected time.

matical problems (calculation of each t_e) and, by adding the calculated expected times for each activity, computes the expected time for each event E, as illustrated in Figure 9-6. Next, the computer identifies those events which determine the longest sequence to meet the end objective—the critical path. Those events not on the critical path must therefore have some *slack* in their timing. Slack is computed by determining the latest time E_L that an event can take place without affecting the events on the critical path $E_x - t_e$, and then subtracting that from an event E not on the critical path ($E_L - E =$ slack). This relationship is illustrated graphically in Figure 9-7. In some instances resources can be reallocated from the slack areas to the critical path.

One of the most useful outputs of this system (for management) is the determination of the possibility of meeting critical schedule dates. These schedule dates, determined or stipulated

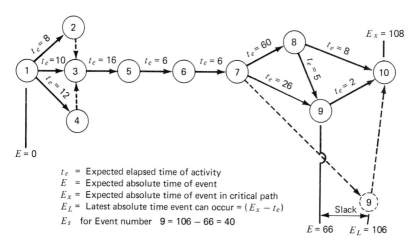

FIGURE 9-7. Determination of slack.

by the customer, usually represent contractual commitments and therefore will, at times, necessitate "trades" between resources and performance specifications, as previously described.

To illustrate the networking process let us assume that a community action group has decided to build a new hospital. A team of planners develops the following list of activities necessary to complete the project:

1/2	Preliminary financing plans
1/3	Preliminary building plans
1/4	Location analysis
3/5	Detailed building plans
5/6	Securing bids
6/7	Review of bids and detailed financing
7/8	Construction
7/9	Selection of staff
8/9	Outfitting the building
8/10	Landscapping
9/10	Orientation of staff

The time needed to complete each activity, t_e is indicated in Figures 9–6 and 9–7. For example, it is estimated that six weeks will be required to secure bids (activity 5/6). The critical path for the project follows the sequence of activities 1/4/3/5/6/7/8/10 and the expected time E_x is 108 weeks. If 108 weeks is not acceptable, the managers would review the program to see what changes could be made. First, each activity on the critical path would be subject to special scrutiny. Next, the slack time for those activities not on the critical path would be considered. Perhaps some transfer of resources would be appropriate, for example, from activity 9/10 where the starting time could be delayed 40 weeks without increasing the total time for the project. Management would have to consider all possibilities, including the addition of more resources from the outside.

PERT/COST

PERT/Cost is a more recent development of the original PERT concept and includes the cost variable as well as time. When resources can be transferred from paths where there is slack to the critical path without adding cost, the decision is relatively simple. Unfortunately, additional costs usually are incurred by adding or redirecting resources to reduce time requirements.

The first step in this analysis is to determine costs. There are different approaches to developing the cost extimates: (1) a single cost estimate of expected actual cost, (2) three cost estimates combined by a formula into expected costs, (3) optimum time-cost curves (used in construction industries and by NASA/DOD Resource Allocation Procedure Supplement), and (4) three separate cost estimates (used in NASA/DOD Time Cost Option Procedure Supplement).[8]

The first method of costing is to make the best estimate of actual costs by a summation of the elements of manpower, material, and other resources necessary to complete the task. Indirect costs then are proportioned to this activity to complete the total cost package.

The second method combines three cost estimates in a manner similar to the three time estimates made in PERT/Time. This adds the element of probability and, assuming that three reasonable predictions can be made, improves the possibility of forecasting the expected cost.

The third approach is the optimum time-cost curve concept. The theory is that a direct relationship exists between time and costs for any activity, and that this relationship can be expressed as a continuous curve. The curve illustrates the relationship of time-cost tradeoffs that might be made. A variation of this method has been to use but two time-cost relationships, that is, for two conditions, normal or crash time. The analyst would determine the cost to complete the task in the minimum possible (crash) time in comparison to the cost for normal time.

The fourth approach provides three possible time-cost-risk combinations from a range of alternatives. The three combinations are called the "most efficient," "direct date," and "shortest time" plans, and are rated respectively as low-, medium-, and high-risk alternatives for accomplishing the project. Managers can evaluate the effect of the three estimates on costs. The selection of the plan to use will depend on the relative weights given to cost, time, and risk for the particular project in question.[9]

The value of PERT/Cost will occur only when actual cost information is reported in time to initiate effective control. When this system can be used with a computer the variations of actual costs from predicted costs can be noted promptly and reported for effective management action.

[8]Don T. DeCoster, "PERT/Cost—The Challenge," *Management Services,* May–June 1964, p. 16.
[9]*DOD and NASA Guide: Pert/Cost,* Office of the Secretary of Defense and National Aeronautics and Space Administration, June 1962, pp. 109–113.

There have been many problems associated with applying PERT/Cost. For example, most companies cannot estimate their costs precisely, the accounting systems are not compatible with the procedure, and personnel and machine capabilities are not available.[10] There is a need for more sophistication in applying these techniques rather than any refinement in the techniques themselves.

APPLICATION OF NETWORK ANALYSIS

Since the development of network analysis there has been an explosive growth in the literature on the subject in the form of articles, studies, reports, speeches, scholarly papers, comments, letters, glossaries, and manuals. By 1963 a bibliography by the U.S. Air Force PERT Orientation and Training Center cited 702 works in the field.[11] Most of the early applications were in the defense and space industry. In 1962, the technique became a requirement for all companies working on research contracts for the Department of Defense or the National Aeronautics and Space Administration. By 1965, a similar requirement was added to many of the production contracts.

The growing interest in PERT and similar techniques has not been limited to defense contractors. Whereas 81 percent of PERT's applications were in government work in 1959, by the end of 1963 50 percent of its uses were strictly commercial, with research and development, construction, and new products planning the three areas where the technique was used most often.[12]

In 1965 Schoderbek published the results of a study he made to determine how many companies were using PERT and CPM, the type of projects where it was used, the characteristics of users and nonusers, and the criteria employed in the decision to use or not to use.[13] Two hundred companies were selected randomly from *Fortune's Directory* of the 500 largest industrial concerns in the United States—returns were received from 186 of the companies. Forty-four percent of the respondents replied that they were using PERT/CPM, and 15 percent indicated that they would be using it within two years.

[10]DeCoster, op. cit., p. 18.

[11]*Bibliography: PERT and other Management Systems and Techniques,* U.S. Air Force, PERT Orientation and Training Center, Bolling Air Force Base, Washington, June 1963.

[12]Steve Blickstein, "How to Put PERT into Marketing," *Printer's Ink,* Oct. 23, 1964, p. 27.

[13]Peter P. Schoderbek, "A Study of the Application of PERT," *Academy of Management Journal,* September 1965, pp. 199–210.

The use of PERT/CPM was found to be correlated to the size of company expressed in terms of total sales, with the larger companies being more consistent users. One of the surprising results of the survey was the number of nondefense projects where network analysis was used; 62 percent of the users were applying it to nondefense projects exclusively.

Recently, many more organizations have made use of CPM. Minnesota Mining and Manufacturing, National Cash Register, Lever Bros., and Diamond Shamrock are using the technique to help in the merchandising of new products. Burlington Northern and Honeywell made use of it in planning a merger; Connecticut Bank & Trust, Hartford, and General Electric found CPM useful in connection with management information systems; International Telephone & Telegraph adopted the technique to train project managers; and Hynes & Diamond, a New York City law firm, uses it to trace the most important elements of the contract suits it handles for corporations.[14]

The application of network analysis has occurred in almost every facet of business and government. The PERT technique has been used in planning and developing internal and external audits in accounting; in integrating and coordinating month- and year-end closing of the ledgers; in planning and implementing revisions of accounting systems, such as standard costs; in preparing the annual report for stockholders, bankers, and governmental agencies; and in planning and controlling the budgetary process.

In finance, network analysis has been used for organizing and determining a priority for the acquisition of capital equipment and the timing of the purchase; in preparing and paying dividends; and in timing and placing new stock and bond issues.

General management applications of this technique have been in the installation and conversion to computer systems; for scheduling unusual operations; for closing down or moving an operation or plant; for installing and integrating a new organizational structure; for long-range planning of management succession; for timing and coordinating a merger; for revising or installing a management reporting system; and for starting up standby facilities.

In the marketing field, PERT has been used in planning advertising media and then in measuring its effectiveness; in implementing sales promotion campaigns; in measuring the ef-

[14]George J. Berkwitt, "Management Rediscovers CPM," *Dun's Review*, May 1971, pp. 57–59.

fectiveness of marketing channels; in entering new marketing areas; in introducing a new product; in realigning sales territory; and in planning special promotions, conventions, and sales meetings.

Applications in production have been in scheduling product tests; planning production and materials flow; planning and implementing maintenance programs; installing major capital equipment; and studying the production process.

Purchasing applications have been used to prepare bills and proposals for materials and parts, and for timing acquisitions or material.

In the transportation field, PERT has been used for coordinating and timing shipment of goods with demand dates, and for measuring the effectiveness of methods for transportation.

The government has planned, coordinated, controlled, and developed weapons systems, defense procedures and contracts; and planned urban renewal projects. Many countries, including the Soviet Union, have made extensive use of network analysis in their planning.

In a study on the possible application of PERT to the field of education, the researchers concluded that the technique could be applied in almost any project where sequential planning was required. The criteria suggested included: Does a specified end objective exist, the accomplishment of which can be determined? Must some schedule date or deadline be met? Is it a complex project? Is there a degree of uncertainty about some or all of the program elements?[15]

There is undoubtedly some relation between the complexity of the project and the advantage of using the latest forms of network analysis. It may follow, therefore, that the technique will gain even wider acceptance as more organizations engage in projects of increasing complexity.

EVALUATION OF NETWORK ANALYSIS

PERT, or any other type of network analysis, is useful in the analysis and design of systems. First, the technique can serve as an effective tool in analyzing the job to be accomplished and therefore provide insights into the resources needed to do the job (system design); second, PERT can serve as an approach for input al-

[15]Desmond L. Cook, *Program Evaluation and Review Technique-Application in Education,* Office of Education, U.S. Department of Health, Education, and Welfare, U.S. Government Printing Office, Washington, 1966, pp. 69–70.

location in the operating system. Finally, it provides a framework and common language for controlling the system.

The PERT system proved to be an excellent communications medium in the Polaris program, not only between the Navy and its contractors, but also within the various contractor organizations. This was accomplished by basic adherence to communication theory; and also to organization, planning, and control theory. The specific facets of the PERT technique responsible for this success may be summarized as follows:

1. The flow network defines all activity to be accomplished. As the network is outlined and each activity is identified and planned, a distinct area of personal responsibility can be described. Thus unassigned areas, or areas of doubtful responsibility, can be identified and resolved as the network is developed.

2. Similarly, problems of coordination among organizations or operating elements within a large organization are quickly identified and resolved during the development of the flow network.

3. The development and biweekly revision of the time estimates for the activities in the PERT network, and the resultant computer outputs, serve as an excellent medium for providing progress information to all organizations and levels of management. Therefore the systems managers continually are notified of any problems which may be developing and are able to activate corrective input.

4. The flow networks, time estimates, and computer outputs serve as continuous stimuli for the program personnel to coordinate their efforts with other affected groups.

In any organization the operating effectiveness of the system depends on the performance of people. The traits or characteristics of human behavior can influence the accuracy and thus affect the operational adequacy of the system. The PERT technique tends to minimize the effects of such behavior. For example, a worker may want to "pad" his work estimates. If PERT is used, he knows that his activity may appear on the critical path, and therefore under the closest scrutiny of management. If he underestimates the time required for the job, he may need additional personnel—again involving management review. Moreover, the fact that he must give optimistic and pessimistic estimates as well as his most likely estimate tends to make his forecast more accurate. Further, with the system in operation and new time estimates being made every two weeks, management will soon discover repetitive overestimates of time required and may, without the knowledge of the individual, apply an "experience" factor to his future estimates. All these "checks and balances," when known throughout the organization, tend to encourage more realistic estimates.

We have discussed the importance of employee participation in planning. Usually those workers involved in creating the plan will make an extra effort to carry it through, since the importance of fulfilling the commitment seems to be a reflection of professional pride and competence. Management has a yardstick to measure the performance of this system—an extremely valuable feature of this technique.

A significant benefit of network planning pertains to the added degree of control it achieves by providing a clearer understanding of the project as a whole and the relationship among the elements.[16]

In spite of the numerous successful applications of these latest network techniques, there are some limitations and problem areas. Schoderbek found the chief problem was lack of motivation. There seemed to be a reluctance among personnel to change to the new system and, likewise, little desire on the part of management to become involved.[17]

Many executives and supervisors have been trained to use static techniques for planning and controlling operations, and have been somewhat successful in using them. A PERT application cuts across traditional functional lines, which may explain some of the reluctance of managers to become involved in its use. We can see from this that PERT "brings in complexities in the practical usefulness of the system that go far beyond the simple pattern of the technique itself."[18]

CPM and PERT cut across traditional lines, and in many organizations no single department will be responsible for correcting problems of scheduling or in identifying costs which are out of line. Therefore, it is essential that network analysis has

---

[16]I. R. Holden and P. K. McIlroy, *Network Planning in Management Control Systems,* Hutchinson Educational Ltd., London, 1970, p. 107.
[17]Schoderbek, op. cit., p. 203.
[18]J. W. Pocock, "PERT as an Analytical Aid for Program Planning—Its Payoff and Problems," *Operations Research,* November-December, 1962, p. 901.

the support of top management if it is to be an effective integration technique.[19]

One common objection to PERT is the cost. The system requires more detailed planning than conventional methods, and the need for a higher degree of skill necessitates the training of personnel in its application. For larger projects, electronic data processing also adds substantial cost. However, if network analysis contributes to the effectiveness and efficiency of the system, the additional cost may be justified. When the technique is used appropriately, it can be a valuable aid in system design, planning, and control.

SUMMARY

Network analysis is a useful managerial technique which can be used to predict or identify the performance of any subsystem for the purpose of design, coordination, and/or control. Each separate segment, or link, of the system is described in relation to other components or activities of the system. A visual representation outlines the task to be accomplished in terms of the resources allocated to do the job.

There are many forms of network analysis: some are simple, and others are complex; some are generalized, while others have been designed for specific types of projects. In general, critical-path scheduling can be considered a basic concept under which specific techniques may be classified.

One popular technique of network analysis is called PERT (program evaluation and review technique). It was created to be used when there is no established system for doing the task, and therefore no exact basis for estimating the required time to complete each task. This technique of management planning and control provides industry with capabilities for program planning, evaluation, and control; program-status evaluation; and simulation techniques for decision-making assistance. The advantages of PERT techniques (which in themselves reflect a systems approach) in the management of complex research and development activities may be summarized as follows:

The sequence and relationship network of all significant

---

[19]Jerome D. Wiest and Ferdinand K. Levy, *A Management Guide to PERT/CPM*, Prentice-Hall, Inc., Englewood Cliffs, N.J., 1969, p. 133.

events in planning how the end objective will be achieved is identified.

The relative uncertainty in meeting or accomplishing all activities in the plan is measured and identified.

The relatively critical condition in areas of effort required to management.

Also, slack areas are shown where some delay will not preclude the meeting of end objectives on time.

The current probability of meeting scheduled dates is provided for management.

A second generation of network analysis techniques has been developed, e.g., PERT/Cost, which go one step further by identifying the alternative trade-off decisions in terms of cost as well as time. When the system to be described is complex, the use of computers is almost a necessity.

PERT has been adopted by companies in defense industries; in fact, its use is required in many government contracts. Network analysis also has proved to be a valuable technique in commercial applications.

QUESTIONS

1. Relate network analysis to the systems approach.
2. Compare and contrast the various acronyms which pertain to network planning and analysis.
3. Define an activity, event, and dummy constraint.
4. What general rules apply to plotting the network?
5. Is it better to make three estimates of activity time? Under what circumstances would your answer be different?
6. How are costs related to network analysis?
7. What advantages of network analysis occur to you? What problems?
8. What situations would be most applicable to this technique?
9. Do you believe this technique will gain wider acceptance in the future? Why or why not?
10. If times of nine weeks for activity 1/4 and sixteen weeks for 7/8 are substituted in Figure 9–6, how would this change E_x for the project?
11. Using the following information plot a network, determine the critical path, and compute E_S for E (11) and for 1–2–4–9–12–13.

Activity	Activity Time, t_e
1–2	5
1–3	8
2–4	6
2–5	4

Activity	*Activity Time, t_e*
2–6	4
3–7	5
3–8	3
4–9	1
5–9	3
6–10	5
7–10	4
8–11	9
9–12	2
10–12	4
11–13	1
12–13	7

PETERSEN GENERAL CONTRACTORS*

Petersen General Contractors was an established construction company doing work in several states in New England. Petersen generally handled small- to medium-sized commercial and industrial construction projects. Some recent projects which the company had completed were a 20,000-square-foot factory building, a four-story office building, and a water filtration plant.

The company was now in the process of preparing a bid for a television station for the erection of a 225-foot-high television antenna tower and the construction of a building adjacent to the tower which would be used to house transmission and electrical equipment. Petersen was bidding only on the tower and its electrical equipment, the building, the connecting cable between tower and building, and site preparation. Transmission equipment and other equipment to be housed in the building were not to be included in the bid and would be obtained separately by the television station. The site for the tower was at the top of a hill to minimize the required height of the tower, with the building to be constructed at a slightly lower elevation than the base of the tower and near a main road. Between the tower and building was to be a crushed gravel service road and an underground cable. Adjacent to the building a fuel tank was to be installed above ground on a concrete slab. A sketch of the tower and building site is shown in Exhibit 9–1.

Prior to preparing the detailed cost estimates, Petersen's estimator met with the company's general foreman to go over the plans and blueprints for the job. In addition to preparing a cost estimate, the estimator was also preparing an estimate of the time it would take to complete

*Source: Albert N. Schrieber, Richard A. Johnson, Robert C. Meier, William T. Newell, and Henry C. Fischer, *Cases in Manufacturing Management,* McGraw-Hill Book Company, New York, 1965, pp. 262–268.

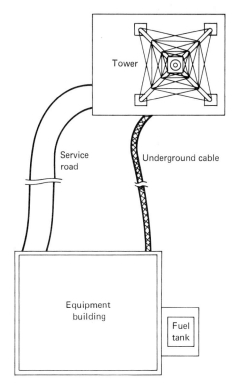

Exhibit 9-1. Television tower and building site plan (not to scale).

the job. The television station management was very concerned about the time factor and it had requested that bids be prepared on the basis of the normal time and cost for completing the job, and also for the fastest time for completing the job and the additional cost that this would entail. The result of the conference between the estimator and general foreman was to determine that the activities shown in Exhibit 9-2 would be necessary to complete the job. It was agreed that the estimator would prepare time and cost estimates for these activities.

In addition to determining the list of activities, the estimator and foreman discussed in some detail how these activities could be sequenced since the list of activities in Exhibit 9-2 did not necessarily indicate the order in which the work could be performed. In the course of the discussion, the estimator made the following notes:

Survey work and procurement of the structural steel and electrical equipment for the tower can start as soon as contract is signed.

Grading of tower and building sites can begin when survey is completed.

After tower site is graded, footings and anchors can be poured.

After building site is graded and basement excavated, building footings can be poured.

EXHIBIT 9–2. **List of Activities for Construction of Television Tower and Building**

a   Sign contract and complete subcontractor negotiations
b   Survey site
c   Grade building site and excavate for basement
d   Grade tower site
e   Procure structural steel and buys for tower

f   Procure electrical equipment for tower and connecting underground cable
g   Pour concrete for tower footings and anchors
h   Erect tower and install electrical equipment
i   Install connecting cable in tower site
j   Install drain tile and storm drain in tower site

k   Backfill and grade tower site
l   Pour building footings
m   Pour basement slab and fuel tank slab
n   Pour outside basement walls
o   Pour walls for basement rooms

p   Pour concrete floor beams
q   Pour main floor slab and lay concrete block walls
r   Pour roof slab
s   Complete interior framing and utilities
t   Lay roofing
u   Paint building interior, install fixtures, and clean up
v   Install main cable between tower site and building
w   Install fuel tank
x   Install building septic tank
y   Install drain tile and storm drain in building site

z   Backfill around building, grade, and surface with crushed rock
aa   Lay base for connecting road between tower and building
bb   Complete grading and surface connecting road
cc   Clean up tower site
dd   Clean up building site

ee   Obtain job acceptance

Septic tank can be installed when grading and excavating of building site is done.

Construction of connecting road can start as soon as survey is completed.

Exterior and interior basement walls can be poured as soon as footings are in.

Basement floor and fuel tank slab should go in after basement walls.

Floor beams can go in after the basement walls and basement floor.

Main floor slab and concrete block walls go in after floor beams.

EXHIBIT 9-3. Television Tower and Building Construction Time and Cost Estimate

Activ-ity code	Activity	Normal time		Fastest time	
		Days*	Cost†	Days*	Cost†
a	Sign contract and complete subcontractor negotiations	5		5	
b	Survey site	6	$ 1,240	4	$ 1,560
c	Grade building site and excavate for basement	8	1,300	6	1,830
d	Grade tower site	30	6,350	21	8,990
e	Procure structural steel and guys for tower	85	‡	85	‡
f	Procure electrical equipment for tower and connecting under-ground cable	120	‡	120	‡
g	Pour concrete for tower footings and anchors	42	8,310	25	11,670
h	Erect tower and install electrical equipment	38	11,350	25	15,620
i	Install connecting cable in tower site	8	1,740	4	1,950
j	Install drain tile and storm drain in tower site	35	3,600	18	5,100
k	Backfill and grade tower site	8	930	4	1,450
l	Pour building footings	29	3,030	21	4,100
m	Pour basement slab and fuel tank slab	14	1,050	11	1,540
n	Pour outside basement walls	34	2,550	30	2,810
o	Pour walls for basement rooms	9	800	7	960
p	Pour concrete floor beams	11	980	10	1,110
q	Pour main floor slab and lay concrete block walls	12	1,860	10	2,240
r	Pour roof slab	15	1,740	13	1,960
s	Complete interior framing and utilities	42	9,750	30	11,800
t	Lay roofing	3	270	2	340
u	Paint building interior, install fixtures, and clean up	19	920	13	1,350
v	Install main cable between tower site and building	35	4,360	25	4,540
w	Install fuel tank	3	180	2	220
x	Install building septic tank	12	630	8	750
y	Install drain tile and storm drain in building site	15	530	10	830
z	Backfill around building, grade, and surface with crushed rock	9	680	7	850

EXHIBIT 9–3. Television Tower and Building Construction Time and Cost Estimate (*cont'd*)

Activity code	Activity	Normal time		Fastest time	
		Days*	Cost†	Days*	Cost†
aa	Lay base for connecting road between tower and building	15	2,560	13	2,970
bb	Complete grading and surface connecting road	8	1,600	5	2,340
cc	Clean up tower site	5	240	3	500
dd	Clean up building site	3	210	2	400
ee	Obtain job acceptance	5		5	

*Days shown are working days only.
†Costs are for direct labor and rental of equipment only.
‡Cost included in Exhibit 9–4.

Roof slab can go on after block walls are up.

Interior can be completed as soon as roof slab is on.

Put in fuel tank any time after slab is in.

Drain tile and storm drain for building go in after septic tank.

As soon as tower footings and anchors are in and tower steel and equipment are available, tower can be erected.

Connecting cable in tower site, drain tile, and storm drain can be put in as soon as tower is up.

Main cable between building and tower goes in after connecting cable at tower site is in and basement walls are up.

Tower site can be backfilled and graded as soon as storm drain, connecting cable, and main cable are in.

Clean up tower site after backfilling and grading is done.

Backfill around building and grade after main cable is in and after storm drain is in.

Clean up building site after backfilling and grading is done.

Following his meeting with the general foreman, the estimator

EXHIBIT 9–4. Estimated Cost of Materials and Equipment

Item	Cost
Structural steel and guys for tower	$23,600
Tower electrical equipment and connecting cable	7,260
Sand, gravel, crushed rock, and cement	5,110
Lumber and millwork	6,400
Drain tile and sewer pipe	3,600
Septic tank, plumbing fixtures, fuel tank, and other hardware	3,300
Other miscellaneous materials	3,320

prepared cost estimates and time estimates for completing the various portions of the job (shown in Exhibit 9-2). Estimates for both the normal time in which the work could be completed and the fastest possible time along with the corresponding costs were made as shown in Exhibit 9-3. The cost figures in Exhibit 9-3 are for the direct labor and equipment use costs only. Estimated costs of direct materials used in construction and purchased equipment to be installed in the tower are shown in Exhibit 9-4. Company experience had shown that for this kind of job indirect labor and other overhead costs could be expected to amount to 65 percent of the direct labor and equipment use cost. The company also customarily allowed 15 percent of the total estimated cost for contingencies. Using this information, the estimator prepared analyses for the job: one for the cost of doing the work at normal rate and one for the cost of doing the job in the shortest possible period of time.

QUESTIONS

1. Working at a normal rate, in how many days can the job be completed? What should the bid be on this basis if Petersen attempted to obtain a profit of 10 percent before federal income taxes?
2. What is the shortest possible time in which the job can be completed? What should the bid be on this basis if Petersen attempted to obtain a profit of 10 percent before federal income taxes?
3. If the job is obtained and the work is to be completed working at a normal rate, what portions of the work should be supervised most carefully to ensure that the job is completed on time? What portions of the work should be supervised most carefully if the contract is let on the basis of completing the job in the shortest possible time?
4. If you were the television station management and felt that the estimated time for completing the job in the shortest possible period of time was still too long, what would you do?
5. What effect would the amount of other work for which Petersen had received contracts have on the bid price for this contract?

CHAPTER 10

Behavioral Aspects of Systems Design

Throughout this book we have considered organizations as man-made sociotechnical systems. This chapter is devoted to a discussion of the behavioral aspects of systems design. A society which places high value on individual freedoms and is geared primarily to the satisfaction of human needs should give adequate recognition to the psychosocial impact of the systems approach.

Application of systems concepts in the design of organizations has a major impact upon participants—blue collar and clerical workers, managers, professionals, and staff specialists. If the concepts of systems design outlined in the foregoing chapters are to be applied for greater organizational effectiveness and efficiency as well as social benefit, recognition should be given to the needs, motivations, and aspirations of all these people. The following topics will be considered:

The behavioral sciences
The human need for systematic relationships
The need for systems change
Behavioral consequences of system changes
Open-systems concept as a basis of human integration
Meeting the human and social problems

THE BEHAVIORAL SCIENCES

The behavioral sciences provide important input for the study of the social factors of systems design. In their study of organizations the behavioral scientists emphasize the psychosocial system with primary consideration for the human participants. The behavioral sciences are relatively recent academic and intellectual disciplines. Much of the work in psychology, sociology, and anthropology is a product of this century, particularly the empirical research. They have provided new insights into human behavior over the whole spectrum of man's activities. Obviously, in this chapter we cannot consider the whole body of knowledge developed in the behavioral sciences. Therefore we will concentrate on those areas which are pertinent to the design of sociotechnical systems.

The behavioral science approach is different from either the quantitative sciences which emphasize economic-technical rationality or the humanities which emphasize human values. As Churchman says:

> There is another kind of scientist who tries to bridge between the economic-feasible approach to the change of systems and the humanist demand for the representation of "real" human values. This is the "behavioral scientist," a man dedicated to investigating what the human being is like in terms of his behavior. This scientist is less interested in model building than he is in the empirical determination of what human beings do and how they make up their minds. It is his belief that the empirical investigation of human behavior will eventually lead to a sound understanding of the nature of the human being and his societies.[1]

To be classified as a behavioral science, a field of study must satisfy at least two basic criteria: (1) it must deal with human behavior and (2) it must use a "scientific" approach. "The scientific aim is to establish generalizations about human behavior that are supported by empirical evidence collected in an impersonal and objective way. . . . The ultimate end is to understand, explain, and predict human behavior in the same sense in which scientists understand, explain, and predict the behavior of physical forces or biological factors or, closer to home, the behavior of goods and prices in the economic market."[2]

---

[1]C. West Churchman, *The Systems Approach,* Dell Publishing Co., Inc., New York, 1968, p. 197.
[2]Bernard Berelson (ed.), *The Behavioral Sciences Today,* Basic Books, Inc., Publishers, New York, 1963, p. 3.

Our discussion of the behavioral aspects of systems design will rely heavily upon the theoretical concepts and research findings of the behavioral sciences. Over the past several decades these fields have contributed significantly to the better understanding of man and his social organizations.[3] Their inputs are vital for designing more effective and efficient sociotechnical systems which also contribute to the satisfaction of human participants.

The Psychosocial System

In Chapter 2 we suggested that the organization can be viewed as composed of several major subsystems: (1) goals and values, (2) technical, (3) structural, (4) psychosocial, and (5) managerial. Individuals in social relationships constitute the psychosocial system in organizations. This system involves many variables including individual behavior and motivation, status and role relationships, group dynamics, and leadership processes. The psychosocial system is affected by changes in goals, technology, and the structure of the organization. For example, the introduction of an automated information system based upon computer technology can have a profound effect upon the people and their social relationships in the organization.

All decisions concerning the design and redesign of systems can have an important impact upon the psychosocial system. This fact should be understood and responded to by the manager. He cannot think of systems design as a purely mechanistic process. One of the manager's most difficult functions is to design effective and efficient sociotechnical systems which integrate the technology and structural requirements with the psychosocial system. The systems approach provides the primary means for achieving this integration between organizational subsystems. As De-Greene says:

> The systems method provides a means for the orderly, integrated, and timely development of systems. Where people are involved, careful consideration must be given to human capabilities and limitations. *When these guidelines are not followed, penalties must be paid in terms of increased costs, decreased performance, slipped schedules, accidents, and loss of life. . . .* When a systems ap-

[3]For an interesting overview of the applications of behavioral sciences in industrial organizations see Harold M. F. Rush, *Behavioral Science: Concepts and Managerial Applications,* Personnel Policy Study No. 216, National Industrial Conference Board, Inc., New York, 1969.

proach incorporating psychological factors is *not* followed in design and management, literally *terrible* things can result at worst, frustrating and costly things at best.[4]

We could discuss many behavioral factors which are important in systems design, such as human physiological and psychological capabilities and limitations; perception, cognition, and learning; formation of values and attitudes; intelligence and decision-making capabilities; group processes; and status and role relationships. Obviously we cannot cover all these aspects and will therefore concentrate on two key elements in the psychosocial system, the motivation of participants and leadership processes.

Motivational Factors in Systems Design

The study of human motivation is concerned with the question of "why do people behave as they do?" In the design of effective sociotechnical systems the manager should be concerned with human performance and those underlying forces which affect behavior. A *motive* is what prompts a person to act in a certain way or at least develop a propensity for specific behavior.

The area of human motivation is highly complex and not thoroughly understood. There are a number of reasons for this complexity. First, the study of human motivation is concerned with "why" people behave rather than the more easily investigated "how" they behave. Second, motives can only be *inferred* from behavior, they cannot be observed directly. Third, similar motives may lead to quite different behavior for different individuals. Fourth, motivation is not only affected by the forces internal to the individual but also by his sociocultural environment. Finally, an individual's motivation changes over time as he faces new challenges, develops new aspirations, and is subject to failures and successes.[5]

With these complexities, we cannot think of human motivation from a mechanistic viewpoint. Mechanical systems are predictable with performance following inputs and transformation processes. It is relatively simple to explain *what* makes the machine perform. It is much more difficult to say *what* causes the individual to perform effectively or ineffectively.

[4]Kenyon B. DeGreene (ed.), *Systems Psychology*, McGraw-Hill Book Company, New York, 1970, pp. 31 and 48.
[5]Chalmers L. Stacey and Manfred F. DeMartino (eds.), *Understanding Human Motivation*, rev. ed., The World Publishing Company, Cleveland, 1965, pp. 1–2.

Fortunately, we are not concerned with all aspects of human motivation and behavior but only with those more limited factors affecting productivity and performance of the organizational system. Specifically, in thinking of the behavioral aspects of systems design, we are concerned with the question of how to motivate individuals to perform their functions effectively within the sociotechnical system. The manager is concerned with the efficient utilization of human resources to achieve organizational objectives.

Traditional management theory assumed a rational-economic individual who was motivated primarily by monetary incentives. The employee was a passive agent who had to be manipulated and controlled by the organizational elite in order to get him to perform. Motivation was achieved through extrinsic inducements (money) rather than through intrinsic forces (the work itself). "Ultimately, then, the doctrine of rational-economic man classified human beings into two groups—the untrustworthy, money-motivated, calculative mass, and the trustworthy, more broadly motivated, moral elite who must organize and manage the mass."[6] This view of human motivation led to the design of organizations which placed limitations and constraints upon individual behavior. Scientific management and the bureaucratic model emphasized the need for strong authority and control over the individual. Emphasis was upon efficient task performance accomplished through the coercion of economic incentives and penalties. Man was viewed as a mechanistic cog in a technical system.

This view of human motivation is not appropriate in most sociotechnical systems in an advanced society. It fails to recognize that man is a complex entity with diverse needs which affect his behavior and performance. The behavioral sciences have contributed to a greater recognition that work is not only the means for man to satisfy his basic physiological needs for goods and services, but also is the vehicle for satisfying higher needs for social interactions, status, and self-realization. The nature of the work and the design of the job have an important bearing on the motivation and satisfaction of the worker.

Many managers and behavioral scientists have come to recognize that the missing element of motivation to work may lie in the character of the work itself. For the mature individual, work

[6]Edgar H. Schein, *Organizational Psychology*, Prentice-Hall, Inc., Englewood Cliffs, N.J., 1965, p. 48.

may be a means of personal growth; it may satisfy his need for achievement, creativity, and self-fulfillment. Work, then, has become more than a means for economic survival, and it is apparent that in this age of affluence with its more sophisticated population, people won't work long or well at a job that offers no challenge or meaning.[7]

There is a growing movement to design jobs to provide more meaningful work and a higher level of motivation and need satisfaction. The term "job design" identifies this approach in which the psychological and social, as well as the economic and technical, factors in the work situation are considered. Many organizations use methods such as job enlargement, job rotation, and job enrichment as means for increasing both productivity and worker satisfaction.[8] These approaches represent a fundamental difference from the traditional view of designing jobs based only upon technical and structural requirements and then "fitting the person to the slot."

We have suggested that the manager should recognize human factors in the design of systems. There is another side to this coin. There is increasing evidence suggesting that people are positively motivated when the organization is designed to fit its environment and to accomplish its tasks effectively and efficiently. This suggests that an appropriate design may provide important psychological rewards for organization members. Morse's research indicates that a high level of human satisfaction can be achieved in organizations with quite different structures, authority relationships, technology, procedures, and leadership patterns. He says:

> Our study suggests a link between organizational characteristics and individual motivation. More specifically, we found that when organizational characteristics suit the kind of task being performed, there is the likelihood of engaging and fulfilling needs for mastery and competence and the likelihood of an individual's attaining high feelings of competence or a high sense of competence.[9]

What are the practical implications of these findings? They

[7]Harold M. F. Rush, *Job Design for Motivation,* The Conference Board, Inc., New York, 1971, p. ii.

[8]For a report on a number of companies which have used these approaches to job design, see ibid.

[9]John J. Morse, "Organizational Characteristics and Individual Motivation," in Jay W. Lorsch and Paul R. Lawrence (eds.), *Studies in Organization Design,* Richard D. Irwin, Inc., and the Dorsey Press, Homewood, Ill., 1970, p. 98.

suggest that systems design is not subject to fixed, mechanistic relationships. Human beings can be motivated to perform effectively in quite different work situations. Management should attempt to design organizational systems which match environmental, technical, and structural requirements with human needs.

Leadership Factors in Systems Design

Just as we have suggested that there is no one best way of designing organizations to achieve maximum human motivation, there is no one most effective pattern of leadership to fit all situations. Leadership is a complex social phenomenon which, although not clearly understood, is a vital consideration in the design of sociotechnical systems.

Leadership can be broadly defined as the ability to influence the behavior of other people. In an organizational context the leader exerts influence in order to accomplish the objectives.

Although a great deal of conceptualization and research has been done on leadership, it is impossible to set forth a general model for effective leadership to fit all situations. We generally favor the *situational,* or composite theory of leadership. This approach emphasizes that the leadership role is always related to the situation. There is an interaction among the personality characteristics of the leader; the environmental forces; the technology utilized; the tasks to be accomplished; and the attitudes, motivations, and behavior of the followers. Thus, the individual who is effective as a top sergeant in the marines might be totally ineffective as an administrator of a social welfare agency. The leadership pattern must fit the situation to be effective. This is, in effect, a composite or an eclectic theory of leadership which takes into consideration all the determinants.

Several research studies have provided new insights into matching leadership styles with the situation. Fiedler has developed a "contingency model" which suggests that the performance of the group is contingent upon the interaction of leadership styles and the favorability of the situation for the leader.[10] He postulates three factors of major importance in determining group effectiveness: (1) the leader's position power based upon his formal authority in the organization, (2) the structure of the task,

[10]Fred E. Fiedler, *A Theory of Leadership Effectiveness,* McGraw-Hill Book Company New York, 1967.

and (3) the interpersonal relationships between leader and members. Based upon these dimensions, individuals could be assigned as leaders to fit the proper niche, and/or groups could be restructured in order to facilitate better leader-member relations. This approach can be summarized as follows:

1. We can change the leader's position power
2. We can change the task structure
3. We can change the leader-member relations

This contingency view suggests the opportunity for the manager to match certain leadership styles with situations where this style will be most effective. This matching process is of major importance in the design of effective sociotechnical systems.

There are many other areas in which the behavioral sciences have made important contributions to our understanding of the human aspects of systems design. While we cannot cover each of these contributions specifically, many of the concepts will be utilized in the following discussion.

THE HUMAN NEED FOR SYSTEMATIC RELATIONSHIPS

In discussing the behavioral aspects of systems design it should not be assumed that people generally resist systemization. Much of man's conscious activities are geared to creating system out of chaos. Man does not resist structuring of his behavioral patterns per se. Rather, the normal human being seeks satisfactory systems of personal and interpersonal relationships which guide his activities. Everyone has been taught or has developed habit patterns which provide a basis for organizing many of his activities. Each human being has, in effect, developed his own unique system for relating a number of diverse activities within a broad operational whole—life's activities. Without systemization, behavior would be random, non-goal-oriented, and unpredictable. Certainly the complex modern industrial society demands more structured human behavior than older, less structured societies.

The discussion should not be confined to talking about the systems by which each individual relates himself to his physical environment. Many of man's actions and much of his behavior are dependent upon his interpersonal relationships. As Sherif and Sherif have written, "Many motives of man are products of social interaction and exposure to sociocultural products. These motives of social origin (sociogenic motives) are revealed in our preferences, in the favorable or unfavorable stand we take toward groups and social issues—in brief in what constitutes our social attitudes."[11]

Thus man is a product of his own motives and aspirations, which are modified extensively by sociocultural factors.

The concept that "no man is an island" merely means that man is a social creature and takes most of his norms and standards of conduct from other members of his society. Everyone has a system of relationships which sets a pattern for his life.

Much has been written of the human consequences of the changes brought on by advancing technology and industrialization. One of the earliest and most pessimistic of these research findings was made at the turn of the century by the sociologist Emile Durkheim.[12] In his investigations he found that rapid industrialization brought on by the industrial revolution had broken down the *solidaire* within social groups. Old family and community relationships were destroyed, and the individual was unable to replace these with new satisfactory social interactions. In this country, Mayo said: "This is a clear statement of the issue the civilized world is facing now, a rapid industrial, mechanical, physiochemical advance, so rapid that it has been destructive of all the historic and social and personal relationships."[13]

The problem in systems design, then, is not one of requiring man to change his total pattern of living and to adapt for the first time to the systematic organization of his behavior. Rather, it is primarily one of man changing from old systems of work and interpersonal relationships to new situations. Because of the rapidity of change, he cannot make the adjustments over extended time periods. Walker says:

> Rapid change has now left most Americans a little breathless. So complex are effects of changing technology that they have overtaken mankind as problems rather than as opportunities. If men are to utilize technology for the good life, they will have to find a substitute for time, which in the past permitted the human organism, and the community, to adjust to the pace of history.[14]

But it should not be inferred that there is just one major

[11]Muzafer Sherif and Carolyn W. Sherif, *An Outline of Social Psychology*, Harper & Row, Publishers, Incorporated, New York, 1956, p. 366.
[12]Emile Durkheim, *Le Suicide*, Librairie Félix Alcan, Paris, 1930.
[13]Elton Mayo, *The Social Problems of an Industrial Civilization*, Harvard University, Graduate School of Business Administration, Boston, 1945, p. 8.
[14]Charles R. Walker, *Modern Technology and Civilization*, McGraw-Hill Book Company, New York, 1962, p. 1.

sociocultural system to which each individual member belongs. Each of us has a number of "interpersonal systems" which have various objectives, perform different functions, and occupy separate places in our lives. Behavioral scientists call this the identification of the individual with the various groups with which he comes into contact. Each of these groups may require the individual to take a different "role." Every position in society carries with it certain norms and expectations of behavior. Thus, a doctor, professor, foreman, or clerk are social roles that have relatively well-defined behavior patterns. Organizations, both formal and informal, have defined roles for participants. "In organizational settings, highly elaborate definitions of positions and roles are transmitted through formal and informal mechanisms. These definitions are intrinsic to the hierarchy and are symbolized in a variety of ways—through dress, physical location, and other status attributes, including age and sex." [15] Role performance is a means for integration within a group.

It is useful to classify individual identification with various types of systems or human groups. It would be impossible to do this for all man's activities. In this respect everyone is unique; no two people have the same set of group associations or systems of interpersonal relationships. We are concerned primarily with the work organization and can classify this identification with various social systems as follows:

Identification with systems external to the organization (*e.g., families, professional associations, community groups, schools*) These systems of interpersonal relationships are unique to the individual and are largely determined by him rather than by the formal organization. However, man's systems of interpersonal relationships cannot be separated into neat categories. Most certainly man's participation and association with such groups as the church or educational institutions can have a profound effect upon his other organizational relationships.

Identification with the organization Identification with the formal organization is one of the strongest systems of interpersonal

---

[15]Abraham Zaleznik, "Interpersonal Relations in Organizations," in James G. March (ed.), *Handbook of Organizations,* Rand McNally & Company, New York, 1965, p. 589. For a discussion of role theory see Erving Goffman, *Encounters,* The Bobbs-Merrill Company, Inc., New York, 1961, and D. J. Levinson, "Role, Personality, and Social Structure in the Organizational Setting," *Journal of Abnormal and Social Psychology,* March 1959, pp. 170–180.

relationships for most individuals. Ask a person what he is, and he will often respond, I work for General Electric, or for IBM, or for the University of Washington. This apparent dominant need to identify and to maintain satisfactory relationships with the formal organization system is an important characteristic of our industrial society.

Identification with functional and task groups   Even within the complex organization, identification is most frequently made within subgroups. For example, I work for the sales department, or I work in accounting, or I am in the Graduate School of Business Administration. Association with these functional groups provides a more refined system of relationships for the individual in his work environment.

Identification with informal groups   We recognize the importance of informal interpersonal relationships and how these affect the formal organizational requirements. With whom do we go to lunch? Who shares our coffee break? These are ramifications of the informal social system which is apparent within every formal organization. To be sure, the formal structure sets the broad framework and pattern within which these informal relationships occur, but the individual has a great deal of latitude in his participation in informal groups.

Although all these systems of relationships are basic to the satisfactions of the individual, the work organization continues to be important. Even though rising productivity and output have reduced time on the job and provided for increased leisure-time activities, our work life remains basic to need gratification. Other social relations cannot be substituted completely. Increasing mobility, both social and geographic, makes it difficult for people to establish enduring friendships. Families often are widely scattered and have become less important as a basis for social activities, identification, and psychological support. Many of our other institutions such as social services, universities, and hospitals have become progressively more institutionalized and, although more efficient, are limited in the means of satisfying human social and status needs. Thus, the work organization continues to be a basic means of social interactions in the satisfaction of certain needs. Levinson says:

> Affiliation with an organization in which a person works seems to have become a major device for coping with the problems result-

ing from these economic, social, and psychological changes. Organizations have recognized and fostered the desire of employees to seek financial security in the organization by means of long service. . . .

Many now have an organizational orienting point. They identify themselves with an organization—whether a company, church, university, or government department. In a man's movement from one neighborhood or community to another, the work organization is his thread of continuity and may well become a psychological anchor point for him.[16]

Many forces are geared to maintaining the system of relationships in the formal organization. For example, the organization structure which places each individual in a hierarchical relationship and specifies his functions and relationships to other people is one of the vital elements in the system. This structure establishes a common set of expectations as to individual performance. The organization establishes the goals to which the interpersonal systems are directed. Broad policies help establish the system of relationships, as well as the more detailed standard operating procedures and methods. Over all, the organization is a *social system* which directly and specifically defines interpersonal relationships for every member.

We have traced some of the interpersonal relationships which tend to systemize individual behavior. It is not inherent within man to resist the systemization of his activities. Just the opposite, in fact; man seeks to establish, in his social relationships, satisfactory and rewarding systems of behavior. "Man apparently neither wants nor has experienced this postulated state of complete autonomy. People have always demanded structure in their lives. With few exceptions, men depend on human relationships, some fixity of structure, routine, and habit to survive psychologically."[17] What then is the major problem in designing systems? It is not one of total resistance to systemization, but of adherence to systems which are already in existence. The crucial problem is ability of the individual and group to change from one type of systematic relationship to another.

A common characteristic in a rapidly advancing society is to make these systems of interpersonal relationships more formal. While many of these systems have been implicit in the past, they

[16]Harry Levinson, "Reciprocation: The Relationship between Man and Organization," *Administrative Science Quarterly*, March 1965, p. 373.
[17]Leonard R. Sayles, *Individualism and Big Business*, McGraw-Hill Book Company, New York, 1963, p. 179.

are now becoming more explicit. This is one of the major precepts of the systems approach: systematic interpersonal relationships are necessary for accomplishing group objectives. Yet, systems should also change.

THE NEED FOR SYSTEMS CHANGE

The design of systems in a modern industrial society requires the integration of many common elements, both human and physical. Scientific and technological advancements have progressed at an accelerating rate and have fostered wholesale changes. It has been necessary to adopt new managerial, organizational, and human relationships in order to meet the requirements of technology and societal change.

Organizations have been the primary institutions for translating scientific and technological achievements into goods and services, fundamental indicators of the standard of living. Every industry has made progress not only in its products but also in the means of production. One of the major consequences has been to increase the size and complexity of organizations which in turn creates internal problems of adjustment. Kennedy states:

> As systems have become larger and more complex, they have created serious economic, political, social, psychological, and even moral problems in addition to technological problems of engineering design and feasibility. But the most important psychological problem relating to systems arises from the necessity to organize people, to acquire them as system components, to select and classify them, to train them, to keep them working for system goals and to bring their performance to a peak to achieve the system goals.[18]

There is a growing interest in social as well as technical change. During the twentieth century we have moved away from the concept of nonintervention in social affairs which stemmed from the "natural law" and "invisible-hand" ideology of the laissez faire doctrine of automatic adjustment. Today the issue concerns the methods used in planning, controlling, and directing the forces of change. "Human interventions designed to shape and modify the institutionalized behavior of men are now familiar features of our social landscape."[19] Increasingly, social

[18]J. L. Kennedy, "Psychology and System Development," in Robert M. Gagné *Psychological Principles in System Development*, Holt, Rinehart and Winston, Inc., New York, 1962, p. 16.
[19]W. G. Bennis, K. D. Benne, and R. Chin (eds.), *The Planning of Change*, Holt, Rinehart and Winston, Inc., New York, 1961, p. 9.

scientists are not only studying the social system but are actively engaged in changing and directing its course.

> Behavioral scientists have been drawn, with varying degrees of eagerness and resistance, into activities of "changing," such as consultation and applied research. "Helping professionals," "managers," and "policy-makers" in various fields of practice increasingly seek and employ the services of behavioral scientists to anticipate more accurately the consequences of prospective social changes and to inform more validly the processes of planning designed to control these consequences.[20]

With advancing technology and the growing emphasis given to increased understanding of the environment, our society and established organizations will undergo dramatic changes in the future. There is no alternative but to adapt to change. We can no longer rely upon structured systems of interference to ward off the problems of social change which will influence us. The primary question from the viewpoint of systems management is to provide a means whereby change can be accomplished with a maximum of benefit to the organization and to the participants and a minimum of penalty to any individual or group. This is the challenge of systems design.

Why People Resist Change

To say that people resist change per se would be an oversimplification of the problem. Certainly, in most activities we welcome and even demand change. Consumers are continually looking for new means and products for expressing their desires for change. Witness the ever-increasing tendency to give formerly standardized products higher style and fashion differentiation. Thus, in many areas, people seem to welcome change. Why, then, is there resistance to change within organizations? Generally, we can make a distinction between these two types of change. The consumers of products have some degree of control over acceptance or rejection of change, whereas, within the organization, changes occur which are beyond the influence or control of individuals. We tend to resist changes in our interpersonal and job relations because our sense of security and the way in which we have been accustomed to doing things are threatened. People frequently resist changes by indifference or outright opposition and rebellion, because most changes result in a disturbance of the

[20]Ibid.

interpersonal equilibrium within the environment in which the individual and social group operates. It is generally not the technological change that is resisted; resistance is generated primarily because of changing sociological relations and because economic well-being may be threatened. In a case study of administering change, Ronken and Lawrence concluded:

> So the problems of "technological change" proved to be the everyday problems of people in an organization, who, like the rest of us, were trying to get along as best they could in the world as they saw it. The increased tempo of change accentuated these problems, and their result was the kind of behavior—"uncooperative attitudes," project delays, and even restriction of output—which has led to the cliché that "people resist change." Looked at in this broader perspective, the story shows unequivocally that the effects of technological change were not confined to technical materials but were critical largely through their effect on interpersonal relationships.
>
> At each stage the introduction of technological change forced readjustments in the social system. Again and again individuals on the projects found that they had to deal with other individuals who were either new to them or stood in a new relationship to them. That these changes in relationships were the major variable in the introduction of the new product emerged as the most insistent uniformity.[21]

Frequently, management is unaware of the full impact of technological change. It looks primarily at the changes in the physical setup and in the physiological requirement for the individuals on the job. For example, it will require new time-and-motion studies, new job specifications, and other manifestations of the physical change in the work. However, even more important are changes in social equilibrium. Generally, any change will alter the informal or formal social hierarchical relationships which exist between people operating in groups. For some people status may be increased, while for others their positions will be apparently diminished. As Roethlisberger points out, "Any move on the part of the company may alter the existing social equilibrium to which the employee has grown accustomed and by means of which his status is defined. Immediately this disruption will be expressed in sentiments of resistance to the real or imagined alterations in the social equilibrium."[22]

[21]Harriet O. Ronken and Paul R. Lawrence, *Administering Changes,* Harvard University, Graduate School of Business, Boston, 1952, p. 292.
[22]F. J. Roethlisberger, *Management and Morale,* Harvard University Press, Cambridge, Mass., 1941, pp. 61–62.

How People Resist Change

Resistance to change can be indicated in many ways. The most evident manifestation of a resistance to change is by complete disassociation of the worker from the job—he quits. This obviously is a major display of resistance and is in a way the easiest to deal with. For the most part employees do not take this alternative, at least not immediately. Frequently they have limited opportunities for change in employment and desire to maintain a continuing relationship with the organization. If an employee stays with the organization, a negative reaction can take many forms ranging from open opposition, rebellion, and even destruction, to apathy and indifference.

The outward manifestations of resistance to change may take many forms which have a direct bearing upon the efficiency of the operation, such as decreased quality or quantity of production, increased absenteeism, tardiness, grievances, and strikes. Unfortunately, it is difficult to trace these concrete results of the resistance back to the original change and to the original cause. Frequently, people do not display resistance in a direct fashion, but their behavior will show its influence in a variety of ways. Nor, in discussing the problem, is it always easy for the superior to determine what really is wrong. People often will disguise their real concern over the impact of change by trying to appear to be rationally motivated in the best interest of the company. It is especially difficult to deal with those who have rationalized their resistance in terms of the organizational benefits. This is one of the chief forms of resistance to change on the white-collar and managerial level.

Because of the many ways of displaying resistance to change and the great difficulty of correcting resistance and moving back into a new, effective equilibrium, it is highly desirable for management to make every effort possible to effectuate the change properly and to facilitate adjustments to it. Giving adequate consideration to the problems of change, both technical and social, prior to the change is much more satisfactory than simply making the change and waiting for the chips to fall.

BEHAVIORAL CONSEQUENCES OF SYSTEM CHANGES

Behavioral considerations are important in the design of sociotechnical systems. In our society with its rapidly changing technology and environmental turbulence, there are many examples of changes which have important behavioral consequences. We have selected three of the more important of these for brief consideration: the automation of production operations, the development of automated information-decision systems, and the microanalysis of complex man-machine systems. The discussion of each of these will serve to illustrate some of the behavioral consequences of these developments.

Automation

Since the beginning of the industrial revolution, with its substitution of mechanical power for human power, there has been an ever-increasing trend toward mechanization. In the early phases of the industrial revolution, this had a traumatic effect upon people. Their lifelong skills were lost; unemployment was rampant; there was a wholesale displacement of workers; and women and children who could operate machines as effectively and at a much lower cost than men were utilized. From these early stages of industrialization rapid advances have been made in minimizing the impact of mechanization on employees. We have come to recognize the importance not only of sharing the benefits of technological improvements, but also of sharing some of the social costs involved. The economy has developed important social innovations, such as unemployment compensation, protection for the employee through legislation, collective-bargaining contracts, and efforts by organizations to retrain and reorient their workers to new technologies.

As we discuss in Chapter 12, automation can be thought of as a further extension of the trend toward mechanization which has been going on over the past few centuries. However, it is even more dramatic and brings into focus a number of new problems. The introduction of automation creates a dramatic and violent change—man is replaced by machines. This is obviously the kind of change which meets greatest resistance from people, and yet it is also the kind of change which is vitally necessary for our economy in order to increase the general welfare.

There is a great deal of interest in the impact of automation on psychosocial systems.[23] Studies suggest that it has had an effect

[23]A few of the investigations of the impact of automation upon people are James R. Bright, *Automation and Management*, Harvard Graduate School of Business Administration, Boston, 1958; William A. Faunce, "Automation in the Automobile Industry," *American Sociological Review*, August 1958, pp. 401–407; Floyd C. Mann and L. Richard Hoffman, *Automation and the Worker*, Holt, Rinehart and Winston, Inc., New York, 1960; and Otis Libstreu and Kenneth A. Reed, "A New Look at the Organizational Implications of Automation," *Academy of Management Journal*, March 1965, pp. 24–31.

upon such factors as the degree and types of skills required, social interaction, motivation and satisfaction, individual autonomy, and supervisory patterns. The issue is still in doubt as to whether automation has an overall positive or negative impact upon the psychosocial system. Several of the studies have indicated that it has had the effect of upgrading skill requirements, increasing autonomy, providing more opportunities for group interaction, and motivating employees through a feeling of participation. Other studies, however, come to opposite conclusions. These differing conclusions suggest that *automation* per se may not have a positive or negative impact. Rather, the effect is determined by how well the new technology is integrated with the psychosocial system.

The managerial system is frequently affected by automation. The advancing technology places new and different demands upon the managerial system, not only for technical skill but also in terms of the administrative and human relations skills required to integrate the various systems. Automation requires that the managerial system perform its functions of planning and controlling differently than would be appropriate for more traditional production. It reduces much of the slack in the managerial decision processes and requires more precise long-range planning.

Automation also has major impacts upon company-union relationships in such areas as employee classification, job evaluation, and pay; education, training, and retraining; job displacement and seniority rights; and the distribution of gains from greater productivity.[24] It would be impossible to suggest all the possible impacts of automation. The changes in work, satisfaction, and group relationships are complex and vary widely in different companies. Generalization as to the total impact, from the present viewpoint, is difficult and perhaps foolhardy.

We can, however, suggest a number of other changes. With automation, the output per man-hour will increase and wage increases will probably result. Furthermore, there will be a continuation of the trend of the past century toward the reduction of hours of work per week, and automation will make this feasible without a reduction in overall productivity. Furthermore, the benefit of automation to labor through better working conditions is significant. Generally, plants will be cleaner, less congested, and safer places to work.

[24]For a discussion of the impact of automation on industrial relations see Edward B. Shils, *Automation and Industrial Relations,* Holt, Rinehart and Winston, Inc., New York, 1963.

Automatic technology, a systems concept, has major implications for our society. First, for man as a consumer, it will offer greatly increased productivity and output, hence a rising standard of living. For man as a producer, there are some difficulties. In this process of change, some individual workers will inevitably suffer losses as a result of displacement, whereas others will benefit as a result of upgrading.

There is a need for adequate measures to ease the hardships on displaced individuals, to train workers with new skills, and to adjust conflicting interest in the enterprise. These are likely to be important issues during the transition to automation. Labor, management, and government agencies responsible for education, vocational training, employment services, unemployment insurance, apprenticeship, wages and hours, and industrial relations are likely to be increasingly concerned with the problems created by advancing technology and automation.

Automated Information-Decision Systems

Automation of material flow has meant some replacement of the decision-making and mental activities of man in organizations. In contrast, white-collar and managerial functions have remained humanized to a major extent. Although there have been typewriters, dictating machines, and other mechanical aids for these functions, much of the actual work has depended directly upon human skills. There has been a continual increase in the proportion of white-collar and managerial positions, whereas the proportion of those engaged in direct production—factory workers and farmers—actually has declined. However, the same kinds of technical developments that led to automation in the factory promise an even more dramatic revolution in clerical operations. This involves two primary phases:

1. The use of automatic electronic equipment for the collection, processing, and comparison of data
2. The application of computers to aid directly in managerial decision-making processes

The most apparent impact is in the first phase, the use of electronic equipment for processing vast quantities of data. However, the second phase, the application of computers in decision making, will have the greatest impact in the future.

Automated information-decision processes will have a profound influence upon the psychosocial system in the organization, primarily upon clerical and white-collar employees. In many ways, the process of replacing clerical workers with data processing equipment is similar to that for workers in the factory. This technology not only replaces some workers but also restructures the jobs, functions, and roles of the remaining workers. The problem will be to motivate clerical personnel and to promote their identification with the organization. Numerous studies suggest that white-collar workers are even more resistant to technological change than blue-collar workers. If "the automated factory of the future will operate on the basis of programmed decisions produced in the automated office beside it," major changes will be required in the psychosocial system of the office.[25]

The trend toward automated information-decision systems will also affect structure. It will require more effective integration of operations across a broad spectrum of functions. It cannot be concerned only with the traditional vertical communication channels based upon the hierarchy but must also consider horizontal and diagonal relationships.[26]

Many early writers suggested that the impact of data processing technology would be to cause a recentralization of decision making in the organization.[27] However, there is little evidence on the extent to which centralization has resulted. Others suggest that it is possible to decentralize operations by providing more complete information to managers at all levels. Instead of moving in one direction, it is likely that the new technology will provide for the centralization of some decisions and for the decentralization of others. The mix of types of decisions and the location of the decision makers will be altered.

There is, however, general agreement that the new information technology will affect the management system. Top management will have to deal with longer-range planning and will need a better perception of how the organizational system interacts with the environment. By programming his more routine, mechanical decisions, the manager will have more time available to deal with the highly variable factors of human motivation and participation. We agree with Ansoff, who says, "Paradoxically enough, the age of change and automation will call for increased management skills

[25]Herbert A. Simon, *The Shape of Automation for Men and Management,* Harper Torchbooks, Harper & Row, Publishers, Incorporated, New York, 1965, p. 76.
[26]Thomas L. Whisler, *Information Technology and Organizational Change,* Wadsworth Publishing Company, Inc., Belmont, Calif., 1970, pp. 63–66.
[27]Typical of this view was that expressed by Harold J. Leavitt and Thomas L. Whisler, "Management in the 1980's," *Harvard Business Review,* November–December 1958, pp. 41–48.

in human relations. In a climate of change, increasing importance will be placed on the manager's ability to communicate rapidly and intelligibly, gain acceptance for change and innovation, and motivate and lead people in new and varying directions."[28]

The advancements in automated information-decision systems may lead to a growing concern over our ability to control this technology. As Whisler suggests:

> It is likely that all of us are at times uneasy about information technology. Only a few people really believe they understand it, and even fewer can directly control its use. As customers and tax-payers, we worry about the consequences of error in computer systems, and fear our inability to eliminate it. As citizens, we worry about a national data bank invading our privacy. Since we can neither understand nor control the behavior of men very well, the appearance of a new technology which we also cannot understand or control adds to our general anxiety; man's anxiety is likely to persist until we understand much more clearly what the technology is and how we can control it.[29]

The systems designer must be prepared to deal with resistance and problems of human adjustment to this new technology. How management handles the human problems will have an important bearing on how effective the new systems are in achieving their potential and will also have an impact upon the well-being of people in organizations and in society.

Microanalysis of Complex Man-Machine Systems

There is an increasing interest in the systematic application of psychological principles to the invention, design, development, and use of complex man-machine systems. Melton describes this as a theory of psychotechnology of man-machine systems and suggests that "it achieves integration of what has heretofore been variously called 'human engineering,' 'human factors engineering,' or 'engineering psychology' on the one hand and 'personnel psychology' or 'personnel and training research' on the other hand. This union comes easily and naturally once the concept of *system* is examined and once the full implications of the concept of the human being as a *component* of a man-machine system are recognized."[30] This detailed approach to the application of psychological

[28]H. Igor Ansoff, "The Firm of the Future," *Harvard Business Review,* September–October 1965, p. 178.
[29]Whisler, op. cit., p. 89.
[30]Arthur W. Melton, in Robert M. Gagné (ed.), *Psychological Principles in System Development,* Holt, Rinehart and Winston, Inc., New York, 1962, p. v.

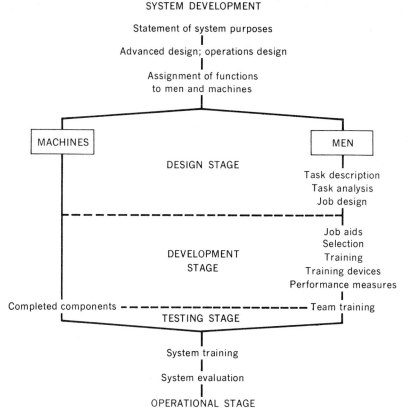

FIGURE 10–1. **Men-machines system development.** [Source: Robert M. Gagne (ed.), *Psychological Principles in System Development,* **Holt, Rinehart and Winston, Inc.,** New York, 1962, p. 4.]

principles to man-machine systems has also been called *ergonomics.* It involves designing machines, tools, and work areas to fit the physiological and psychological capabilities of human beings.

This research on integrating human factors directly into complex technical and mechanical systems was stimulated by the Air Force and the National Aeronautics and Space Administration.[31] For example, in the Apollo space capsule, it was necessary to consider the whole man-machine system and to integrate human capabilities with the physical equipment. The first stage is to determine the purpose, or mission, of the system and to develop an advanced operational design. From these, together with inputs about the current state of technological knowledge, decisions are

[31]For a discussion of these developments see Kenyon B. DeGreene (ed.), *Systems Psychology,* McGraw-Hill Book Company, New York, 1970.

made about the components of the total system and the way in which they can be connected to fulfill the system's mission. This leads to the assignment of functions to men and machines. Figure 10–1 is a model of man-machine systems development.

Psychotechnology has important implications. The basic assumption is that man should be considered one of the major components of a complex man-machine system rather than merely a user of the system once it is developed. It denies that system development is purely an engineering problem—psychological and social problems must also be considered. "Any reasonably complex system requires a true interaction between man and the other parts of the system, which may be machines, other men, or combinations of these. Some way must therefore be found for thinking about the functions of machines and the functions of men within a framework which makes possible the relation of these two kinds of functions to common goals—that is, to system goals."[32]

This micro approach to man-machine system development has major implications for many advanced military and space programs, and this is where most of the current research is taking place. As a result of these studies, a great deal more will be learned about the interrelations between man and technology, which will help in the design of future man-machine systems.

OPEN-SYSTEMS CONCEPT AS A BASIS OF HUMAN INTEGRATION

The *open-systems concept* offers a basis for more effective management of human and social factors in large organizations. Management does not deal with static structures but with the dynamic interrelationships of individuals, groups, and physical factors. An increasing number of researchers and writers express the view that organization theory and management practice should be based on the open-systems approach. For example, the psychologists Katz and Kahn use this concept as a framework for their study of organizations. In their preface they state:

> In our attempts to extend the description and explanation of organizational processes we have shifted from an earlier emphasis on traditional concepts of individual psychology and interpersonal relations to system constructs. The interdependent behavior of many people in their supportive and complementary actions takes

[32]Robert M. Gagné, "Human Functions in Systems," op. cit., p. 35.

on a form or structure which needs to be conceptualized at a more appropriate collective level. Classical organization theory we found unsatisfactory because of its implicit assumptions about the closed character of social structures. The development of open-system theory, on the other hand, furnished a much more dynamic and adequate framework. Hence, our effort, in the pages to follow, is directed at the utilization of an open-system point of view for the study of large-scale organizations.[33]

Similarly, Likert uses the systems concept in the development of his "new theory" of management and Sayles adopts the open-systems view in his study of managerial behavior.[34] These are just a few examples; across the entire spectrum of academic specialties dealing with organizations and management we find the systems approach emerging as the dominant model. Although the early systems approach was geared to technical and engineering operations, it is now being used increasingly as a basis for the study of behavioral aspects of organizations.

Limitations of Traditional Views

In Chapter 2 we noted that the classical assumptions on human behavior in organizations are based upon the bureaucratic theory of Max Weber, the scientific management approach of Frederick Taylor, and the administrative theory of Gulick, Urwick, Mooney and Reiley, and others. This traditional view emphasized the hierarchical structure, legitimate authority, vertical communications patterns, span-of-control considerations, and line and staff relationships. It attempted to structure human behavior to meet organizational requirements. In contrast, the systems approach views individuals and groups, with their motivations, interactions, and values, as vital subsystems of the total organization. The structuring of behavior under the traditional approach may be somewhat appropriate in highly regularized, routine activities and in organizations which are very stable; it is not feasible for dynamic systems subject to change. Shepard says:

> Bureaucratic structures are designed to do programmable things in a stable, predictable environment. More and more, programmable things can be mechanized and automated. More and more, the en-

[33]Daniel Katz and Robert L. Kahn, *The Social Psychology of Organizations,* John Wiley & Sons, Inc., New York, 1966, p. vii.
[34]Rensis Likert, *New Patterns of Management,* McGraw-Hill Book Company, New York, 1961, and Leonard R. Sayles, *Managerial Behavior,* McGraw-Hill Book Company, New York, 1964.

vironment is unstable and rapidly changing. The present need is for modes of organization which permit rapid adaptation to changing circumstances; the search is for ways in which people can organize for innovative, unprogrammable activities. The main point of this chapter is that a more humanistic organization theory than we have known in the past is required, and that it is realizable in practice.[35]

We feel that the systems approach offers opportunity for the "more humanistic organization theory" which Shepard envisions.

Need for New Relationships

Traditional management theory emphasized the scalar chain of command and vertical relationships to the neglect of horizontal and diagonal networks. Even the line and staff concept provided only a limited means of dealing with communications outside the vertical channel. The systems approach is based on establishing information-decision networks including all relationships— vertical, horizontal, and diagonal. The discussion in Chapter 13 on program management indicates the importance of these networks in the management of complex systems. We believe that new organizational requirements will result in a continuing decline in the emphasis on hierarchy and increasing reliance upon horizontal and diagonal information flows. One of the consequences of this transition will be the ability to integrate more completely the goals of individuals and the organization through better motivation, task orientation, and reward structures.

Integration of Activities around Systems and Subsystems

Systems design involves the establishment of project and facilitating subsystems to accomplish certain tasks or programs. Under this approach the network of human interdependence required to accomplish a given task is based on shared responsibility of the participating members of the subsystem. In contrast, the traditional organization is geared to functional performance and the integrating force is authority. Instead of gearing participant activities to rule obeyance and closely structured behavior, the systems approach provides a basis for active participation in meeting task requirements. The manager is looked upon as a resource person who can help the group meet its goals as well as a source of au-

---

[35]Herbert A. Shepard, "Changing Relationships in Organizations," in James G. March (ed.), *Handbook of Organizations,* Rand McNally & Company, Chicago, 1965, pp. 1141–1142.

thority and control. Thus, the systems approach provides the framework by which the newer concepts of motivation, leadership, and participation can be applied effectively within the organization.

Interaction-Influence System

The systems approach has been used by Likert in the development of a concept of management he calls the "interaction-influence system." He suggests the development of highly effective work groups linked to other such groups into the larger organizational system. There is an overlapping of these groups so that a multiple "linking-pin function" provides additional channels through which information and influence can flow. Basic to the development of his "interaction-influence" system was research which suggested the need for a newer theory of organization and management that would develop highly coordinated, motivated, and cooperative social systems. In describing the organization operating under this new theory he says:

> The organization consists of a tightly knit, effectively functioning social system. This social system is made up of interlocking work groups with a high degree of group loyalty among the members and favorable attitudes and trust between superiors and subordinates. Sensitivity to others and relatively high levels of skill in personal interaction and the functioning of groups are also present. These skills permit effective participation in decisions on common problems. Participation is used, for example, to establish organizational objectives which are a satisfactory integration of the needs and desires of all members of the organization and of persons functionally related to it. High levels of reciprocal influence occur, and high levels of total coordinated influence are achieved in the organization. Communication is efficient and effective. There is a flow from one part of the organization to another of all the relevant information important for each decision and action. The leadership in the organization has developed what might well be called a highly effective social system for interaction and mutual influence.[36]

Collaborative-Consensus Systems

Closely related to Likert's views are those expressed by Shepard. He suggests that organizations can operate under two broad approaches. The "coercion-compromise" system relies heavily upon an internal system of command, on authority and obedience, and

[36]Likert, op. cit., p. 99.

on bureaucratic regulation for governing the actions of participants. "In others, the authority system is rarely appealed to for
resolving conflict, solving problems, or making decisions. These
organizations approach, in their functioning, systems of collaboration and consensus."[37] There are many adverse consequences of
the coercion-compromise system, such as canceling-out processes
where the energies which might be directed to meeting organizational goals are consumed in attempts by individuals and groups
to control, counteract, or exploit one another. There are also a number of other forces which reduce the effectiveness of this approach.
By contrast, he sees the development of a system of collaboration
and consensus as a means for more effectively meeting organizational and individual goals. He says:

> The commitment of members of collaboration-consensus systems
> is to one another's growth, and to superordinate goals on which
> their growth in part depends. . . . Control is achieved through
> agreement on goals, coupled with a communication system which
> provides continuous feedback of results, so that members can steer
> themselves. . . .
>
> In consensus-collaboration systems, good management is
> understood to be the emergent product of adequate working rela-
> tionships among the organization's members. Improving and per-
> fecting the communication, control, and decision-making networks
> within the organization is, first of all, a problem of improving work
> relationships among managers so that they will use the systems
> they develop.[38]

Likert's interaction-influence system and Shepard's collaboration-consensus sytem with their humanistic orientation are
compatible with our systems approach. They express dissatisfaction with the classical view as a basis of human collaboration in
organizations and suggest the need for new theories. Open-systems concepts provide a more fruitful avenue for the development
of these new approaches.

New Managerial View

The systems approach suggests a new role for management. In the
traditional view the manager operated in a highly structured,
closed system with well-defined goals, clear-cut relationships,
tight controls, and hierarchical information flows. In the open-
systems view, the organization is not static but is continually

[37]Shepard, op. cit., p. 1128.
[38]Ibid., pp. 1128–1129.

changing to meet both external and internal disturbances. The manager's role is one of developing a viable organization, meeting change, and helping participants establish a dynamic equilibrium.

The systems concept does not provide a prescription for making a manager's difficult and complex job easier. Rather, it helps him to understand and operate more effectively in the reality of complex, open systems. It suggests that operations cannot be neatly departmentalized but must be viewed as overlapping subsystems. Leadership patterns must be modified, particularly when dealing with professionals and highly trained specialists, and motivation must be directed toward active, willing participation rather than forceful subjugation. These and other forces suggest a different role for the manager. Sayles says:

> A systems concept emphasizes that managerial assignments do not have these neat, clearly defined boundaries; rather, the modern manager is placed in a network of mutually dependent relationships. All the strands of the net are not alike; some impose one pattern of initiation and response upon him, some impose very different tempos and rhythms. . . .
>
> Successful managers recognize these dynamics and seek to shift their own behavior, both as a means of detecting changes in the system and responding to the changes that are identified. Rather than becoming frustrated by rules that are always changing, where one is not automatically given the resources needed to do a job (the dimensions of which are in flux), the sophisticated manager recognizes these as hallmarks of the world in which he must live.[39]

MEETING THE HUMAN AND SOCIAL PROBLEMS

Even though the systems approach provides a more effective basis for motivating and integrating the activities of organizational participants than traditional management approaches, there remain problems in transition from an old to a new system. The application of the systems approach does create change and consequent resistances. What can management do to help organizational members make the transition and reach a new and better equilibrium? How can changes be made effectively and efficiently? We agree with Shepard that the coercion-compromise approach is much less effective in initiating and gaining acceptance of change than is the collaboration-consensus approach. In fact, one of the major advantages of this latter method is that it is geared to change rather than stability. However, given a managerial orientation

[39]Sayles, op. cit., pp. 258–259.

toward the collaboration-consensus approach there still remain questions of specific means for making changes.

Leavitt suggests that there are a number of approaches to organizational change:

> One can view industrial organizations as complex systems in which at least four interacting variables loom especially large: task variables, structural variables, technological variables, and human variables. If one takes such a view, he can go on to categorize major applied approaches to organizational change by using three of the same variables: *structural* approaches to change, *technological* approaches, and *people* approaches.[40]

We have discussed a number of the technical and structural approaches to change in such areas as quantitative techniques, network analysis, and organizational design. The human approach to organizational change has received increasing emphasis in recent years.[41] This view tries to change organizations by first modifying the behavior of participants. It is suggested that changing human behavior will result in modifications in the structure and in the development of technical innovations.

In reality, it is quite difficult to categorize separately these several approaches to organizational change. Most efforts to effect change should deal with the interactions between technology, structure, and people, and should therefore integrate all three approaches. Katz and Kahn suggest that there is a major error in assuming that the primary method for organizational change is through changing individuals. In discussing the people approach to change and its limitations they say:

> Its essential weakness is the psychological fallacy of concentrating upon individuals without regard to the role relationships that constitute the social system of which they are a part. The assumption has been that, since the organization is made up of individuals, we can change the organization by changing its mem-

---

[40]Harold J. Leavitt, "Applied Organizational Change in Industry: Structural, Technological and Humanistic Approaches," in James G. March (ed.), *Handbook of Organizations,* Rand McNally & Company, Chicago, 1965, p. 1144.

[41]Some examples of this approach are seen in Paul R. Lawrence, *The Changing of Organizational Behavior Patterns,* Division of Research, Harvard Business School, Boston, 1958; Robert H. Guest, *Organization Change: The Effect of Successful Leadership,* Richard D. Irwin, Inc., Homewood, Ill., 1962; E. Ginzberg and E. Reilly, *Effecting Change in Large Organizations,* Columbia University Press, New York, 1957; and W. G. Bennis, K. D. Benne, and R. Chin, *The Planning of Change,* Holt, Rinehart and Winston, Inc., New York, 1969; Richard Beckhard, *Organization Development: Strategies and Models,* Addison-Wesley Publishing Company, Reading, Mass., 1969; and Gordon L. Lippitt, *Organizational Renewal,* Appleton-Century-Crofts, New York, 1969.

bers. This not so much an illogical proposition as it is an oversimplification which neglects the interrelationships of people in an organizational structure and *fails to point to the aspects of individual behavior which need to be changed.*[42]

In order to initiate organization innovations most effectively, they suggest that consideration be given to changing individual behavior and also to direct structural or systemic alterations. The following methods are available to bring about organizational change:

> The use of information—The supply of additional cognitive inputs to the participants concerning the nature of the change and its impact on them. However, information alone is not a source of motivation and this method is of limited effectiveness unless combined with other approaches.

> Individual counseling and therapy—These methods attempt to help the individual gain new insights and changes of attitudes which will alter his behavior.

> Influence of the peer group—A third, and often more effective, approach to organizational change is through the influence of the peer group. Peers do exert strong influences on individual behavior and can help in bringing about change.

> Sensitivity training—This approach is closely related to the peer-group approach. This method helps the individual to better understand his own attitudes and feelings through processes of group interaction and can help him adapt to change.

> Group therapy in organizations—The essence of this approach is to have the organization change itself by means of group processes occurring at every level in the organization. The first step is the improvement of people's understanding of their organizational interrelationships and their own personal motives. A further objective is organizational restructuring by responsible organizational participants.

> Feedback and group discussion—This procedure involves the feedback of information from research and surveys to various organizational families, each consisting of a manager and his immediate subordinates. There is integration through linking processes which provide a communications network covering the organizational hierarchy.

> Systemic change—This approach is not directed at changing individuals but requires the direct manipulation of organizational

[42]Katz and Kahn, op. cit., p. 391.

variables. One example would be the attempt to change the hierarchical distribution of decision-making power in an organization. Another is the attempt to provide the best fit between the social and technical systems and to introduce into the organization changes needed to attain this fit.[43]

The first four methods listed are directed at altering individual behavior as a means of effecting organizational change. The latter three approaches are directed more toward modifying role and structural relationships. In our view each of the above approaches provides a useful method for achieving organizational change. There is no set pattern which is most effective in all cases. The manager's role is one of recognizing the dynamics of change in complex man-machine systems and of adopting approaches which will minimize the disruptions and enhance the development of a new equilibrium which is more effective and efficient.

SUMMARY

The behavioral sciences are concerned with the study of social factors of systems design. Over the past several decades behavioral scientists have contributed significantly to the understanding of man and his social organizations. Their inputs are vital for designing more efficient and effective sociotechnical systems which also contribute to the satisfaction of human participants.

Motivational factors play an important part in the design of jobs and the work situation. Many organizations have used such methods as job enlargement, job rotation, and job enrichment as means for increasing both productivity and worker satisfaction.

Leadership is a complex social phenomenon which is also a vital consideration in the design of organizations. Although there are various theories of leadership, the situational theory seems most appropriate. This approach emphasizes that the leadership role is always related to the situation. There is an interaction between the personality traits of the leader, the performance requirements of the task, the organizational climate, and environmental forces, as well as the attitudes, needs, and behavior patterns of the followers.

People do not resist systems per se. Rather, the normal human being seeks satisfactory systems of interpersonal relationships which guide his activities. The problem in systems design is not one of requiring man to change his total pattern of living and

[43]Ibid., pp. 392–451.

to adapt for the first time to the systematic organization of his behavior. Rather, it is primarily one of man changing from old systems of work and interpersonal relationships to new situations.

A dynamic society must expect and even welcome change; it is through change that better material and social welfare is achieved. Generally, it is not technological change which is resisted; resistance develops primarily because of changing social relations and because economic well-being is threatened. Resistance to change can take many forms, ranging from quitting, open opposition, and rebellion to apathy and indifference.

There are many examples of systems changes which have important behavioral consequences. Three of the more important are the automation of production operations, the development of automated information-decision systems, and the microanalysis of complex man-machine systems. Each of these has created many problems of adaptation for human participants. Increasingly, the manager as systems designer should recognize and deal effectively with the consequences of these changes to the psychosocial system.

The systems approach offers a basis for more effective management of human and social factors in organizations. Management deals with the dynamic interrelationships of individuals, groups, and physical factors; the systems approach provides the basis for understanding and operating with these complex interrelationships. The organization is not static, but is continually changing to meet both external and internal demands. The manager's role is one of developing a viable organization, meeting change, and helping participants establish a dynamic equilibrium.

Overall, we are not pessimistic and do not think that the implementation of the systems approach will have major adverse effects upon individuals or society. Rather, we view the implementation of this concept as offering greater material rewards and providing more opportunities for human satisfaction.

QUESTIONS

1. Why are behavioral aspects important in the design of sociotechnical systems?
2. Discuss the importance of motivational factors in systems design.
3. What is meant by the situational theory of leadership?
4. What is the relationship between the systemization of human behavior and organizational participation?
5. Outline the major social groups with which you are identified. How does your "role" differ in each of these groups?

6. Do you believe the work organization is assuming an increasingly important basis of human identification and need satisfaction?
7. How have technological changes affected man's social organizations?
8. Why do people resist change? How do they show this resistance?
9. What are the impacts of automated information-decision systems on people in organizations? What do you forecast for the future?
10. What is meant by psychotechnology and what is the importance of its development?
11. In what ways can the systems approach provide a basis for dealing with human problems in complex organizations? What are its major limitations?

Acme Aircraft Corporation*

George Bruster took an engineering job with the Acme Aircraft Corporation soon after his graduation from State Engineering College in June, 1961. He was initially assigned the responsibility of supervising a group of engineers and engineering aides involved in conducting experimental test programs on various models of airplanes and airplane components.

Prior to his graduation, Bruster had spent several summers working for Acme Aircraft and had worked part-time for this organization for a period while attending school. At the time of his permanent employment he had held every position in the testing group other than that of crew chief. Because of his previous experience he was assigned the position of crew chief—an unusual assignment for a "new" engineer.

The average size of a testing crew was seven to ten individuals, of whom five were usually graduate engineers and the remainder engineering aides and technical assistants. The responsibilities of the crew chief included the over-all planning and coordinating of the test programs with which his group was involved. Approximately half of the crew chief's responsibilities were administrative rather than technical; and because of the nature of his responsibilities, the crew chief often was not the engineer on the crew who had the most experience or the greatest technical knowledge. Often older engineers, specialists in electronics or design, for example, would be working on crews headed by younger, less experienced engineers. This type of arrangement had rarely created friction in the past—especially as the older specialists were usually not interested in accepting responsibility for anything but their particular part of a testing series. In addition, crew membership was constantly changing as crews

---

*From *Human Elements of Administration: Cases, Readings, Simulation Exercises* by Harry R. Knudson, Jr. Copyright © 1963 by Holt, Rinehart and Winston, Inc. Reprinted by permission of Holt, Rinehart and Winston, Inc.

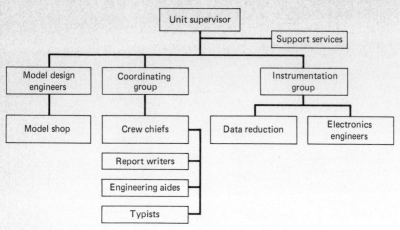

Exhibit 10-1. Organization chart of a testing unit.

were disbanded and reformed as tests were completed and new tests undertaken.

Exhibit 10-1 is an example of the organization of a typical testing unit.

On November 1, 1961, George Bruster's group was assigned the project of testing a new model component for an experimental aircraft which Acme was developing. It was only the second major assignment that George's group had had since he took over as crew chief in June. This particular test series was of prime importance, for the results of the tests would be instrumental in providing data upon which Acme would base its design proposal to government representatives. If the company could provide an acceptable design, it would be in a favorable position eventually to gain a large—and profitable—production contract.

The unit supervisor stressed the importance of this particular series of tests to George and informed him that the entire testing group was under considerable pressure from top management to get quick and accurate results. Top men from the model design and instrumentation groups had been assigned to the tests, as well as one of the best report writers in the coordinating group.

Because of scheduling problems regarding the test facilities available at the Bristol plant of Acme—the "home" office of the test group headed by Bruster—arrangements were made for the current series of tests to be conducted at the Culver City facilities of Acme. Culver City was located approximately 900 miles from Bristol; and while the Culver City operations were organized in the same manner as those at Bristol, the operations were run autonomously because of the physical distance between the two facilities. Thus, while Bruster and his crew would actually conduct the tests, they would be using the equipment and facilities of the Culver City operation.

George Bruster arrived at the Culver City test facility on November

7 to coordinate with the people there and make final test arrangements. After determining that the test was scheduled for December 1 and that his crew would receive the full cooperation of the local facility, he went to the data reduction group to arrange for the computer processing of data that would result from the test. The head of the data reduction unit, Gil Harmon, introduced George to the chief programmer, Dick Jones, with whom he was to work throughout the data reduction process.

George explained the importance of the test and showed Dick the type of information that would be required as final data from the digital computers.

After studying the information for a few minutes, Dick said, "I'll have to write a new program in order to give you the information you want. None of our present standard programs are capable of handling this job."

"How long will it take to write a new program?" George asked.

"Oh, I could probably have it finished by the fifth of December. That's the last day of your test, so it will be done in time to reduce your data."

"That won't do!" George exclaimed. "We must have data from day to day all during the test. This proposal is red hot, and we must analyze our data on a day-by-day basis. That's the only way we can be sure we are taking the right approach in our test program. Each day's testing will be dependent on the data from the day before."

"So, what do you think? Can you have your program finished by the first?"

"Well, I dunno," mumbled Dick. "I might be able to finish by the first if there are no hitches in the program, but things seldom go that smoothly."

"But it is possible to finish by the first?" insisted George.

"It's possible, but I have other important programs to work on. Everything would have to work properly the first time."

"This project is so important it just has to be done on time. We don't have any choice but to plan it for the first of the month."

"Okay, I'll give it all the effort I can. With a little luck it will probably be ready for the first."

"Swell," concluded George. "I'll count on it."

After concluding all pretest arrangements, George returned to Bristol. During the remainder of November he was in frequent telephone communication with Culver City. All preparations were progressing satisfactorily and Dick Jones assured George that the program would be finished by the last day of November.

On November 30 George and his crew arrived at Culver City. The test was to begin the next day.

George found everything in readiness for his test, except that the data program was not quite finished. He went to Dick Jones and asked what the hold up was.

"No holdup," Dick replied. "The program will be completed by the end of the day, and we can check it out on the computer first thing in the morning. If everything checks out okay, we will be able to run your data from the first day's testing sometime tomorrow night. So you'll have your data the next day, just as you requested."

"What happens if everything doesn't check out?" asked George.

"It'll take a little while to iron out any bugs that may show up. But it shouldn't hold us up much; a few hours maybe."

"Will you be able to work overtime on this if it becomes necessary?"

"I think so. We should be able to get your data for you one way or another, so don't worry. We'll let you know if we run into any major problems."

George was reassured and returned to his hotel satisfied that all was in readiness for the start of his test the following day.

The testing groups existed as staff units. As such, they conducted tests at the request of line and project groups who were in need of the particular information. It was the usual practice for the group requesting a test to send along a representative to make whatever decisions regarding the test program that might come under the jurisdiction of the line organization.

The requesting group for this test had sent along their senior project engineer, Richard Wallen, because of the importance of the test. Wallen was a fairly new supervisor but was well qualified technically. He was a "driver," worked his subordinates hard during rush programs such as this, and had a reputation of sometimes "rubbing people the wrong way" in order to achieve an immediate goal.

Wallen was directly responsible to the division general manager for the success of the program. One of his major concerns was whether or not the final data would be ready on a day-to-day basis. He asked George about it the night before the test.

George replied, "Dick Jones told me everything would be ready on time. The odds are real slim that anything would go wrong; and if something went wrong, it would only slow us down a couple of hours."

The following day the data from the first shift of testing was turned over to Jones for processing. However, the program did not check out properly and Jones was unable to give George his data the following day.

The same situation occurred the next two days of testing, with Jones unable to make his program work despite working several hours overtime each day.

On the fourth day the results were no better. Three hours after the testing shift was completed Wallen and Bruster went to see Jones. When they found that Jones had gone home, Wallen "blew his top" and told George Bruster to telephone Jones at his home and demand to know why he wasn't at the office working on the programing problem.

A few minutes later Gil Harmon, head of the data reduction unit, received a worried phone call from Jones, who quoted George as saying, "If you don't get down here and start working on this program, it may cost you your job!"

Harmon passed on this information to Conners Simpson, who was instrumentation supervisor at Culver City. Simpson was shocked and angered at the attitude the visiting group was taking toward one of his men. He immediately phoned Wallen and demanded an explanation. He told him in no uncertain terms to "lay off" his men and also told Wallen to follow the proper chain of command and notify him first next time there was a problem. In addition, Simpson stated that he "had no intention of letting Jones come down and work on your damn program. Jones has been working twelve hours a day for the past week and has several other problems to deal with also. Besides, it's too late to salvage much of the data."

Before he hung up the phone, Simpson told Wallen, "This thing has gone too far. I'm going to take it to the boss and get it ironed out first thing in the morning. I want you and your crew chief to meet me, Jones, and Harmon in the boss's office at eight o'clock tomorrow morning."

The meeting was held, but the test series was considered unsatisfactory by all involved. The group had failed to get the desired information, and additional tests would have to be rescheduled at considerable cost in time and money.

The meeting proved to be a unique experience for George Bruster. Wallen denied outright that he had told George to use the strong language in speaking to Jones that had upset everyone so badly.

George could only reply that he thought that such language was Wallen's intent. George subsequently left the meeting shaking his head unhappily and trying to understand how the whole affair had deteriorated into such a mess.

QUESTIONS

1. What were George Bruster's functions as crew chief? What was his "authority" in this situation?
2. What was the nature of the communications network in this case? How did this contribute to the problems?
3. What means were provided to facilitate coordination? How could more effective coordination be achieved in a complex situation such as this?
4. How effective was the planning process in this case? What might be done to improve planning on similar projects in the future?
5. What type of leadership patterns are evident in the case? Were they appropriate to the situation?
6. What are the advantages of this rather flexible organizational structure? What are the disadvantages?
7. Do you think Acme Aircraft would function best as a "coercion-compromise" or a "collaborative-consensus" system? Why?
8. How does this case relate to the discussion of the "new managerial view" in the chapter?
9. How do you explain the rather intense reaction on the part of Conners Simpson and the other people at Culver City at the end of the case?
10. How would you help George Bruster understand how "the whole affair had deteriorated into such a mess"?

PART **3**

The body travels more easily than the mind,
and until we have limbered up our imagination
we continue to think as though we had stayed home.
We have not really budged a step until
we take up residence in someone else's
point of view.

John Erskine, *The Complete Life*

Managerial Applications

INTRODUCTION   It can be enlightening to look at the world around us through the eyes of others. In this section of the book the reader is invited to play the role of a manager (as a systems analyst and designer) and review these chapters with reference to the concepts and techniques developed in Parts 1 and 2.

We have selected examples which we think are of general interest to managers. However, our purpose in reviewing these applications is more than descriptive; it is our belief that these illustrations will help strengthen the philosophy of managing by system.

Chapter 11 is concerned with flow systems for both goods and services. For example, material flows are traced from the raw material stage through various transportation, storage, and transformation stages through to the ultimate consumer. The concept of inventories is described as a means of decoupling the flow system and facilitating transformation and transportation processes. Of particular importance is the point of view of the total flow system and the need for balance among the various segments involved.

Chapter 12 discusses automation and describes a recent development in producing machines—numerical control. In this system the operation of machines is planned and controlled through programmed instructions recorded on tape, usually as a digital code. It is an example of a structured, closed-loop system where inputs are measurable and outputs are predictable.

Chapter 13 deals with the program-management concept, a philosophy of management which emphasizes the importance of timely integration of all aspects of a weapon, space, or other system, from the establishment of operational requirements (perception of need) through design, production, delivery, and utilization. This chapter illustrates the application of the systems approach in managing large-scale, complex programs.

Chapter 14 is concerned with planning-programming-budgeting systems (PPBS). The general concept is described and its development is traced in the Department of Defense and other government agencies. The applicability of this managerial approach to states, cities, and universities is illustrated. Future prospects and problems are also considered.

Chapter 15 reviews the role of data processing in keeping track of organizational transactions, as well as in providing information for managerial decision making. A data processing system —collecting, processing, comparing, and analyzing—provides information for coordinating organizational activities, including strategic and operating subsystems. The electronic computer facilitates sophisticated systems of data processing, provided it is used as an integral component in a system capable of utilizing its potential. Integrated data processing and real-time systems are also discussed.

CHAPTER 11

Flow Systems — Goods and Services

There are countless interrelationships among the many activities involved in the process of material flow. For example, decisions made in manufacturing affect the purchase of raw materials and the sale of finished goods. Decisions made in selecting a mode of transportation may affect packaging, warehousing, and production. However, many firms operate within functional boundaries; each function is carried out as an entity, and performance is measured by the department manager's effectiveness and efficiency in his own particular activity.

Recently a number of companies have reorganized their operations to manage and control the movement of materials as a single integrated system, from the raw material source through the many stages of processing and including the distribution of the finished product. In this chapter we shall review this approach under the following topic areas:

Increasing complexity in distribution and production
Increasing cost of distribution
The total flow system
Planning the transformation
The function of inventories
Service systems

Service flow systems
Integrating systems

INCREASING COMPLEXITY IN DISTRIBUTION AND PRODUCTION

The problems associated with efficient performance of distribution and production activities have expanded geometrically in relation to the expansion in the variety of colors, sizes, and models of products being distributed. There are problems of anticipating demand, geographic dislocation of inventories, maintaining adequate stock for customer service, control of inventory, and production planning.

Problems of Anticipating Demand

The problems of anticipating demand, planning inventories, and scheduling production of a product line in total are simple in comparison to the problems associated with predicting and planning specific segments of the product line. More specifically, an appliance manufacturer can determine the sales potential for refrigerators based on past experiences and economic conditions. When this potential demand must be translated into sales by size, model, and color, the problem becomes more complex. Past experience has limited value and, furthermore, it is difficult to predict trends effectively. Much of the overproduction and subsequent distress selling in appliances and other products is traceable to the difficulty of anticipating demand when a large variety of products is manufactured.

Geographic Dislocation of Inventory

Experience has shown that there is no pattern of consistency in the demand for various colors, sizes, and models of products within regions of the United States market. When regional inventory planning is based on past experience, it is not unusual to find that consumption patterns have shifted and inventories are in the wrong locations. Colors or models which sell in a region one year may not sell in the same proportion the following year. As a result, transshipments of inventories—with the additional costs—are sometimes necessary in order to balance supply with demand.

Maintaining Adequate Stocks

One of the specific problems associated with efficient performance of the distribution function is the maintenance of adequate stocks at the regional warehouses, distributors, and retailers in order to serve the market promptly. As the variety of products increases the problem becomes more complex. Inventories should be sufficient to provide adequate selection, but middlemen are reluctant to assume the risks associated with large inventories. To illustrate, two units of each model, size, and style of a single television manufacturer may represent an investment in excess of $50,000 for a retailer.

Control of Inventory

As suggested before, the problems associated with controlling inventories are intensified as the variety of items is increased. The growth and change in product-line characteristics in both consumer and industrial products have resulted in more items for the distribution system to handle and stock. More items mean less volume per item and correspondingly higher unit processing, handling, and transportation costs.

In a study to measure the effect of increased product variation on the amount of inventory required, it was concluded that an increase in variety from one to three items (with total sales remaining the same) necessitated an increase in field inventories of 60 percent; in the same study, if total sales increased 50 percent, inventory requirements increased 100 percent.[1]

These figures, typical of companies with a wide market for their products, illustrate the effect of small-volume items on inventory control. Yet, as companies have expanded the variety of their product lines, the number of small-volume items has increased. Studies based on the records of a large number of firms distributing consumer and industrial products revealed that a relatively small percentage of items—usually 10 to 20 percent—account for about 80 percent of sales, while about half of the items account for less than 4 percent of sales.[2] This is a critical factor in inventory control because the slow-moving items usually contribute much more than their proportionate share of inventory cost.

[1] John F. Magee, "The Logistics of Distribution," *Harvard Business Review*, July-August, 1960, pp. 90–91.
[2] *Ibid.*, p. 91.

Production Planning

The increased efficiency and reduced cost resulting from production have made a significant contribution toward improving the standard of living in the United States. Mechanization, assembly lines, specialization, and, more recently, automation have resulted in productivity increases in manufacturing activities which have outstripped progress in distribution activities. The trends described above, however, tend to restrict the potential contribution of improved manufacturing techniques to further cost reduction.

As more and more companies succumb to the trends of market segmentation, product differentiation, and product variety, the opportunity for mass production—with its inherent advantages—is reduced. While the total number of units to be produced has increased, the number of identical units tends to decrease as a company increases the variety of colors, styles, sizes, and models. Instead of an assembly-line production of a large number of identical units, the manufacturing process becomes a series of shorter runs of dissimilar products. Economies of continuous runs are reduced as new setups and changes become normal procedure. Estimates of demand for the various products must be substituted for estimates of total demand in the determination of production planning and production scheduling. Liaison and communications between the manufacturing and distribution functions within companies become more important than in the past.

INCREASING COST OF DISTRIBUTION

As products are differentiated and the variety of products increases, several elements of marketing cost increase. Advertising and sales promotion expenditures are necessary to stimulate demand for the various products in the line. Under policies of product development for market segmentation, sales promotional appeals must be directed at the various submarkets. In addition, it may be necessary to expand the sales force and increase expenditures for sales training.

The process of handling orders becomes more complex and costly because a larger number of relatively small orders are substituted for fewer large orders. Consequently, costs associated with order handling and filling back orders are increased.

Decreasing the size of orders often results in a larger number of small shipments from manufacturing plants and warehouses to the market. As a result, unit transportation costs are increased.

These examples illustrate the effect of the increased variety of products on marketing costs. Actually, the entire marketing process becomes more complex and therefore more costly. Goals of improving efficiency or of controlling marketing costs become more difficult to attain.

Inventory costs include warehousing, insurance, taxes, handling, capital costs, and obsolescence. These combined costs represent a substantial part of the total cost of distribution. Any steps that can be taken to reduce the amount of inventory required have an immediate and significant effect upon physical-distribution costs.

Much of the added inventory cost is traceable to the obsolescence that develops from the addition of new products, engineering changes, and the regular introduction of new models. Technological obsolescence as a result of these changes is a significant price to pay for the progress and sales promotional values of regular style and model changes and has become an accepted cost of moving ahead in dynamic industries. No precise data are available on the cost of inventory obsolescence. There is no doubt, however, that this factor constitutes a definite problem and a major cost. For example, one of the daily activities at a parts depot of a large vehicle manufacturer is the scrapping, or returning to a central warehouse, of parts that have been designated obsolete.

The problems and costs of inventory obsolescence, while they vary considerably among different classes of products, also arise in relationships between manufacturers and middlemen. In general, when a product line is long, contains a variety of items, or contains slow-moving items, it is necessary to offer obsolescence protection and/or return privileges to distributors and retailers in order to encourage them to carry an adequate inventory.

All the costs mentioned are readily identified, but often difficult to measure. There is still another category of costs which may not be recognized. "The costs which derive directly from the waste, inefficiencies, and duplications possible in a distribution system should obviously not be, as they so frequently are, overlooked. These are the costs that result from not having the right goods at the right place at the right time." Possibly the largest of these costs pertains to lost sales.

In order to identify and analyze the relationships existing among the factors of production and distribution, it is helpful to consider the total system within the concept of the flow process.

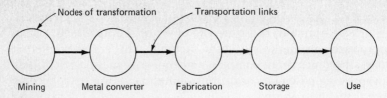

FIGURE 11-1. A flow network.

THE TOTAL FLOW SYSTEM

The reader may find it useful to think of the total flow system as a network of nodes, linked together by transfer systems. Some form of transformation takes place at each node, e.g., processing, storage, or packaging. The links between nodes are the means of mobility between subsystems which contribute utility through a flow or transfer process. Figure 11-1 illustrates a flow network with the first node representing a mining operation. The ore is transferred to a node where it is converted to ingots, shipped to a node where the ingots are transformed into fabricated parts, moved to a storage node, and finally delivered to the user. Most systems of production and distribution would require a very complex network to represent the process and flow accurately.[3]

Transformation and Service Nodes

With reference to transformation and service, we should consider the capabilities, capacity, and cost characteristics of each node. Nodes may be specialized, performing only a single function, or they may have the ability to perform a variety of functions, perhaps on a number of different types of units or transactions flowing through them. Specialized nodes are more likely to be suited to continuous processing operations while nodes with general-purpose capabilities are more frequently associated with one-at-a-time, short-run, or batch-type operations. For example, a crude oil refinery node is a special-purpose processing facility designed for continuous processing of crude oil with limited capability for altering the mix of inputs and outputs. In contrast, a fabrication facility such as a machine shop would have capabilities for producing various types of parts, and successive lots processed through them are likely to be quite different.

[3]See Paul A. Wassmansdorf, "Identifying and Controlling the Costs of Physical Distribution," in Hale C. Bartlett (ed.), *Readings in Physical Distribution*, Interstate Printers & Publishers, Danville, Ill., 1970, p. 63.

The measurement of the capacity of a service or transformation node involves consideration of the basic operating rate in the node and the length of time that the facility operates. Some facilities, such as electric generating plants, are designed for continuous operation, but may not be utilized continuously. In determining the size or number of facilities to be incorporated in the system, comparisons should be made between the marginal costs of higher utilization rates and the costs of providing additional facilities to be operated at lower rates of utilization. A factor affecting capacity, particularly of general-purpose facilities, is the amount of time lost in process change (setup time) as different entities flow through the facilities. Where this time is appreciable, capacity is reduced accordingly. Operating policies, then, determine in part the capacity of a service or transformation node.

Fixed and variable costs are relevant in selecting the number of transformation or service nodes with similar capabilities to include in a system. Technological advances often offer opportunities for lower variable cost of operations but usually with higher fixed costs. Where volume is high enough in the system, choices may be made between providing a single facility with high capacity, high fixed cost, and low variable cost or a number of facilities with smaller capacity, low fixed cost, but higher variable cost.

Storage Nodes[4]

Within the operating system, storage nodes interrupt the flow in portions of the network, and permit a degree of temporary imbalance between preceding and succeeding activities. The storage node acts as a buffer so that activities do not have to be coordinated precisely and linked tightly with one another. Management reduces the problems of coordinating flow through the network by using storage nodes; but a penalty is paid for the gain in organizational flexibility—additional costs are accrued for providing storage or waiting facilities, handling charges, and capital investment in inventories. The capacity of a storage node determines the amount of decoupling that can be obtained. In effect, organizational flexibility is purchased by providing storage nodes in the network. Management can increase flexibility by providing more costly storage nodes of higher capacity, but eventually a point is

[4]See Richard A. Johnson, William T. Newell, and Roger C. Vergin, *Operations Management—A Systems Concept,* Houghton Mifflin Company, Boston, 1972, pp. 71–76.

reached at which marginal savings obtained by decoupling the network are not sufficient to offset the marginal costs of storage.

In addition to the organizational justification for storage nodes, such nodes also serve as points at which units moving through the network can be aggregated, stored, disaggregated, and mixed together as necessary. For example, in a distribution system storage nodes may perform the function of bringing together shipments from different sources, regrouping them into mixed lots, and sending them out through the next link in the network. The airline terminal in the air transport system serves a somewhat similar function in that it provides a place where passengers arriving by auto and plane can be disaggregated and reaggregated into loads suitable for outgoing transportation links. The terminal also provides a place for storing passengers, the entities moving through the system, until such time as suitable transportation links are available.

Transportation Links[5]

Transportation links may provide intermittent movement of units in the system as in the case of passenger aircraft in an airline system, or flow may be continuous as in a pipeline. We also can characterize transportation links by their capacity for handling different types of entities.

Physical characteristics such as maximum load and speed of movement determine the maximum capacity of a transportation link. The degree to which maximum capacity is utilized through maximum loading and minimum delays determines the actual capacity. Less than maximum utilization may result, for instance, when the design of the transportation link is not matched to the unit flow in the system. Cargo aircraft are often underutilized when space in the cargo compartment is exhausted before maximum weight-lifting capacity is reached.

The physical characteristics of transportation links are important to the overall network because they impose constraints on operations at preceding and succeeding nodes. Cost characteristics of transportation links must also be analyzed in terms of the impact on the total operation of the network. A link which offers the lowest transportation cost does not necessarily result in minimum cost for the system. Such things as the amount of in-transit inventory required and the impact of the speed and responsiveness of

[5]Ibid, pp. 354–358.

the link on operations at preceding and succeeding nodes must be considered. In a spare parts supply system, for example, it may be more economical to maintain a single inventory of parts at a central location and air freight the parts to locations of demand rather than to maintain separate inventories at various geographical locations and ship parts to these dispersed storage nodes by a cheaper but slower mode of transportation. Airlines frequently find that, for many items, a single location or a few central locations for a spare parts inventory can provide nearly the same parts availability as multiple locations, and with a much smaller total inventory investment. However, in order to determine the lowest total-system cost and at the same time maintain an effective system, the overall network should be analyzed. This requires a large amount of planning.

PLANNING THE TRANSFORMATION

The planning process consists of the development of a series of plans or schedules with successively shorter time horizons. Firms forecast and also plan conversion to some extent when they determine the proper capacity and design of factory buildings, warehouses, railroad systems, etc. A consideration of scheduling is necessary in the selection of equipment and processes to ensure that the processes selected are the most economical for the anticipated level of operations. After facilities are acquired, scheduling at a more detailed level is required to plan the best level of operations and employment throughout the year. Finally, monthly, weekly, and even daily schedules are developed to describe in detail the precise activities of individuals and facilities.

A manufacturing firm producing goods requires two types of operating schedules. The manufacturer needs schedules of the aggregate or total level of production for the intermediate time span of up to twelve months in order to plan for the hiring of people, acquisition of raw materials, and creation of inventories. Short-term schedules of perhaps less than a month's duration are then developed within the constraints of the aggregate schedule. The short-term schedules assign individuals and facilities to produce specific products and services, and are based upon up-to-date information about orders and inventory levels.

The necessity for planning aggregate production, employment, and inventory levels arises because of uneven time patterns of either inputs or outputs. If inputs were available at a uniform price throughout the year and if sales requirements were spread evenly, the optimal schedule would be to produce at the average demand level with no seasonal inventory buildup and no necessity for hiring and layoff, or for overtime to adjust employment to the production schedule. Unfortunately, most firms contend with some seasonality in the demand for their products. In industries which produce products such as boats, toys, lawn mowers, farm equipment, and antifreeze, as much as 80 to 90 percent of annual sales may occur in less than half the calendar year. Even necessary items such as food and clothing, which have a more stable consumption pattern, often exhibit an appreciable degree of seasonality.

Some organizations also face the constraint of an uneven rate of raw materials input. For example, fruit and vegetable canneries receive all their input of each basic product within an interval of a few weeks out of each year. They pack all their output within a few weeks because of the spoilage rate of the raw material. Such schedules give rise to high cost because the firm must maintain expensive equipment which it uses for only a small part of each year.

The alternatives open to the organization with a seasonal demand pattern are more numerous because of the ability of the firm to supply products over time through the use of inventories. At one extreme, the firm can meet each change in demand with a change in the production rate, accomplishing this by hiring and laying off employees and by the use of overtime and idle time. At the other extreme, the firm can maintain an even production and employment pattern and accommodate the seasonal sales pattern by building up inventories during the slack sales periods and reducing them during the peak times. Other alternatives consist of all combinations of the two extremes, using some inventories and having some variation in the production and employment rates.

Cost of Smoothing Production

Specific penalty costs are associated with all the alternatives for smoothing production. Level production schedules result in large stocks of seasonal inventories with their related storage and carrying charges. Overtime operations usually require a 50 percent wage payment premium and result in additional inefficiency when large increments of overtime are scheduled. Idle time may be even more costly. Changing the employment level may be relatively simple in some firms where a low skill level is required, but extremely expensive in firms where several months of training may be necessary in order to bring employees to an acceptable level of productivity. In addition, a schedule which utilizes a varying transformation rate will require more capacity than a stable pattern.

It is no simple matter to arrive at accurate cost estimates. The estimation problem is complicated because the costs do not remain constant and may vary considerably over a short period of time. Three critical factors are suggested as determinants of the total incremental costs of changing production and employment levels:[6]

1. The production output rate and inventory and employment levels of the period about to end, that is, the point of departure
2. The magnitude of the change in the production rate, the employment level and the inventory level
3. The length of the period of the production schedule

The current operating level represents some point in the total production-cost curve of the firm. This cost curve is not a straight-line function; the marginal costs vary throughout the curve. For example, if a firm has been operating at 75 percent of normal single-shift capacity, a 10 percent increase in the production rate can be accomplished by hiring more workers. If the firm had been operating at 100 percent of normal capacity, however, an increase of the same magnitude might require a second-shift operation, and increased supervision in addition to hiring more workers. Similarly, a reduction in the production rate from the 100 percent level could be accomplished by a small reduction in the work week, or by laying off personnel with the lowest seniority and lease skill. If the production rate were down to 50 percent of normal capacity, however, further reductions in employment might necessitate laying off highly skilled employees whom the firm may not be able to rehire at some later time.

Large increases in the employment level will require more intensive recruiting, covering a wider geographic area and the hiring of some people without the desired skills. Thus, the cost per employee hired may increase as more are hired. The same relationship will hold with respect to reductions in the employment level. There is usually some attrition plus those recently hired who can be layed off at little cost to the firm. Larger layoffs may require some restructuring of the organization and direct penalty costs because of union restrictions and state unemployment compensation laws.

[6]See R. E. McGarrah, *Production and Logistics Management,* John Wiley & Sons, Inc., New York, 1963, pp. 110–113.

Earlier in the chapter, several references were made to the significance of inventories in the flow process. The basic function of inventories in relation to their cost is of great importance in the analysis of the total flow system. The following discussion presents the function/cost relationship in some detail.

THE FUNCTION OF INVENTORIES

Organizations provide goods or services for other organizations or individuals. Those which provide services lack the flexibility in the temporal and spatial dimensions possessed by the organizations which produce goods. A group of medical doctors cannot treat disease and injury until a patient brings the unique input of himself to the organization for treatment. The doctors must be located and keep hours convenient to some segment of the population in order to receive this unique input. The organizations which produce the medications and equipment used in treating the patient can, however, produce them at any convenient time and location. The use of inventories creates this flexibility.

Inventories are located at a variety of points in the operating system. All goods are produced from materials which originally existed in their natural state as animal, vegetable, and mineral matter. Some organizations convert the natural matter into raw materials such as lumber, iron and steel, hides, and so forth. Other organizations begin the conversion of raw materials into industrial and consumer goods. In producing complex products, such as computers or jet airplanes, hundreds of different organizations may be involved in converting and assembling the product and some individual components may pass through several organizational entities. After the physical transformation is completed, other organizations transport and transfer ownership of the products, often through several stages, until the product reaches the hands of the ultimate consumer.

Inventories provide the basic function of "decoupling" the operations involved in converting inputs into outputs. They allow both time and spatial separation between production and consumption of products and between the many nodes or operations within the operating system.

Economic development provides increased output and efficiency through specialization. In the caveman's society, each person produced all his own goods—food, clothing, and a few simple utensils. In modern industrialized societies, each individual produces only a minute fraction of the goods he consumes. Such a society cannot operate without large stocks of inventories. The high degree of specialization necessitates geographic and temporal separations. Inventories provide the buffer which allows these separations to exist. The tremendous advance in the standard of living during the last century in the advanced economies is due as much to changes in production methods, such as specialization and division of labor, as it is to technological invention. The time span required for producing an object such as an automobile from the conversion of raw material to final delivery would undoubtedly run into years. Yet, a person can purchase a new automobile in a matter of minutes because of the existence of inventories. Inventories also provide separations which allow economical levels of operations. Instead of requiring production of a single unit each time one is consumed, products can be produced in batches, thus achieving economies in handling and transporting the goods and setting up production processes.

Since inventories tie up assets, firms must keep them at a reasonable level. Additional direct charges accumulate because of storage space requirements, insurance and taxes, and so on. Firms, therefore, cannot afford to keep unrestricted inventories at every point in the production process despite the benefits they bring. Even with closely controlled inventories, manufacturing firms often find that as much as 25 to 50 percent of their total assets are invested in inventories. Moreover, wholesalers and retailers occasionally find as much as 75 to 80 percent of their assets in inventories.

All types of business and other organizations maintain some inventories. Manufacturing firms, whose primary task is the physical conversion of goods, maintain large stocks of raw materials and semifinished and finished goods. Marketing firms, such as wholesalers and retailers, accumulate finished goods, maintain them at locations, and provide them at times convenient to their customers. Financial institutions, transportation firms, governmental organizations and other institutions that deal primarily in providing services rather than products still require stocks of office and operating supplies, cash, and so forth.

Inventory Costs

The benefits obtained from the proper use of inventories are not obtained without penalty. There is a rather substantial cost of carrying inventories. A firm should consider the cost of capital which could be earning a return if invested elsewhere. In making this estimate, a firm takes into account the liquidity and risk involved. Money tied up in inventory is quite liquid—it may be converted into cash in a fairly short time, if the need arises. Most firms have more investment opportunities, which will earn returns in excess of the borrowing interest rate, than they can obtain funds to finance. Hence, a firm should charge inventories with an opportunity cost equivalent to the expected return on other investments with comparable risk and liquidity; a rate usually in excess of the borrowing rate.

Inventory is also subject to spoilage, obsolescence, and deterioration. Many firms carry fire insurance on inventories. Even when none is carried, the inventory carrying cost rate should reflect the existing risk of fire loss. Warehouses and storage areas must be built and maintained for the inventories. Space charges may include depreciation of racks, fixtures, and other handling and storing devices. Generally, these costs are apportioned uniformly among the various stored products on the basis of some percentage of the product's dollar value. Although a more accurate allocation of these costs may be on the basis of storage space required, such information is usually not readily available within the firm's normal data processing system. Generally, a cost-based allocation is sufficiently accurate for inventory decision-making purposes within the firm since some correlation does exist between inventory cost and product value.

When all the elements of cost are added together, the total annual carrying cost is often within the range of 20 to 25 percent of the inventory's value. The inventory carrying cost is normally treated as a linear cost function. Thus, a firm with a 25 percent carrying cost maintaining an average inventory of $1,000,000 would have an annual inventory cost of $250,000.

The benefits obtained from carrying inventory accrue at a decreasing rate. That is, a firm obtains large economies from adding the first units of inventory, but as the firm adds more inventory the cost reductions become smaller. Although a firm may obtain $500,000 in annual benefits per year from the first $1,000,000 of inventory held, the second $1,000,000 may produce only $100,000 worth of savings in other areas. Thus, relatively small inventories produce a large rate of return with the return becoming smaller as the size of the inventory is increased. The main decision problem in inventory control is to determine at what point the cost of carrying inventory outweighs the benefits which the inventory produces.

Most products and materials are sold or consumed individually or a few units at a time. However, in order to decrease the amount of ordering, shipping, and handling, the products are purchased or produced in larger quantities. Determination of the optimal quantity to produce or purchase often is accomplished through the use of an economic production (or order) quantity formula which relates the cost of storage or production to the rate of use.

SERVICE SYSTEMS[7]

In goods-producing systems, the use of inventories dampens the effects of irregularities in the time patterns of inputs and outputs. Service systems, however, usually depend upon a unique input provided by the beneficiary of the service, and conversion or production cannot take place until that unique input is available. Inventories of services cannot be accumulated.

Because of the inherent time dependence of production in service systems, they typically cannot achieve the same level of efficiency in utilizing the time capacity of people and facilities as goods-producing systems can achieve. Some service systems approach full utilization of their resources by scheduling the arrival of the unique inputs provided by the "customer." Systems which provide medical (a doctor's office) and legal (lawyer's office) services and some transportation systems (scheduled trains, buses, and the like) fall into this category. The apparent internal efficiencies of these systems are substantially reduced when the time spent waiting by the "customer" before being served is considered. In other service systems, such as highways, hospitals, and supermarkets, very little control over the arrival of the "customer" exists and it may be necessary to provide sufficient capacity to serve peak loads even though peak load conditions exist only a very small proportion of the time and most of the facility remains idle most of the time.

The institutions providing service cannot, unfortunately, accumulate inventories of the services that they provide. Their inability to accumulate inventories prevents the service industries from making the rapid strides in increasing efficiency and output that have occurred in the production of physical products. Banks must maintain sufficient facilities and people to handle peak-hour loads even if they remain idle the remainder of the day. The railroads and the airlines must move their trains and planes on schedule even if only one-fourth of the seats are occupied. Contrast this

[7]Ibid. pp. 406–407.

to the factory in which lawn mowers can be produced all year long, although almost all of them are sold in a period of four or five months each year. The service industries continue to require a larger and larger portion of the total work force partially because they cannot automate operations and accumulate inventories of services.

Service Systems with Noncontrollable Inputs

The vast majority of service-producing systems exercise little control over the time of arrivals to the system. Although individual arrivals may follow specific time-behavior patterns, the overall pattern of arrivals for many service systems is completely random. Arrival patterns give rise to queuing or waiting lines when they occur with some type of time distribution. Service or transformation is performed, again, over some kind of a time pattern, and the individuals leave the queuing system. Because of the uneven patterns of arrivals and service times, waiting lines are formed from time to time.

Waiting lines are encountered frequently in normal daily existence. One joins a waiting line for service at a department store or a supermarket checkout counter, at a traffic stoplight, or at a bank. In other cases, the arrivals are things rather than people. For example, applications for entrance arrive at the admissions office of a university, orders for production arrive at a factory, and jobs arrive at a computer center for processing. In some cases, the service center goes to the waiting line. When someone calls a repairman to fix a home appliance, the repair order call joins the repairman's waiting line of jobs where it remains until the service center or the repairman reaches that point on the waiting line. The above are just a few examples. A very wide variety of situations fits the general waiting-line model.

When the flow of materials and the flow of service are considered together, the analysis reflects the systems approach. The following material on service flow, or the service cycle, represents this point of view.

SERVICE FLOW SYSTEMS

In distribution systems it is usual to think of service flow as the time it takes for delivery from the warehouse to the customer. However, the service cycle in reality includes the total time after the need for goods is recognized until the goods are available. Figure 11-2 shows a complete service cycle.

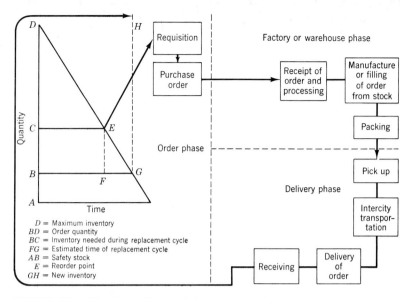

FIGURE 11-2. The three phases of the service cycle.

Service can be divided into three parts: (1) the order phase, (2) the warehouse phase, and (3) the delivery phase. The order phase includes all activities of the buyer necessary to communicate the need for a product to the seller. Specific activities include recognition of the need to order or reorder, the paper work involved in writing a requisition and purchase order, and the transfer of the order to the vendor. If the vendor's representative calls on the buyer and gets the order, the transfer of the order to the plant or warehouse would still be a part of the order phase of the service cycle.

The warehouse phase includes the activities needed to get the order ready for shipment, e.g., the receipt and processing of the order; the planning, scheduling, and manufacturing or the filling of the order from stock; and the packing of the order for shipment.

The delivery phase involves the physical transfer of the product from the seller to the buyer. The delivery from plant or warehouse to the shipper, the transfer to the buyer's location, and the receipt and processing of the incoming shipment are activities of the delivery phase of the cycle.

The lead time between recognizing the need and the satisfaction of that need therefore includes all the activities outlined. Some of these activities are carried out by the customer, some by the seller, and the rest by outside agencies. The buyer can reduce total lead time by accelerating the activities within his operation or by bringing economic pressure on the seller to improve that portion of the service cycle which the seller controls.

Delivery Service and Sales

Most customers would like to have manufacturers, or their representatives in the distribution system, maintain all inventories beyond current requirements and locate these inventories close at hand. This relieves the customers of carrying safety stocks; the reorder point could approach zero inventory. Customers need carry only those inventories consistent with ordering in economic quantities. The manufacturer has the prime responsibility for forecasting demand, maintaining safety stocks, and giving the customer prompt delivery service from decentralized inventories.

How much are sales influenced by the amount of service the seller provides? Or stated in other words, will there be an increase in sales if the seller provides better service? Most experts believe there is a direct correlation between sales and service, and the simplest representation of this is a straight-line, or linear, relationship. Figure 11-3 shows that an individual firm can increase its share of the market if it improves its delivery service relative to other companies in the industry.

The share of the market equals the service time multiplied by a constant. When the change in service time does not result in as great a change in sales, the constant is less than 1. A firm seldom operates at the extremes of no service or perfect service; reasonably good service is provided by the typical firm.

When a firm is operating at either extreme of the service-time cycle, there is no longer a linear relationship. As service time ap-

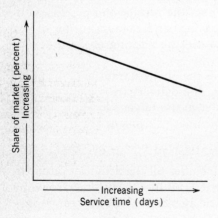

FIGURE 11-3. Relationship between service time and share of the market.

FIGURE 11–4. Relationship between service time and share of the market for extremes of service.

proaches zero, the curve tends to become horizontal; the increase in sales realized by a decrease in service time from near perfect to perfect probably would be less than a similar rate of improvement in the intermediate portion of the scale. Similarly, change in service from poor to very poor may have little effect on sales. Figure 11–4 illustrates the tendency of the sales-service curve to flatten out at either end of the scale.

Another factor also must be considered. Changes in sales as a function of service would not be constant or incremental, but would occur in steps. For example, a manufacturer would tend to initiate a significant improvement in service time in order to produce a psychological impact on the customer. A significant improvement, such as a reduction from ten to six days, would be more desirable than a gradual change from ten to six days over a long period of time. Figure 11–5, therefore, would be more descriptive of the service-time—sales relationship.

The relationship of the change in sales to the change in serv-

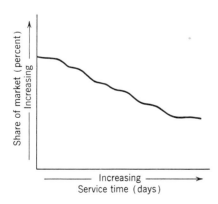

FIGURE 11–5. Relationship of service time to sales with significant changes in service time.

ice will vary in different industries, depending on competition and the possibility of product substitution. However, the important points suggested from this analysis are that (1) service changes at either extreme have little effect on sales, and (2) a service change must be significant to have a psychological impact on the customer.

Improving Service

One method of improving customer delivery service is to reduce the time cycle by storing inventories in many locations close to the point of need. This implies, first of all, that someone has been able to forecast what and where the need will be. The real test of forecasting is the accuracy of the forecast in comparison with what happens and the ability to isolate distinct variables so that major errors may be recognized and corrected. As suggested earlier, when variables are added, the problem of measurement becomes more complex and the accuracy of the forecast more doubtful.

It becomes apparent, therefore, that when inventories are decentralized and the amount of inventory stored depends on the forecast for that region, additional inventories must be stored to offset the unreliability of the forecast. In fact, inventories must increase more than proportionally to provide for all contingenies. Figure 11-6, a probability table, illustrates this point.

If the demand during the lead time is 1 and the product is ordered when the stocks have declined to 1 unit, 50 percent of the time there will be a stockout. When a company wants to provide stock in almost every situation (99.999 percent of the time), the reorder point would occur when the stocks are reduced to 9 units. However, the rate of increase of the order point is not as great when the demand during lead time is larger. Therefore, as service is improved by increasing the number of decentralized storage units, the inventories necessary to provide this service increase dramatically and the cost increases accordingly.

FIGURE 11-6. Service-policy Effect on Order Point and Inventory Shows Order Point for Each Service Policy.

	Order point, order-service policy, percent				
Demand during lead time	50	90	95	99	99.999
1	1	3	3	4	9
10	10	15	16	19	29
100	100	113	117	124	153
1,000	1,000	1,037	1,050	1,075	1,158
10,000	10,000	10,112	10,152	10,232	10,500

FIGURE 11-7. Number of Days for 50, 90, and 100 Percent of Orders to Flow through Service Cycle.

	50 percent completed	90 percent completed	100 percent completed
Order phase	1.0	3.0	11
Warehouse phase	.8	4.3	6
Delivery phase	2.0	3.7	5
Total service cycle	4.7	7.5	14

A second and more logical approach to the customer-service problem is to maintain customer-service levels consistent with the demand of most customers, but accomplish this objective through a more efficient system of distribution. One plan is to centralize distribution points and gain savings through smaller inventories, less paper work, and greater control and still maintain equivalent service levels. This can be done by improving each phase of the service cycle and combining the three phases into an effective total system.

When the total service cycle is considered, a business firm may find that it is not getting prompt service from decentralized storage points. A study was made of the service cycle of a firm which supplied products to retail stores. Orders were traced from the time the customer dispatched the order until the goods were delivered to the customer. The results were rather startling. Figure 11-7 shows the cycle time necessary to complete 50, 90, and 100 percent of the orders sampled.

The company believed that it was providing daily deliveries to its customers, but the study indicated that only 50 percent of the orders were in the hands of the customer 4.7 days after the customer placed the order. It was 7.5 days before 90 percent of the orders completed the service cycle, and 14 days before all deliveries were made.

This suggests the need to integrate the flow of materials and service as a total system.

INTEGRATING SYSTEMS

Firms commit thousands and even millions of dollars which may or may not produce a profit, depending on the acceptance of the product in the market.

A major reason for making production commitments far in advance of sales is the material-flow cycle. Market planning provides the basis for production planning, which in turn establishes material requirements; materials are purchased, delivered to the plant, inspected, and transferred to stores. A protective cushion of time is added for each step of this flow process, tending to allow the maximum time which any step might take.

Finished products may go into temporary storage, then to the shipping department, sometimes to branch warehouses, to wholesalers and/or retailers, and finally to the customer. This outbound movement is replete with multiple handling and costly delay before the product is placed in the hands of the consumer.

The longer the flow-cycle time, the further in advance the commitments must be made relative to producing a given item. The longer the cycle, the greater the opportunity for competitors to develop a new product which may capture a larger share of the total market.

Certain phases of the external distribution system have been studied intently, and optimal warehouse location patterns as well as optimal routing and scheduling patterns have been developed. In many cases, however, the confines of the problem have been rather narrow, with simplifying assumptions being made concerning the effect of factors at either end of the subsystem. The effect of changes within the system upon external elements usually has been ignored. Further, the broader aspects of the total system have not received much attention, principally because of the organizational structure of the typical business firm.

Traditionally, most organization has been vertical and hierarchical, with authority and responsibility resting in individual functions. Superior-subordinate relationships have been established on a functional basis, with orders and instructions going down the line and reports and requests going up the line. Recently, this traditional approach has been questioned in reference to its suitability for overall efficiency of the operation. For example, the flow of material and information in the typical manufacturing operation tends to be horizontal, cutting across the vertical structuring of functional authority.

The problem is that most companies organized in the traditional functional fashion are not set up to take advantage of conceptualizing the total flow process. First of all, management should reevaluate its organization and reconstruct it as a network of systems.

Recently a number of companies have reorganized their operation to manage and control the movement of materials as a single integrated system, from the raw material source through the many stages of processing and including the distribution of the finished products.

The systems approach involves (1) reviewing the need for the function in terms of the objectives of the system, and (2) determining its cost and contribution in relation to other necessary functions. For instance, packaging costs could be reduced by using new kinds of materials or packaging machinery. However, a more basic approach would be to investigate the relationships among packaging, transportation, handling, and advertising; this may reveal the desirability of changing, or eliminating, the packaging function. In another case it may be more profitable to allow manufacturing output to fluctuate, because selling costs may be reduced more under this kind of policy than the additional costs incurred when production is geared to demand.

Every activity in the flow of materials should be considered as a segment of a total system. The contribution of each component and subsystem could be ascertained by measuring its output; its efficiency is determined by comparing this measure of output against a measurement of resource input. This kind of evaluation would point out areas of inefficiency and enable management to adjust its operation to meet changing conditions.

These are illustrations of relationships which exist among a few functions. The matrix of relationships among all the functions relative to converting and transferring raw materials to the market provides a whole new field of exploration.

Simulating the Network

The best way to study material flow is by simulation. Since the analysis is concerned with the overall flow of material and information, and since it contains a number of separate and diverse functions, it would be extremely difficult to create a mathematical equation to define the total system. Therefore analysis structured toward optimizing the total-system operation seldom would be meaningful. Simulation, on the other hand, would allow the researcher to reproduce the system under study via a series of simplified algebraic equations set up to represent the various levels and flows of material, information, and manpower.

A number of benefits accrue to the researcher and the manager when a simulation study is undertaken of the total from raw material to consumer. First of all, since those persons involved in making decisions in the operation as a whole must verbalize their decision-making process to the researcher, they cannot avoid becoming better acquainted with their own operation. The explicitness with which the activities and decisions must be set forth for a simulation model forces those involved to define their own functions clearly. Often this activity in itself can result in benefits which more than offset the time and cost involved in the research project. Once the system has been simulated by a number of simplified and fairly straightforward equations, a number of days, weeks, or years of activity can be generated, and the results of these operations can be compared with actual results for the same period. In this way the critical points in the model can be compared and their realism evaluated. The model as verbalized by the decision makers may turn out to be quite different from the actual operating system. When the simulation results are compared with some actual operating data, the decision makers involved see where their perception of the process was wrong.

The model of the total system, including accumulation of raw materials, production, and distribution, can be used to evaluate changes in given policies. A policy change can be made in any one segment of the total process, and the impact of this change can be evaluated by the simulated operating results. This tool gives management an opportunity to test and evaluate proposals without running the risk of actually installing new approaches and absorbing the necessary costs associated with system changes.

Changes in the various segments of the total system can be programmed and "run" over a period of time in order to discover which parts of the total flow are most sensitive to change. If wide fluctuations result at a particular point because of what were considered minor policy changes in another area, management has a good clue for subsequent decision making and/or more detailed investigation.

Typically, the system simulation which can be used for describing an entire operation will be a relatively closed system. This means that the operation is simulated with little participation by outside individuals or other external variables; that is, policy changes or alternative decisions are programmed into the simulation model at relatively few points.

When the simulation program is used for demonstration or training, it may allow outside decision makers to participate. In this case the decision makers who are external to the simulation process must make key decisions which are processed by the computer. In accordance with the basic program and the choices of the "players," the results of the operation are simulated. This can be a valuable exercise in that it forces the people involved to make decisions in a dynamic environment and also to think about all the various factors involved in the distribution system.

It is quite obvious that the use of simulation techniques,

particularly for large-scale operations, would not be possible if it were not for the availability of large-scale electronic computing equipment. While the design of simulation systems is not overly complicated and does not involve a great deal of sophisticated mathematics, a vast quantity of variables and a large number of equations are involved. Although the equations are simple to manipulate, there can be many thousands of them and they all must be computed for each time period involved in simulating the operation. With the computer these calculations are simple, and elaborate system simulations are possible.

SUMMARY

The distribution of goods and services has become increasingly complex. Because of the increasing variety of products being produced, it has become more difficult to predict demand. Inventories often are stored in the wrong market area, and must be larger to accommodate the uncertainty of demand. All this adds to the increasing cost of goods and services.

It is useful to regard the flow system of goods and services as a network of nodes, linked together by transfer systems. At most of these nodes transformation and/or service takes place. Other nodes are used to decouple or interrupt the flow of the network, to permit a degree of temporary imbalance between preceding and succeeding activities in the network. Transportation links provide movement of the entities in the system between the various nodes.

The scheduling process provides the timing of activities between the nodes and also the detailed planning of activities within the nodes. The relation of planning relative to the need for the product will affect the regularity of the transformation cycle. An alternate to producing directly for need is to produce at a regular rate and inventory or store the excess production for the cyclical demand. Obviously inventory of production incurs some additional cost which may be countered by the additional cost of operating at an irregular rate of transformation.

Inventories are located at various points in the operating system. They may be raw materials, goods in process, or finished products. They provide the basic function of "decoupling," the operations involved in converting inputs into outputs. Such factors as opportunity cost, spoilage, obsolescence, deterioration, and handling are included in the total cost of carrying inventories.

In service systems it is not possible to decouple a network

through inventories, and when inputs arrive at a noncontrollable rate, the system must be programmed to handle peak loads. The customer is concerned with the amount of time it requires to provide a service and, in distribution systems, this includes the operations of ordering, preparation of the order, and delivery. In some instances the service cycle has a direct connection with the sales that can be made for a product.

The individual phases of the external distribution system have been studied intently, and many improvements are apparent. The greatest potential for improvement may be to consider the entire network or system and to integrate the activities of the various nodes. Systems simulation can be employed as a basic tool of analysis.

QUESTIONS

1. What problems have been magnified by the increasing complexity in distribution and production?
2. What part do storage nodes play in the systems network?
3. Give an example of (a) an intermittent transportation link and (b) a continuous transportation link.
4. How does the uneven input to the transformation node affect planning? Give an example where this situation may exist.
5. What kinds of costs are incurred by smoothing production? What are the benefits?
6. What is the basic function of inventories?
7. What kinds of costs are incurred by having inventories?
8. What is the major difference between product and service transformation in the network system?
9. What relation exists between service and sales? Give an example of how the availability of a product for delivery may have influenced your decision to purchase.
10. Explain the probability table (Figure 11-6). What is the significance of this table to inventory policy?
11. Describe the three phases of the service cycle. Which phase is the most important to the purchaser?
12. What relation does the organization have to the ability to integrate systems?
13. How might a researcher simulate a distribution system? Prepare an illustration from your own experience.

O-Nut, Incorporated*

Jim Powers, Art Gross, and Fred Hatch respectively had just been appointed president, operations manager, and financial secretary of O-Nut, Incorporated, which had just taken over the entire assets of the OK Orchard Development Company. The assets consisted of 1,000 acres of planted land containing approximately 65,000 eight-year-old "O" nut trees; 2,000 acres of cleared unplanted land suitable for the growing of "O" nut trees; sufficient buildings and equipment to support the existing operation; and a substantial supply of office, maintenance, and operating supplies. Approximately 10 days prior to the transfer of ownership to O-Nut, Incorporated, the OK Orchard Development Company had completed the harvest of its second annual crop of "O" nuts. They obtained a yield of approximately 2½ million pounds of unshelled nuts and had contracted for the sale of the entire amount for $325,000.

OK Orchard Development Company was organized and operated by a group of three enterprising and aggressive businessmen for the purpose of growing, processing, and distributing "O" nuts for a heretofore undeveloped world market. The company was established on a modest capital base but had been unable to raise sufficient additional capital on satisfactory terms. As a result it was not in a position to carry out its original plans to develop its own processing and distribution facilities. Projected profits, based on the sale to existing processors of the two crops of "O" nuts previously obtained, indicated a long-run return on their investment that was substantially less than originally appeared possible under a fully integrated growing, processing, and distribution operation. In addition, the rapidly expanding yield potential of the 65,000 trees could

*Source: Albert N. Schrieber, Richard A. Johnson, Robert C. Meier, William T. Newell, and Henry C. Fischer, *Cases in Manufacturing Management,* McGraw-Hill Book Company, New York, 1965, pp. 232–243.

quickly overburden existing processing facilities and possibly upset the stable market price for raw "O" nuts.

Rather than subject themselves to this risk or surrender their independence by merging with a larger company or by floating a large common stock issue, the owner-managers of the OK Orchard Development Company decided to sell their interests to the United Nut Growers (parent company of O-Nut, Incorporated). The price obtained repaid their total investment and provided a modest return for their efforts. The terms of the sale were for payment of one-third on the day of transfer of ownership and the remaining two-thirds in five equal annual installments.

The sales agreement stated that the three owners of the OK Orchard Development Company would remain in their current positions in an operating but non-policy-making capacity for three months after the official transfer agreement was signed. This was designed to provide an efficient and smooth transfer of operations to the new management. Although not included in writing, negotiators for O-Nut, Incorporated, stated that their firm would retain as many operational employees in their current positions as possible after the transfer had been effected. The negotiators, however, were careful to qualify this statement by stating that this promise was not to imply the mandatory continuance of any current company objectives or policies regarding operating practices, working conditions, or wages. This information was communicated to the employees of the OK Orchard Development Company by the original owner-managers.

"O" nuts varied in size from a filbert to a medium-sized walnut and had a texture and taste distinctly different from any currently commercially available nut. Some people likened its taste to that of an almond or chestnut, whereas others claimed it tasted similar to a filbert or brazil nut. "O" nuts could be used for party, dinner, and cocktail treats; as an ingredient or topping for cakes, pies, cookies, ice cream, and numerous other desserts; as a garnish for meats, fish, and fowl; and as an addition to various salads. A paperback book of "O" nut recipes, endorsed by a world-famed chef in a major hotel in Jamaica, was available upon request for chefs, dietitians, housewives, and others who were interested in using "O" nuts.

The discovery of the "O" nut as an edible fruit was made by Dr. Jim Adams in the late 1800s. Until 1922, however, when the first sizable commercial plantings were made, the "O" nut tree was valued primarily for its ornamental qualities and the majority of the plantings were sold for such purposes. A small portion of the plantings was used for growing "O" nuts. These generally resulted from an overoptimistic estimate of nursery requirements for ornamental plants.

For many years the primary market for "O" nuts was local natives and inhabitants of nearby islands who ate the nuts in their natural uncooked state. It was not until a group of agricultural economists took an active interest in the commercial use of "O" nuts that their potential value as a delicacy became apparent. In 1942, when the OK Orchard

Development Company was formed, there were only 1,200 acres of "O" nut trees under cultivation. A majority of these trees were approaching a state of maturity, and the production of raw unshelled nuts approximated 150,000 pounds. Many of these trees were originally planted to be sold as seedlings and not for the production of nuts. The yield of most trees at this time was as low as one-fifth to one-tenth of the expected yield of the varieties developed and subsequently planted by the OK Development Company.

Few new plantings were made between 1942 and 1948 because of World War II and the numerous and more fruitful opportunities available to investors during that period. In addition, the existing, rapidly maturing trees provided a supply of "O" nuts which was neither easily harvested nor disposed of profitably in view of existing labor, equipment, and transportation problems. In the mid-1950s the OK Orchard Development Company sensed a change in existing conditions and, on the basis of an expected major increase in the demand for "O" nuts, purchased 3,000 acres of timberland suitable for growing "O" nut trees. Within a few years 1,000 acres of this land had been cleared and planted with approximately 70,000 newly grafted "O" nut trees. This planting represented a potential increase of tenfold or more in the future supply of "O" nuts and temporarily discouraged newcomers from entering the field.

At the time the OK Orchard Development Company sold out to O-Nut, Incorporated, there were approximately 2,500 acres of "O" nut trees under cultivation. Excluding O-Nut, Incorporated, the largest of the growers owned 400 acres of 3- to 5-year-old trees in the non-bearing stage. These trees were of a variety similar to those being grown by O-Nut, Incorporated. The remaining 1,100 acres under cultivation were owned by 13 independent firms and consisted of 500 acres of 7- to 9-year-old currently bearing trees and 600 acres of mature and over-mature low-yield trees. In addition to O-Nut's 2,000 acres of cleared land, other producers had available an additional 1,000 acres of land suitable for growing "O" nut trees. The 600 acres of low-yield trees could be converted to the latest varieties of high-yield trees by regrafting. Such trees would be of bearing age within 4 to 5 years after regrafting, which would be at least 3 years prior to any yields available from new plantings made at the same time.

A major foreign nut producer was known to have been investigating the profit potential of "O" nuts. If this firm decided to enter the field it was conjectured that it would do so by purchasing numerous mature and overmature orchards, including connecting lands, and thus be able to substantially increase yields within 5 years from the entry date into the field. The financial capabilities of this foreign firm equaled or exceeded those of O-Nut, Incorporated, and its parent company, United Nut Growers.

Original plantings of "O" nut trees were made by grafting cuttings from prize growing stock to select 2-year-old nursery grown rootstock. These trees yielded their first fruits in 7 to 8 years after their grafting date. Planting could also be accomplished by regrafting to mature rootstock resulting in initial yields within 4 to 5 years after the regrafting was made. No appreciable difference in the overall yield pattern appeared to exist between new grafts and regrafts except for the approximately 3-year difference in time between grafting and initial yields. Due to the need for more careful grafting and extensive root pruning and culturing required by regrafts, the original cost of regrafting was approximately double that of purchasing and planting newly grafted trees which currently averaged $10 per tree. Part of this difference was recovered by the reduced maintenance resulting from the shorter non-bearing period of regrafted trees. Once a regraft was attempted, whether successful or not, further regrafting was inadvisable. The survival rate for new grafts was approximately 90 to 95 per cent, as compared to 70 or 80 per cent for first regrafts. For second, third, or additional regrafts the survival rate approached zero. Under ideal conditions a maximum success rate of less than 25 per cent had been achieved on second regrafts. Tree removal costs were estimated to average $5 per tree when regrafting or replanting previously planted areas.

"O" nut trees reached a maximum height of 45 feet and were planted approximately 25 feet apart. Somewhere between the eleventh and thirteenth year (the eighth and eleventh year for regrafts) the trees had to be thinned by 50 per cent to provide 35 feet of space between trees. If adequate spacing of trees was not provided, excess shading resulted and the nuts did not ripen properly. Experience indicated that as much as an 80 per cent loss in a crop could occur from overshading. Exhibit 11-1 gives the expected average-yield pattern for "O" nut trees of the variety existing on O-Nut, Incorporated, properties. Research with new varieties of "O" nut trees had developed trees with yields up to 25 per cent greater than those currently existing in O-Nut orchards. Indications were that further research might develop even more bountiful varieties. No other significant differences in the overall yield pattern or maturity rate had appeared.

EXHIBIT 11-1. Expected Yield Pattern for O-Nut, Incorporated, Trees (Yield in pounds per tree).

Age	Yield
1-6	0
7	20
8	40
9	80
10	100
11	120
12	160
13	160
14	140
15	140
16	120*

*Fifteen percent annual decrease for all subsequent years.

Harvesting of "O" nuts was seasonal in nature and occurred during the months of September, October, November, and December. The mature nuts fell to the ground before being harvested. Since the nuts could not safely be allowed to remain on the ground more than sixty days without significant deterioration, they were harvested twice during the season.

Harvesting was done by handpicking nuts that had fallen to the ground. The majority of pickers were women between the ages of thirty and forty-five years. Harvesters were generally employed on a four-month basis and recruited through ads in the daily newspapers. Since worker qualifications included only a willingness to work and a strong back, applicants were given a minimal screening before being hired. The major elements in the screening process were a check of previous employment records with the firm, a check with the local police, and a physical examination to detect any back, leg, or neck injuries which might hinder the worker. Upon employment each harvester was given a pair of shoes, a pair of gloves, and a harvesting bag. This equipment was either new or used, depending on what sizes were available in used equipment. Employees were expected to return this equipment at the end of the season. Any equipment that was lost was paid for by the picker at a price equal to the company's cost of the equipment. The average cost of hiring, equipping, and terminating was approximately $30 per employee. The cost was relatively independent of whether the employee worked the full four months or some shorter time. Full-term employees generally wore their equipment quite ragged, whereas short-term employees often absconded with their equipment.

Harvesters were paid on an hourly basis and received a wage of approximately $1.38 per hour with no fringe benefits. The expected output was 1,100 pounds of nuts per picker per day. The labor market had been extremely favorable for the employer but was becoming increasingly tight as the overall production of "O" nuts increased and demand for harvesters increased. The future labor market was expected to become less favorable to the employer unless mechanical harvesting, which was still in an experimental stage, was quickly introduced and accepted.

Two of the larger and older orchards, partially owned by an orchard equipment producer, were experimenting with a newly designed mechanical harvester. Several of the existing "O" nut producers were considering a changeover in harvesting techniques pending conclusive evidence regarding the economics of mechanical harvesting. To date only preliminary results and engineering specifications were available. A fully documented report on the results of the experiments conducted was expected to be completed and released within three months. Some preliminary cost figures provided by the equipment manufacturer were included among the records of the OK Orchard Development Company.

The figures indicated that to facilitate the use of a mechanical harvester the ground surrounding each tree had to be leveled, graded, and surfaced with a 4-inch layer of pea gravel or volcanic ash. This required several tons of gravel per tree and was estimated to cost $300 per acre complete, including grading, leveling, gravel, and surfacing. This special preparation was required because of the rocky nature of the soil (3- to 6-inch-diameter rocks). The mechanical harvester accomplished its task by scooping up to a ¼- to ½-inch layer of gravel including any fallen nuts, separating the nuts from the gravel by a screening process, and re-depositing the gravel. Once applied the gravel surfacing was estimated to last a minimum of 20 years. When the surface became too thin, a 1- to 2-inch layer of gravel could be added to the top of the existing surface. The need for a 4-inch initial layer arose from the need to cover the numerous rocks in the orchards.

The price of a mechanical harvester which the equipment manufacturer had proposed to OK Orchard was $40,000. It was designed to harvest 20 to 25 acres per day depending on the planting configuration. The proposed mechanical harvester had a specified capacity of over 2½ times that of the two experimental harvesters in existence and was recommended on the basis of future needs. The differences in the initial cost and operating cost were substantially less than 2½ times that of the lower capacity machines. The price quoted was 1½ times that of the smaller machine and operating and maintenance costs were estimated to be only 80 per cent greater. A machine of intermediate capacity was not considered practical as it would require the same number of operating personnel and would provide a negligible original cost saving.

The harvester required three full-time operators and when moving from one area to another had a maximum speed of 5 miles per hour. Considering the difficulty of retraining competent skilled help on a part-time basis it was recommended that these employees be hired on a full-time basis and be used elsewhere during the non-harvesting season. This was consistent with the experience of most employers who found it advantageous to maintain truck drivers and similarly skilled personnel on a full-time basis even though this skill could be utilized for as little as 25 per cent of the employee's total activities. This, however, presupposed that the employee could be used to perform some useful secondary task when not occupied in performing his primary function. It was estimated that employees capable of being trained to operate and service the proposed mechanical harvester could be found and retained at a wage rate of approximately $2.50 per hour. In view of the difficulty in retraining skilled help on anything but a day shift basis and the added risk to the equipment and the operators resulting from nighttime operation, single-shift operation of the harvester was recommended. The equipment required daily maintenance and cleaning of approximately 4 man-hours. This could be performed by one to four individuals in substantially the same number of total man-hours of effort. It was felt that several of the currently employed individuals could perform this task. Gasoline, oil, and other operating and maintenance expenses were estimated at $5,000 per year per 8-hour shift. This cost would increase proportionately for any usage beyond the estimated 40 hours per week. Current delivery time for the proposed piece of equipment was 8 months from the order date.

Total single shift capacity of "O" nut processing plants was approximately 3,000,000 pounds of raw nuts per year. Approximately 80 per cent of the existing processing facilities was owned or controlled by a single distributor. "O" nut growers were responsible for delivering their harvest to a local pickup point where they were graded, weighed, and transferred to railroad cars which delivered them to the processing plant.

"O" nuts arrived at the processing plant in a paperlike husk. The husks were removed by tumbling the nuts in a high-velocity wind chamber. After this the nuts were placed in large dehydrators where they remained for at least two weeks. Once dehydrated the nuts could be kept for ten to fourteen months, which allowed the remaining processing to be conducted throughout the year rather than being required immediately following the harvesting period. Between the husking and dehydrating operations all nuts were inspected visually and any defective nuts removed.

After dehydration the nuts were graded for size and weighed into 300-pound batches to enter the final processing. The nuts proceeded to one of seven cracking machines, each machine being set up to process a specific size range. Good nuts were separated from spoiled nuts, shells, and other foreign matter by a flotation process. The good nuts sank to the bottom of the tank, whereas shells and other foreign matter remained on top. Immediately after flotation the good nuts were partially dried in a large centrifuge and, after another visual inspection, each batch passed through a flash dehydrator where any remaining traces of water or excess moisture were removed. After this second dehydration each batch was laboratory tested for moisture content, taste, and other properties. The nuts were then ready for roasting, final inspection, salting, and packaging. After roasting, the nuts were no longer separated by size and were processed in a continuous rather than a batch type process. Final packaging consisted of vacuum packing the processed nuts in unlabeled glass jars. Labels were applied just prior to shipping the processed nuts to local and regional distribution points. The approximate retail selling price of processed "O" nuts was $2.50 per pound.

Information obtained from the more successful of the two small independent processors indicated that the smallest economic unit of processing capacity was 400,000 pounds of raw nuts per shift per year. Larger plants essentially consisted of multiples of this basic unit of capacity. The current cost per basic unit of capacity (400,000 pounds of raw nuts per year) was $375,000, excluding building and installation costs. Processing costs, excluding the cost of raw nuts, averaged $0.05 per pound of raw nuts. This was equivalent to approximately $0.25 per pound of packaged nuts, since the weight loss due to shelling, dehydration, roasting, and inferior-quality nuts averaged 80 per cent of the initial gross weight of the raw nuts. Due to the difficulty of obtaining sufficient quantities of skilled help, most processing plants also operated on a single-shift basis. The independent processor, however, from whom the majority of the cost information was obtained, was operating on a two-shift basis. Due to maintenance and other problems the second shift was from 20 to 25 per cent less productive than the first shift.

The only quantitative information immediately available for making a reasonable long-range estimate of potential "O" nut sales was current and past sales of other varieties of nuts and condiments. After examining a substantial amount of data the following conclusions were drawn:

1. From a purely objective standpoint, i.e., nutritional value, taste, stability, etc., "O" nuts were comparable to other common nuts such as walnuts, filberts, pecans, and almonds.
2. From a marketing, promotional, and processing standpoint the "O" nut industry was 15 to 25 years junior to any of the major nut industries.
3. With efficient promotion techniques and good fortune the "O" nut industry could achieve the current status of the major nut industries within 10 to 15 years.
4. A reasonably attainable 3- to 5-year goal for "O" nut sales would be a sales rate equivalent to that of filbert sales (16,000,000 pounds of raw nuts per year).
5. An optimistic yet potentially attainable 10- to 15-year goal for "O" nut sales would be a sales rate equivalent to that of walnut sales (160,000,000 pounds of raw nuts per year).
6. To achieve either of these goals "O" nuts would have to be made available in a variety of forms and prices comparable to that of the currently major nuts on either a weight or volume basis.

Exhibit 11-2 is an abbreviated balance sheet for O-Nut, Incorporated, immediately after acquisition of the assets of the OK Orchard Development Company. At the time of transfer, the OK Orchard Development Company employed 35 full-time employees who received an average pay of $2 per hour. These employees were nonunionized al-

EXHIBIT 11-2. Balance Sheet, January 1.

Current Assets		Current Liabilities		
Cash	$ 125,000	Payables	$	45,000
Securities	2,000,000	Other		5,000
Receivables	4,000	Total	$	50,000
Inventories	40,000			
Goodwill........	1,000	**Fixed Liabilities**		
Total	$2,170,000	OK Orchard Development		
		Company.....................		3,000,000
Fixed Assets		**Net Worth**		
Trees...........	$2,950,000	100,000 shares common stocks		
Equipment	150,000	(100 percent owned by		
Buildings.......	125,000	United Nut Growers and		
Land...........	1,275,000	Processors)		3,620,000
Total	$4,500,000			
Total assets	$6,670,000	Total liabilities and net worth		$6,670,000

though a majority were believed to favor a union shop. During the non-harvesting season these employees performed such tasks as pruning, fertilizing, spraying, and maintaining the grounds and equipment. It appeared that they could continue to carry out this function as long as the number of trees under cultivation did not exceed 65,000. During the harvesting season these employees assisted in the harvest by acting as field supervisors and recorders, by operating local collecting stations, and by operating a shuttle service between the pickers and the local collecting stations and between the local collecting stations and the processor's pickup point.

It appeared that unless mechanical harvesting was adopted these tasks could not be performed by the 35 full-time employees after an annual yield of 5,000,000 pounds or more was achieved. The mechanical harvester would eliminate the need for field supervisors and recorders. Local collecting stations, nevertheless, would have to be retained unless a road system capable of supporting large trucks was installed throughout the orchard. However, the shuttling of nuts from the single mechanical picker to the collecting station would be considerably more efficient than from the many handpickers. An opinion had been expressed that if mechanical picking was adopted the current full-time non-harvest work crew could support the full potential harvest of the 65,000 trees currently under cultivation.

The only other major expense of operating the orchard was for materials required to maintain the trees and grounds. This amounted to approximately $2 per tree per year and was expected to slowly increase until the trees reached full maturity, at which time it would probably level off at approximately $2.40 per tree per year.

United Nut Growers and Processors of Jamaica, Incorporated, as full owners of O-Nut Incorporated, directed Jim Powers and his management team to carry out the following objectives:

1. Become the world's leading integrated producer, processor, and distributor of "O" nuts and "O" nut products
2. Attain and secure an industry leadership position by becoming and remaining the world's most efficient and low-cost producer, processor, and distributor of "O" nuts and "O" nut products
3. Promote the growth and profit potential of the "O" nut industry to the greatest extent economically feasible
4. Design an initial five-year program which would operate within the bounds of sound financial policy and limit the issuance of additional common voting stock to 80 per cent of that currently outstanding

QUESTIONS

1. Prepare annual estimates for 10 years for the following: physical characteristics (trees, yields, seasonal employees, etc.); profit and

loss statement; and balance sheet. The estimates are to be based on the following assumptions:

a. No additional trees are planted.

b. No existing trees are regrafted.

c. All yields are as shown in Exhibit 11-1.

d. Trees must be thinned to 35-foot spacing after the harvest at age twelve.

e. Harvesting is done manually at existing wages and production rates.

f. All raw nuts produced can be sold at $0.13 per pound.

g. Costs for purchasing, grafting, planting, and maintenance of "O" nut trees are capitalized until the initial year of yield of the trees (year 7 for new grafts and year 4 for regrafts).

h. Capitalized costs on trees are depreciated at a rate of 10 per cent per year until full depreciated, starting with the year the trees begin to produce a yield. If a tree is cut before it is completely depreciated, the remaining book value is immediately charged to current expenses.

i. Tree maintenance costs are charged to current expenses after the trees begin to produce a yield.

j. The marginal tax rate is 48 per cent of taxable profits.

k. Executive salaries and expenses remain at $45,000 per year.

l. O-Nut's indebtedness is interest-free if retired on schedule.

m. Depreciation to be on a straight line basis at the rate of 10 per cent per year for buildings and 15 per cent per year for equipment.

n. All other factors remain constant.

2. Based on their current operating situation, prepare an estimated monthly cash flow statement for the first year of operations for O-Nut, Incorporated. Assume harvest receipts are received at the end of October and December and estimated taxes are paid on a quarterly basis.

3. Prepare a projection of the potential production of raw "O" nuts for the total industry for the next ten years, assuming no new plantings.

4. What factors must be given consideration in developing an overall plan of operation?

5. What investment opportunities are available to O-Nut, Incorporated? What are the approximate funds available? How would you proceed to evaluate each investment opportunity?

6. Assume that current manual harvesting methods and costs remain constant. What rate of return is indicated by converting to mechanical harvesting? Do you recommend a change to mechanical harvesting? Why or why not?

7. Assume that new trees would be planted at 25- or 35-foot intervals and that items (c) through (n) of question 1 apply. What would be the maximum long-run rate of return available from new plantings for:

    a.   Replanting cycle using new trees only

    b.   Replanting cycle using regrafts

    Specify the cutting years for each alternative used to obtain your answers.

8.   What are the factors you should consider and how would you go about determining an overall optimal plan on a long-term basis? Clearly identify what "optimal" means in this situation.

9.   Evaluate the policies of operating the processing plants on a single-shift or multiple-shift basis.

10.   What problems does O-Nut face and what strategy should they follow to "become the world's leading integrated producer, processor, and distributor of 'O' nuts and 'O' nut products"?

CHAPTER 12

Automation and Numerical Control

Automation is an important application of the systems approach in industry. It is a term which describes the control of machines by machine—a natural evolutionary step in man's continuing efforts to achieve technological progress. Before an automated operation is designed, it is essential to consider the entire operation as an integrated system and relate the impact of new tools on other subsystems of production and distribution.

Numerical control (N/C) is one example of automatic processing which is engineered to achieve standards of performance impossible under other forms of manufacture. We have selected N/C as an example of an automated production system because it illustrates the functions of planning, organizing, controlling, and information flow as they pertain to a closed-loop system. Further, this is an example of automation which offers great promise as a production system of the future. The following topics are covered in this chapter:

Automation and systems
The decision to automate
Numerical control
System flow

AUTOMATION AND SYSTEMS

Automation is one of the best-known applications of systems. It requires an overall systems approach to integrate the operations of the business firm (e.g., perception of the product mission, product research and development, engineering and design, processing, distribution methods, and other facilitating activities) into an operational man-machine system. Successful automation means more than adopting a new production process for an existing product; it may require, for example, a complete redesign of the product to complement the automated system. One of the best-known examples of the need to redesign occurred in the production of electronic equipment, when printed circuits and dip soldering replaced more conventional assembly operations.

Distribution also is affected by the automation of production lines. Automation often results in the standardization of the product and limits the flexibility of output. Consequently, the distribution system of the organization must integrate its activities closely with those of the automated production system. Further, fixed costs increase as the company substitutes capital for direct labor. The automation must be used at high capacity for an extended period of time if the capital investment is to be recovered.

Definition of Automation

We have discussed the broad philosophy of automation as an application of the systems approach. Inasmuch as automation represents a philosophy or concept rather than the specific application of certain techniques, it is difficult to present a precise definition—it is a word of many meanings. The term was coined by Del Harder and the Ford Motor Company in 1946 to denote the introduction of a new type of mechanized equipment. To him it described the automatic transfer of in-process work from one machine to the next without human aid.

Herbert A. Simon supported this view when he wrote: "Automation is nothing new; it is simply the continuation of that trend toward the use of capital in production that has been a central characteristic of the whole Industrial Revolution."[1] Using the same argument, Jaffe and Froomkin state that both mechanization and automation will cause changes to occur in the process and/or the output, often oriented toward reducing man-hour activity and the need for workers. Any development of this type, they believe, is more properly referenced under the general term *technological change*[2].

In contrast, John Diebold regards automation as a basic change in production philosophy—a frame of reference which considers an industrial process as an integrated system from the introduction of the raw material to the packaging of the complete product. Diebold maintains that the real essence of automation may have been obscured in that ". . . it is, more than anything else, a concept or a way or approach in solving problems, and that it makes a considerable departure from many accepted practices of management."[3]

Other writers have defined automation very precisely, however. For example, Bernard Karsh states that it is "the accomplishment of a work task by an integrated power-driven mechanism entirely without the direct application of human energy, skill, intelligence, or control."[4]

These definitions of automation range from a description of supermechanization to a continuous flow process, where machines replace the energy of man in direction, operation, and control. Rather than limit the discussion to a single definition of automation, it is preferable to think of automation as a total concept. Using this frame of reference, the basic features of automation include:

1. The replacement of the human operator in a step or steps of a process
2. The increased employment of feedback control—both theory and techniques—to the design and operation of automation systems
3. The use of sensing, decision, and computing elements to replace human operators, implying machines with a higher "intelligence" content and ability to control a process

[1]Herbert A. Simon, *The Shape of Automation for Men and Management,* Harper & Row, Publishers, Incorporated, New York, 1965, p. 6
[2]A. J. Jaffee and Joseph Froomkin, *Technology and Jobs,* Frederick A. Praeger, Inc., New York, 1968, pp. 16–17.
[3]John Diebold, *Beyond Automation,* McGraw-Hill Book Company, New York, 1964, p. 54.
[4]Bernard Karsh, "Work and Automation," in Howard Boone Jacobson and Joseph S. Roucek (eds.), *Automation and Society,* Philosophical Library, Inc., New York, 1959, p. 387.

4. A broad "systems" approach to new developments, viewing operations as a complex of men, materials, machines, methods, and money, rather than an array of isolated components[5]

Advanced automation may be regarded as the phenomenon of machine controlling machines, i.e., a machine or device measures the output of the processing machine, makes sure that it is following programmed instructions. Feedback is a required element in this philosophy of automation; the output of the system is measured continually in terms of the item being controlled, and the input is modified to reduce any divergence or error toward zero (Chapter 4). Advanced automation, therefore, is an example of a closed-loop system where control is built into the system, and the system is operated without the need for external direction. It is an illustration of a structured system with each component arranged in precise order; the output can be predicted and measured, and the operating efficiency of the system is easy to determine.

Rethinking for Automatic Systems

An official of the automobile industry was once asked if he thought the final assembly of automobiles could be automated. He replied that it would never happen during this century; applications of automation would be confined to the subassembly divisions of the plant. It is obvious, however, that the automobile manufactured today was designed to be hand-assembled, whereas future automobiles could just as well be designed to be assembled by machine. Although the automation of assembly lines has lagged behind, there is some evidence that this is changing. Reference to this new trend is made in the discussion of Detroit-style automation and direct numerical control.

Automation involves a process of complete *rethinking*: the attitude of mind which enables one to get outside of a problem that seems insoluble and approach it in a new and perhaps entirely different way. Rethinking the product resulted in the printed circuit for the electronics industry. This made it feasible to mass-produce radios and television sets by a semiautomatic process. By standardizing a basic module it was possible to develop and produce machine-made resistors, capacitors, and tube mounts. This principle helped solve the problem of the manufacturers who had found it difficult to standardize the many sizes and shapes of

[5]Eugene M. Grabbe, "The Language of Automation" in *Automation in Business and Industry*, John Wiley & Sons, Inc., New York, 1957, pp. 21–22.

resistors and condensors so that these units could be adapted to the printed circuit.

Another example of product redesign involved a cooking stove. Before installing the automatic machinery, a manufacturer had been selling two price lines and offering eight different styles in each price category—sixteen product variations in all. It was not economical to make so many different styles with the new machinery, but by redesigning the product it was possible to reduce all sixteen varieties into one basic body. Different variations were created from this basic body by arranging the heating elements in various ways and adding special features to some models. Shortly after the installation of the automatic machinery, competition forced the introduction of another price line, but again, it was possible to vary the panel and a few accessories to achieve the necessary change.[6]

Often it is necessary to analyze how a product is being made, with the thought of developing new processes which would be easier to automate. The net result might be a plantwide system of automation similar to an oil refinery.

In all types of automation it is necessary to rethink the entire operation as a system and integrate it as a whole. Of the numerous applications of the philosophy of automation, three broad applications stand out: Detroit-style automation, process control automation, and office automation. These are discussed briefly in the following sections. A more comprehensive discussion is presented on a specific example of automation (numerical control machines) later in the chapter.

Detroit-style Automation

Detroit-style automation describes that type of manufacture which typically has been applied in the mass production of standardized parts or components. When the term was first published in a report on the pioneering work at Ford, it was defined as "the art of applying mechanical devices to manipulate work pieces into and out of equipment, turn parts between operations, remove scraps, and to perform these tasks in the time sequence with production equipment so that the line can be wholly or partially under pushbutton control as strategic stations."[7]

[6]John Diebold, *Automation: The Advent of the Automatic Factory*, D. Van Nostrand Company, Inc., Princeton, N.J., 1952, p. 44.
[7]Ruppert LaGrande, "Ford Handles by Automation," *American Machinist*, Oct. 21, 1948, pp. 107–122.

Detroit-style automation of plant operations may range from a single line of automatic equipment (e.g., milling machines which are fed and cycled continuously with automatic handling) to complete production facilities where components are fed, positioned, adjusted, sorted, assembled, and tested automatically. Detroit-style automation has been introduced in the metal-working, component-manufacturing, and assembling types of industries, e.g., automotive, primary metals, fabricated metal products, machinery, transportation equipment, paper manufacturing, and electrical and electronic equipment industries.

Detroit-style automation applies the systems approach. Groups or sequences of operations, automatic mechanisms or machines, and control and handling devices are brought into a single man-machine system in a continuous operation. In the electrical field, for example, one manufacturer produces motors of various horsepower on two automated lines. More than a hundred standard models are produced in batches, each model being turned out once in two weeks. The equipment for this plant took over two years to design, build, and get into operation.

Another significant example of automation involves the automatic manufacture of roller bearings. The production rate is now many times the rate produced by more conventional production systems.

Most radio and television manufacturers are using printed circuit boards and assembling components to these boards automatically. This has required the redesign of most of the components in order that they may be integrated into the printed circuit. In most instances, the components are inserted into the printed circuit boards automatically, and the connections are soldered as the board moves through a molten solder bath and are tested automatically as the board proceeds along the production line.

One of the last segments of the production system, the assembly line, now is being automated. The Smith-Corona Marchant Company uses an automatic machine to assemble typewriters and eliminate hand labor. A major United States clockmaker has automated an entire line which can put 6,000 clocks together in a day. In the automotive industry a unique machine assembles spark plugs and inspects and packs them for shipping.

Basically, Detroit-style automation is utilized for items produced in large quantities. It has been geared to the concept of high-volume production with few variables. Although it is not as glamorous as those examples of automation which incorporate feedback control with a closed-loop system, Detroit-style automation is a more rudimentary example of the application of the systems approach and is of fundamental importance in the mass-producing industries.

Automation in the Process Industries

Automation has been applied in most complete form in the process industries. The process industries are those that handle bulk solids, liquids, or gases in some form and modify these materials either by physical or chemical means to produce a finished product with the desired properties. Many of these processes are strictly physical in nature. Some are chemical, and some are combinations of the two.

The implementation of the systems concept and automation in the processing-type industry has been made possible by the development of process control computers which receive information, perform mathematical computations, make comparisons and evaluations resulting in decisions, and provide output information signals for process control. By the use of computers it has been possible to automate the many process industries under the closed-loop concept, with feedback.

One of the earliest applications of the computer to process industry was in a refinery. In the system the computer receives a vast number of inputs, including flow rates, temperatures, pressures, and gas compositions. The computer performs calculations and initiates several independent control actions and optimizes performance of the total system, given the various inputs and the required outputs. The computer (1) determines the maximum reactor-inlet pressure; (2) distributes the available feed materials to five parallel pairs of reactors to take advantage of any differences in catalyst activity; (3) determines the amount of water to be injected into the catalyst activation; and (4) when needed, determines the amount of unreacted material which should be returned to the reactor inlet.

Other than petroleum and chemical facilities, process automation has not been introduced as rapidly as predicted. A factorywide closed-loop system requires the integration of machinery, instrumentation, and computers. Unfortunately many companies do not have the size and diversity to supply process automation for an entire application. Having different companies supply segments of the total system has caused innumerable problems, particularly in integrating the systems.

The future for process automation is not dark. The problems that have delayed its general adoption will be solved, and substantial growth may follow. However, the automation of material flow for an entire company is a utopian concept. While closed-loop subsystems may include large segments of the total operation, the human element still will be needed for many tasks, e.g., programming and maintenance.

Office Automation

The third example of automation is the application of the systems concept to information-handling and decision-making problems in the office. Mechanization in the office once was limited to man-machine systems, such as the typewriter, adding machine, and so forth. Later machines performing several operations appeared, such as the typewriter combined with the adding machine, complex bookkeeping machines, and finally punched-card accounting machines. The recent development of electronic data processing machines has provided managers an opportunity to engineer better systems of data recording, information processing, and decision making.

The computer is the "star" of office automation, and because it is big, fancy, and impressive it has been accepted as a prestige symbol. Moreover, its potential as a machine can be appraised (perhaps not accurately) by the nonscientists, the business executive, the engineer, military personnel, and teachers.

> Advances in radiant energy, solar energy, thermonuclear conversion, in metallurgy, in astrophysics, or in molecular chemistry may be in process of opening avenues of basic importance to industrial development. The company official and the operating engineer do not get excited about such advances, because they cannot understand them. But the computer they can understand, and they can begin to plan creatively with respect to it. The fact that the computer can thus capture the creativity and imagination of the non-scientists bodes well for its future, but also it accounts in part for an overvaluation in contrast with other potential avenues of development.[8]

In the future the difference between the factory and the office operation will become less distinct, for there is a trend toward integrating the information processing of the office and automatic

[8]Robert A. Solo, "Automation: Technique, Mystique, Critique," *The Journal of Business*, April 1963, pp. 166–178.

factory. This is another example of the development of increasingly complex, integrated systems. These applications are discussed more completely in Chapter 15, Data Processing Systems.

THE DECISION TO AUTOMATE

The participants in a conference on automation concluded that automation is necessary if we are to meet the needs of society. They suggested that a combination of economic factors and human resistance to change has impeded its adoption in many areas where it could be beneficial, and pointed out that in every application automation should be studied, planned, applied, and controlled with great care.[9]

Most installations are introduced as labor-saving devices. One company, for example, has a machine that turns out three million piston-rod subassemblies annually. A single operator now is doing the same work which previously required twenty men on the assembly line.[10]

The charge most commonly levied against automation is that it creates unemployment. There is some evidence that job opportunities have not been reduced in total and that many new jobs were created during the period of high economic activity in the 1960s. To say that technological change does not bear major responsibility for the general level of unemployment of particular persons in particular occupations and locations is unrealistic, however.[11]

Labor cost savings are the most significant factor in the decision to automate, although they should always be considered in conjunction with other objectives. One large manufacturer decided to install automatic machines to wire electronic equipment components. The machines performed the operation at about one-half the cost of doing it manually, and paid for themselves in approximately one year. The wiring machine occupied only 40 percent of the space; reduced wiring errors, testing, and correcting at the final stage of production; improved working conditions by eliminating tedious, repetitive jobs; and permitted faster, easier, and less expensive engineering changes.

[9]Hugh D. Luke, "The Challenge of Automation," in Ellis L. Scott and Roger W. Bolz (eds.), *Automation and Society,* Center for the Study of Automation and Society, Athens, Ga., 1969, p. 14.
[10]T. O. Prenting and M. D. Kilbridge, "Assembly: Last Frontier of Automation," *Management Review,* February 1965, p. 7.
[11]Howard R. Bowen and Garth L. Mangum, *Automation and Economic Progress,* Prentice-Hall, Inc., Englewood Cliffs, N.J., 1966, p. 53.

A large warehouse was automated to eliminate the cyclical labor demand and the resulting errors, breakage, pilferage, and confusion which resulted from the rapid increase in personnel. Under the new automated system, temporary labor was needed only rarely and the labor savings paid for the installation in four years.

Costs are not always easy to identify or measure. In addition to a comparison of obvious direct and indirect cost data, such factors as the reliability of tooling and machines are significant. Moreover, information on volume, labor content, and time are pertinent to the analysis. Finally, consideration of output, design stability, and space required by the facility are important criteria in automation decisions.

In general businessmen tend to underestimate the costs associated with automation. Perhaps labor-saving characteristics of the machine are considered as savings, but if the labor union does not allow workers to be replaced, there is no reduction in labor cost. On the other hand, if the machine has greater output it still may be possible to reduce labor costs per unit. Another cost that frequently is ignored is the cost of installing automatic equipment. For example, the machines may require related changes in heating, cooling, and wiring systems. Also the entire operation might be shut down during the installation. Finally, extensive costs could be involved in training personnel to use the new equipment.

Two factors are contributing toward the trend to automate: (1) the increasing knowledge about automation, and (2) the economic necessity for it. As we learn more about automatic machinery the principles of application become clearer to the user, and management then is prepared to make further advancements. Price competition from domestic and foreign producers often forces a decision to automate. A stage is reached when cost reductions are impossible without additional capital investment in facilities.

There is no point in automating just for the sake of automating. Management should ask what the machines are expected to accomplish, and even more basic, what the long-run demand might be for the output being automated. If a company buys new machines, and then adapts them to an existing system, there is little possibility of achieving the potential effectiveness and efficiency possible from a total-systems approach.

The best approach is to analyze potential applications in direct reference to the unique characteristics of the industry in question. For example, the production of single continuum items such as oil, wire, and sugar presents different problems in automatic production from discrete objects such as radiator castings, automobile engines, or a complex electric motor. The problems of automation vary with the characteristics of the end product, the materials used, and the nature of the components. When the output volume is small or uncertain and/or the chances of product-design changes are great, the risk of introducing Detroit-style automation may be substantial. One approach is to construct special-purpose systems and write off the cost of such a system quickly. Another approach is to use a more flexible automated system. Numerical control is an example of automation where flexibility is achieved by automating the basic functions of production. It may be possible in the future to link these basic machines into a processing line and manufacture an entire product automatically. If a different product were required, it would be necessary only to change the instructions and sequence of operations.

NUMERICAL CONTROL

Numerical control represents a recent development in making machining operations more automatic. It is an example of a closed-loop system which incorporates inputs of technical information in the form of a numerical code to instruct the processor (the producing machine) to perform a complete work cycle. The basic concept was advanced many years ago by Joseph Jacquard when he used punched cards to control textile looms. The perforations in the cards activated mechanical devices which controlled the operations of the looms. These remarkable machines were exhibited in Paris in 1801. Since that time many other devices have been built to operate on the same principle, e.g., the player piano. The machines of today use electronic devices to transfer information and activate the operations.

Numerical control originated as a result of a study sponsored jointly by the Parsons Corporation of Traverse City, Mich., and the United States Air Force. The Parsons Corporation had experienced difficulty in the manufacture of propeller-blade inspection templates, and it was hoped that some form of automatic machine control could provide a solution to this problem.[12] In March 1952,

---

[12]*Design, Development and Evaluation of a Numerically Controlled Milling Machine,* MIT, Servomechanisms Laboratory, Final Report, D.I.C. 6873, Cambridge, Mass., 1956.

the construction of the first numerical control milling machine was completed and later in the same year, this machine was demonstrated to representatives of the airframe industry and to a group of machine-tool builders.

The construction of a second machine was completed in May 1955. The design of this machine incorporated a number of refinements which eliminated many of the difficulties experienced in the operation of the first model. This industrial protoype machine was built under the sponsorship of the Giddings & Lewis Machine Tool Company of Fond du Lac, Wis. In 1957, the first numerical control skin and profile mills were delivered to the airframe industry. The acquisition of additional N/C equipment has been steady since that time.

Figure 12−1 is a photograph of the world's first machine tool to be automated and controlled by the medium of magnetic tape—the Giddings & Lewis spar and skin milling machine. Shown on the machine's table is an integrally ribbed skin for the North American F-100D Super Sabre. Seen at the right are the

FIGURE 12−1. Giddings & Lewis spar and skin milling machine. (Photograph courtesy of Giddings & Lewis Machine Tool Company, Fond du Lac, Wis.)

system's magnetic-tape playback and machine control units which operate all machine movements.

The N/C Process

Numerical control machines use electronic devices to transfer information and to activate and control each operation. The instructions are recorded on punched cards, magnetic tape, or paper tape and can control the sequence of machining operations; machine positions; speed, distance, and direction of movement of a tool or work piece; flow of coolant; and even the selection of a proper preset cutting tool for each operation. The recorded media (cards or tape) are loaded in a control unit and a system of electronic interpreting devices is programmed to drive the machine tool through the operations and movements outlined in the instructions. The operator starts, stops, loads and unloads, and observes the operation of the machine. He can change instructions after an operation has been completed by removing the roll of tape from the control unit and adding another tape programmed to describe a different operation. The whole process is much like playing a tape stereophonic sound system.

The difference between N/C and conventional machine tools can be illustrated by comparison. In general purpose machine tools, e.g., the man-operated lathe, the instructions on direction, speed, and distance the tool must travel when machining a particular part are performed by the operator who reads these instructions from blueprints or work orders. A more advanced conventional machine is specialized and has the instructions about sequencing, positioning, and tool travel built into the operation so that identical parts can be produced in quantity. In order to produce another product on this machine it would be necessary to change the mechanical or electrical control devices and add new templates, jigs, and fixtures for the different product. Numerical control, in contrast, is extremely flexible. Moreover, it incorporates feedback control so that programmed instructions can be followed precisely.

Numerical control systems are classified under two basic functional types—positioning and continuous path. A positioning system sequentially locates the tool at specified points of the work, and at these points the machine tool performs an operation. The locus or path of the tool between the points of operation is relatively unimportant and unspecified, because machine operations are not conducted during these intervals. Positioning systems are used to control machine tools such as the drill and jig bore which perform operations only at specified points on a work piece. In drilling, for example, the drill spindle is positioned at a single specified point; the proper drill size, speed, and feed selected; the drill advanced to cut a hole to the proper depth; withdrawn when completed; and repositioned to cut at the next point of work.

Continuous path machining is accomplished when the location points become closer and closer together, until the machine operations are continuous with the movement of the tool rather than only at specified points. This system is used to control such tools as the lathe and milling machine. The problem is to control a cutting tool which requires frequent changes in movement along two or more axes. This requires a more complex control system than is necessary in positioning numerical control.

SYSTEM FLOW

The work flow in the production of parts generally goes through six stages: (1) engineering drawing, (2) production planning, (3) tool design, (4) tool fabrication, (5) machine setup, and (6) machine operation. Various systems of numerical control require different components, media, and arrangement of functions. It is difficult, therefore, to relate the stages of numerical control to a conventional system of planning and manufacture. In Figure 12–2 the work flow procedure is illustrated by sixteen steps—from the source data (step 1), to the machining of the part (step 16). Most of the steps listed in this example of N/C work flow involve the conversion of data into other media, the processing of the data, and the checking of the converted or processed data against the original program sheet. The recent trend is to condense this list by greater computer utilization in planning and preparing machine instructions, and by standardizing media and control systems. The usual methods of planning, fixture design, tool design, and work scheduling must be dealt with. Further, the path to be followed by the cutting tool must be determined, together with speeds, feeds, tool sizes, checking points, and other machine functions which are to be accomplished during the processing cycle. It should be noted that there are two kinds of information generated, dimensional data defining the path geometry and information concerned with the processing aspects of the job, e.g., feed rates, sequence of cuts, and tool size.

NUMERICAL CONTROL

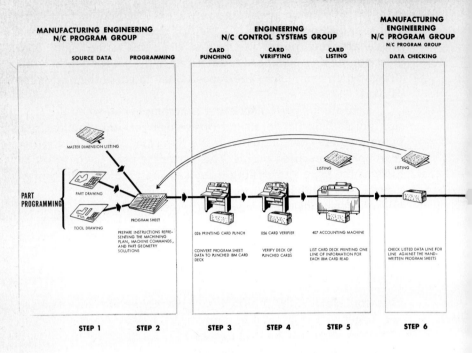

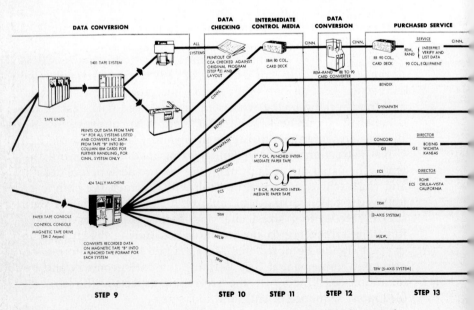

FIGURE 12-2. Numerical control work flow. (Courtesy of the Boeing Company.)

WORK FLOW

ENGINEERING
N/C CONTROL SYSTEMS GROUP

DATA CONVERSION   **DATA PROCESSING**

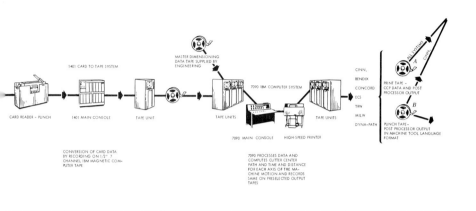

MASTER DIMENSIONING
DATA TAPE SUPPLIED BY
ENGINEERING

1401 CARD TO TAPE SYSTEM

CINN,

BENDIX

CONCORD

7090 IBM COMPUTER SYSTEM

ECS

TRW

MILW

DYNA–PATH

PRINT TAPE –
CCP DATA AND POST
PROCESSOR OUTPUT

PUNCH TAPE –
POST PROCESSOR OUTPUT
IN MACHINE TOOL LANGUAGE
FORMAT

CARD READER – PUNCH   1401 MAIN CONSOLE   TAPE UNIT

TAPE UNITS

7090 MAIN CONSOLE   HIGH-SPEED PRINTER

TAPE UNITS

CONVERSION OF CARD DATA
BY RECORDING ON 1/2" 7
CHANNEL IBM MAGNETIC COM-
PUTER TAPE

7090 PROCESSES DATA AND
COMPUTES CUTTER CENTER
PATH AND TIME AND DISTANCE
FOR EACH AXIS OF THE MA-
CHINE MOTION AND RECORDS
SAME ON PRESELECTED OUTPUT
TAPES

STEP 7   **STEP 8**

N/C MACHINE
CONTROL MEDIA   **NUMERICALLY CONTROLLED MACHINE TOOLS**

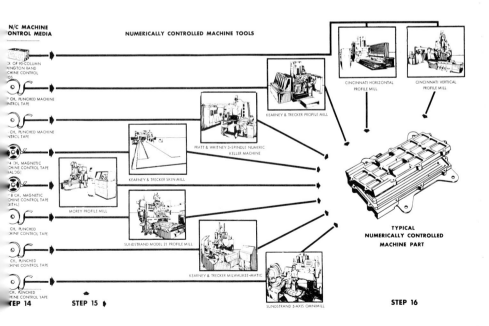

CINCINNATI HORIZONTAL
PROFILE MILL

CINCINNATI VERTICAL
PROFILE MILL

K OF 90-COLUMN
REMINGTON RAND
MACHINE CONTROL
CARDS

CH, PUNCHED MACHINE
CONTROL TAPE

CH, PUNCHED MACHINE
CONTROL TAPE

4 CH, MAGNETIC
MACHINE CONTROL TAPE
(ANALOG)

8 CH, MAGNETIC
MACHINE CONTROL TAPE
(DIGITAL)

CH, PUNCHED
MACHINE CONTROL TAPE

CH, PUNCHED
MACHINE CONTROL TAPE

CH, PUNCHED
MACHINE CONTROL TAPE

KEARNEY & TRECKER PROFILE MILL

PRATT & WHITNEY 3-SPINDLE NUMERIC
KELLER MACHINE

KEARNEY & TRECKER SKIN MILL

MOREY PROFILE MILL

SUNDSTRAND MODEL 21 PROFILE MILL

KEARNEY & TRECKER MILWAUKEE-MATIC

SUNDSTRAND 3-AXIS OMNIMILL

**TYPICAL
NUMERICALLY CONTROLLED
MACHINE PART**

STEP 14   **STEP 15**

STEP 16

FIGURE 12-3. Operational Flow under Conventional and Numerical Machine-Tool Control

Operation	Conventional	Numerical control
Design and drawing of part	Presentation of engineering data in form of drawing of part with dimensions expressed in conventional blueprint form.	Conversion of engineering blueprint data in form of sketch of part with dimensions expressed in rectangular coordinate form.
Planning of methods	Selection and general description of machining operations and tooling. Preparation of general setup instructions.	Selection of parts or portion of parts for numerical control machining and general descriptions of machining operations and tooling.
Tooling	Design and fabrication of jigs and fixtures.	Design and fabrication of jigs and fixtures.
Programming	Programming is not done under conventional control.	Preparation of manuscript and control tapes. Use of computer as aid for continuous tape control. Preparation of specific setup instructions. (Determining and coding detailed manufacturing steps and instructions which describe in sequence exact cutting operations, machine motions, and functions such as feeds, speeds, and direction and distance of table travel.)
Machining machine-tool setup	Planning and setting up correct sequence of machining operations according to blueprints or other general instructions. Selection and manual adjustment of speeds, feeds, direction, and distance of table travel and other machine controls. Mounting tooling.	Mounting tooling and control tape specified by setup instructions.

FIGURE 12-3 (*con't*)

Operation	Conventional	Numerical control
Machine-tool opera-tion	Loading workpiece into machine. Tending and adjusting machine during work cycle. Unloading workpiece.	Loading workpiece into machine. Tending and observing the machine during work cycle. Unloading workpiece.

Source: *Outlook for Numerical Control of Machine Tools,* United States Department of Labor, Bureau of Labor Statistics, Bulletin No. 1437, March 1965, p. 34.

The change in work patterns can be appreciated by an examination of Figure 12-3. It illustrates the operational flow under conventional and numerical control of machine tools.

Programming Numerical Control

In the early stages of the development of a numerical control programming system, the time required for computer program debugging more than equaled the time required for manual planning. Consequently, an effort was made to minimize programming time by developing subroutines for carrying out the steps in the computation process.

Most complete programs were used less than ten times; therefore the approach was to set aside and reuse the appropriate portion of an old program whenever it could be adapted to a new program. The subroutine was given a number to which the programmer could refer when incorporating it in the system he was designing. Early experience indicated that a major portion of each new program could be created by referring to a library of subroutines from former programs.

The library of subroutines solved many of the problems encountered in program design but created others. Before long the library became large, and the difficulty of selecting the appropriate subroutine for a new program and of modifying it according to current needs increased.

Often the subroutines used were similar. This led to a different approach, that of using a single generalized program which could be adapted to fit each particular case. The first step in this approach is to determine the common factors so that a skeleton program can be devised. The computer then proceeds to make the necessary calculations and translations. It is sufficient to say that the technical aspects of devising a systematized solution to the problems of programming data for the computer are extremely complicated.

The Aerospace Industry Association adopted a standardized system called APT (Automatically Programmed Tools), which is a collection of computer programs for eliminating most of the tedious mathematical operations associated with designing numerical control applications. To produce a part using the APT system the programmer analyzes each design in terms of its geometric forms, e.g., straight lines, circles, ellipses, and parabolas. Then, in the APT language, the programmer describes the part geometry and motions to be accomplished by the numerically controlled equipment.

The computer translates these instructions, makes the necessary mathematical calculations, and automatically produces the coded instructions for the machine-controlled equipment. The use of the APT system of programming has reduced the planning time significantly.

EVALUATION OF NUMERICAL CONTROL

Numerical control is being applied with some success. However, there are evident difficulties which can be traced in large part to the rapid development of this concept. The problems and criticisms so far encountered can be summarized as follows:

1. There is a high capital investment required for the purchase of the machines and supporting equipment. This criticism applies more to continuous path systems than to positioning operations.
2. The cost of establishing suitable computing and programming facilities is great. The programming requires a high level of skill, particularly in devising new routines.
3. There is a lack of compatibility among the various systems designed by competitive machine manufacturers. Even the media are not standardized (cards or tape). A National Aerospace Standard (NAS 943) does exist, however, for punched tape, and this form of machine input is generally accepted as the most desirable.
4. Preparation of magnetic tapes for the machine tools can be a time-consuming process.
5. Machine-tool operators, programming errors, and machine malfunctions are the prime sources of parts re-

jections when they occur. This is usually because of a lack of adequate techniques for checking tapes and the inexperience of some programmers, operators, and maintenance personnel.

6. The numerically controlled machines operate at standard machine speeds. They must be utilized to a greater capacity than conventional machines, therefore, if an economic advantage is to be gained.

7. Maintenance of these machines is more complicated, and it requires special training and equipment.

8. Quality control has been a problem. An unusual amount of time has been required to check a finished part of irregular design.

9. Equipment is being developed so rapidly that the user may install machines where the development will continue after installation. This is time-consuming and expensive.

10. Many shop supervisors and workers are reluctant to accept numerical control.

Many of the problems or criticisms of N/C which were stated relate to first-generation machine design, the difficulty of preparing machine instructions accurately, and the large initial capital investment. Machines are being designed, however, which will perform more accurately and with fewer breakdowns. Moreover, most machines will soon be controlled by compatible systems. Problems associated with information preparation are a function of the skill of the program-engineering group. These problems will decrease as that group gains experience and adopts improved techniques of programming. Numerical control machines are expensive, but the costs must be reviewed relative to the cost of the entire system and relative to the capabilities and productivity of the system.

Numerical control has many advantages which are present in most applications and which tend to offset the high capital investment of this equipment. These advantages may be summarized as follows:

1. Extreme accuracy is available on the more complicated shapes and larger parts. These are the kinds of parts which are the most difficult to manufacture with man-operated equipment.

2. The equipment is flexible. More than one machine of the same type can be operated from the same tape. The

machines may be adjacent to each other or at different and remote locations.

3. Shorter lead times may be planned to get a part into production in certain cases since some of the traditional operations are eliminated, e.g., tool fabrication.

4. There is less scrap due to the greater accuracy of the system and the reduction of machinists' errors.

5. It is not necessary to store large inventories of tools, jigs, and templates. Tapes can be stored outside of the factory area and require but a fraction of the space needed by templates.

6. It takes less time to prepare the machine for operation than the setup time required with the conventional machine.

7. Fewer skilled operators are required, even on close-tolerance jobs.

8. The machine can duplicate parts on succeeding runs within close tolerances. This is important in the production of interchangeable parts.

9. Normally, fewer inspections are required, and experience indicates that only the first part needs 100 percent inspection.

10. The machine can operate continuously without interruption, except for maintenance.

It should be pointed out that numerical control machines can perform work which would be impossible to perform with conventional machines. In addition, the productivity of these machines is greater than that of conventional machines in most applications. The real value of these automated systems, however, can be tested only in specific applications.

It is difficult to compare N/C with a conventional system, for different kinds of planning and information preparation are involved. It is not sufficient to consider the operation of the machine unit alone, but instead the total system cost must be measured and compared. The justification for N/C must be tested for each potential application.

IMPACT OF NUMERICAL CONTROL

Numerical control will have a definite impact on many functions of those industrial firms that use it. Certainly the engineering department will be affected by this development.

Engineering

In the near future many companies using N/C will change traditional drafting practices. It will be possible to discontinue drafting in many designs, for the tape will become the new form of record. Tape records will be supplemented by photographs of engineering sketches and pictures of oscilloscope images stored on microfilm.

Mathematics will gain in importance, for much of the actual testing of a new design will be accomplished mathematically. The engineer's job will be to transfer the design and operating requirements into computer language as a mathematical function. The computer will complete the task.

Manufacturing

The production of parts will become highly technical because of more refined design techniques. Shop managers will need a technical background. The production shop will be backed by a group of engineers who will solve production problems. Minor design problems, tooling problems, cutter problems, machine application, and problems in manufacturing technique will all be a part of this group's work load.

Other manufacturing activities affected will include scheduling of processing, as lead time is reduced and machine utilization becomes critical; control of quality with new inspection devices; and change of product design to conform to the capabilities of the new equipment.

Numerical control will have a definite impact on the nature of the functions performed and also on the man-hours required to perform each function. The change is evident in Figure 12-4, which identifies three case studies of man-hour requirements using conventional and N/C machines. All three studies illustrate the reduction of man-hours required for tooling and machining, while case 2—the only one where planning time has been identified—shows the increased time required to perform that function.

N/C equipment will tend to change the level and significance of the decision-making process in production. The decision on machine selection must be made early in the planning process, and once made it is costly to change. Moreover, scheduling decisions become more important as every attempt must be made to utilize this high-cost equipment. Finally, it is more precise to preprogram decisions on machine feeds, speeds, and tooling rather than to rely on the machine operator.

System Design

The effect of N/C will be felt throughout the entire company. However, the principal effect will be reflected in systems design. This concept will change the traditional requirements of work and information flow. The language of data transmission, the components in the system, and the control features of the system can all be different, which will free the design from past limitations. For

FIGURE 12-4. Three Comparative Case Studies of Man-Hour Requirements: Conventional and Numerically Controlled Machining

Case Study 1. Multiple operation of drilling, reaming, and tapping, 914 parts

Operation	Conventional methods		Numerical control		Percentage difference in man-hours, numerical control vs. conventional
	Man-hours	Per-cent	Man-hours	Per-cent	
Total	3,424	100.0	818	100.0	−76.1
Planning	(na)	(na)	(na)	(na)	(na)
Tooling	485	14.2	83	10.1	−82.9
Design	149	4.4	15	1.8	−89.9
Fabrication	336	9.8	68	8.3	−79.8
Programming (control data and tape preparation)	0	0	16	2.0	
Machining (machine-tool setup and operation)	2,939	85.8	735	89.9	−75.0

Source; U.S. Army, Ordnance Weapons Command, *Ordance Corps Study of Numerically Controlled Machine Tools,* Headquarters Ordnance Weapons Command, Joliet, Ill., 1960, p. 32.

Case Study 2. Skin milling, 4 parts

Operation	Conventional methods		Numerical control		Percentage difference in man-hours, numerical control vs. conventional
	Man-hours	Per-cent	Man-hours	Per-cent	
Total	6,848	100.0	3,249	100.0	−52.6
Planning	320	4.7	960	29.5	200.0
Tooling	5,952	86.9	1,896	58.3	−68.1
Design	912	13.3	216	6.6	−76.3
Fabrication	5,040	73.6	1,680	51.7	−66.7
Programming (control data and tape preparation)	0	0	321	9.9	
Machining (machine-tool setup and operation)	576	8.4	72	2.2	−87.5

Source: Peter D. Tilton, *Retrofit Applications of Numerical Control for Machine Tools,* Stanford Research Institute, Calif., 1957, p. 61.

Case Study 3. Drilling, 40 parts

Operation	Conventional methods		Numerical control		Percentage difference in man-hours, numerical control vs. conventional
	Man-hours	Per-cent	Man-hours	Per-cent	
Total	41.8	100.0	20.0	100.0	−52.2
Tooling	27.1	64.8	12.7	63.5	−53.1
Design	2.7	6.4	2.7	13.5	0
Fabrication	24.4	58.4	10.0	50.0	−59.0
Programming (control data and tape preparation)	0	0	1.2	6.0	
Machining (machine-tool setup and operation)	14.7	35.2	6.1	30.5	−58.5

Source: *Friden Flexowriter for Numerical Control*, Friden, Inc., Rochester, N.Y., 1961, p. 22.

example, much of the processing and technical information will be combined as a single input of information, and these inputs will occur in a language compatible with machine usage. A different type of person will be planning the operation of a more structured and predictable system. Further, it will be a system which is capable of adjusting to changing market demands without confusion or time lag.

APPLICATIONS

The number of N/C machines has increased dramatically; almost every metal-fabricating firm of any size now uses them. Whereas a majority of the early applications were of the positioning type of numerical control, recently the continuous type has made substantial gains in usage.

N/C has been particularly popular in the aerospace and machine-tool industries and these industries probably will continue to be important users of this equipment. These two industries are characterized by producing small quantities of a wide variety of parts, and tooling time constitutes a high proportion of the total cost of production. In the aerospace industry the trend has been to design N/C machines with high power and low speed in order to achieve greater accuracy in the production of parts. By necessity, the machines have become larger and heavier, the controls more refined and adaptable to a variety of situations. For example, the controls can be sensitive to thicknesses of the material and can change speed to compensate. When the material is thinner or softer than standard, the speed of the machine can be increased automatically to improve operating efficiency.

The general acceptance of N/C by the large aerospace firms has had a significant impact on the smaller firms in the industry. In many instances the small firms have been forced to install N/C equipment in order to maintain their qualifications as acceptable suppliers.

The automobile industry also has made increasing use of N/C. In that industry it is used primarily to produce the basic tools for production runs. It used to take nearly two years to get ready to produce a new model, but with N/C the preparation can be accomplished in a much shorter time.

N/C has been given credit for large productivity gains and cost savings, but the return on investment would improve significantly if the downtime, the time the machines are not operating, could be reduced. Failure to utilize the machines to their capacity affects their efficiency and their ultimate acceptability to potential users. In many instances the machines are not operated correctly, are the wrong machines for the specific job, or are poorly maintained.

The machine tool industry has recognized the importance of educating the customer about both the potential of the machines and how to achieve the potential once the machines are installed. Not only is it necessary to convince the customer that N/C is a necessary development, but it is essential to provide the technical instruction and assistance so that the machines can be placed into productive operation sooner and operated closer to maximum efficiency. Manufacturers are now providing the expertise so that expected results can be realized, and supplying a complete line of technical assistance and maintenance service. This is particularly important for the small shops.

The following list of guidelines show how a user can make a good start with N/C tools:[13]

> *Use the builder's know-how* and experience. Take all people concerned with the machine to the builder's plant for broad backgrounding. Most have developed worthwhile programs in this line.
>
> *Don't underestimate* the problems. Electronic maintenance is not for good old Joe the electrician.
>
> *Set up* one man and/or department to run the show with full authority and responsibility.

[13]T. M. Rohan, "Education Curbs N/C Frustrations," *The Iron Age*, Sept. 26, 1968, p. 65.

Select men for training in operating programming and maintenance with extreme care. Tool builders stand ready to help you select them with aptitude tests you can give and grade yourself. And they have loads of preparatory material to send your man ahead of time so he gets more out of his training at the plant.

Don't skimp on a few days or weeks of extra training. The man will be running a tool worth $150,000 or more. Consider including a back-up man for training because the No. 1 man will probably soon get promoted.

Don't compromise the new tool by keeping old lot sizes, quantities, tooling and other limitations and even charging them against the new unit.

Let foremen who will run the machine participate in buying decisions—at least to having extent of veto power if he knows it won't do the job.

Make foremen aware of indirect savings in less tooling, less inventory, faster handling design changes and less downtime and idle time on machine.

Recognize machine tool builder's intent to assume central responsibility. Do not by-pass him and communicate with control builders, for instance. Inform them early of problems, not in panic.

The real benefits from N/C will occur when the systems approach is used to integrate planning and operation into a more complete system. Such an approach has been developed; it is called direct numerical control.

DIRECT NUMERICAL CONTROL

Recent developments in computer and N/C technology have made the automated metalworking factory a reality. A new system, direct numerical control (DNC), uses a computer to prepare the controller programs and the instructions to produce specific parts, and for monitoring simultaneously the actual operation of several machines. The data on machine status and output are recorded automatically, analyzed, and distributed to manufacturing management. This information can be used to schedule the operation of machines. Figure 12–5 shows the information flow of DNC.

To illustrate this concept, assume that the computer already has prepared the design instructions for many parts and the sequence of machine operations necessary to produce these parts. This information is stored in the computer's memory. As an order for a part is received, the computer can determine what machine is available and then schedule the production run. When the time for that particular production run arrives, the computer com-

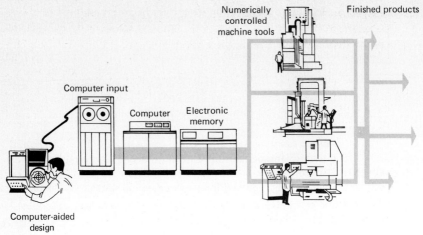

FIGURE 12-5. Information and work flow—direct numerical control.

municates the instructions on how to produce the part directly to the machine, and then monitors its output. As the order for one part is completed, another is made ready for production.

In the typical N/C system the computer prepares the tape for the manufacturing operation and the signals recorded on the tape actually direct and control the operation of the machine. With the computer in direct communication with the producing machines (DNC), the automatic planning and controlling of diverse machine-shop activities is possible.

The DNC system has several advantages over tape-controlled N/C. For instance, the process of cutting and proofing each new paper tape is no longer required. "One plant, says John C. Garrett, of GE's Manufacturing Automation Systems Operation, uses 7-million ft. of tape a year, of which it discards 5½-million ft."[14] Obviously, the elimination of tapes would make a significant saving.

"With a DNC system the steps to prepare the program are the same, except that the procedure is different in that a part programmer can interchange information with the machine system in a process of testing and optimizing the process."[15] The system incorporates a cathode-ray tube display and a keyboard so that a programmer may write changes into machine instructions instantaneously and then check them. This assists the programmer in improving the instructions and takes much of the

[14]*Business Week*, "Computers Move into the Machine Shop," Sept. 19, 1970, p. 88.
[15]Philip H. Reagan, "Multi-machine Automation by Direct Numerical Control," *Computer Decisions*, July 1970, p. 32.

wasted motion out of the machining process. The savings could be substantial. "Optimized programs alone, say experts, should increase the utilization of numerical control machines by 15% to 25%."[16]

The reliability and accuracy of numerically controlled tools should also increase. The elimination of the tape-reading function on a chip-cutting machine, for example, lifts a delicate system out of an environment where contamination is common, thus eliminating errors.[17]

Many advocates of DNC suggest that better management planning and control may be the most significant advantage of the system. For example, gains can be achieved by proper scheduling. "Parts that are manufactured in batch lots spend only about 1 percent of their time being machined, and the rest of the time either traveling around the shop or queued up waiting to be worked on."[18] Prompt status reports can identify problems early, or assure management that the work is going according to plan.

Although several manufacturers have installed DNC systems, there has been no great rush to place orders. Part of this reluctance to use such equipment may be due to the great variety of systems being introduced, and to the many choices available to the user. The choices vary from adopting the most advanced systems to alternatives that propose the modification of existing equipment. For example, one firm is advertising a system that simplified the programming of some parts programs and adds equipment which permits the user to modify the program right at the machine. Even though there has been some reluctance to adopt DNC, the automatic factory in metalworking is now a distinct possibility.

SUMMARY

Automation is a term which describes the control of machines by machines—a closed-loop system where control is built into the system. Automation may be applied to a single task, or it may be an integrated, companywide system. A companywide system (without people), however, is a utopian concept. Automation involves a complete process of rethinking, i.e., the attitude of mind which enables one to get outside of a problem that seems insoluble and approach it in a new and perhaps wholly different way.

Numerical control may be defined as a specific kind of auto-

[16]*Business Week,* op. cit., p. 88.
[17]*Business Week,* "From Design to Finished Product," Dec. 30, 1967, p. 90.
[18]Allan T. Demaree, "Kicking the Doldrums at Cincinnati Milacron," *Fortune,* December 1970, p. 32.

matic system which controls the movements of an operating mechanism by means of previously programmed instructions coded on media such as punched cards, punched tape, or magnetic tape.

After the feasibility of numerical control had been established, it was decided to install this type of equipment in the aircraft industry, where close tolerance, complex manufacturing problems, short lead times, and increasing costs were prevailing characteristics.

The work flow of the system includes engineering drawing, program engineering, process-tape preparation, control-tape preparation, and machine operation. Various systems of numerical control, however, require different media, components, and arrangement of functions.

There is some question whether or not numerical control is economical. Each application must be reviewed and evaluated on its own merits, but numerical control can provide better quality at reduced cost in many instances. Further, it has a degree of flexibility impossible in the typical man-operated machine inasmuch as it can perform a greater variety of tasks.

Numerical control will make a significant impact on current engineering and manufacturing practices. However, the greatest impact will be reflected in terms of systems design. It will free the traditional processing system from outdated concepts and illustrate principles of system design useful in other business applications. Direct numerical control has made the automatic factory possible in the metalworking industry.

QUESTIONS

1. Define automation.
2. Why is it often necessary to "rethink" a product before automation? Give an example.
3. Describe each type of automation reviewed in the book.
4. What factors are pertinent in a decision to automate?
5. What is numerical control? What is the difference between continuous path and position machines?
6. How does N/C change the work flow in production planning and operation?
7. What problems of criticisms have been associated with N/C?
8. Of the advantages to N/C listed in the text, which do you believe are the most significant?
9. How does DNC differ from N/C? What advantages may it have?
10. Make a prediction of the application of N/C in the future.

CASE:

The Hitonic Machinery Corporation*

The Hitonic Machinery Corporation ranked among the upper ten firms in the production and sales of machine tools and equipment in the United States. Over the past several years there had been a major shift in production and sales from conventional machinery to numerically controlled machinery. Although there was still good reason to expect a further shift toward numerically controlled equipment, definite indications were appearing that a balance between the sales of conventional and numerically controlled equipment was approaching. This was evidenced by the fact that sales of conventional machinery were holding their own while sales of numerically controlled machinery were increasing, but at a decidedly lower rate.

Insofar as the manufacturing activities of The Hitonic Machinery Corporation were concerned, the amount of manufacturing activity generated by a sales dollar of conventional equipment was considerably greater than that generated by a sales dollar of numerically controlled equipment. This was partly due to the fact that the numerical control portions of the numerically controlled machinery were purchased from outside the firm, and partly due to the fact that engineering and development costs for numerically controlled machinery represented a greater proportion of the total cost than for conventional machinery. Furthermore, all numerically controlled machinery was built on a semicustom basis, whereas the greatest portion of conventional machinery was built to standard specifications.

However, if one looked only at the basic machine, there was surprisingly little difference in the parts comprising the two types of ma-

*Source: Albert N. Schrieber, Richard A. Johnson, Robert C. Meier, William T. Newell, and Henry C. Fischer, *Cases in Manufacturing Management,* McGraw-Hill Book Company, New York, 1965, pp. 163–170.

chinery. Given a part at random it was difficult to know whether the part in question would eventually become part of a conventional or a numerically controlled machine. Conventional machines had been produced over a much longer time period and were much more uniform in design than numerically controlled machines. As yet no two completely identical numerically controlled machines had been built except to satisfy a single order. Conventional machinery was in a relatively stable technological state; numerically controlled equipment was continually undergoing major technological change.

In reviewing the performance of his firm over the past decade, M. O. Ree, president of The Hitonic Machinery Corporation, had much to be satisfied about. During this transition period Hitonic had grown from a secondary position to that of a leading producer in the machine tool industry. Ree attributed a major portion of his firm's success to aggressiveness in the design, development, and production of numerically controlled machinery. In successfully carrying out this transition, a major portion of the technical and managerial resources of Hitonic had been devoted to this single end. Ree realized that this had caused a certain lack of attention to less immediately important organizational and operational problems of the firm.

One specific area that Ree felt had received inadequate attention over this period was that of facilities planning and modernization. This oversight was intentional and was less critical than might be expected. Hitonic had completed a major modernization program just prior to the introduction of its numerically controlled line of equipment. At that time considerable new equipment had been added. The quality of Hitonic's current manufacturing facilities was still above average for the machine tool industry. To remain a leader, however, in the machine tool field on both a product and price basis, Ree felt this area required renewed attention.

One anomalous fact particularly troubled Ree. Although Hitonic was a major producer and seller of numerically controlled machinery, they utilized a very small proportion of such equipment in their own manufacturing processes. Several numerically controlled machines were included in Hitonic's manufacturing facilities, but it could not be stated that they comprised a really significant portion of their total manufacturing capability. In addition, a substantial amount of the capacity of this equipment was used for experimental and sales purposes. Less than 10 percent of the parts made by the firm had any processing done on a numerically controlled machine. With this in mind it appeared to Ree that a study to determine the economic advantages of adding additional numerically controlled equipment to the existing facilities was in order. Because of the high initial cost of numerically controlled equipment and the tight production schedules required by the demand for such equipment, Ree felt that it would be advisable to attempt to determine both the company's immediate needs and the medium- to long-range needs for such equipment.

J. L. Crow, controller for The Hitonic Machinery Corporation, strongly supported Ree's feelings with regard to the need for determining the firm's long-run facility needs. He stated that the firm was financially strong but that rapid expansion and high design and development costs were making long-range planning of any major expenditures increasingly necessary.

M. A. Gnett, director of numerically controlled equipment sales, saw two additional uses for the long-run forecast of the firm's need for numerically controlled equipment. First, although it was theoretically possible to perform almost any machining operation on a numerically controlled machine, there appeared to be a limit to the proportion of such operations which could be performed economically in any given situation. Knowledge of where this point might be would give Hitonic's sales organization some feeling as to the true saturation point for numerically controlled equipment, would assist in making long-range sales forecasts, and would provide useful information relative to the proper approach in selling numerically controlled equipment. Also it would provide a means of determining whether or not additional products and designs should be added to the existing line. Gnett agreed that a quantitative figure might be difficult to obtain and undoubtedly would be subject to error. However, it appeared to him that estimates with a reasonable foundation would be superior to pure, unfounded conjecture.

The second use which Gnett foresaw was in the development of a sound methodology for establishing the saturation point for individual firms. Repeatedly Gnett had received requests from customers to assist in making long-range predictions of their needs for numerically controlled equipment for purposes of financial planning. On each occasion Gnett had to admit that he had no answer except to quote the relative proportions of numerically controlled equipment possessed by specific firms and also to state that they were all increasing this proportion. This, of course, did not assist those firms which already possessed the highest proportions of numerically controlled equipment in their field. Most important from a sales point of view was the fact that these specific firms were the ones usually desiring to determine their long-run needs.

With all these reasons in mind Ree organized an operations research team from among his staff and assigned them to the project of developing a systematic routine for determining Hitonic's immediate and long-run needs for numerically controlled equipment. S. M. Ample, head of facilities and equipment planning, was appointed director of this operations research team. In attacking the problem the group proposed to devise a scheme specifically suited to their own firm and, on the basis of the results obtained, to decide whether or not to attempt to generalize the scheme to make it adaptable to the needs of a wider range of firms. Two months after having been assigned to the task, Ample's group submitted their first official report outlining their approach to the problem. Exhibit 12-1 summarizes the basic elements of their proposed methodology and approach to the problem.

EXHIBIT 12-1

(The following is a brief summary of the first report submitted by the operations research group of The Hitonic Machinery Corporation outlining their proposed method for the determination of an economic saturation point for numerically controlled equipment.)

The initial task of the operations research group was to determine if any previous attempts had been made to arrive at such a figure or its equivalent. A review of current literature and other available sources of information was made with little success. To simplify the problem, and thus get more immediate useful results, it was decided that a specific solution would be attempted prior to seeking a general solution to the problem. It was felt that early practical results would encourage more studies of this type, whereas a prolonged delay in arriving at useful results could easily cause the project to lose momentum and be displaced by projects of a more immediate but less important nature. It was also felt that the experience gained in determining a specific solution would serve as a useful guide in developing a general solution procedure.

In addition, the operations research group decided to design the procedure so that a minimum amount of original data would have to be collected; i.e., the study would minimize the need for new data which were not available within the firm's current data reporting system or in its historical records. It was realized, however, that some original data would have to be collected, particularly cost estimates for operations currently being performed on conventional machinery but suitable for processing on numerically controlled equipment.

The specific problem selected was to determine Hitonic's own short- and long-run saturation ratio for numerically controlled equipment. The saturation ratio was to be defined as the maximum proportion of the total work load (expressed in conventional machine hours) that could economically be performed on numerically controlled machines Because of the similarity in manufacturing methods used to produce the various mechanical parts required for the numerous classes of machines (milling, boring, grinding, etc.) and types of machines (conventional and numerically controlled), it was suggested that the facilities mix required by kind of operation was *constant,* even though the product mix *varied.* If the hypothesis of a constant facilities mix was valid, the task of determining the saturation ratio would be greatly simplified.

The essence of this hypothesis was that the proportion of the total work load for each work center had remained constant in the past and would continue to remain constant in the future. For purposes of testing the hypothesis the total work load and the work load of each work center were to be adjusted to include both the actual work performed within the company and any machining work that had been subcontracted. Work centers were the established administrative units composed of groups of machines capable of performing similar operations. The logic of the hypothesis was based on the assumption that a far greater change in

Hitonic's product mix, in terms of both *classes* and *types* of machinery produced, had occurred in the past ten years than was expected to occur during the next fifteen to twenty years.

If the constant-facilities-mix hypothesis was acceptable, it appeared possible to determine the overall saturation ratio by analyzing a simple sample of parts. If, however, facility requirements had significantly changed over time because of changes in the product mix or other factors, it appeared that the overall saturation ratio would also change over time. Under these conditions, the satisfactory prediction of future overall saturation ratios might require that many samples of parts be taken in order to determine individual work-center load factors for each product class and to determine saturation ratios for each work center. The work-center load factor represented the average proportion of the work load associated with a given product which was performed by a given work center. It was even conceivable that separate saturation ratios for each work-center-and-product combination might be necessary. Since the acceptance of a constant-facilities-mix hypothesis would substantially reduce the cost and time required for the study, it was recommended that the potential validity of this hypothesis be tested statistically.

Two approaches for determining the past validity of the constant-facilities-mix hypothesis were to be considered: (1) a series of chi-square tests and (2) a linear-regression analysis. The basic data available were histories of eight years of monthly work loads (expressed in actual machine hours) for each work center.

The initial step for the chi-square tests was to determine for the *over-all* eight-year period the proportion of the total work load performed within each work center. These ratios were to be called "eight-year ratios." For the first set of chi-square tests the eight-year period was to be divided into four successive two-year periods. For each two-year period the "expected" work load for each work center was to be calculated by multiplying the total work load for the period by the appropriate eight-year ratio for each work center. A simple chi-square test was to be performed to determine if the *expected* work loads of the work centers for each period were sufficiently similar to the *actual* work loads to support the constant-facilities-mix hypothesis. If this test failed to support the hypothesis, a similar chi-square test was to be performed in which the eight-year period would be divided into two successive four-year periods. This test would be less conclusive than the first test, but was recommended in order to reduce the possibility of rejecting the constant-facilities-mix hypothesis because of some unusual short-term condition which might have existed during specific two-year periods but which would be unlikely to persist over the longer four-year periods.

In the event that *either* of the chi-square tests failed to support the constant-facilities-mix hypothesis, a linear-regression analysis would be performed. This analysis would consist of determining whether the variation in the proportion of the total work load performed in each cost center possessed any recognizable trend with respect to time. A linear-regression equation, with time as the independent variable, would be calculated for the proportion of the total work load performed within each work center. The time coefficients for these equations were to be statistically tested to determine if they were significantly different from zero. If so, they would be reviewed to determine what practical consequences, if any, might result from still accepting the constant-facilities-mix hypothesis.

If on the basis of the chi-square tests and the linear-regression analysis the constant-facilities-mix hypothesis was rejected, a recommendation would be made to reconsider the cost of the project, since a more expensive approach would probably be necessary. After allowing for this possibility, however, the remainder of the report was based on the tentative assumption that the constant-facilities-mix hypothesis would prove acceptable.

It was impractical to determine the percentage of work currently economical to process on numerically controlled machinery on the basis of a 100 per cent analysis. A sampling scheme appeared necessary, and it was suggested that approximately 200 parts be selected for the sample. This amounted to approximately 2 per cent of the number of active parts fabricated by Hitonic. The sample was to be selected by randomly determining a part number and selecting every fiftieth part number thereafter until the full sample size was attained. Only parts which had been produced during the immediate 12-month period were to be included in the sample. Part numbers which were selected by the basic sampling procedure but did not meet this criterion were to be replaced by suitable part numbers.

Every operation of each part selected was to be analyzed to determine the relative economy of producing the part on a numerically controlled machine as compared to processing the part on a conventional machine. For most of the parts the tooling, setup, and average production costs for processing on conventional equipment were available. For a few jobs the tooling, programming, setup, and average production costs were also available for processing on numerically controlled equipment. Whatever information required for such comparisons that was lacking was to be estimated by the process engineering department.

From these estimates the total processing requirements represented by the sample were to be separated into three classes:

1. High savings through numerical control processing
2. Moderate savings through numerical control processing
3. Marginal and negative savings through numerical control processing

Because of the magnitude of the programming costs and the volume requirements of particular parts, it appeared that the relative economy of producing the part on a numerically controlled machine might well depend on whether or not conventional tooling was already available. With this in mind it was recommended that all parts be analyzed under two conditions: first, under the condition of the actual current situation regarding tooling; and second, under the assumption that no tooling existed for either type of processing. The saturation point determined under the first condition would represent the short-run saturation point, and the saturation percentage determined under the second condition would represent the long-run saturation point.

Since it appeared that it would take several months to accumulate and carry out the calculations suggested in the previous discussion, no further planning had been completed. Detailed plans regarding additional aspects of this study and future studies were to be delayed until the results of the current phase of the project were obtained and evaluated.

The report also noted that the preliminary estimate of the overall cost of the proposed study was $10,000.

QUESTIONS

1. Is the proposed study worth undertaking at the estimated cost? If so, is the design of the study satisfactory?
2. What advantages will Hitonic achieve by having a knowledge of the saturation point for numerically controlled equipment for its own operations?
3. Will the solution technique proposed have wide applicability or be primarily restricted to Hitonic's own operation?
4. If the proposed tests support the constant-facilities-mix hypothesis, does it follow that the percentage of the total work load which can be done economically on numerically controlled equipment will also remain stable?
5. What different environmental and technological conditions prevail with regard to numerically controlled equipment as contrasted to conventional equipment?
6. Assuming an acceptable result is obtained by completing the proposed study, what problems with regard to achieving an optimum amount of numerically controlled equipment remain unsolved?
7. Realizing that there is a substantial amount of judgment involved in making the necessary cost estimates and other decisions required by the proposed study, what kind of bias if any might be anticipated?
8. Are the recommended tests of the constant-facilities-mix hypothesis adequate, or can they be improved?
9. If the constant-facilities-mix hypothesis was not acceptable, why would the cost of developing an overall saturation ratio be so greatly increased?

CHAPTER 13

Program Management

This chapter is concerned with the application of the systems approach in coordinating the development, production, and utilization of large-scale man, material, and machine systems. Generally, the discussion will focus on the program management of large systems which are combinations of a number of major subsystems. We will discuss several military, space, and civilian applications of program management. The following topics will be discussed:

> Impact of advancing technology
> Large-scale integrated systems
> Definition of program-management concept
> Functional stages in program development
> Organizational modifications
> Program management at NASA
> The matrix organization
> Other applications of program management

IMPACT OF ADVANCING TECHNOLOGY

Before the industrial revolution in Western Europe and America, scientific knowledge was rarely, or at best slowly, translated into useful applications for the material betterment of man. Since 1850, however, the lag between the discovery and application of scientific knowledge has been decreasing. Moreover, a growing share of scientific and technological effort has been devoted to applied research. Thus science has become a pervasive force in modern society, having widespread influence over all of man's activities.

Technological advances in the United States have been introduced at an increasing rate. A substantial portion of the new technology can be attributed to the great increase in expenditures for research and development. In 1947 research and development expenditures totaled $2.1 billion; by 1971 they had risen to nearly $28 billion. The amount of funds contributed for research and development by private industry and educational institutions has increased, but federal participation in research and development has been even greater. In 1971 the federal government provided a staggering $15 billion, 53 percent of the nation's research funds.[1]

It is becoming increasingly apparent that modern science and technology can create major economic and social changes. Thinking only of the past decade, we can see how advancements in nuclear energy, space exploration, computers, television and other communication systems, surgical techniques (such as heart and other transplants), development of drugs for the control of human behavior, and advancements in genetics have affected our society. And, the impacts are accelerating. Although technological change had major effects in the past, the current and future consequences are much greater.

> It is in the pervasive influence of technology that our contemporary situation seems qualitatively different from that of past societies. . . . This quality of finality of modern technology, and the degree to which our time is oriented toward and dependent on science and knowledge, have brought our society, more than any before, to explicit awareness of technology as an important determinant of our lives and institutions. As a result, our society is coming to a deliberate decision to understand and control technology, and is therefore devoting significant effort to the search for ways to measure the full range of its effects. It is this prominence of technology in many areas of modern life that seems novel in our time and deserving of explicit attention.[2]

A phenomenon of modern industrial society is the development of large-scale, complex organizations for the accomplish-

---

[1]*Federal Funds for Research, Development, and Other Scientific Activities,* National Science Foundation, Washington, D.C., 1965, and *National Patterns of R&D Resources—Funds and Manpower in the United States, 1953–1971,* National Science Foundation, Washington, D.C., 1970.
[2]Emmanuel G. Mesthene, *Technological Change: Its Impact on Man and Society,* New American Library, Inc., New York, 1970, pp. 25–26.

ment of specific purposes. This development is closely related to technological change. Large social organizations are the primary creators and users of technology. They are, in effect, the social mechanisms for the utilization of the developing knowledge from the sciences.

The rapidly advancing technology has taxed man's organizational and administrative abilities. As major scientific projects become more complex, the problems of management increase greatly. Scientific advancement in a complex society has required increasing specialization among men and organizational units. The integration of specialized functions for effective organizational performance is a critical management responsibility; this is where the systems approach is particularly useful.

With new product ideas continually pushing the state of the arts, plus rapid obsolescence, the management functions of planning, organizing, and controlling are crucial. Figure 13–1 shows the relationship between useful product life and the time required for research and development behind that product. Accelerating technology has led throughout history to shorter life spans for each new generation of products. Planned obsolescence has become a byword in modern industrial society. In addition, the amount of time and money required to design and develop the product and set up production facilities has increased. This longer development cycle has made the management function of long-range planning and systems design mandatory in order to minimize the risk of expending valuable resources on a project with little or no chance of success.

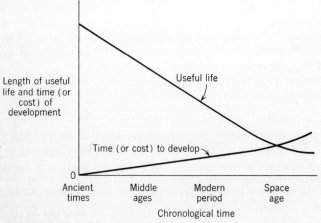

FIGURE 13–1. Relationship of useful product life to length of time (or amount of money) it takes to develop and produce the product.

This relationship is apparent with military and space systems; the cost of research and development programs has skyrocketed. Furthermore, advances are so rapid that some are obsolete even before they are operational. Although not as spectacular, the rapid pace of change in the civilian sector is also apparent. For example, within a period of less than ten years, black-and-white television went through the cycle of market introduction to market saturation. Market expansion and demand for new products, together with increasing research and technological advancements, have been major forces fostering an environment of change and the attendant necessity for more effective systems management.

LARGE-SCALE INTEGRATED SYSTEMS

There have been numerous examples of the application of the systems approach to complex problems of integration of human and material resources. A good example of the necessity for systems management for the successful accomplishment of a large venture can be seen in the development of the nation's transportation facilities. In establishing railroads, for example, it was necessary to integrate such diverse functions as the securing of railways, rolling stock, and fuel; the building of lines, bridges, tunnels, stations, and terminal facilities; the training of personnel and the accomplishment of this under political and competitive pressures. Successful establishment of the nation's transportation network required effective systems management of all these and many more components.

As another example, we might examine the early stages of commercial television. It was not sufficient for manufacturers to design and produce a workable television set; standardization of frequencies and other aspects had to be achieved among manufacturers, broadcasting had to be standardized, network cables had to be installed, interest and demand had to be stimulated (with early programming by manufacturers), and distribution and service channels had to be established. With all these functions necessary for successful performance of the entire system, it is little wonder that there was more than twenty years time lag between the first successful receiver and its widespread use.

We could point to many other applications of the systems approach as it has been applied to civilian sectors in our society, such as the construction of roads or the building of dams and other large-scale, complex activities. Even though these civilian projects are of major magnitude, they do not approach the complexities involved in the management of military and space systems.

One of the earliest and most successful applications of the systems approach was in the development of the atomic bomb— perhaps one of the major scientific efforts in history—which covered a period of five years, cost over $2 billion, and required the energy and talents of many of America's leading scientists. Certainly, the scientific and technological achievements were indispensable in making the project successful. However, the importance of the management functions in bringing together the vast complex of materials and human resources should not be underestimated. A combination of scientific and technological knowledge, together with competent managerial and organizational abilities, was integrated into a coordinated system to reach the goal.

Many of the large-scale systems are associated directly or indirectly with national defense, space exploration, atomic energy, or some other federally sponsored procurement of research and development programs. With a national defense budget of $77.5 billion for fiscal year 1972 and $3.2 billion for The National Aeronautics and Space Administration, over $80 billion was spent for these purposes.[3] Thus, the federal government is the major customer for the large-scale systems. However, Echo and Telstar satellite communications systems are examples of such programs sponsored by private industry. Other commercial programs in the use of atomic energy for power and propulsion are also evident.

These examples of the application of the systems approach to broad managerial problems were forerunners of what has come to be termed the *program-management concept.* This concept called for the systematic integration of a vast number of technologies, industries, human and material resources, and other subsystems into an integrated whole toward the accomplishment of objectives.

DEFINITION OF PROGRAM-MANAGEMENT CONCEPT

The program-management concept is a dynamic philosophy geared to changing managerial requirements in the research, development, procurement, and utilization of large-scale military, space, and civilian systems. With the advent of newer, more complex programs, military services, other government agencies, and private companies have had to adapt their organizations to augment traditional structures. Pressures of technological innovations

---

[3]*The Budget of the United States Government, 1972.* Government Printing Office, Washington, D.C., 1971, p. 83.

and time requirements have made it necessary to establish *centralized management* agencies whose primary responsibility is to provide *overall integration on a systems basis* of many diverse functional activities. Various terms have been used to designate these integrative management agencies, such as *systems management, program management, weapon-system management,* and *project management.* Although there are some differences in these terms and their meanings, they have a thread of commonality—the integrative management of a specific program on a systems basis. For example, Cleland says:

> The project manager acts as a focal point for the concentration of attention on the major problems of the project. This concentration forces the channeling of major program considerations through an individual who has the proper perspective to integrate relative matters of cost, time, technology, and total product compatibility. The project manager is personally involved in critical project decisions concerning organizational policy including: cost and cost estimating; schedules; product performance (quality, reliability); commitment of organizational resources; project tasking; trade-offs involving time, money, and performance; contract performance; and total production integration.[4]

We are using program management as the generic term to describe these approaches. It will be useful to consider the evolution of program management in more detail.

Evolution of Program Management

The program-management concept has evolved from systems-engineering approaches employed to meet complex industrial- and military-product applications over a number of years. Systems engineering—the invention, design, and integration of the entire assembly of equipment as distinct from the invention and design of the components, and geared to the accomplishment of a broad objective—is a concept which has been fundamental to practical engineering since the beginning of the industrial revolution. One of the earliest applications of systems engineering in the United States was geared to military procurement. During the War of 1812 Eli Whitney was commissioned to provide rifles for the young republic and developed a complex system (for that time) for the design and interchangeability of component parts. This fos-

---

[4]David I. Cleland, "Why Project Management?", *Business Horizons,* Winter 1964, p. 83.

tered, much as modern systems engineering, the design of new equipment and methods of production.

The term *systems engineering* has been utilized in recent years to describe engineering systems which are larger, more complex, and more difficult to engineer than any of those in the past. For industrial and military products up through World War II, systems engineering was involved mainly in integrating existing subcomponents into a final product. Design was geared to steady improvement rather than explosive breakthroughs. Interchangeability between components became a major consideration in design and engineering.

One of the key elements in systems engineering today is the design of the product for a mission without complete assurance that the necessary components will be forthcoming. The function now involves—whether for military or industrial products—the coordination of research and development of subcomponents, as well as the integration of these subcomponents in the production phase.

One of the major problems in systems design for a large-scale, highly complex product such as a weapon system lies in coordinating machines and materials and in establishing organizational relationships for the necessary decision making and dissemination of information to the complex array of groups whose efficient performance is vital to the project. This coordination is achieved through a *system of information flow*. The system of information flow is established less rigidly when there are rapid technological changes and product innovations.

Systems engineering (the integration of the physical components of an assembly) and information systems (the establishment of a communications network between the various functions whose performance is necessary for successful product mission) are major elements in overall *systems design* as discussed in Chapter 7. Program management has evolved because of the need to design more effective organizational systems to deal with the complex managerial problems.

Program management was used during the 1950s for the Air Force's advanced aircraft, missile, and space systems, the Navy's nuclear submarine project, and the National Aeronautics and Space Administration's space programs. The terms *weapon-system management, project management,* and *program management* were used to describe these approaches. As the need for managing the development and production of systems with such missions has broadened in scope, the term *program management* has gained wider usage.

In program management the scope of the mission is often more extensive than the boundaries of the organization which has primary responsibility for mission accomplishment. Therefore, persuasion rather than formal authority may be necessary in order for the program manager to coordinate activities. In contrast, systems management as set forth in Chapter 6 pertains to those systems that are designed to operate within defined boundaries of authority and control.

Where Is Program Management Appropriate?

The program-management approach is most appropriate in large-scale endeavors which are new and require unique combinations of human and material resources. Although there are obvious differences between such large-scale endeavors (for example, between the development of the national space program, the creation of an effective national transportation system, the development of a multinational business organization, or the creation of the Tennessee Valley Authority) there are certain similarities in all large-scale endeavors. James E. Webb, former Administrator of NASA, suggests a number of these:

> *First,* they are ordinarily undertaken as a result of a significant change in the environment—social, political, technological, military, or other—that raises a new and urgent need or presents a new opportunity.
>
> *Second,* interaction between the environmental situation and large-scale endeavors is a continuous and often turbulent process.
>
> A *third* very important common feature of large-scale endeavors is that organizing, administering, reorganizing, and administering the reorganized structure provide the key to the effectiveness and usefulness of such endeavors, rather than the invention of entirely new machines or processes.
>
> *Fourth,* large-scale endeavors do not generally require new organizational and administrative forms, but the more effective utilization of existing forms.
>
> *Fifth,* all large-scale endeavors have a number of unusually complex managerial requirements. They depend on men with special, often unique, skills, men of high intelligence and creativity, men trained in a variety of disciplines, men who by their nature raise unique problems for management.
>
> *Sixth,* another common denominator of large-scale endeavors is the necessity of a continuing "critical mass" of support. There must be enough support and continuity of support to retain and to keep directly engaged on the critical problems the highly talented people required to do the job, as well as to keep viable the entire organizational structure.

Seventh, large-scale endeavors are increasingly concerned with the utilization, and often the development, of advanced technology and the application of new knowledge. Most require doing something for the first time and have a high degree of uncertainty as to precise results.

Eighth, all large-scale endeavors have important secondary and tertiary effects beyond those associated with the prime objective. These alter the environment and significantly impact events generally.

Ninth, a number of intangibles characterize the large-scale endeavor. They are essentially investment enterprises representing a willingness of a group or a society to give up resources in hand for future returns that may be long delayed in realization. They are ordinarily unusually challenging from the standpoint of their uniqueness, their promise, or the urgency of their need, and they tend to appeal to creative instincts on the part of supporters and participants.

Tenth, large-scale endeavors, whether public or private, invariably loom large in the public eye. They are subject to constant watchfulness on the part of supporter and opponent alike.[5]

Although these characteristics occur in varying degree in different large-scale endeavors, they do describe a general pattern of relationships. A little reflection suggests that the SST (supersonic transport) was one such large-scale endeavor which had these characteristics.

One of the major requirements for the organization and administration of large-scale endeavors with the above characteristics is the development of a managerial system which is quite different from traditional, bureaucratic organizations. Management of such large-scale programs requires the integration of a large number of factors, some in conflict, into a cohesive and dynamic whole geared to keeping the total system moving toward objective accomplishment. Webb suggests some of the features of this managerial system:

> Executives within such large-scale endeavors thus have to work under unusual circumstances and in unusual ways. They cannot function in accord with the simplified scheme of traditional enterprises. . . . In the large-scale endeavor the man himself must also be unusual; he must be knowledgeable in sound management doctrine and practice, but able to do a job without an exact definition of what it is or how it should be done; a man who can work

[5]James E. Webb, *Space Age Management,* McGraw-Hill Book Company, New York, 1969, pp. 59–63.

effectively when lines of command crisscross and move in several directions rather than straight up and down; one who can adjust to, and be himself, several bosses at the same time; one who can work effectively in an unstable environment and can live with uncertainty and a high degree of personal insecurity; one willing to work for less of a monetary reward than he could insist on elsewhere; one who can blend public and private interests in organized participation to the benefit of both.

More than anything else the executives within a large-scale endeavor must be able, one by one and all together, to see and understand the totality of the job that the endeavor is designed to do. Each must see and understand the relationship of his evolving and changing individual assignment, and of the functions and people involved in that assignment, to the whole job and its requirements.[6]

Program management is an approach which attempts to deal with the difficult organizational and managerial problems associated with such large-scale endeavors. Before looking at the organizational modifications required in this approach, it is useful to consider the various stages in the development of a large-scale program.

FUNCTIONAL STAGES IN PROGRAM DEVELOPMENT

A convenient step in understanding the evolution of program management is the *product-mission concept.* Any product, civilian or military, can be thought of as having a mission to perform. Often, in the civilian economy, one of the problems is the determination of the right product mission and the development of promotional materials which will enhance the ability of the product to fulfill its mission in the eyes of the consumer. Briefly, to fulfill the product mission it is necessary for the manufacturer to perceive a need, to design or develop a successful product, to produce it efficiently, to stimulate demand for this product, to provide for distribution through channels necessary to reach the consumer, and perhaps to educate the potential users in the proper utilization of the product. The accomplishment of a successful mission for the product can be viewed as a systems management problem much broader than just physical production.

The same functions have to be performed for successful mission accomplishment for the simplest product and for the most complex space or weapon systems. The major differences are not in the types of functions to be performed, but rather in the com-

[6]Ibid., pp. 136–137.

plexity and integration of these functions. Five basic functions are necessary for successful mission accomplishment:

1. Perception of need
2. Design
3. Production
4. Delivery
5. Utilization

Within each of these primary functions there are numerous subfunctions, many of which have increased so much in complexity and importance that they frequently are considered to be separate functions; however, it is useful to think of broad functions first and then to discuss more detailed subfunctions so that the interrelationships can be discerned. For purposes of illustration we will discuss a weapon system, such as Polaris.

Perception of Need

Perception of need for a new or different weapon system is influenced by many strategic and political considerations. Consideration has to be given to the current and possible future technological and military capabilities of potential enemies. It also requires a thorough assessment of the political situation, particularly the implications of military preparedness upon foreign policy. The broad perception of need must be narrowed by consideration of what is desired, tempered with an evaluation of the current state of the art, a forecast of future technological feasibility, and a consideration of economic factors. There is a strong likelihood of conflict among the various objectives. This conflict must be resolved at the national level.

Design

Once the initial stage of perception of need is accomplished, the next stage is research, development, and design. Given a broad military mission, there are generally numerous alternative solutions for the successful accomplishment of that mission. The design function includes setting forth alternative solutions, developing designs, evaluating alternative solutions, and selecting the final design. Obviously, experimentation and testing of components and overall systems are performed in each of these stages. Once the design has been determined, the next step is production.

Production

The function of production includes the establishment of manpower and physical facilities, selection of component suppliers and sources of raw materials, testing and inspection of parts and components to meet quality specifications, assembly of components into final products, and testing and performance analysis of final products. The coordination of all these subfunctions is a vital part of the production process.

Delivery

This is the function of transferring ownership physically from producer to user. For military products this function is accomplished by a program of testing and reevaluation. In the civilian economy, distribution of the finished product usually is more complex, however, requiring major effort on the part of the producers. Military producers, on the other hand, deal directly with ultimate users.

Utilization

The function of utilization is performed most frequently by the military services, although private industry may participate to a limited extent. This function includes such things as training of personnel, development of facilities for operations, logistics, maintenance and repair, modernization, and retirement.

These five functions—perception of need, design, production, delivery, and utilization—are basic for mission accomplishment. Regardless of the product or the time period, they have to be performed by some agency. Essentially, then, program management integrates the performance of all these primary functions necessary for successful mission accomplishment.

The development of highly sophisticated weapon and space systems required more effective decision making. The Department of Defense was among the first to make extensive use of systems analysis (see Chapter 6). Systems analysis had its antecedence in the military operations analysis of 1939–1945. However, operations analysis dealt mainly with "tactical" problems that involved the immediate use of equipment in operations, primarily the function of effective utilization. In contrast, systems analysis deals with longer-range problems and integrates all functions required for mission accomplishment.

Although systems analysis makes use of quantitative approaches, it also involves nonquantifiable inputs. Hitch suggests the broad, integrative nature of systems analysis for military applications as follows:

> Systems analysis at the national level, therefore, involves a continuous cycle of defining military objectives, designing alternative systems to achieve those objectives, evaluating these alternatives in terms of their effectiveness and cost, questioning the objectives and the other assumptions underlying the analysis, opening new alternatives, and establishing new military objectives.[7]

A basic part of this process is "cost/effectiveness analysis," which compares alternative ways of accomplishing national security missions and then determines the way that contributes the most for a given cost or achieves a given objective at the least cost.

The National Aeronautics and Space Administration also has used systems analysis in its decision making. It established an Office of Systems to analyze all the various missions, systems, and equipment being considered for the man-in-space endeavor. One of the first assignments of this office was to analyze systematically the complex problem of deciding upon a mission mode for Project Apollo, the manned lunar landing program.

Systems analysis provides the means for consideration and integration of all functions necessary for successful mission accomplishment and emphasizes the optimization of total-systems performance. It also provides for evaluating alternative means of mission accomplishment in terms of costs and effectiveness. It is an important prerequisite to efficient program management.

ORGANIZATIONAL MODIFICATIONS

In the traditional organization with a limited and well-established product line, the president and other chief executives can perform the "program-management functions." However, with new and complex programs involving new product designs and technologies and requiring the coordination of many different functional departments, the president's office alone cannot provide the necessary integration. Under these circumstances it is usually necessary to establish a specific organizational agency, operating at a lower level, to facilitate this coordination.

[7]Charles J. Hitch, "A Planning-Programming-Budgeting System," in Fremont Kast and James Rosenzweig (eds.), *Science, Technology, and Management,* McGraw-Hill Book Company, New York, 1963, p. 64.

Program management involves the appointment of one individual, the program manager, who has responsibility for the overall planning, coordination, and ultimate outcome for the program. He usually is superimposed upon the functional organization and the imposition of this integrating agency tends to create new and more complex organizational relationships. In some ways authority and responsibility for the performance of certain tasks are not as clear-cut as under the functional structure. Actually, each method of organizing, functional or program, has advantages. The functional approach makes sure that specialized activities are performed adequately for a variety of programs. With functional authority it is possible to balance the performance requirements over a variety of programs and to maintain clear-cut vertical control over the activities performed. However, there is a weakness in the lack of a strong source of authority that will ensure the timely integration of all functions for a single program.

Program management attempts to minimize this defect. However, it creates difficulties in eliciting the most effective performance of each function over a broad program complex while at the same time maintaining proper balance among all functions on a given program.

Authority and Responsibility

The authority and responsibility given to the program manager varies widely in different organizations and programs. In some cases he has very little authority and operates primarily as an expediter. In others, particularly with large-scale weapon and space systems, he has authority over the entire operation with the various functional operations subordinated to him. In most situations, however, his role lies somewhere between these extremes. The essence of program management is that it is interfunctional and is often in conflict with the normal organization structure.[8]

> The program manager cannot operate effectively if he relies solely upon the formal authority of his position. Success is more likely to depend upon his ability to influence other organizational members. Because he is a focal point in the operation, he does have informational and communications inputs which provide him with a strong basis of influence.

[8]For an interesting discussion of some of the human problems created by program management see Clayton Reeser, "Some Potential Human Problems of the Project Form of Organization," *Academy of Management Journal*, December 1969, pp. 459–467.

Emphasis on Horizontal and Lateral Relationships

The program manager's authority and influence flow in different directions from hierarchical authority. They flow horizontally across vertical superior-subordinate relationships existing within the functional organization. Throughout the program, personnel at various levels and in many functions must contribute their efforts. For each new program, horizontal and lateral information-decision networks must be established which differ significantly from the existing networks based upon the established structure. The organization should be sufficiently flexible to allow for evolving relationships and networks as program requirements change.

Special Role of Program Manager

Under the program-management approach new organizational relationships are established. The following listing by Cleland summarizes the special role of the program or project manager which differentiates him from the traditional manager:

1. As a manager he is concerned with accomplishing specific projects that require participation by organizations and agencies outside his direct control.
2. Since the project manager's authority cuts through superior-subordinate lines of authority, he conflicts with the functional managers who must share authority in their functional areas for the particular project.
3. As a focal point for project activities, the project manager enters into, on an exceptional basis, those matters necessary for the successful accomplishment of the project. He determines the *when* and *what* of the project activities; the functional manager, who supports many different projects in the organization determines *how* the support will be given.
4. The project manager's task is finite; after the project is completed, the personnel directly supporting the project can be assigned to other activities.
5. The project manager oversees a high proportion of professionals; consequently he must use different management techniques than in the simple superior-subordinate relationship.
6. His diverse and extraorganizational activities require unification and integration directed toward the objective of the project. As a unifying agent for the total management function he has no line authority to act but depends on other manifestations of authority to attain the objective. Thus the directing function is somewhat less important from the perspective of the project manager. What direction he does accomplish is through the functional managers supporting him.

7. The project manager does not normally possess any traditional line authority over the line organization involved in creating the goods or services.[9]

The program manager thus has a unique role in the organization, one which is subject to substantial conflict and ambiguity.[10] Many of the organizational and managerial modifications are illustrated in the following discussion of program management at NASA.

PROGRAM MANAGEMENT AT NASA

The National Aeronautics and Space Administration (NASA) was created in 1958 and given primary responsibility for research and development in civilian space efforts. NASA was given a fivefold mission:

1. To formulate specific national objectives and develop a comprehensive program for the study and peaceful utilization of space.
2. To conduct research leading to practical solutions of problems of aeronautics and space flight.
3. To develop and operate appropriate vehicles for scientific investigation and practical utilization of space for peaceful purposes.
4. To arrange for participation by the scientific community in planning and conducting scientific flight of aircraft and space vehicles.
5. To provide for the widest practical and appropriate dissemination of information concerning these activities and results.[11]

In early 1961 the national space program was changed dramatically with the announcement of the objective of a manned lunar landing and return by 1970, the Apollo program. This major policy decision reflected upon NASA's entire operations. During the 1960s NASA's yearly budget was in excess of $5 billion, and the number of direct employees was over 34,000. In addition, approximately 300,000 people employed by industry, universities, and research organizations were working on NASA projects.

Since the successful landing of Apollo 11 on the moon and the safe return of the astronauts to earth in August 1969, NASA's activities have been gradually scaled down to an estimated ex-

[9]David I. Cleland, op. cit., p. 82.
[10]David L. Wilemon and John P. Cicero, "The Project Manager—Anomalies and Ambiguities," *Academy of Management Journal*, September 1970, pp. 269–282.
[11]*1962 NASA Authorization*, Hearings before the Committee on Space and Astronautics, House of Representatives, 86th Cong., 1st Sess., 1961.

penditure level of $3.2 billion in fiscal year 1972. However, this still represents a major national commitment of resources. The volume of expenditure and level of effort for these space programs are much greater than for other major national efforts such as the atomic bomb program during World War II and the accelerated ballistic missile program during the late 1950s and early 1960s.

NASA's overall program includes four major areas: manned space flight, space science and application, advanced research and technology, and tracking and data acquisition as shown in Figure 13–2. Integrating the complexity of programs, with the great variety of missions, into an effective and viable organization is difficult. The program directors and their staffs are responsible for program budgeting and funding, for setting up each approved project, for milestone reporting, for establishing the technical guidelines that must be accomplished, and for reviewing and evaluating progress on a continuing basis with the field centers. They serve as the focal point within NASA for integrative management on a program basis.

Manned Space Flight Program

The organization and management of the manned space flight program is unique in NASA's operations. During 1961, after NASA

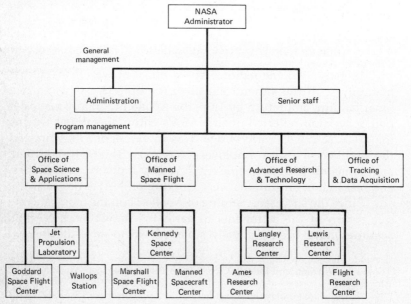

FIGURE 13–2. Organization of National Aeronautics and Space Administration.

had set down the objectives of its newly expanded program for lunar exploration, a team of management specialists analyzed other experiences, such as the Manhattan Engineer District, the Navy Special Projects Office, and the Air Force systems management approaches. These alternative organizational plans were appraised and reviewed by NASA officials. Based on this study, an organizational plan was designed to provide unified program management. The objective was to bring all important functions for each major program grouping within a single office and so facilitate prompt decisions.

The Director of the Manned Space Flight Program was given direct responsibility for the institutional operations of the three centers primarily concerned with manned space flight: the Manned Spacecraft Center, the Marshall Space Flight Center, and the Kennedy Space Center. The other NASA elements also worked with the Director of Manned Space Flights on any project that supported the manned space program. They continued to report through other program offices for work unrelated to manned space flight. In the manned space flight program, a management council was established which consisted of the directors of the Office of Manned Space Flight and the senior officials of the three research and development centers. This management council met monthly and provided the key communication and integration for these centers.

The Office of Manned Space Flight consisted of four program offices for the overall direction of Gemini, Apollo, mission operations, and advanced manned missions programs. These offices were responsible for management. For example, the Gemini and Apollo program directors were charged specifically with the responsibility for producing the required spacecraft, vehicles, and facilities on schedule and within costs. These responsibilities included planning and schedules, budgets and cost control, systems engineering, design, test, and performance evaluation necessary to ensure the achievement of program objectives.

The above discussion indicates that NASA has made substantial use of the program management approach as a basis for integrating highly diverse and complicated activities. This was particularly true in the Manned Space Flight Program. The success of the moon landing in 1969 and of the later Apollo missions is, in part, a tribute to the success of this managerial approach.

The Office of Manned Space Flight continues to use the program-management approach. Figure 13-3 shows the current organization of this office and indicates that as the older programs, such as Mercury and Gemini, were completed, new program

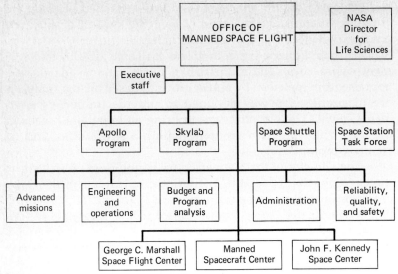

FIGURE 13-3. Organization of the Office of Manned Space Flight.

offices were established. Program management is being used for Skylab, the country's first manned orbital space station, and the more sophisticated Space Shuttle and Space Station. These new programs will utilize management approaches based upon those developed for Apollo and earlier manned space flight programs. We foresee the continued development of more sophisticated managerial approaches necessary to keep pace with the rapidly advancing technology and increasing complexities of space endeavors.

THE MATRIX ORGANIZATION

The emphasis in this chapter on program management should not be construed as an indication that it is necessarily the best way of organizing all projects. Actually, this approach is most effective when an organization is dealing with a small number of large systems. When an organization has a variety of projects, ranging from large to small, it is often desirable to use a mixed organization. For programs of major magnitude a program-type management may be established, but the smaller, less significant projects may be carried out by the functional organization.

When an organization is dealing with numerous smaller projects, a *matrix* organization may be used where there are well-established functional departments which have special skills and capabilities for performance on a variety of projects. Essentially, projects flow through the functional complex and receive the services of these specialized departments as shown in Figure 13–4. The matrix organization represents a compromise between the traditional functional organization and the full-scale program management form.[12]

The Navy uses this approach for many of its small-scale projects. The National Aeronautics and Space Administration has a mixed organization. The Office of Manned Space Flight has authority over the research and development centers for integration of the Manned Space Program. In most of the other smaller projects, the various program offices have less authority and control. In these cases a good deal of responsibility is assigned directly to the research and development centers.

There are many examples of the use of the matrix form in industry. The Systems Group of TRW, Inc., has developed a matrix organization for many of its aerospace and other high-technology projects. TRW Systems' business is in the application of advanced

[12]For a more detailed discussion of the matrix organization see John F. Mee, "Matrix Organization," *Business Horizons,* Summer 1964, pp. 70–72, and Fremont A. Shull, *Matrix Structure and Project Authority for Optimizing Organizational Capacity,* Southern Illinois University, Business Research Bureau, Carbondale, Ill., 1965.

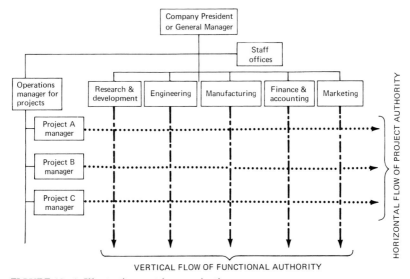

FIGURE 13–4. Illustrative matrix organization.

technology. In order to maintain its capabilities to deal with sophisticated technology, it needs to maintain laboratories and other specialized groups with a critical mass of skilled scientists and technicians. At the same time it is dealing with several hundred projects which have to be phased through the organization. Therefore, TRW Systems uses the matrix form which retains the highly specialized technical and staff departments but provides for the establishment of a project office for each customer program. The project manager has overall management responsibility for all project activities and directs these activities through the project office. It is the central point for all projectwide activities such as schedules, cost and performance control, system planning and engineering, and contract management. Employees are assigned from the specialized technical and staff departments to participate on the project team. An individual may work on a single project for a length of time or he may provide support to several projects at the same time.

This matrix organizational form at TRW Systems meets the two basic requirements of retaining specialized departments with a high level of technical expertise, but also providing for the planning, coordinating, and control of each project. It does provide a flexible structure within which people and resources can be allocated. However, it is not a simple managerial system and there is substantial role ambiguity and intergroup conflict. TRW Systems has utilized organization development and other programs to help provide the interpersonal climate necessary to make the matrix organization work.[13]

OTHER APPLICATIONS OF PROGRAM MANAGEMENT

Although program management has been used primarily in the defense and aerospace sectors, it will find increasing application in many other areas. Steiner and Ryan suggest forces that will influence this trend: "Our projection of greater use in the commercial world is predicated on several bases: increased sophistication of customer needs, increased complexity and size of business, increased pace of technological change, increased involvement of the Government as a customer in nondefense areas, and the changing needs of people in organizations."[14]

[13]"Teamwork through Conflict," *Business Week,* Mar. 20, 1971, pp. 44–50, and "The Systems Group of TRW, Inc.," *Behavioral Science: Concepts and Management Applications,* National Industrial Conference Board, Inc., New York, 1969, pp. 157–171.
[14]George A. Steiner and William G. Ryan, *Industrial Project Management,* The Macmillan Company, New York, 1968, pp. 158–159.

Essentially, the program-management approach is applicable to those large-scale endeavors characterized previously in this chapter. Several of the automotive firms utilized this approach in, development, and production of new products such as compact cars. Commercial aircraft companies have followed the program-management form in the development and production of their products. Many organizations have utilized a modification of this approach in the form of product managers to integrate their production and distribution functions.

Program management also will find increasing applications in the noncommercial sectors dealing with problems such as transportation, urban renewal, health care, crime and delinquency, and pollution. There are many major social problems which require new administrative and organizational arrangements to facilitate their solution. We foresee that the program-management approach may be one method for achieving the necessary planning, coordination, and control of complex endeavors. The difficulties of applying this approach to these social problems will be even greater than those applications discussed in the foregoing sections. Application of the program-management approach for dealing with broader social problems will require the coordination of many public and private organizations—it will be inter-organizational in nature. For example, in the establishment of metropolitan community health systems, the program-management function would require the coordination of activities of many hospitals, public health agencies, private physicians, etc. The program-management function would be difficult, requiring the integration of many separate organizations and individuals. However, the pattern for this development has been established in our large national space and military programs.

SUMMARY

There have been numerous examples of the application of the systems approach to complex problems of integration of human and material resources. The development of the nation's railroad transportation system and, more recently, the introduction of commercial television are typical examples. One of the earliest and most successful applications of the systems approach in the military sphere was in the development of the atomic bomb during World War II.

These examples of the application of the systems approach to broad managerial problems were forerunners of what has come to be termed *program management.* The program-management concept is a dynamic philosophy geared to changing managerial requirements in the research, development, procurement, and utilization of large-scale military, space, and civilian systems. It is geared to the integrative management of a specific program on a systems basis. It has evolved because of the need to design more effective organizational systems to deal with the complex managerial problems.

Program management requires organizational modifications, emphasizes the integrative aspects, and requires the development of effective lateral information-decision networks. The essence of program management is that it is interfunctional and is often in conflict with the normal organization structure. Under this approach it is often difficult to establish clear-cut authority relationships, and the program manager must use persuasion rather than formal authority in carrying out his activities.

A prime example of program management is seen in the organization of NASA's Office of Manned Space Flight. This office provided the planning, coordination, and control of the numerous activities required for the successful Apollo and other manned space flight programs.

The matrix organization represents a compromise between the traditional functional organization and the pure program-management form. It is generally used when the organization has a variety of projects which must flow through the functional complex and receive the services of these specialized departments. This approach has been used by NASA, the Navy, and industrial organizations such as TRW Systems.

The trend toward the use of program management will continue. It will be applied to the solution of many of our social problems, such as transportation, urban renewal, and health care. Program management, most apparent in military and space activities, is the vanguard of more complex systems which will evolve in the future.

QUESTIONS

1. How is advancing technology related to the development of program management?
2. Why is the view of product missions important in program management?
3. Using the listing of functions required for mission accomplishment, set forth a plan for the introduction of a new commercial product.
4. Make a list of large-scale endeavors which fit the characteristics listed on pp. 395 and 396.

5. What is program management and why has it evolved?
6. How does the "authority" of the program manager differ from traditional line authority?
7. How does the matrix organization differ from the traditional functional organization? What are its advantages and limitations?
8. Through the cited references and other library resources, investigate the program management for a specific National Aeronautics and Space Administration program.
9. Discuss applications of program management in industry.
10. Discuss the application of program management to large-scale social problems. Make a list of some of the problems where this approach might be appropriate.
11. Why might interorganizational program management be more difficult than intraorganizational program management?

CASE:

Atlas Electronics Corporation (A)*

SPYEYE PROJECT—ORGANIZATION

Company History

Atlas Electronics Corporation was organized by a group of engineers and scientists who pioneered electronic research and development for the Office of Scientific Research and Development during World War II. After the war, members of this group joined together to form a private company to continue their efforts.

From the start, Atlas earned a reputation among government and corporate customers as a leader in advanced electronic techniques and systems. Its present capabilities cover a wide spectrum of electronic applications and skills, including aviation systems, radar, space payloads, communications, and electronic warfare (reconnaissance and counter-measures). Atlas has continued to distinguish itself for advances in the state-of-the-art and for superior quality on numerous prototype and initial operational equipments developed for U. S. government agencies. Full 95% of its business is on government R & D contracts, whether directly or for prime government contractors.

Atlas' success is largely due to the competence, dedication and stability of its staff. Of its 3,000 employees, over half have engineering or scientific degrees. Approximately 15% of these have advanced technical or MBA degrees or are working toward them. The primary resource of

*This case was developed and prepared by Dr. William R. Lockridge, Associate Professor, Graduate School of Business Administration, C. W. Post Center of Long Island University. Reprinted by permission. All names have been disguised.

management is the brainpower of these men, who are professional specialists in diverse fields.

Company Organization

Atlas Electronics Corporation is a typical engineering company organized along functional lines. Its functional engineering departments are oriented to various technical disciplines and are staffed with engineers, scientists and technicians who work on developing advanced techniques and in the support of projects.

The departmental organization structure starts with the department head and goes down the line through the section heads, group leaders and supervisory engineers, to the scientists, engineers and technicians who are doing the detail work. The department heads report to John Doan, Executive Vice President. Communications, approvals and directions flow through this organization in an orderly manner. Each level is under the supervision of the level above it and normally will not operate without higher level approval and direction.

Atlas has three engineering functional departments: an Antenna Department, a Receiver Department, and a Data Systems Department. Each of these is responsible for developing advanced techniques, performing engineering, and for giving support to R & D projects in its technical area. The organization of each of these departments is shown in Exhibits 13–1 to 13–3.

In addition, Atlas has a Manufacturing Department (Exhibit 13–4), which does fabrication, assembly and testing of production units. This Department also reports to John Doan. Purchasing, accounting, personnel

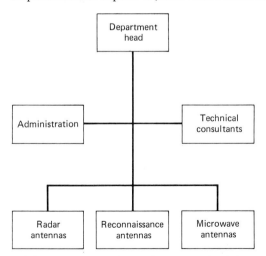

Exhibit 13–1. Atlas Electronics Corporation (A), Antenna Department.

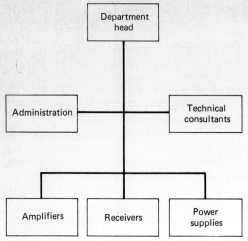

Exhibit 13-2. Atlas Electronics Corporation (A),
Receiver department.

administration, and other services are performed by various company staff departments not shown in the Exhibits.

From time to time, Atlas sets up an ad hoc Project Management to handle a large R & D contract. This is a semiautonomous group consisting of a project manager and other personnel drawn from the functional organizations in the company. It has complete responsibility for meeting all of the requirements of the contract, but it gets the work done in the functional departments. At the end of the project it is dissolved.

The Project Management assigns technical tasks to each supporting

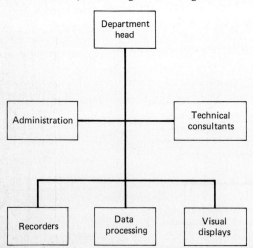

Exhibit 13-3. Atlas Electronics Corporation (A),
Data Systems Department.

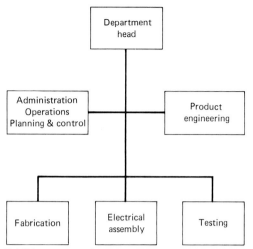

Exhibit 13-4. **Atlas Electronics Corporation (A),**
Manufacturing Department.

department to perform. To a limited extent, it is permitted to cut across organizational lines so that it can deal with the people doing the work without having to go through the whole hierarchy of their functional organizations. It handles scheduling and overall cost control; it deals with subcontractors and maintains liaison with customers; and it coordinates all of the technical inputs and "hardware" from the supporting organizations into the overall system which is delivered to the customer.

The people who are literally transferred to the Project Management are mostly of a supervisory or senior category and report directly to the project manager. Their function is to advise him in their respective technical disciplines, to cooperate with him in managing the project, and to give "work direction"[1] to the personnel in the functional departments who are doing the work. The Project Management staff cannot directly supervise the work of the department personnel because these workers report in line to their department head. The department head may be on the same level or a higher level than the project manager. Consequently, the project manager has the problem of getting the utmost in effort from people who are responsible to someone else for pay raises, promotion, performance and other aspects of line relationship.

Spyeye Project

As the result of a successful competitive proposal, the government has awarded Atlas an R & D contract for an airborne reconnaissance system

---

[1]"Work direction"—definition of the goals, specifications and constraints (budget, schedule, etc.) for a technical task, as distinguished from detailed supervision of the work to perform it; the "what" to do, not the "how" to do it.

called "Spyeye." The system consists of an antenna, a receiver, an amplifier and visual read-out equipment. This is an advanced system requiring the development of specific equipment whose performance characteristics are beyond the existing state-of-the-art. Atlas agrees to produce a prototype model in 9 months. Following acceptance by the government, it agrees to produce 5 operational systems within another 6 months.

The contract is for a firm fixed price of $6 million, of which $5.6 million is the estimated target cost and $400,000 is Atlas' fee. The contract has a profit-sharing incentive whereby the government and the contractor share any cost-saving below the $5.6 million on a 90/10 percent basis. It also provides penalties on the contractor for overrunning the cost, for late delivery, and for failure to meet performance specifications. The government will debit Atlas dollar for dollar against its fee for any cost overrun, and will assess it $200 for every day of late delivery. Various penalties, up to 20% of the fee, are provided for failure to meet technical performance specifications.

Project Support

The Spyeye project requires support from many functional areas throughout the company. It needs technical advice, engineering and "hardware" from the reconnaissance section of the Antenna Department, the amplifier and receiver sections of the Receiver Department, the visual displays section of the Data Systems Department, and the fabrication, assembly and testing facilities of the Manufacturing Department. (See Exhibits 13–1 to 13–4.)

Alternatives for Project Organization

Company management has to decide whether to organize Spyeye as an ad hoc Project Management, or to handle it through one of its functional departments. Two men are available to lead the project, but the one selected will depend on the choice of organization. These men are Howard Datson and Burt Saunderson.

Howard Datson, 55, is head of the Receiver Department. He has been with the company since its inception and has built his department to the largest in the company. Datson and his group were responsible for numerous innovations in the receiver line and have kept the company ahead of most of its competition in that field.

Datson put in a strong plea to the President, Homer Skillton, to let the Receiver Department manage Spyeye as a project within its functional organization. "My department has been in existence since this company started," he said. "We've a well-trained staff with a lot of managerial and technical know-how. We'll have to do the bulk of the development anyhow. And I'm sure we can handle the interfaces with the other departments without any trouble."

Datson went on to express some of his personal feelings about the alternative of setting up a Project Management. "You must recognize that we've built the reputation of this company on the technical capability and quality performance of its functional departments. I personally dislike becoming a 'service' organization to a group who will be here to-day and gone tomorrow. Also, it'll probably be managed by someone who is not as technically oriented as any of our department heads."

"One thing I want to make particularly clear," he continued, "no-body's going to come into my department and tell my men how they must do their work. They report to me and my supervisors and we're the ones who call the shots."

Burt Saunderson, 45, is a section head in the Antenna Department and has held that position for six years. He started as a project engineer twelve years ago and worked up through the group leader level to section head. A year ago he was relieved of his functional assignment and was appointed Project Manager in an ad hoc Project Management for an R & D project called "Moonglow." Moonglow was much smaller than Spyeye, but it had many of the same characteristics, such as the support from several different functional departments, a fixed-price, and penalties for failure to meet cost, schedule and performance specifications.

Saunderson and his Project Management group had successfully completed the Moonglow project. They had delivered the system on time, and the performance was satisfactory to the customer, although the equipment deviated slightly from the specification. They also had been able to increase the company's fee $1\frac{1}{2}\%$ by bettering the targeted cost. But Moonglow was now over and the people on it had to be reassigned.

While waiting for a new assignment, Saunderson served as bid manager on the Spyeye proposal to the government and was responsible for having come up with the reconnaissance system which the government finally bought. He felt he was the logical one to head up the Spyeye Project, if President Skillton decided to organize it as a Project Management. Accordingly, Saunderson sent a memorandum to Skillton outlining his reasons for this type of organization, which were, in essence as follows:

1. The project involves four of the company's operating organizations. If management is established in any one of these, the company would have the awkward situation of one functional department directing the activities of others who are on a parallel with itself in the company organization structure.

2. The project involves more than mere technical development. Cost, schedule and technical performance all must be evaluated and balanced to produce the optimum overall result. A functional department, steeped in its own technology and hampered by its organizational structure, would lack the objectivity to view the overall project problem in perspective and to meet the ever-changing operational crises which arise from day to day.

3. The project does not involve pure research. It requires some in-

novation in the techniques area which can be done by the supporting functional departments. But someone will have to develop the overall system and that can best be done by a Project Management.

4. The project will add little to the long range technical capability of the company. What it needs is an organization to "get the job done,"—an organization which can use the technical support of the functional organizations without causing any permanent disruption in the company's organization structure.

President Skillton recognized that both men had good arguments.

QUESTIONS

1. What are the basic differences between the role and activities of a functional engineering department and a Project Management unit?
2. What are the advantages and disadvantages of a Project Management structure over a traditional functional organization?
3. Under what conditions would it be most appropriate to form a Project Management structure to handle an R&D project?
4. How would you organize the Spyeye Project if you were President Skillton? Why?

Atlas Electronics Corporation (B)*

SPYEYE PROJECT—OPERATIONAL PROBLEMS

Spyeye Project Management

President Skillton met with Executive Vice President John Doan to discuss the Spyeye Project. "John, I've decided to organize Spyeye as a
Project Management instead of assigning it to any of the functional
departments. It's too big and too complex and it'll be in trouble from the
start. I don't want to upset the stability of any department by temporarily
expanding its personnel and giving it a coordinating job to handle."
(See Exhibits 13-5 and 13-6.)

Project Manager

"But this creates some problems on which I'll need your help," he continued. "The first is the selection of a Project Manager. He's got to be at
home in the front office talking about budgets, time schedules and corporate policies and also at home in the laboratory talking about technical
research and development problems. Of course, we can't expect him to
double as a member of top management and a scientist equally well, but
he's got to know what can be done technically and be enough of a
business man to get it done within the contract."

"I'm thinking of Burt Saunderson for the job. But I'd like your

---

*This case was developed and prepared by Dr. William R. Lockridge, Associate
Professor, Graduate School of Business Administration, C. W. Post Center of Long
Island University. Reprinted by permission. All names have been disguised.

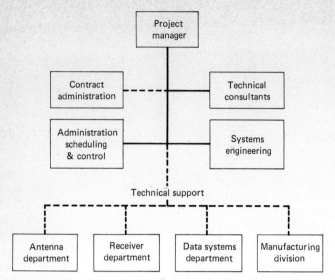

Exhibit 13-5. **Atlas Electronics Corporation (B), Spyeye Project Management.**

opinion of him. Burt's a graduate engineer with a BS and MS in electrical engineering. From his earliest training, he's dealt with scientific analysis. He's accustomed to working objectively with tangible things. But as a Project Manager, he'll have to marshall pieces of preliminary or tentative information, juggle several problems at once, compromise one requirement for the benefit of another, and make decisions that are often based on experience and judgment rather than on specific knowledge.

"Another thing," Skillton continued, "as a section head, Burt's accustomed to having direct-line authority over the people in his department doing the work. They do as he says. But as a Project Manager, he'll have to win the cooperation of the supporting department heads and their staffs to get things done. This kind of management means dealing with human nature, and Burt will have to put a lot of emphasis on human factors to succeed."

"Well, I feel his performance on the Moonglow Project shows he can do the job," Doan replied. "I'd rather have him than one of our department heads. Each of them is a professionally dedicated individual, highly skilled in the techniques of his field. What we need here is a different breed of cat—a manager who can run a business, rather than a professional who is endeavoring to optimize a technical advance."

Project Manager Authority

President Skillton then raised another point. "No matter who we appoint, we've got to give him sufficient authority to get the job done. But we've a delicate situation here. We can't permit him to step in and tell a department head how to run his department. Yet we must give him sufficient status to compel their respect and cooperation. I'll have him report to you. This will place him on the same organizational level as the department heads who are supporting the project."

"That's OK with me," Doan replied. "After all, I've other project managers reporting to me and I try to treat them and the department heads alike."

"Of course, Burt will have overall management of Spyeye and will assign technical tasks to each supporting department," Skillton continued. "But these will be in the nature of subcontracts with budgets and schedules which he'll have to negotiate with each department head and on which he'll obtain their commitment. He can tell them what to do, but not *how* to do it. This will keep design development in the functional departments where it belongs."

"But I'm not too happy about this arrangement," Skillton reflected, "because it gives the Project Manager little control. So when Burt meets with a problem that requires some pressure on a supporting department, he'll have to come to you, if he can't reach an agreement with the department head."

"Well, I'll have to assume that as my responsibility," Doan replied.

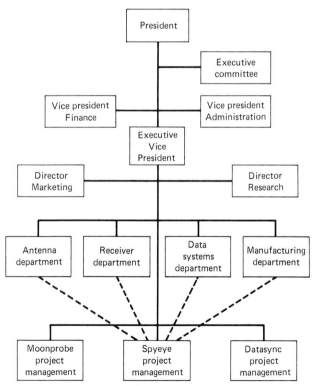

Exhibit 13-6. Atlas Electronics Corporation (B), Spyeye Project.

"All the operations report to me and it's my job to see that any conflicts are resolved in the best interest of the company."

Project Staff

"Another problem we have to consider," Skillton continued, "is how we'll staff the Spyeye Project Management. Obviously, it should be with supervisory or senior technical people from the departments skilled in the project techniques. But each of these departments needs these people in its own operations. I don't want to step in and direct any department head to transfer people to the Project Management. Burt will have to convince each department head that it's in the best interest of the company and the individual concerned to transfer him. Personally, I feel that it broadens a man's experience and capability to be assigned to a project for a while."

Project Support

President Skillton meditated for a moment and then continued, "In mulling over the problem, John, it appears to me that if we could induce each department head to set up a Spyeye support group as a sub-project within his own department, responsible solely for support to the Spyeye Project Management, it would overcome some of the weakness of the ad hoc organization concept.

"This would, in effect, create a 'project within a project,' headed by a project leader who would take his 'work direction' from the Project Management staff rather than from his own departmental supervision. I think this would cut across the organizational lines to implement the interfaces between the Project Management and the supporting groups, and I feel it would inspire a team spirit on the project. At the same time, it would preserve the status of the functional department supervision, because detailed supervision of the work would remain with them. I want you to see if the Spyeye support can be organized in this manner," he concluded. (See Exhibit 13–7.)

Employee Morale

Skillton and Doan had another problem which neither of them had discussed. That was, how to maintain employee morale under the structure of "two bosses" which the Spyeye Project Management created.

Jack Davis was a group leader in the Data Systems Department before he was transferred to the Spyeye Project Management. His new assignment required that he be the operational communications link between the project and his "home" department. He gave "work direction" to Abe Marks who was the project leader heading up the Spyeye Project group in the Data Systems Department.

Jack and Abe were having lunch together in the company cafeteria. "I can't keep from wondering what'll happen to me when the project's over," Jack remarked. "Will I be transferred back to the Data Systems Department? If so, will I have lost ground by my temporary absence? Or will they assign me to another project? I don't see anything new coming in and I don't like it. Believe me, I keep looking around."

"I've my problems, too," Abe replied. "While I'm still in the department and report to Joe (his section head), I'm working exclusively on the Spyeye Project. I like the assignment. I feel I'm part of the project team, and when that equipment starts flying out there, I'm sure they'll give me credit for my part. But how does this affect my status and salary?

"When it comes time for rate review," he continued, "will Joe know how I'm doing? Burt knows more about my work than Joe does. Will they talk to each other, or will I be dropped in the crack?"

"I'm in another bind," Abe continued. "Often I have to decide what's best for the project as against what's best for the department. Should I do what the project needs to meet its contract or be loyal to the department's policies and standards? If I 'bite the hand that feeds me' where'll I wind up?"

"I guess these are some of the risks we have to take," Jack philosophized. "Some guys prefer the challenge of strict technical development. Others want the action of a project. Personally, I feel that this project assignment will broaden my experience, or I wouldn't have taken it. But I can't help but worry about what it'll do to my future."

Burt Saunderson didn't hear this conversation, but he knew that these feelings persisted with personnel working on the project, either on his staff or in the supporting departments. He wondered how he could induce these men to keep their "eye on the ball" and devote their full effort to the project when they were worrying about their personal futures.

Performance Problem

Seven months after the project started, Saunderson noted from his progress reports that the Receiver Department still failed to meet the technical performance specification on the receiver. The specification required a band spread from 1000–10,000 mc. The breadboard model would only operate at 1050–9200 mc.

Time was getting short and he had to take prompt action. Investigation disclosed that it was doubtful if the circuit, as designed by the Receiver Department, would ever meet the specification. Consequently, it did not appear advisable to spend more time on it. Saunderson's technical staff advised him that the addition of another transistor on the lower end and the substitution of a 2QXR tube for a transistor at the upper end would cure the situation. Both of these would increase the cost and the tube would change the configuration of the "black box." His project administrator advised him that the project could absorb the cost and the customer said that the slight change in the configuration was not important. But here an obstacle arose. The Receiver Department was not satisfied with the quality of the 2QXR tube and refused to use it.

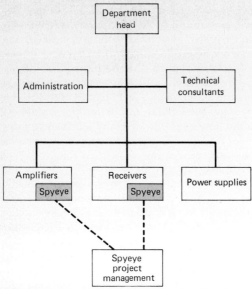

**Exhibit 13-7. Atlas Electronics Corporation (B),
Receiver Department, Spyeye project support.**

Saunderson met with Datson to discuss the problem. "Howard, we've got to do something to get that receiver up to spec. Time's getting short. We'll get socked $200 a day for late delivery and they'll take a slice of our fee for failure to perform. Now, I know you hate to use the 2QXR, but it'll do the job long enough to meet the life requirements and will satisfy the customer. We've got to give somewhere or we'll be in serious trouble."

"Yeah, I know how you feel," Datson replied, "but I've got to preserve the quality reputation of the company. After all, we obtained Spyeye because of our reputation for quality as much as for our technical competence and favorable price. If I do anything to impair that image it'll only hurt us in the long run."

QUESTIONS

1. What are the personal qualifications required of a good project manager? How do these differ from those required of a functional department head?
2. What would you do to give the Spyeye Project Manager sufficient authority to get the job done without usurping some of the authority of the supporting department heads?
3. What can the Spyeye Project Manager do to overcome the handicap of a lack of supervision and control of the work on the project?

4. What arguments can the Project Manager use to induce the functional department heads to release some of their employees for transfer to the project-management staff?

5. What are typical employees' fears about working on the project-management staff? How can these concerns be lessened?

6. What are the advantages to an individual of working on the project-management staff?

7. Do you believe that the project approach involves more "participative" management by its staff than does a functional organization? Why?

8. If a conflict arises between a technical project requirement and the policy or standard of a supporting functional department, who should make the final decision? If you were the executive vice president, John Doan, how would you reconcile the conflict on the receiver design?

9. Is the project-management form more flexible in handling an R&D project than a functional departmental organization? If you were a customer, how would you prefer to have your R&D project handled from an organizational standpoint?

CHAPTER 14

Planning-Programming-Budgeting Systems

The development of planning-programming-budgeting systems is an application of the systems approach. PPBS is a comprehensive process for creating a more effective decision-making system for public agencies. Initially developed by the Department of Defense between 1961 and 1965, it was extended to all departments of the federal government in 1965. Since that time similar systems have been initiated by states, cities, universities, local school districts, hospitals, and other organizations. This chapter covers the conceptual foundations of PPBS, traces its evolution and expansion, and sets forth the basic steps in the process. Several examples of the application of PPBS are given, as well as consideration of its future potential and problems. The following topics are included:

Concepts and terminology
Developing a program structure
Planning and program analysis
Linking the planning and budgetary processes
Expanding applications of PPBS
Future prospects and problems

CONCEPTS AND TERMINOLOGY

The development of the planning-programming-budgeting system (PPBS) represents one of the most important and comprehensive examples of the application of the systems approach to the management of complex organizations. PPBS was initially developed by the Department of Defense between 1961 and 1965.[1] This new systems management approach proved so successful that in 1965 the President directed that it should be introduced into all departments of the federal government. Since that time, PPB systems have been developed by numerous states, universities, hospitals, local governmental agencies, and other organizations.

It is difficult to set forth a simple definition of PPBS. Essentially it represents a comprehensive process for creating a more effective decision-making system for public agencies. In many ways it is similar to comprehensive long-range planning approaches developed by business enterprises.[2] The Subcommittee on Economy in Government of the Joint Economic Committee suggests the comprehensive nature of the planning-programming-budgeting system as follows:

> The principal objective of PPBS is to improve the basis for major program decisions. Program objectives are identified and alternative methods of meeting those objectives are subjected to systematic analysis comparing costs and benefits. Cost and benefit data reflect future as well as current implications of program decisions. The budget is the financial expression of the underlying program plan and translates program decisions into appropriate requests.
>
> PPBS focuses on the output of programs whereas traditional budgetary approaches tend more or less inevitably to emphasize expenditure inputs. It assesses as fully as possible the total costs and benefits, both current and future, of various alternatives. It endeavors to determine rates of return for programs, as well as the rate of return that may have to be foregone when one program is chosen over another.[3]

[1] For a discussion of the development of PPBS within the Department of Defense see Charles J. Hitch and Roland N. McKean, *The Economics of Defense in the Nuclear Age,* Harvard University Press, Cambridge, Mass., 1960, and Charles J. Hitch, *Decision-Making for Defense,* University of California Press, Berkeley, Calif., 1965.
[2] For a discussion of this view see George A. Steiner, "Program Budgeting: Business Contribution to Government Management," *Business Horizons,* Spring 1965, pp. 43–52.
[3] *The Planning-Programming-Budgeting System: Progress and Potentials,* Report of the Subcommittee on Economy in Government, Joint Economic Committee, 90th Cong., 1st Sess., December 1967, p. 1.

Essentially then, PPB is a systematic approach which attempts to establish goals, develops programs for their accomplishment, considers the costs and benefits of various alternative approaches, and utilizes a budgetary process which reflects program activities over the long run rather than on a yearly basis.

When the President of the United States encouraged the use of PPBS in all government agencies in 1965, he called it a "revolutionary" new systems. However, the basic logic of such an approach seems so apparent that one wonders why it represented such a departure from the past. To understand, we should consider the traditional budgetary process in the federal government and most other public agencies.

In the past, government agencies developed their budget requests on an annual basis for their particular needs. These budgets served accounting and administrative control purposes, but were not appropriate for long-range planning. For example, in the Department of Defense, the various military services sent their budgets to Congress to review the requests and made appropriations. The budget categories were based upon expenditure inputs such as personnel and capital goods requirements and did not reflect the output of major program activities. Many weapon-systems programs involved the utilization of resources from various departments and agencies. Under this traditional budgetary system it was difficult to determine the actual cost of any program activity. Furthermore, because the budget was developed on a yearly basis, it was impossible to determine the total cost of those programs which were extended over several years. This budgetary system also made it difficult to ascertain with any degree of assurance the total benefits of various governmental programs. Obviously, the executive branch and Congress found it impossible to determine the cost/benefit relationship between various suggested programs at the time they had to make appropriations for expenditures. With increasing demands upon various levels of government for efficient public services, such an ineffective approach became unacceptable.

PPBS attempted to remedy the defects of the former budgetary system and to link the planning-programming-budgeting subsystems into a more comprehensive and effective decision-making system. More specifically, within the federal government, PPBS is designed to:

1. Make available to top management more concrete and specific data relevant to broad decisions

2. Spell out more concretely the objectives of government programs
3. Analyze systematically and present for agency head and Presidential review and decision possible alternative objectives and alternative programs to meet those objectives
4. Evaluate thoroughly and compare the benefits and costs of programs
5. Produce total rather than partial cost estimates of programs
6. Present on a multi-year basis the prospective costs and accomplishments of programs
7. Review objectives and conduct program analyses on a continuing, year-round basis, instead of on a crowded schedule to meet budget deadlines[4]

It should be emphasized that PPBS is a continuous process with no exact starting and ending points. However, for purposes of description, we will start with the development of objectives and the establishment of a program structure.

DEVELOPING A PROGRAM STRUCTURE

The first stage in the development of a PPB system is the clear delineation of the agency's primary missions. No governmental or other organization can pursue *all* the alternative objectives which might be considered desirable. Under PPBS the various governmental agencies are required to specify their missions for accomplishment. In systems terminology, this represents a focus upon system outputs rather than inputs or the transformation processes. Just what is each agency trying to accomplish? Although this may appear to be a logical approach for any organization, there are many factors which have restricted precise consideration of missions, particularly in governmental agencies. The organizational structure of most governments is not mission-oriented. In many cases, different agencies have similar or overlapping missions.

Under PPBS each government agency establishes its primary missions and then sets forth its more specific objectives. These missions frequently are stated in rather general and relatively abstract terms. For example, the missions of the U.S. Department of Agriculture are

The programs of the Department of Agriculture seek to provide an adequate supply of food, fiber, and timber; maintain farm

[4]*Bulletin No. 66–3,* Bureau of the Budget, Executive Office of the President, Washington, D.C., Oct. 12, 1965.

income; improve the nutritional level and protect the health of the entire population; and promote the continuing development of rural areas.[5]

Similarly, the Department of Defense's mission is to provide for national security. However, these broad statements of missions are too general to provide operational guidelines for agency activities. It is necessary to translate these broad missions into more specific objectives and programs.

The next step in PPBS is to set forth a specific *program structure* for the accomplishment of objectives. "An early and essential step for each agency is the determination of a series of output-oriented categories which, together, cover the total work of the agency."[6] In the federal government, an agency program structure normally includes three levels of classification; program categories, program subcategories, and program elements. These three levels are described as follows:

> *Program categories* are groupings of agency programs (or activities or operations) which serve the same broad objective (or mission) or which have generally similar objectives. For example, a broad program objective is improvement of higher education. This could be a program category, and as such would contain federal programs aiding undergraduate, graduate, and vocational education, including construction of facilities, as well as such auxiliary federal activities as library support and relevant research programs.
>
> *Program subcategories* are subdivisions which should be established within each program category, combining agency programs on the basis of narrower objectives contributing directly to the broad objectives for the program category as a whole. Thus, in the example given above, improvement of engineering and language training could be two program subcategories within the program category of improvement of higher education.
>
> *Program elements* are usually subdivisions of program subcategories and comprise the specific products (i.e., the goods and services) that contribute to the agency's objectives. Each program element is an integrated activity which combines personnel, other services, equipment and facilities. An example of a program element expressed in terms of the objectives served would be the number of teachers to be trained in using new mathematics.[7]

[5]*The Analysis and Evaluation of Public Expenditures: The PPB System,* vol. 2, part IV. "The Current Status of the Planning-Programming-Budgeting System," A Compendium of Papers Submitted to the Subcommittee on Economy in Government of the Joint Economic Committee, 91st Cong., 1st Sess., 1969, p. 742.
[6]*Bulletin No. 66–3,* op. cit.
[7]Ibid.

It is evident that the development of a program structure represents an application of the systems approach. It starts with the most comprehensive program and then develops subsystem elements which contribute to program accomplishment. While program categories and subcategories represent broader grouping of activities, program elements are the more specific and measurable activities. Program elements should produce clearly definable outputs which can be measured.

Examples of Program Structures

In the federal PPBS each agency develops its own program structure. There are frequently wide variations in program structures for different agencies, but this should be expected because of the wide variety of missions and objectives. In the pioneering program structure established by the Department of Defense, over 1,000 program elements were classified into the following nine major program categories: Strategic Retaliatory Forces, Continental Defense Forces, General Purpose Forces, Airlift and Sealift, Reserve and Guard, Research and Development, General Support, Retired Pay, and Military Assistance. Since its establishment this program structure has been modified to reflect new missions of the Department of Defense.

Figure 14-1 shows the major program categories and subcategories for the Department of Health, Education, and Welfare for fiscal year 1970. There were four major program categories: education, health, social and rehabilitation services, and income maintenance. Each of these is divided into several subcategories which in turn are divided into program elements. Program elements are not shown; but to illustrate, under the program category of Education and the subcategory of Development of Vocational and Occupational Skills, there are three program elements: (1) improving the education of the general population, (2) improving the education of the economically and socially disadvantaged, and (3) improving the education of the physically and mentally handicapped.

The development of a program structure for a large and complex agency such as the Department of Health, Education, and Welfare is obviously a difficult task. However, it should be emphasized that the creation of a program structure is not an attempt to make greater complexity out of an inherently simple activity. This department and other governmental agencies are engaged in a large number of complex activities which are very difficult to

FIGURE 14-1. Program Structure of the Department of Health, Education, and Welfare, Fiscal Year, 1970

Program Category and Subcategory
Education:
Development of basic skills
Development of vocational and occupational skills
Development of academic and professional skills
Library and community development
General research (nonallocable research)
General support
Health:
Development of health resources
Prevention and control of health problems
Provision of health services
General support
Social and rehabilitation services:
Improving individual capability for self-support
Improving the social functioning of individuals and families
General development of social and rehabilitation resources
General support
Income maintenance:
Aged assistance
Disability assistance
Other individual and family support
General support and increasing knowledge

Source: *The Analysis and Evaluation of Public Expenditures: The PPB System,* vol. 2, part IV, "The Current Status of the Planning-Programming-Budgeting System," A Compendium of Papers Submitted to the Subcommittee on Economy in Government of the Joint Economic Committee, 91st Cong., 1st Sess., 1969, p. 746.

administer. The development of a program structure is an attempt to provide a more effective total system. It is geared to make clear definitions of agency programs, to construct program objectives, and to develop output indicators which are used to measure program effectiveness. Although the development of the program structure is just the initial step in the establishment of a PPB system, it should be very valuable in the planning and implementation of more effective governmental activities.

One further contribution stemming from the development of program structures for each governmental agency should be elaborated. Viewed from the highest level of overall administration of the federal, state, or local government, the creation of program structures by each agency assists in the comprehensive planning and implementation of all governmental activities. It provides a basis for interagency analysis and for national policy determination. It helps both the President and Congress in assessing those program activities which meet national objectives. It should help in the elimination of duplication and waste in the use of resources.

PLANNING AND PROGRAM ANALYSIS

Once the missions, objectives, and program structure of the agency have been delineated, the next step in PPBS is program analysis. This step is concerned with the effective and efficient accomplishment of program objectives. An essential part of PPBS is the appraisal of alternative means for the accomplishment of objectives and the evaluation of the costs and benefits of these alternatives.

Traditional government planning-budgetary processes made it very difficult to evaluate various alternatives for objective accomplishments. The true costs of various programs were frequently obscured by the complex accounting and budgetary system which focused upon fiscal controls. Furthermore, the benefits of various programs, and the alternatives, were rather imprecise estimates based primarily upon the judgment of the agency. The introduction of the PPB system brought with it many new analytical techniques and approaches for the more systematic evaluation of programs, their costs, and their anticipated benefits.

Systems Analysis

The term *systems analysis* has the broadest connotation in describing the process of evaluating alternative courses of action in the allocation and utilization of resources to meet agency objectives. Quade describes systems analysis as follows:

> Systems analysis might be defined as inquiry to aid a decision-maker choose a course of action by systematically investigating his proper objectives, comparing quantitatively where possible the costs, effectiveness, and risks associated with the alternative policies or strategies for achieving them, *and formulating additional alternatives if those examined are found wanting.* Systems analysis represents an approach to, or way of looking at, complex problems of choice under uncertainty, such as those associated with national security. In such problems, objectives are usually multiple, and possibly conflicting, and analysis designed to assist the decision-maker must necessarily involve a large element of judgment.[8]

As this description suggests, systems analysis does not just

---

[8]E. S. Quade, *Analysis for Military Decisions,* The Rand Corporation, Santa Monica, Calif., 1964, p. 4.

deal with lower-level, "tactical" problems where precise quantitative techniques can be applied. It also can be used at the highest level of national decision making where judgmental factors are important. As indicated in Chapters 6 and 8, system analysis can be ascribed to any orderly analytic study designed to help a decision maker identify a preferred course of action from among possible alternatives.

The federal PPBS specifically calls for the use of systems analysis in the development of *Special Analytic Studies* which provide agency heads, the executive branch, and Congress with information for making decisions concerning alternative ways of achieving program objectives. There is no established format nor length for these studies—they vary with the agency and subject matter involved. Such studies can be economic analyses, sociological evaluations, data collection efforts, mathematical models, and other approaches appropriate to the particular issue. These studies provide the basis for more specific determination of missions, objectives, and programs and for the evaluation of alternative approaches.

Cost/Benefit Analysis

Cost/benefit analysis can be considered as a specific application of systems analysis. Other terms, such as cost/effectiveness and cost/utility analysis have been used to describe similar approaches. Cost/benefit analysis is specifically geared to a comparison of alternative courses of action in terms of their costs and their effectiveness in attaining a specific objective. This type of analysis is most appropriate when dealing with *program elements* as described earlier where there is a definable and measurable agency activity.

Cost/benefit analysis involves the systematic examination and comparison of alternative courses of action that can be taken to achieve specific objectives for some future time period. This examination of alternatives involves the assessment of the cost (in terms of economic resource cost) and the benefits (utility or gains) pertaining to each of the alternatives being compared. Frequently, the problem is one of maximizing the benefits with a fixed cost or conversely, minimizing the costs for a specific program benefit.

The concept of cost/benefit analysis is deceptively simple in theory, but exceedingly difficult in practice. It can be simple when applied to a relatively closed system; for example, if the objective is to build a specified highway with minimal construction costs.

However, if we enlarge the problem to consider a broader system the analysis is much more difficult; for example, if we consider all the economic and social costs of the construction of the highway against all the economic and social benefits. How does the highway affect the general ecology of the region? What impact does it have upon esthetic values? How does it benefit or harm the "quality of life"? It is obvious that these broader considerations can create very complex analytical problems where many judgmental considerations enter into the assessment of costs and benefits.

In other agencies, such as the Department of Health, Education, and Welfare, which deal specifically with "human" factors, the costs and benefits of the various program elements are particularly difficult to measure. For example, what are the costs/benefits of the various programs allocating resources to higher education, to disease control and prevention, to welfare programs, and to accident prevention programs? Interestingly, this agency has attempted to move toward the application of cost/benefit analysis to many of these programs. For example, Figure 14–2 shows the results of a study which examined eight alternative methods for reducing injuries in motor vehicle accidents. In spite of the many difficulties and problems associated with this analysis, the results

FIGURE 14–2. Analysis of Motor Vehicle Injury Control Alternatives 1968–1972 by the Department of Health, Education, and Welfare

Program	PHS* cost† ($ millions)	Savings* ($ millions)	Benefit/ cost ratio	Deaths averted	Cost per death averted
Seat belt use	$ 2.0	$2,728	1351.4‡	22,930	$ 87
Restraint devices	.6	681	1117.1	5,811	100
Pedestrian injury	1.1	153	144.3	1,650	600
Motorcyclist helmets	7.4	413	55.6	2,398	3,000
Reduce driver drinking	28.5	613	21.5	5,340	5,300
Improve driver license	6.1	23	3.8	442	13,800
Emergency medical services	721.5§	1,726	2.4	16,000	45,000
Driver skills	750.5	1,287	1.7	8,515	88,000

*Public Health Service.
†Discounted.
‡Numbers have been rounded to a single decimal point from three decimal points; therefore ratio may not be exact result of dividing column 1 into column 2 as they appear here.
§Includes $300 million state matching funds.
Source: Elizabeth B. Drew, "HEW Grapples with PPBS," *The Public Interest*, Summer 1967, p. 16.

are interesting.[9] The highest benefit-to-cost ratio and the lowest cost-per-death-averted was shown to be associated with the program to encourage people to use seat belts. In contrast, the development of emergency medical services and programs to improve driver skills had a low benefit-to-cost ratio and a high cost-per-death-averted.

The Department of Health, Education, and Welfare conducted additional studies to compare the benefits and costs for various other programs. A summary of these studies is shown in Figure 14–3. Again, it is apparent that programs to eliminate auto accidents generally had the highest benefit-to-cost ratios as compared to disease control programs. It is obvious that many problems of interpretation exist from the examination of the informa-

---

[9]For a discussion of these problems see, Elizabeth B. Drew, "HEW Grapples with PPBS," *The Public Interest,* Summer 1967, pp. 9–29.

FIGURE 14–3. Benefit/Cost Data for Selected Programs of the Department of Health, Education, and Welfare, 1968–1972.

Program	1968–1972 HEW and other direct costs* (millions)	1968–1972 savings direct and indirect* (millions)	Benefit/ ratio cost†
Seat belt use	$ 2.0	$2,728	1351.4
Restraint devices	.6	681	1117.1
Pedestrian injury	1.1	153	144.3
Motorcyclist helmets	7.4	413	55.6
Arthritis	35.0	1,489	42.5
Reduce driver drinking	28.5	613	21.5
Syphilis	179.3[1]	2,993	16.7
Uterine cervix cancer	118.7	1,071	9.0
Lung cancer	47.0‡	268	5.7
Breast cancer	22.5	101	4.5
Tuberculosis	130.0	573	4.4
Driver licensing	6.1	23	3.8
Head and neck cancer	7.8	9	1.1
Colon-rectum cancer	7.3	4	.5

*Discounted.
†Numbers have been rounded to a single decimal point from three decimal points; therefore ratio may not be exact result of dividing column 2 into column 3 as they appear here.
‡Not discounted.
Source: Elizabeth B. Drew, "HEW Grapples with PPBS," *The Public Interest,* Summer 1967, p. 21.

tion in these tables. They do tend to place a "cost on human life," something which we all have difficulty in accepting. Furthermore, they reflect primarily the "economic" costs and benefits and do not consider other social aspects. Certainly, we would not want to stop support of cancer research because it had a low benefit-to-cost ratio. We would want to consider this information with a *great deal of caution* in the determination of program objectives and in the allocation of resources. Nevertheless, the information generated from these cost/benefit studies is useful in looking at program alternatives. Although this information is incomplete and subject to differing interpretations, it does move in the right direction toward more effective resource allocation. It would seem better to have such information available, to be used wisely and with judgment, rather than to operate by guesses and hunches.

Multiyear Planning and Analysis

One of the key features of PPBS is the extension of the program planning and analysis over a long time span. Under the traditional budgetary process, planning and analysis was limited to the annual budgetary cycle. However, most government programs continue for a longer term and appropriate program evaluation should consider the costs and benefits accordingly.

Under the federal PPB system, each agency is required to develop comprehensive *Program and Financial Plans* (PFPs) which cover the outputs, costs, and financing of all agency programs for the next five years. The PFPs also include the two preceding years and thus cover a total of seven years. They are intended as a bridge to relate annual budget allocations more closely to longer-term plans and priorities and thus provide a means for more realistic evaluation of the various programs. The years beyond the budget year are included to show the future implications of past and current decisions. The PFP shows, on the output side, the expected benefits of multiyear programs and, on the cost side, the future financial requirements that result from sequential program decisions made up through the budget year.

This move toward program planning for a five-year period rather than the traditional annual budgetary period has created difficulties for many governmental agencies. In effect, it extends the planning horizons and forces the agency to deal with many future uncertainties which were ignored in the past. In many ways this extension of the planning time period under PPBS is similar in impact to the development of comprehensive, long-range planning in business organizations. Longer-range planning has become more vital for governmental agencies and businesses but its implementation creates many difficulties.

LINKING THE PLANNING AND BUDGETARY PROCESSES

Conceptually, the PPB system provided a complete linkage between the development of a program structure, the planning and analysis of programs, and the budgetary process. In many state and local governments this attempted integration is apparent by the use of the term *program budgeting* to identify this entire process. In spite of this conceptual linkage, there are many discontinuities between the planning-programming phase and the budgetary process. In the federal government and in many state and local governments this discontinuity remains as one of the major problems in the implementation of a comprehensive PPB system. These difficulties stem from a number of forces, such as the traditional emphasis of budgetary systems, the problems in developing a budget based upon programs, and the difficulties involved in the interface between the executive and legislative branches in government. Many of the problems are associated with the attempt to superimpose the new PPB system upon an existing budgetary process.

Traditional Budgetary Process

Traditional budget systems in governments are based upon agencies rather than programs. The approach to the development of annual budgets involves the agencies listing financial requirements by line objectives or cost elements, indicating past-year actual expenditures, current-year estimates and actual expenditures, and estimating expenditures for the next budget cycle. Essentially, this process concentrates upon the inputs of resources necessary for the functioning of the agency and gives little consideration to the outputs. The emphasis in the process is not upon program planning but, rather, upon the management of ongoing activities and financial control over the disbursement of funds. There is an inherent conflict between the utilization of the budget for planning vis-à-vis financial control purposes. Colm suggests this diversity of purposes:

> It was important to recognize that the budget, not only serves program appraisal, program formulation, and program execution

functions, but also legal, political, and managerial control functions. The latter historical functions explain the fact that the accounting system, which is the basis for all government operations in most countries (including the developed countries), is poorly designed to serve planning purposes.[10]

This discontinuity is compounded because the budget is the basic economic document of the government. It is virtually the only source of information concerning the cost implications and resource allocations of government choices among alternative program expenditures. Because the traditional budget has achieved such preeminence as the economic document of the federal and other governments, any comprehensive PPB system must strive for a more effective interface between it and the other phases of the system. The successful development of PPBS calls for a major modification in the budgetary process and in the budget document itself.

Developing a Program Budget

Integration of planning and the budgeting process can be accomplished more effectively through the development of the budget on a program basis. A great deal of time is already spent in the preparation of the budget document. Shifting to a program budget would reallocate this effort toward long-run goal setting and planning and away from the emphasis upon financial controls. Ideally the budget document would be based upon the stipulation of the major program activities of the government with direct expenditures related to the attainment of the program objectives, irrespective of the administering agency. The emphasis in the program budget would be on forward planning rather than fiscal control of expenditures. One of the primary goals should be to convert the annual routine of preparing a budget into a conscious appraisal and formulation of future programs.

It should be emphasized that this shift toward program budgeting requires a substantial change in the informational inputs necessary to make the process effective. Under PPBS the generation of this essential information should be done during the planning-programming phases and then made available in a usable form for the budgetary process. The program budget should be the document which indicates the amount of resources re-

---

[10]Gerhard Colm, *Integration of National Planning and Budgeting,* National Planning Association, Washington, D.C., 1968, p. 33.

quired to accomplish the plans developed during the planning-programming phases. Furthermore, the program budget should be extended from the current annual period to include longer-term projections of expenditures on a program basis. Generally, the program budget and associated program analyses should cover at least a five-year period, and in some cases should extend even longer. Because of the intrinsic uncertainties in long-range planning, these longer-run projections of program expenditures would be subject to annual review and modification. But, these annual changes should take place in the context of a long-range perspective rather than from a short-term, yearly viewpoint. Even when an effective PPB system is developed which integrates the various phases, many problems of coordination between the various branches of government will remain.

Interface between Executive and Legislative Branches

In most governmental agencies, the development of the PPB system has been initiated by the executive branch. In the federal government, the President directed his executive agencies to comply with PPBS requirements. There are continuing difficulties in coordinating the system with congressional requirements. While the executive arm may carry on the planning-programming and budget preparation activities, it is Congress which actually makes the appropriations for carrying out the programs. The development of a sophisticated PPBS may be very useful for the executive branch but still not meet the needs of the legislature. PPBS may actually represent a threat to the legislative branch because it makes the traditional congressional role of watchdog over the executive branch more difficult. The utilization of long-range planning, systems analysis, and other approaches under PPBS may introduce additional complexities in the national decision-making process. If Congress is to perform its role effectively, it, too, must increase its knowledge base and develop more appropriate information for its own decision-making function. If the executive branch has the resources and information for effective strategic planning and program development but the legislative branch does not, a major discontinuity can develop. This appears to be happening in the federal government. The Subcommittee on Economy in Government of the Joint Economic Committee said:

> If Congress is to increase the effectiveness with which it reviews and scrutinizes program and appropriations decision, it must move with dispatch to establish an Office of Economic Evalu-

ation and Analysis to provide all Members of Congress with objective and independent program studies and policy analysis. This Office should be staffed with competent economic analysts and should assist all congressional offices and committee staffs in gaining access to information on the costs, benefits, and distributive impacts of program and policy alternatives.[11]

This recommendation would provide Congress with a separate and independent staff to carry on strategic planning and program analysis. While this may seem to be a duplication of effort, it is necessary if the separation of functions between executive and legislative branches is to be maintained. Congress should have sufficient resources and information for analysis if it is to carry out its national policy-making and appropriations functions. National policy issues are too complex and resources are too limited to allow an unsophisticated decision-making process. Both the executive and legislative branches need the best possible analytical and informational basis for these decisions.

These problems of integrating the budgetary process with PPBS and the interface between the executive and legislative branches are indicative of the difficulties in initiating a new system for diverse and complex governmental operations. However, we should not be too critical because the introduction of PPBS has been difficult. PPBS represents the attempt to develop a more comprehensive system of strategic planning, resource allocations for programs, and managerial and financial control over expenditures for complex organizations. It should be emphasized that PPBS should never be considered as an inflexible, perfectly designed mechanistic system. It must be designed as an innovative, adaptive organic system which responds to change.

EXPANDING APPLICATIONS OF PPBS

In the foregoing discussion we have emphasized the application of PPBS by the federal government. This is natural because much of the original development of this approach came from the Department of Defense and other federal agencies. However, PPBS has spread to many other organizations—states, cities, universities, school systems, hospitals, etc. We cannot cover all of these applications but will provide several illustrations.

---

[11]*Economic Analysis and the Efficiency of Government,* Report of the Subcommittee on Economy in Government of the Joint Economic Committee, 91st Cong., 2d Sess., February 1970, p. 13.

It should be emphasized that it is impossible for these organizations to apply the federal PPBS directly. While the basic steps of establishing missions and objectives, developing a program structure, planning and program analysis, and integration with the budgetary process are appropriate to many types of organizations, the actual implementation should take into consideration the unique circumstances applicable to the organization.

Utilization of PPBS by States

A 1968 survey found that twenty-eight states were developing PPBS.[12] Since that time other states have initiated this system. Many of these programs were encouraged by grants from the federal government to help develop more effective planning and budgetary systems at the state and local level. The federal PPBS has served as the general model for these systems. However, there are wide variations because of the many different organizational, administrative, and political elements unique to the different states. Therefore, there is no "typical" state PPB system. The system being developed by the state of Washington serves as one illustration of this approach.[13]

Early in 1967, the governor of the state of Washington requested a review of the state's planning and budgetary process with the view of developing an integrated planning and budgetary system. This led to the development of a PPB system and its initial implementation in the 1971–1973 biennial budgetary process. The system follows closely the approach set forth in the foregoing sections: (1) the development of a program structure, (2) the initiation of program planning, and (3) the creation of a program budget.

It is quite evident that the introduction of such a system cannot be accomplished rapidly. There are many problems associated with obtaining agreement on an appropriate program structure, recruiting sufficient trained manpower with skills in program planning and analysis, and tying the system in with the existing budgetary process. Implementing the PPB system will take time; however, progress is being made and this approach will have an increasing impact throughout the entire state government.

[12]*Innovations in Planning, Programing, and Budgeting in State and Local Governments*, A Compendium of Papers submitted to the Subcommittee on Economy in Government of the Joint Economic Committee, 91st Cong., 1st Sess., 1969, p. 2.
[13]The material for this section is taken from *Program Financial Planning*, Office of Program Planning and Fiscal Management, State of Washington, Olympia, Wash., May 1970.

Utilization of PPBS by Cities

Many cities, especially the larger ones, have moved toward the development of PPB systems. Philadelphia initiated PPBS in 1966 and New York City began developing its system in 1967. Again, the general model followed by most cities is patterned after the federal PPBS. The initial step is the development of a basic program structure which reflects all activities of the city government. Figure 14–4 shows the program structure adopted by Philadelphia for their 1968–1969 budget. This structure served as a basis for the allocations of funds, by programs for the budget period.

Again, as is true with the federal and state governments, PPBS has not come easily for the cities. It represents a comprehensive and complicated system which requires extensive planning, analysis, and coordination of activities. Furthermore, inasmuch as PPBS represents a new system for the allocation of limited resources, it is bound to become involved in the interplays of the political processes. This is true at all governmental levels.

Utilization of PPBS by Universities

PPBS is also being applied at the level of the individual organization.[14] Many universities are developing such systems. With growing enrollments and higher costs there have been many pressures from legislatures, trustees, alumni, and other groups to develop more effective means for planning and resource allocation. Many universities have turned to PPBS to find answers to their decision-making dilemmas.[15] But, PPBS has not come easily to the universities. Difficulties occur in defining the objectives of the institutions; the university serves many roles for students, faculty, alumni, local, state, and national governments, and other interest groups. Thus, it has numerous objectives which are frequently in conflict. Furthermore, while it is relatively easy to measure the inputs of expenditures necessary to maintain the university, it is very difficult to measure the outputs in terms of meeting these diverse objectives.

Another difficulty stems from the basic nature of the deci-

[14]For example PPBS has even been applied by local school districts. See Harold I. Steinberg and Robert A. Nielsen, "PPBS for a School District," *Management Controls,* July 1971, pp. 136–143.
[15]For a discussion of the applications of PPBS to universities see Paul W. Hamelman, "Missions, Matrices and University Management," *Academy of Management Journal,* March 1970, pp. 35–48, and James S. Dyer, "The Use of PPBS in a Public System of Higher Education: Is It Cost-Effective?", *Academy of Management Journal,* September 1970, pp. 285–300.

FIGURE 14-4. PPBS in the City of Philadelphia

Program Framework Adopted for 1968-1969 Budget

A. Community development:
  Housing
  Economic development
  Institutional development
  Neighborhood renewal
  Urban beautification
  General support
B. Transportation:
  Mass transit
  Streets and highways
  Traffic control and enforcement
  Off-street parking
C. Judiciary and law enforcement:
  Crime prevention
  Patrol and apprehension
  Criminal prosecution
  Judiciary and court administration
  Detention and rehabilitation
D. Conservation of health:
  Personal health protection and promotion
  Healthful environment
  Comprehensive medical care
E. Public education:
  Higher education
  Supplemental education
F. Cultural and recreational:
  Provision of cultural and recreational opportunities
G. Improvement of general welfare:
  Child care
  Care of the aged
  Improvement of intergroup relations
  Emergency preparedness
  General assistance
  Consumer protection
  Veterans' affairs
H. Services to property:
  Fire protection
  Water services
  Water pollution control
  Sanitation services
I. General management and support:
  Legislative
  Administration and management
  Financial
  Legal
  Employee development and welfare
  Voter registration and elections
  Property and records management
  Planning

sion-making processes in academia. Students have substantial discretion in the selection of their major areas of concentration and courses of study. Individual subject areas represented by the faculty have an important part in the development of courses, curriculums, and areas of research. Decentralized decision making and individual autonomy are highly valued in the academic setting.

Universities of the past can be characterized as being responding systems rather than planned systems. They have responded to the demands and needs of students, faculty, legislatures, professional associations, the federal government (particularly in the area of research), and other groups. They characteristically have not engaged in comprehensive planning to chart their own future course. And many participants in academia like it that way. But the demands for all organizations in our society to utilize scarce resources more effectively to accomplish socially prescribed goals are forcing universities to adopt more systematic planning. The increased use of PPBS reflects this trend.

The starting point for the application of PPBS to the university is the development of a program structure which relates to the primary missions of the institution. Figure 14−5 illustrates the program classification structure used by the Western Interstate Commission for Higher Education. This structure sets forth the primary educational programs of the university as (1) instruction, (2) organized research, and (3) public services. These are further divided into subprograms, program categories, program subcategories, program sectors, and finally program elements as shown in Figure 14−5. The support programs are similarly divided. This program classification structure is being adopted by many institutions of higher education, including the University of Washington. Theoretically, this arrangement will help the university focus on the primary outputs of the various programs.

The development of a program structure such as the one illustrated in Figure 14−5 is about as far as most universities have gone with implementing PPBS. A great deal needs to be done in finding appropriate output measures of performance. The next steps of program analysis and the utilization of cost/benefit studies are just being initiated. There remain many problems in linking planning-programing with the budgetary process. The difficulties associated with the utilization of PPBS in universities are not just a reflection of the resistance by administrators, faculty, and students to the "rationalization of the organization"; they also reflect the great complexities of the system—both internally and

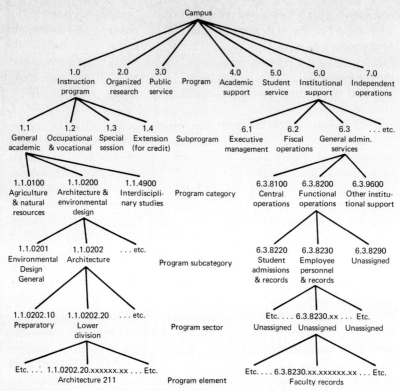

FIGURE 14-5. University program classification structure nomenclature developed by Western Interstate Commission for Higher Education.

in its relationships to the social environment. But, slow progress is being made, and we foresee that the PPB system will become a more effective approach to planning and resource utilization for universities.

FUTURE PROSPECTS AND PROBLEMS

In this chapter we have suggested that PPBS represents a comprehensive application of the systems approach. PPBS attempts to integrate many complex governmental activities which formerly were only loosely tied together; there has been substantial discontinuity between the planning-programming and budgetary phases. PPBS attempts to bring these phases together into a more effective overall system. We should not be surprised that the implementation of PPBS has been slow and difficult and that many conflicts have arisen over its usage. It should be recognized that PPBS does not create the complex problems associated with governmental operations. Hopefully it is not creating the confusion but, rather, trying to deal with the complexities which already exist. As Kahn suggests:

> In effect, program budgeting, as does any governmental effort, faces the problem of all planning: it represents an attempt to introduce rationality into a world of interest groups, bureaucratic rigidities, informal organization, politics, and many uncertainties. If the planner is at all times clear that his mission and capability are not to eliminate all of these, but rather to optimize the rational component in the process, he can work comfortably and usefully. . . .
>
> In short, we have found no nostrums or panaceas, but rather helpful tools and constructive perspectives for the social planner. The analyses projected do not *make* the decisions and never will; they may serve to sharpen intuition and enhance judgement.[16]

We agree with this view that PPBS can never become the only system for governmental planning and program implementation. However, it can be a useful part of the overall system which includes many other elements, constraints, and inputs.

Various critics of PPBS are concerned that it will be used as an administrative technique to replace other processes in our society.[17] They suggest that decisions concerning basic governmental policies and the allocation of national resources are complex—involving elements of a rational planning approach, as well as political processes. Decisions regarding such major issues as the allocation of resources for national defense, space exploration, foreign aid, national health programs, and environmental improvement should not be based solely upon a highly rationalistic decision-making system but should be subject to the influence of democratic political processes. This view suggests that attempts to develop a comprehensive PPBS controlled by the executive branch may be in conflict with these political processes. Although we can understand these concerns, we do not think there is an inherent conflict between the development of more effective planning and decision-making systems such as PPBS and the democratic process. In fact, PPBS can be viewed as an effective *means* for the implementation of the *goals* of our society. This system can help provide the necessary informational inputs which serve as the basis for more knowledgeable decision making on the part of

---

[16]Alfred J. Kahn, *Theory and Practice of Social Planning*, Russell Sage Foundation, New York, 1969, p. 261.
[17]For example see Aaron Wildavsky, "Rescuing Policy Analysis from PPBS," *Public Administration Review*, March/April 1969, pp. 189–202, and Nicholas Golovin, "Social Change and the 'Evaluative Function' in Government," *Management Science*, June 1969, pp. B-461–B-480.

citizens and their elected representatives. We do not believe that a modern democracy can operate effectively with ill-defined goals and crude informational inputs. PPBS can help in the establishment of strategic policies and in the effective utilization of resources toward their accomplishment.

Need for Social Indicators in PPBS

There are some problems concerning the nature of the information available for PPBS and other governmental decision-making approaches. We continue to rely strongly upon economic indicators as measures of performance in our society. New measures of performance are needed and are being developed to measure social performance. In the past, sophisticated measurements in the economic-technical sector have been developed (National Income and Product Accounts). There is a growing interest in the development of national social indicators and a program of social system accounting.[18] Development of such a system of social accounts will help in evaluating the performance of agencies and organizations in the accomplishment of social goals. These social indicators could be tied in with PPBS to provide a much more meaningful basis for measuring performance in accomplishing social goals rather than relying only on the economic measures which are currently utilized. Although detailed discussion of this development is beyond the scope of this chapter, this trend will have major significance in the development of a comprehensive system for national policy decisions. This development follows the establishment of national economic accounting during the earlier part of this century and is a natural evolution toward providing information necessary for more effective national planning and allocation of resources.[19]

PPBS and national social accounting are a reflection of the utilization of a systems approach at the national level in our society. While most of the illustrations in this book of the application of this approach have been at the level of the individual

[18]For a discussion of these trends see Bertram M. Gross, *The State of the Nation*, Tavistock Publications, London, 1966; Raymond B. Bauer, *Social Indicators*, the MIT Press, Cambridge, Mass., 1966; U.S. Department of Health, Education, and Welfare, *Toward a Social Report*, Government Printing Office, Washington, D.C., 1969; Nestor E. Terleckyj, "Measuring Progress towards Social Goals: Some Possibilities at National and Local Levels," *Management Science*, August 1970, B-765–B-777; and "Social Goals and Indicators for American Society," *The Annals of the American Academy of Political and Social Science*, May 1967 and September 1967.

[19]For further discussion see Michael Springer, "Social Indicators, Reports, and Accounts: Toward the Management of Society," *The Annals of the American Academy of Political and Social Science*, March 1970, pp. 1–13.

organization, these new developments are indicative of its use in a broader framework. Since the inception of this book in 1962, we have seen the systems approach being applied to more complex organizational and interorganizational activities. The extension of this approach to the national level and the entire society should not be surprising—but it is moving more rapidly than we could have anticipated a decade ago.

SUMMARY

Comprehensive planning-programming-budgeting systems developed by governmental agencies represent an important application of the systems approach. PPBS was initially developed by the Department of Defense and in 1965 was extended by presidential directive to all departments of the federal government. Since that time, PPB systems have been initiated by numerous states, universities, hospitals, and local government agencies.

PPBS is a systematic approach which attempts to establish goals, develops programs for their accomplishment, considers the costs and benefits of various alternative approaches, and utilizes a budgetary process which reflects program activities over the long run. This system developed because of the many problems and incongruities in traditional governmental planning and budgetary processes.

The first stage in the development of a PPBS is the clear delineation of the agency's primary missions. Attention is focused upon the outputs of the system rather than upon resource inputs. The next step sets forth a specific structure for delineating the agency activities into program categories.

Once the missions, objectives, and program structure of the agency have been delineated, the next step in PPBS is program analysis. This step is concerned with the effective and efficient accomplishment of program objectives. An essential part is the appraisal of alternative means for the accomplishment of objectives and the evaluation of the costs and benefits of these alternatives. Systems analysis and cost/benefit analysis are used at this stage. One of the key features of PPBS is the extension of the program planning and analysis for a long time span, typically five years.

Conceptually, PPBS provides a complete linkage between the development of a program structure, the planning and analysis of programs, and the budgetary process. One of the major difficulties in implementing this system has been in adapting the budget process to this approach. Difficulties stem from a number of forces, such as the traditional emphasis of budgetary systems upon short-term financial controls, the problems in developing a budget based upon programs, and the difficulties involved in the interface between the executive and legislative branches in government. The successful development of PPBS calls for major modification in the budgetary process and in the budget document.

Since its development by the federal government, PPBS has spread to many other organizations—states, cities, universities, school systems, hospitals, etc. It is necessary for these organizations to adapt the system to their own unique circumstances.

PPBS represents one of the most comprehensive applications of the systems approach. It attempts to integrate many complex organizational activities which were only loosely tied together. Because of the comprehensiveness of the approach and the many governmental units involved, the implementation of PPBS has not been easy. The development of national social accounting will aid in providing better informational inputs for PPBS.

QUESTIONS

1. In what ways does the development of PPBS represent an application of the systems approach?
2. What is your definition of PPBS? How is it similar or different from comprehensive, long-range planning used by business organizations?
3. How does PPBS differ from traditional governmental planning and budgeting systems?
4. What is meant by a program structure? Do you see any difficulties for governmental agencies in delineating their activities in terms of specific programs? Give examples.
5. Do you agree that the development of a program structure forces greater emphasis upon the outputs rather than the inputs of the system? Why?
6. What are the problems and implications of the extension of governmental program planning for five years into the future?
7. What are the major problems in linking the planning and the budgetary process under PPBS?
8. Why might there be conflict between the executive and legislative branches over the application of PPBS?
9. Would the program structure developed for the city of Philadelphia set forth in Figure 14-4 be appropriate for the city in which you live? Is your city currently applying PPBS? How?
10. Do you think the program classification set forth in Figure 14-5 would be appropriate for your university or college? Does the institution in which you are a student utilize PPBS? How?

The New York State Planning, Programming and Budgeting System*

Introduction

Since 1964, New York State has been developing a Planning, Programing and Budgeting System (PPBS) which systematically relates the expenditure of funds to the accomplishment of planned goals. As stated by Governor Nelson A. Rockefeller in an address to his Cabinet on February 28, 1967: "The overall goal of the Planning, Programing and Budgeting System in New York State is to provide a mechanism by which alternative goals, programs and expenditures of State government can be organized, analyzed and summarized for presentation to State policymakers to provide them with a more objective basis for making policy decisions." The Governor has given the Division of the Budget and the Office of Planning Coordination (the State's planning agency) the prime responsibility for implementation of PPBS. Over the past 4 years these two central executive staff agencies have worked closely with other State government agencies in the development of PPBS.

PURPOSES AND PROGRAM

The PPB System is intended to strengthen the State's decision making process by focusing attention on the following important questions:

*Source: Innovations in Planning, Programing, and Budgeting in State and Local Governments, A Compendium of Papers Submitted to the Subcommittee on Economy in Government of the Joint Economic Committee, 91st Cong., 1st Sess., 1969, pp. 48–52. Presentation by David A. Seyler, Director of Budget Planning, Division of the Budget, New York State.

1. What are the objectives of State programs?
2. What is being accomplished by State programs in terms of their objectives?
3. How do programs and their alternatives compare in terms of their costs and benefits?
4. Who benefits from each program?
5. What are the future implications of State programs both in terms of cost and benefits, and in terms of their effect on overall State development?

In order to accomplish our PPB objectives, it has been found necessary to initiate several management improvement efforts as well as some changes in the State's resource allocation decisionmaking process. These include the development of a New York State program structure, increased emphasis on program analysis, initiation of a program plan reporting system and some specific changes in the State's executive budget process.

In the development of the New York PPB System, one of the initial steps was the development of a Program Structure. The purpose of a program structure is to provide a framework for resource allocation decisionmaking. It establishes the basic classification scheme for the marshalling of information required for program analysis and policy decisions.

The program structure highlights the government's fundamental objectives and the competing and complementary programs involved in achieving them. Programs with common objectives are grouped together to facilitiate consideration and analysis of major policy questions.

The New York State program structure has been developed at two levels. At the central governmental level, programs are grouped into major functions—Governmental Affairs, Education, Health, Transportation and Travel Safety, Social Development, Housing and Community Development, Business and Industry, Natural Resources, Recreation and Cultural Enrichment, and Personal Safety. Each of these major functions is subdivided into subfunctions on the basis of objectives. For each agency a program structure has been developed which relates the specific program activities that produce goods and services for society to the State's objectives. The program activities are grouped into subcategories and the subcategories grouped into program categories. Each program subcategory relates to one of the statewide subfunctions.

In the development of the New York State program structure, the following criteria have been considered:

1. The program structure should be end-product oriented; it should be useful for agency and central executive decisionmaking.
2. It should permit the comparison of alternative methods of pursuing each objective.

The program structures for the individual agencies were developed cooperatively by the individual agencies and the central staff. State agencies have been urged to begin the collection of data on the goods and services produced by their programs, the costs of their programs, and the accomplishments of their programs in terms of their objectives and to utilize this data in program decisionmaking and budget justification.

In addition to the development of a program structure, major emphasis is being placed on the scheduling and execution of program analysis throughout State government. Program analysis is being pursued at both central staff and agency levels.

The Division of the Budget is analyzing major issues. This analysis identifies and describes the major features of a significant problem facing State government. It addresses such questions as: What is the problem, what are the objectives and evaluation criteria, what are the current activities, who is involved, what are the political and other significant factors, how do the costs and benefits of the alternatives compare and what recommendations for follow-up are feasible?

For example, the New York State Business Advisory Council in conjunction with the New York State Division of the Budget and the Department of Education is beginning a systematic analysis of urban education in the ghetto. The purpose of this study is: (1) to determine the feasibility of utilizing systems analysis to provide solutions in difficult social areas, and (2) to provide some basic guidance in solving one of the State's most difficult problems.

Because many of the major problems facing the State transcend agency lines, the Division of the Budget has found it necessary, in addition to performing program analysis, to develop an analytical framework to relate the outputs of individual agencies to overall State objectives. This is done by: (1) defining the major problem areas, (2) examining the State's overall objectives, (3) indicating the needed information to determine how well we are meeting the objectives, (4) identifying the different agencies involved, (5) defining the methods and procedures necessary to get the information, (6) selecting areas for more detailed analysis, and (7) describing ways of improving the decisionmaking framework within the Division of the Budget.

Individual agencies are also being asked to study the effectiveness of their various programs. Several studies are now underway which should provide a mechanism for both evaluating the effectiveness of current agency activities as well as developing suggested solutions to pressing agency problems. In many instances, the studies undertaken by the agency are similar to the analysis being done by the central staff. It is hoped, however, that agency studies will be able to develop more detailed information on the costs associated with various alternatives.

On the basis of the approved program structure, each agency submits to the Division of the Budget and the Office of Planning Coordination an annual Program Plan Report. The Program Plan Reports are submitted to the central staff agencies on July 1. They are later revised, if necessary, to correspond to the agency's budget request, which is submitted in September.

The Program Plan Reports present, for authorized programs and for proposed program changes, statements of program objectives of 5-year projections, program size indicators (estimates of the quantity of goods or services to be produced), program effectiveness measures and 5-year projections of personnel, fiscal and capital requirements. In addition, for a proposed program change, agencies list the alternatives they considered before adopting the program change and state the criteria for selecting the chosen alternative.

The Program Plan Reports also contain a description of proposed effectiveness studies and a departmental summary. The suggested effective studies in the Program Plan Reports assist the central staff in scheduling program analysis efforts throughout State government. The departmental summary summarizes both the major objectives and problems of the agency.

The Program Plan Reports are analyzed by the Office of Planning Coordination to determine the impact of agency program plans on the State comprehensive planning process. This linkage of PPB to State comprehensive planning is a unique feature of the New York State system. Program plans are also analyzed by the Division of the Budget as a framework for resource allocation decisions.

The PPB System has had a significant effect on the budgetary process. It has led to revisions in the format of the Executive Budget and, more importantly, in the types of information used in budget decisionmaking.

The conversion from a budget presented in object terms to a program budget began in 1962 when a program presentation format was included in the Executive Budget for a group of selected agencies. The development of the New York State PPB program structure has led to the redefinition of State programs on the basis of objectives. In this year's Executive Budget, to the extent possible, the program presentation has been made to conform to the PPB program structure.

In addition to the changes in the format of the Executive Budget, procedures have been developed to insure that the information contained in the program plan reports and the recommendations derived from program analysis are used in the budget decisionmaking process. For example, forms have been devised for use by the Governor in reviewing budget recommendations that present to him the following types of information for each major program: The objective of the program in terms of its impact on society, its current status, its projected output level, and the alternatives considered in developing the recommendations.

While much progress has been made in the development of New York State's PPB System, much remains to be accomplished. Now that the components of the system have been established the challenge facing State agencies and the central staff in New York is how to better utilize these developments to improve budgetary decisionmaking.

Several efforts have been initiated to improve the utility of PPB for decisionmaking. Plans are being developed by the central staff and individual State agencies to: delineate more clearly the objectives of the New York State PPB system; determine the steps to be taken in the next several years to achieve these objectives; and recommend specific activities that can be undertaken in the current year to make the PPB System more usable. In the development of these plans care is being taken to insure that the PPB System improvements are related to the total management process of the State. This means the coordination of PPB developments with improvements in governmental research, accounting procedures, long-range planning and program evaluation.

New York State policy makers have exhibited a receptiveness to the application of analytical techniques to government problems, as witnessed by the aforementioned systems analysis of urban education. The challenge facing analytical staffs at the central and agency levels is to provide analysis which is meaningful and useful for policymaking. The major focus in New York State's PPB System will now be on providing this analytical support for policymaking.

While New York State has developed program structures for individual agencies and for the State as a whole, considerable effort must be applied to the development of meaningful ouput information. Until units of output can be determined for specific programs, it will be impossible to provide governmental executives information that indicates the extent to which program objectives are being accomplished. The development of meaningful output information is closely related to the problem of performing useful program analysis in State government. The absence of detailed information on program output is perhaps the most serious deterrent to the utility of program analysis.

One of the most serious constraints to the full development of a PPB System is the lack of a trained staff. New York State has conducted numerous staff training seminars on PPB development for agency and central staff personnel. Our future plans call for training programs oriented toward the development of in-depth analytical capability, for both central and agency staffs.

The success of PPB in a governmental jurisdiction depends upon the commitment of governmental executives to the goals of PPB. Equally important are the willingness and ability of policymakers, administrators, planners, and budget personnel at all levels of government to utilize it for budgetary decisionmaking. The ultimate test of PPB will be the extent to which it assists decisionmakers in continously improving the effectiveness of their programs to meet the changing needs of society.

QUESTIONS

1. Do you think that PPBS can help in meeting the governor's goal of providing "a mechanism by which alternative goals, programs and expenditures of State government can be organized, analyzed and summarized for presentation to State policymakers to provide them with a more objective basis for making policy decisions"?

2. What is your evaluation of the criteria which were established for the development of the New York State program structure?
3. Why was it necessary for the Division of the Budget to develop an analytical framework to relate the outputs of individual agencies to overall state objectives? Why couldn't this be done by each agency separately? What is your evaluation of the seven-step procedure which was developed to accomplish this purpose?
4. What are the primary purposes of the Program Plan Reports?
5. What has been the impact of New York's PPBS on its budgetary process?
6. Why would it be so difficult to develop meaningul output information for the various state programs? Give examples.
7. Why might the state have difficulty in developing a trained staff for the implementation of PPBS? What types of academic training would be most useful for people who were assigned to work with PPBS?
8. Has your state developed a PPB system? If so, in what ways is it similar or different from the system used by New York State?
9. Assume that you are responsible for implementing a PPB system in your state. How would you approach the problem of gaining acceptance (enthusiastic support?) on the part of potential users?

CHAPTER **15**

Data Processing
Systems

Systems concepts have been applied extensively in data processing; indeed the term *data processing system* has widespread usage.
Data processing serves two primary functions: (1) recording transactions and maintaining files concerning the basic activities of the
organization, and (2) providing timely and meaningful information which facilitates managerial coordination of material and
human resources toward objective accomplishment. In this chapter
we will explore in some detail the development of data processing
and its implementation via systems concepts. We shall structure
this discussion around the following topics:

> Automating information flow
> Data processing
> Evolution of equipment
> Electronic computers
> Electronic data processing (EDP)
> Integrated data processing (IDP)
> Real-time systems
> The computer utility
> Current and future developments

AUTOMATING INFORMATION FLOW

The trend toward more sophisticated mechanization has involved using machines to replace human effort. The net result has been an increase in productivity or output per man-hour.

Mass-production-oriented processes have utilized systems concepts in order to coordinate and control the movement of raw materials and component parts through manufacturing facilities. Managerial decision making in such an environment necessarily has been geared to an overall systems approach. Automation is an additional step in the long line of technological innovations. As emphasized in Chapter 12, automation has different shades of meaning to different people. However, a common element includes the concept of energy harnessed to a mechanical process which is carried on without human intervention. It implies self-adjusting control, which is maintained by comparing desired or planned results continually with actual performance, adjustments being made according to the determined differences.

The term *automation* also has been applied to the flow of information necessary to guide the production process. Thus automation can be applied in two different ways: (1) the processing of the product and (2) the processing of information necessary to produce the product. This latter function sometimes has been referred to as *office automation*. The activity to which automation is applied, in this case, is data processing. The ultimate, from the standpoint of automated systems, would entail a production process controlled completely from start to finish on the basis of preestablished criteria and by means of an information-decision system which can be implemented without human intervention. Later in this chapter, we shall consider some examples which have such goals. However, before looking at specific applications, it will be useful to discuss the concept of data processing in general and the evolution of equipment which has facilitated advancement in data processing systems.

DATA PROCESSING

Facts are the raw material for the function of data processing. In the modern organization the number of potentially relevant facts for decision making at various levels can be overwhelming. Therefore, only the most pertinent facts can be reported in the normal course of operations. One of the prime purposes of the data processing function is that of screening, collating, arranging, and relating the various facts that are collected in day-to-day operations in order to develop meaningful information for managerial decision making.

Facts and Information

Many facts are generated daily both inside and outside the organization. Only a few of these are of interest to management. The information-decision system should be designed to garner pertinent facts and screen out those that are unwanted or unusable. Moreover, it is likely that additional processing is necessary before meaningful information is available. Translating absolute sales dollars by territory into percentage figures provides useful information. Ratio analysis may be important in other cases, or sophisticated manipulations such as correlation analysis might be applied to source data. The exception principle (referring only non-routine cases to a superior for decisions) is an example of the use of small amounts of pertinent information rather than massive amounts of factual data.

The concept of a data processing system serving to translate facts into information is illustrated in Figure 15–1. Three basic elements are involved: input, processing, and output. The input is represented by facts or data.[1] The processing includes the element of control in order to guide the manipulations, some means of storage of data and a way of applying arithmetic and/or logical operations to the data. The output is represented by information

[1]As defined in Chapter 5, data are facts obtained through empirical research or observations. The terms are often used interchangeably.

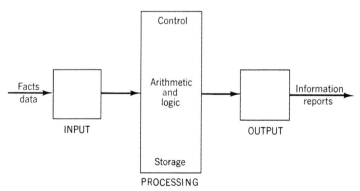

FIGURE 15–1. A data processing system.

which might come in a variety of forms, including management reports. This representation of a data processing system is appropriate, regardless of the elaborateness of equipment utilized in the various stages. We shall discuss this aspect in more detail in a later section. First, however, it would be useful to distinguish scientific and management data processing.

Data Reduction

Since our definition of data processing was general, referring to the translation of facts into information for every purpose, the term data processing obviously applies in both management applications and scientific computations. However, other terms can be used to provide a clearer picture of the various types of data processing. Normally, *computing* applies to typical mathematical calculations which are carried out by a computer. In the precomputer era this was called *calculating.* The age of computers also ushered in the term *data reduction.* It stems from the processing of voluminous facts, often generated in experimental situations, into a meaningful form. In a sense, the data are "reduced" to manageable proportions and information is gleaned which is used in subsequent calculations or decision making.

Problems of mammoth proportions in the scientific fields actually fostered the development of large-scale electronic computing equipment. Today there are computers of all sizes used in scientific computations and data reduction. In terms of numbers of programs, such usage outnumbers those in the management data processing area. However, the number of hours involved in the latter exceeds that spent on scientific computations and data reduction.

File Maintenance

Most managerial data processing can be viewed as a file-maintenance job. For example, companies maintain a file of employee records which are updated periodically in payroll processing. Current information is collected and translated into a form suitable for input into the data processing system. It is processed in conjunction with the perpetual file, and both an updated file and current-output information (in this case payroll checks) are generated. During the processing other exceptions may be uncovered and noted for management's attention during the output phase.

Inventory processing also may be considered a file-maintenance operation. In this case, the "file of people" is replaced by a file of part numbers or numbers for finished inventory. Similarly, an accounts-payable data processing application can be thought of as a file of customers. For labor-cost distribution the file might be job numbers. In all these cases an updated file is maintained summarizing transactions connected to either a part number, an employee, a customer, or a supplier. Current activities are processed in conjunction with the file, a new file is generated, and current output also is developed. Simultaneously, any exceptional situations can be noted for managerial attention.

Basic Steps

A number of steps normally are involved in any data processing application, but they can be summarized in four basic categories as follows:

Collect
Process
Analyze
Decide

The collection of data can be relatively straightforward, or it can be complicated, depending on the sources involved. Collection of data may involve verbal communication, handwritten notes, formal source documents, or machine-sensible media. Depending on the complexity of the data processing system and its equipment, the data collected may require translation into a proper form for input. The processing phase includes such functions as sorting, collating, calculating, and summarizing. These tasks may be carried out in various ways.

Although both the analyze and decide phases might be considered as part of processing, they are sufficiently distinct to be discussed separately. The result of processing facts or data is information which can be used in making decisions. Normally, information is used in comparisons with expected values, past performance, competition, or other yardsticks in order to present a meaningful picture for management. These comparisons provide a basis for managerial decision making, the fourth phase in the data processing cycle. Decisions lead to actions and also provide guidelines which serve as inputs in subsequent cycles.

An Example

In order to understand the concept of degrees of complexity in data processing systems, we shall look at an example. Visualize a small, family-owned delicatessen. At the beginning of the month cash on hand amounts to X dollars. During the month purchases of supplies are made out of this fund and sales are made to customers, with the proceeds being added to the fund. At the end of the month the fund is tallied and is found to amount to Y dollars. The collection of facts in this situation is represented by the series of expenditures and receipts over the month. However, in this case it is conceivable that none of the individual transactions are recorded and that the only observable facts are the starting and the ending amounts.

Notice that the processing phase in this data processing system can be handled with a stubby pencil and the back of an old envelope. The facts for input include the figure recorded as the amount in the till at the beginning of the month (X) and the current amount in the till (Y). These facts are entered into the processing operation. The figure for X has been stored on a piece of paper in the drawer throughout the month. The figure Y has been accumulating as a file of cash throughout the month. Both facts then are entered into storage on the piece of paper being used to process the data. The control element in the processing phase is in the mind of the delicatessen's proprietor. He carries out the steps of deciding which is the larger, X or Y, and writing that one down near the top of the paper. He then writes the smaller of the two below and performs a subtraction operation to get the net difference. A combination of the paper, the pencil, and the proprietor provides the setting and tools for the arithmetic operations. The output of the processing operation would include a figure for gross profit or loss, which might be written on a separate sheet of paper and filed. Also, a new figure would result, representing the level of cash in the till; this figure becomes the X for the subsequent month.

A comparison might be made of the current month's results as against previous months, as against expected performance, or as against the performance of the delicatessen across the street. Such comparisons might lead to a decision to maintain the status quo, or it could lead to alternative courses of action. Normally, the analyze and decide phases of this data processing operation would be implicit; that is, a manager probably would not consciously "decide" on the alternative courses of actions. Rather, he most likely would continue his normal procedures unless something quite drastic happened during the month.

Many refinements could be considered if the size of the operation warranted it. A larger business might keep more detailed records of purchases and/or sales. Also, it might employ some mechanization in the processing phase such as an adding machine or possibly a desk calculator. With such equipment we see the addition of storage capacity in the mechanical equipment and the arithmetic ability which such equipment obviously provides. On the other hand, control in such a data processing system would still rest with the human being involved in the processing. However, a set of control procedures might be established at a higher level and handed down to a machine operator, who would refer to such instructions in the processing phase. Regardless of the mechanization involved in the processing phase or of the form of input or output data, the data processing system always involves the collection, processing, analysis, and decision phases. Furthermore, its primary function is one of translating facts into meaningful information for managerial decision making.

Modern large-scale enterprises obviously employ data processing systems which are much more elaborate and sophisticated than that described above. The development of such systems has depended to a considerable extent on the equipment available.

EVOLUTION OF EQUIPMENT

Going back in history, an extremely important invention for facilitating information flow and data processing was paper. Such "equipment" permitted the maintenance of records. Records of facts could be filed and updated periodically when the need arose. The written record increased the size and reliability of data storage, thus transcending human memory and vocalizing ability. Even with records, however, the human element remained responsible for data input, control, and output.

The invention of the typewriter allowed even more elaborate record keeping by increasing legibility and providing a means for multiple copies. The invention of calculating devices to add, subtract, multiply, and divide was also an important step in facilitating data processing. Such devices provide a faster, more accurate approach to arithmetical operations.

Combination calculator-typewriter machines were developed for bookkeeping and accounting operations. Such machines allow performance of multiple operations: the preparation of statements, ledgers, and journals. Another giant step in the evolution of equipment facilitating data processing was the development of electromechanical punched-card equipment. The use of punched-hole patterns as a programming device was conceived as early as 1801 for a loom in which weaving of textiles was performed according to punched-hole patterns. The player piano is operated on the same principle. When it took nine years for the Bureau of the Census to compute the 1880 census, it became evident that a radically new approach was needed. It was estimated that by using traditional methods the computations on the 1890 census would not be completed until the 1900 census had been taken. Herman Hollerith, an employee of the Census Bureau, devised a code and applied the punched-hole concept to cards which could be sorted mechanically. Holes punched in various positions on a card represented individual items of data. The control of sorting and other operations was obtained by means of electrical contacts through the punched holes.

Referring to Figure 15-1, the facts or data would be represented in punched cards as input to the processing phase. Such input would be keypunched from numerous sources in the data collection phase of the cycle. The cards themselves provide a storage medium for data. Also, there are storage elements in the tabulating equipment in order to facilitate the accumulation of totals, subtotals, and other similar bits of information. The control element is a wired board with instructions which are triggered by control punches in the cards themselves. The electromechanical equipment provides limited arithmetic and logic operations. The output in such a process is usually in the form of a printed report which can be expanded or contracted according to the needs and wishes of management.

ELECTRONIC COMPUTERS

A computer is "a machine that manipulates symbols in accordance with given rules in a predetermined and self-directed manner. Speaking more technically, an automatic computer is a high-speed, automatic, electronic, digital data-processing machine."[2] A discussion of the adjectives involved in the above quotation is helpful in understanding the equipment, or "hardware," involved in electronic data processing. The electronic computer was developed primarily to provide a faster means of computation in scientific problems, particularly in the World War II period. Earlier calculators had been able to supplant human effort and improve productivity manyfold. However, the speed of computation

[2]Ned Chapin, *An Introduction to Automatic Computers*, D. Van Nostrand Company, Princeton, N.J., 1957, p. 4.

was limited by movement of mechanical parts, thus imposing a relatively low upper limit on ultimate speeds of calculation. A significant principle for electronic computers is that the flow of electrons, acting as signals in the circuitry of the equipment, is susceptible to direction and control. Numbers and alphabetic characters are symbolized by electronic pulses or other manifestations. The controlled movement, or flow, of these symbolic signals provides the basic framework for electronic computers.

Another important adjective is "high-speed," since speed of computation was one of the prime goals. The speeds obtained to date by electronic computers are extraordinary and promise to increase even more in the future. Increasing computational speed plus larger and larger storage, or memory, devices makes the electronic computer an extremely versatile tool for use in any data processing system.

The term *digital* is used in contrast to *analog,* which describes an important group of computing machines which use a physical analogy as an approach to the problem being studied. The physical analogy is constructed electronically within the computer's work area. The digital computer, on the other hand, is based on symbol manipulation and counting (the binary number system).

The term *automatic* refers to the self-controlling aspects of electronic computers, which have internally stored programs, or lists of instructions, that determine the sequence of operation in a processing or computational routine. These instructions are predetermined in the sense that human effort is required to plan and set forth in detail all the steps involved in any processing job. Once the program is designed, it acts as the control element in the data processing system. During processing, the program itself can be modified, again according to predetermined rules, and hence provide directions according to the situation which input data represent. It is this quality which parallels the feedback control concept of production automation and that has led to describing electronic data processing as office automation. The concept of internally stored, self-adjusting programs for controlling operations sets the electronic computer completely apart from predecessor equipment. In this sense it is not just an additional step in the long line of increased mechanization. It provides a new dimension for data processing and allows much more sophisticated and imaginative systems of information flow.

The electronic computer offers tremendous potential as a management tool. It can do work (suited to its talent) faster and more economically than any other equipment. It is more accurate than people or other machines in use. It can easily perform calculations previously considered impractical, if not impossible, in the area of operations research and analysis. But most important, the electronic computer offers a rare opportunity to expand the scope of current mechanized information flow.

It is a potent tool which might well be used for expanding the scope of current systems; this is the most significant contribution of the electronic computer to business data processing. Because it is such a potent tool and represents such an advance over its forerunners (electromechanical equipment), it provides analysts with a real opportunity for redesigning systems of information flow.[3] Concerted effort should be focused on the long-range aspects of the data processing function in order that optimum results may be obtained from such a potent tool. A complete reevaluation of a company's system of information flow should be undertaken in order to provide a proper frame of reference for the applications put on the computer. If each such application is related to the overall plan (or information-decision system), the ultimate result should be a more integrated data processing system. The starting point for the necessary reevaluation should not be the current system; the analysis should start from scratch without reference to present systems or machines.

State of the Art: Hardware and Software

The collection phase of electronic data processing may be expected to progress in three stages:

1. Visible source material will be prepared by the same methods as heretofore (handwritten, typed, etc.) and converted to machine-sensible information (punched cards, magnetic tape, etc.) prior to processing.
2. Original source material both visible and machine-sensible will be prepared simultaneously; for example, the perforated tape produced as a by-product of a typewriter operation.
3. The source data will be machine-sensible only; for example, the use of employees' keys to punch a time clock, no visible time card being produced.[4]

[3]For a detailed discussion of potential problems, see M. Valiant Higginson, *Managing with EDP: A Look at the State of the Art*, American Management Association, New York, 1965, pp. 29-30.
[4]International Business Machines Corporation, *The Auditor Encounters Electronic Data Processing*, p. 13.

It is interesting to note the preoccupation with the collection and preparation of data for input to the computer. Processing, primarily in terms of computer capabilities, seems to be no problem. Indeed, we have equipment today which seems adequate in terms of computational speed or storage capacity. Sophisticated computer programs are being developed continually to include more and more analysis and decision-making functions. The real stumbling block to implementation of information flow remains the collection, transcription, and transmission of data suitable for input to central processing units.

The manufacture of peripheral equipment is the fastest growing segment of the computer hardware industry. In fact, some experts estimate that by 1975 peripheral equipment will account for 75 percent of the cost of a typical computer installation. The faster, more powerful third-generation computers have expanded data processing applications significantly and created "a surging demand for all kinds of machines that speed up the flow of data in and out of computers—disc and tape drives, printers and plotters, robot reading machines, and terminals with keyboards and TV-like screens."[5] The emphasis on improving peripheral hardware stems from the tremendous gap in speed between central processing units which operate electronically and input-output devices which have heretofore been largely electromechanical. "Even in the best-run computer installation, the central processor often is not used 20 per cent of the computing time."[6] Therefore, it is obvious that devices which will decrease the ratio of input-output time to overall processing time will be well received.

Most companies have progressed from punched-card accounting to electronic data processing. In some cases the existing applications were transferred "as is" to the new media. In the case of medium-scale computing equipment, punched cards have remained in some installations as the only input-output media. Often the existing systems and procedures are utilized with only minor improvements and refinements. Obviously, this approach is the most straightforward and probably the easiest. On the other hand, it might not lead to as much improvement as could be obtained through a systems design effort which starts from scratch and ignores existing procedures and practices.

[5]Gene Bylinsky, "The Computer's Little Helpers Create a Brawling Business," *Fortune*, June 1970, p. 85.
[6]Ibid.

For many years IBM has focused attention on the word *think* as the key to success in business, particularly systems analysis. In the field of electronic data processing a stronger case might be made for emphasizing the word *rethink*. The concept involves the substitution of *significantly new* systems or methods rather than the incremental improvement of existing systems.

Some computer people assert that the most effective electronic-data processing installations seem to develop from operations that originally were manual rather than mechanical. This is reasonable because the computer performs the various steps of a program in essentially the same way as a person does. Each record or item is processed completely as a unit (in the file-maintenance approach), rather than bit by bit, as is the case of punched-card systems. Similarity to the human approach allows a great deal of imagination in design connected with electronic data processing. High-speed computers should force analysts to rethink the entire flow of paper work and reporting in order to utilize expensive and powerful equipment.

The task of developing the minutely detailed program of procedural steps is arduous, time-consuming, and often frustrating. The earliest programs were written directly in a language the machine could use to perform the arithmetic and logic operations specified. Each instruction had to be coded and stored in a specific location in the computer's memory. Each step included a reference to a location where the next instruction could be found. Keeping track of used and unused space allotted to the program was a tedious task. Simplifying the programming chore has been the focal point of much research and development over the past decade. This aspect of data processing is called *software* and its development has paralleled, to a degree, that of the hardware.

Software includes all the programming systems used to facilitate effective and efficient utilization of computer hardware.[7] McCracken would broaden the definition to include manual development and training sessions as well.[8] Software research and development has been an extremely important part of electronic data processing because programming systems have augmented systems-design capabilities even more than equipment sophistication. The first improvement involved intermediate symbolic codes which the programmer could use to develop a set of instructions. These instructions were processed by an assembly program

---

[7]"The Changing Software Market," *EDP Analyzer*, July 1966, pp. 1–12.
[8]Daniel D. McCracken, "The Software Turmoil,"*Datamation*, July 1962, p. 22.

which prepared a set of machine-language steps for actual data processing operations.

The development of subroutines also made programming easier. Sets of instructions for typical calculations were developed in modular form and inserted into a larger system of program steps where needed. Libraries of subroutines have been accumulated by manufacturers and users over the years. Most computers have special instructions which incorporate subroutines automatically in programs by means of simple reference statements.

Another phase of software development is presented by compilers or translators which are similar to assembly programs but usually much more complex. The trend has been to make the language used by the programmer as simple as possible, thus requiring a more complex compiler or translator program to develop the machine-language instructions (object program).[9] For scientific computations which may be carried out only once, the efficiency of the object program is not critical. Numerous programs are likely to be compiled and it is more important that the compiler program itself be as efficient as possible. For business data processing, compiling time is not nearly so critical. In this case the object program must be as efficient as possible because it is used repeatedly. For example, the goal in business data processing is to have standard, efficient programs for everyday tasks such as sorting and merging records.

The development of programming languages has progressed rapidly over the last decade. FORTRAN IV (Formula Translation), COBOL (Common Business Oriented Language), ALGOL (Alogorithmic Language), and BASIC (Beginner's All-purpose Symbolic Instruction Code) are widely used. There have been numerous suggestions for standardization in order that program packages may be used on a variety of computers. Some progress has been made but much remains to be done.

NPL (New Programming Language, later PL-I) was designed to meet the need for a language that could be used for both business and scientific applications. The absence of arbitrary restrictions allows the programmer to devote most of his effort to problem description and to express with freedom the procedure for its solution. The objective was to develop a language which would

---

[9]The goal may be to allow the programmer to write in his own inimitable, ungrammatical style with sloppy punctuation and misspelled words. With a minimum of constraints he may be able to concentrate on the problem and achieve a truly creative solution. The compiler would have to be ingenious in order to translate such a description into an effective and efficient object program.

enable programmers to write more diverse application programs than heretofore possible.

A number of special-purpose languages have been developed for specific classes of problems, for example, investigations into artificial intelligence, linguistics, human behavior simulation, and a variety of problem-solving techniques requiring manipulation of nonnumeric or symbolic data. List processing capability is the central theme for IPL-V (Information Processing Language), LISP, and SLIP.

For another particular application, simulation, IBM developed GPSS (General Purpose Systems Simulator). SIMSCRIPT, a similar development by the Rand Corporation, is a pretranslator for FORTRAN IV. CLS (Control and Simulation Language), SIMPAC, and DYNAMO are other examples.

Undoubtedly many companies have developed their own programming language or modified standard packages to fit particular needs. While some data processing systems are implemented by special-purpose equipment, standardization of hardware is more common. There is a broad base of common programming systems—subroutines, assemblers, and compilers—as well as many tailor-made, intracompany innovations which represent individualized software packages. Moreover, there is still considerable freedom for innovation in designing data processing systems; the ingenuity shown by systems designers or programmers is still a crucial element.

Growth in the importance of software parallels that in peripheral equipment in overall data processing systems A significant amount of money can be spent in developing software. And, certainly, it is important to tailor-make systems to fit the needs of the individual organization. However, large-scale, complex, data processing applications often can benefit from some or all of an established and proven program, which may be available through the following sources:[10]

Computer users
Computer manufacturers
Independent software companies
Nonprofit software companies
Divisions of large hardware manufacturers (e.g., aerospace firms)
Universities
Consulting and accounting firms
Service bureaus

[10]"The Changing Software Market," op. cit., p. 1.

Professional groups (e.g., ACMs SIGPLAN group)
Computer users groups (e.g., SHARE)

Normally software comes with the purchase of hardware. However, the user may need additional or more sophisticated routines. In such a case he may lease or buy software from independent companies that have developed proprietary packages—either computer programs or computer-based services.[11]

Research and development has been focused on alleviating the tedious, time-consuming, and often frustrating task of preparing machine-language or object programs. Sophisticated and readily available software allows the programmer more time and facilitates his efforts in implementing data processing systems efficiently.

All in all, the state of the art in *utilizing* electronic computers in data processing has not kept pace with the technological innovations (both hardware and software) of the sixties. The gap may widen in the future unless more attention is given to the creative design of systems of information flow.

ELECTRONIC DATA PROCESSING (EDP)

An electronic data processing system is depicted in abstract fashion in Figure 15-2. Note the obvious similarity between this representation and that of a data processing system in general; that is, there are five basic elements, including input, output, operation, storage, and control. The larger circle represents the total system with connection to the environment via input and

[11]Ibid., p. 5.

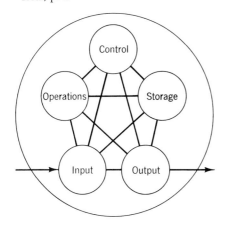

FIGURE 15-2. An electronic data processing system.

output media. These media could include punched cards, punched paper tape, magnetic tape, optical scanners, high-speed printers, typewriters, or console instructions.

The operations element of the electronic data processing system involves arithmetic and logical manipulations described earlier. Storage facilities include magnetic cores, magnetic drums, magnetic disks, and auxiliary storage via the use of magnetic tape. The control element includes the program which covers, in minute detail, the steps to be taken in the processing operation. Each element in the electronic data processing system is connected to every other element. It is this phenomenon that provides the significant advantages found in electronic systems over predecessor systems; these interrelationships allow the entire system to function as one unit. Given this electronic data processing system, what are some of the typical applications that have been developed?

Payroll

For many large companies the initial application designated for electronic data processing has been payroll. In the first place, it is one of the major data-handling jobs and offers a fruitful area for cost reduction. Second, it is often the most "routinized" processing job, hence giving the impression that payroll would be the easiest application to convert to EDP. At first glance, paying people seems like a simple, straightforward task. However, the conversion never seems to go quite as smoothly as expected.

There are a large number of transactions involved in a typical payroll application. Also, the processing job turns out to include more than just multiplying hours worked times rate per hour and writing a check for the resulting amount. For example, records must be kept of such items as year-to-date earnings, year-to-date withholding tax, year-to-date social-security payments, vacation, and sick leave. Numerous deductions must be taken into account: life, medical, and accident and health insurance; savings bonds; credit union; and others. Each day sees changes such as new hires, terminations, and transfers, or different rates, locations, names, and tax codes. In addition, requests for vacations and/or pay in lieu of time off must be processed, as well as sick-leave transactions. All in all, there is a seemingly infinite number of steps involved in what appears to the uninitiated as a relatively straightforward task. Because each and every possibility must be accounted for in programming the computer, the task becomes quite tedious.

Whereas in a manual system the individual could act with only partial information, the computer must have *all* the facts. Without *all* the facts, the computer is either stymied or else it generates erroneous output.

The employee master record tape, including all the various items of information mentioned above, plus current data, serve as input for payroll processing. Output from the processing includes payroll checks, reports on earnings and deductions, termination checks, an updated master record, and information for processing labor-cost distribution.

Inventory Control

Inventory applications involve keeping records of all material issued in manufacturing operations. The precomputer approach might have been one of keeping inventory in Kardex visible-tip records. Such records are replaced by magnetic tapes in electronic data processing applications. Information from a material requisition is keypunched and eventually fed into the computer, where the transaction is carried out and a record of the activity is produced. It is designed to be filed behind the item ledger card to show the up-to-date information concerning usage and current balance. After sufficient activity (a predetermined number of transactions), a new-item ledger card is produced which replaces the old card plus the interim lists of activity. This application is obviously in *stage 1* since the initial records are hand-created and eventually translated into a medium suitable for input through an electronic computer. Advancement to *stage 2* would require something like a perforated tape created simultaneously with the initial material requisition. Such a tape could be used to produce the major portion of subsequent records required for input to the computer and for other purposes. To arrive at *stage 3,* a direct hookup between stores and inventory would be required. Information punched in the manufacturing record could be transmitted via data-transmission equipment and lines to the magnetic-tape storage of the central installation. The ultimate in this approach would be the use of some type of file computer,[12] on line at all times, in order that random access to the status of each and every item may be available immediately.

---

[12]A file computer is distinguished by a vast amount of storage capacity, usually allowing random access to any item stored. It is so named because complete "files" of information can be stored internally and transferred from storage to arithmetic and logic units with great speed.

Accounts Payable

For an accounts-payable application, a combination of stages 1 and 2 can be found. The goal in the overall material-records system involves the integration of the processing of requisitions, purchase orders, etc., with the processing for accounting distribution and the inventory control. Purchase orders usually are made from a requisition. A control file (ledger card) can be established with a perforated tape punched as a by-product. The tape can be converted to cards, and the cards to magnetic tape. With the master file on magnetic tape, the processing is done via a combination of magnetic tapes and punched cards. Basically, visible records are produced as previously, with conversion to machine-sensible media for input to the computer (stage 1). However, the intermediate steps include elements of stage 2, simultaneous production of perforated tapes and hard copy. The outlook for stage 3 operations, similar in concept to the ultimate in control applications, is long-range but certainly not impossible.

INTEGRATED DATA PROCESSING (IDP)

The concept of integrated data processing emphasizes a common organizational data base which can be used for many processing applications.[13] Data are collected once and converted to a form (magnetic disks, e.g.) which will be readily accessible for subsequent processing. One goal is to provide the means to produce subsequent documents or information with a minimum of human intervention, thus cutting time, effort, and errors.

The perforated tape is used most often as the common-language element of an integrated data processing system, and it can be produced by cash registers, typewriters, bookkeeping machines, desk calculators, teletype setters, and others. It can actuate some of these same pieces of equipment plus punched-card machines and computers. In more sophisticated computer systems, the initial recording may be directly on magnetic tapes or disks.

In order to eliminate the handling of cards and paper tapes between initial recording and input to computer systems, some type of direct data transmission system must be utilized. Many present and potential users of such devices are evident, such as multiplant companies with central data processing, companies

[13]An organizational data base requires both (1) a set of common data definitions (and a means of enforcing the use of these definitions within the organization) and (2) the provision for access to any data item for any processing program. "Creating the Corporate Data Base," *EDP Analyzer*, February 1970, p. 3.

with widespread sales offices, and companies with scattered, in-plant recording stations. Overall systems might include a large central computing facility with many remote input-output devices. Or, it might involve a number of small computers linked to each other by high-speed data communication facilities. In the latter case, parts of the overall data base may be stored in the centralized computer system with provisions for access from any other part of the total system.

Data transmission within integrated processing systems typically is over leased telephone lines. This is likely to be the case for some years to come.[14] However, microwave relays can be used and, in the future, satellites and laser beams may be used for long-distance data transmission.

An Example of IDP

Facts concerning the amount of time a person spends on various activities can provide the data base for several processing applications—job and man time, job status, shop load, and labor standards. The benefits which would accrue from automating the data collection and preparation phase are obvious. In each case the source data could be machine-sensible only with the original information recorded directly on a magnetic tape or disk.

With regard to job and man time for payroll purposes, the employee clocks in and out by using his badge and some coded information contained in a work order. The first requirement is a machine to prepare a unique badge for each employee. Likewise, a corner of the work authorization must be prepared by a similar machine. Insertion of both the badge and the work order into the point-of-activity recorder provides the information necessary to account for what the employee does during the time he is in attendance. Flexibility can be achieved by allowing additional information to be inserted by a keyboard. Data transmission media are necessary to connect the point-of-activity recorder with central storage. The magnetic-tape reader will receive the badge identification, the job work order number, variable data, and location code from the point-of-activity recorder. It will record these data on tape with the time recording of the activity in language acceptable to a data processing system. Also, all data recorded on tape will be verified with the original input data to ensure positive recording.

[14]"Future Trends in Data Communications," *EDP Analyzer,* April 1969, p. 2.

The resulting tape is similar to a typical payroll input tape. It can be prepared automatically by the computing system from data received over the transmission lines directly from the work areas. This means the elimination of the time and effort previously spent in transporting the data to the payroll department plus the time and effort spent at the point in preauditing, key punching, verifying, balancing, and converting cards to tape. After the payroll input tape is developed, the processing is the same as before, pay checks and labor-cost distribution being the most important output. Additional reports for factory use are available on a current basis, thus fulfilling, in part, other important objectives.

Source recording for payroll and labor-cost applications is a first step toward a system of integrated data processing. Payroll, labor-cost distribution, accounts payable, material records, production control, and many other applications can all be processed electronically, using data collected and prepared for input to the computer via source recording and data transmission. As interdependent applications are tied together, duplication will be eliminated. The success of some companies in implementing the first phases of such an approach lends some credence to the long-run goal of an overall system of information flow utilizing electronic data processing as the core.

Integrated data processing sometimes connotes or implies a total systems approach. While this may be a useful goal, it is probably not realistic. Linking all of the information flow necessary for an entire organization is still extremely difficult, if not impossible, regardless of the sophisticated hardware and software available. Moreover, even if such an approach were possible, it may not be practical or even desirable. The important thing is to structure the system so that key bits of information are available on a timely basis for managerial decision making. It may be appropriate to set aside portions of the system deliberately for manual operation and to design the human element into the system at crucial points —particularly in the strategic and coordinative subsystems of the organization.

REAL-TIME SYSTEMS

Most data processing applications are examples of batch processing; that is, facts or data are collected manually or electronically over a period of time and then merged with a master file in a processing run. Such processing might take place biweekly, weekly, daily, or even at shorter intervals. However, batch processing implies that the system is not completely up to date at every possible moment. Real-time processing, on the other hand, involves updating the master file or description of the current situation with every transaction, regardless of how frequent. For example, a wholesaler's inventory might be kept entirely in the magnetic storage of a file computer. As orders are received and processed, the inventory status is updated immediately. Thus a perpetual inventory record is maintained which is current in terms of transactions at any given point in time. Information on stockouts is obtained as an exception printout at the first possible moment. Also a purchase order is printed as soon as the reorder point is reached. If transactions were collected for a week and then processed, serious gaps could be present in the information necessary for managerial decision making.

In describing "real-time management control," Malcolm states:

> In using a computer as an integral on-line controlling device, the term "real-time control, communication, and information system" has evolved as a system design concept. By this is meant that the information is transmitted instantaneously, without conversion, into a centralized computer, which processes it, compares it with predetermined decision criteria and issues instructions to men and/or machines for corrective or purposeful action. This may be thought of as "real-time control." Further, the computer by means of direct outputs informs affected parties of this information as it is developed. This is "real-time communications." Lastly, suitable condensations of the above information are prepared, transmitted and displayed to higher levels of management for broader system decisions. This is "real-time management information."
>
> The meaning of the word "real-time" lies in the fact that information is used as it develops and that elements in the system are controlled by the processed information immediately, not after the fact or by making periodic forecasts of the expected future state of the system.[15]

Real-time management information-decision systems are still in the development stage. In most cases, only part of the total system incorporates the real-time feature. In the military area, however, examples are available which indicate the general concept involved and the feasibility of ultimate systems in civilian manage-

[15]Donald G. Malcolm, "Exploring the Military Analogy: Real-time Management Control," in Donald G. Malcolm, Alan J. Rowe, and Lorimer F. McConnell (eds.), *Management Control Systems*, John Wiley & Sons, Inc., New York, 1960, pp. 190–191.

ment applications. The most familiar application is that of the SAGE (Semi-Automatic Ground Environment) system.[16]

SAGE is a continental air command and warning system designed to maintain a complete, up-to-date picture of the air and ground situation in the continental United States and other parts of North America. It was designed to control modern air-defense weapons rapidly and accurately and to present appropriately filtered pictures of the air and weapon situations to Air Force personnel who conduct the air battle. The SAGE system includes numerous radar installations and a widespread interconnected network of air-defense direction centers which receive information from numerous sources and process the information rapidly on electronic data processing equipment. Elaborate means are available for displaying pertinent information to human decision makers stationed at the direction centers in order to issue battle orders controlling interceptor aircraft and other weapons in the air-defense system.

A block diagram of the SAGE system is shown in Figure 15–3. It illustrates the manner in which human and automated decision making takes place, the closed-loop feedback of control and monitoring of information, and the central role of the computer. Malcolm summarizes the data processing features of the SAGE system as follows:

1. Use of a general-purpose information processing and computing device with large and readily available information storage capacity and with very-high-speed computing capability.
2. Automatic real-time transmittal of control and other operational information in digital form through a versatile output system that sorts information according to destination and acts as a buffer between computing cycles and transmitting equipment.
3. Use of a large integrated computer program of some 100,000 instructions which includes and ties together 100 subprograms and handles thousands of types and varieties of information, controls the sequence of operations of all subsystems, performs all information handling and computing tasks, and assists in evaluation of alternatives and in decision making.[17]

Several objectives for information-decision systems are brought to mind by the SAGE example. Management by exception is a must in large-scale systems where voluminous facts are

[16]Ibid., pp. 187–208.
[17]Ibid., p. 201.

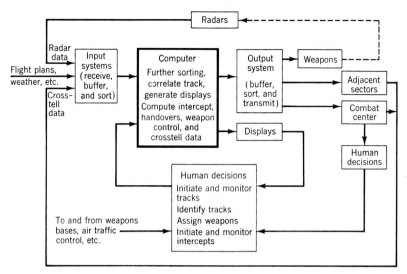

FIGURE 15-3. Conceptual system design of SAGE. (Source: Donald G. Malcolm, "Exploring the Military Analogy: Real-time Management Control," in Donald G. Malcolm, Alan J. Rowe, and Lorimer F. McConnel (eds.), *Management Control Systems,* **John Wiley & Sons, Inc., New York, 1960, p. 200.)**

generated continuously. Only a few of these facts are pertinent for managerial decision making; hence the bulk of the data generated within the system must be screened before it is reported to decision makers at key points.

Airline reservation systems are examples of real-time information systems in private industry. The problem involves matching customer demand with an inventory of seats scheduled for future flights. It is desirable to process inquiries about the availability of space in a matter of seconds in order to make the system practical from a customer's standpoint. The system accepts inquiries from numerous points—city ticket offices, airport ticket counters, airport check-in positions, airport standby control, and by telephone. A request initiates a sequence of processing steps which checks the availability of seats, reports status, and updates the inventory if a sale is made. The real-time reservation system for an airline is actually a small part of the total information system for the company. However, it does perform an exceedingly crucial function and hence deserves the considerable attention that has been devoted to it. In addition, the reservation system for a given company often must be interrelated with those of other airlines when a passenger changes planes in order to complete his journey. Such a supersystem of multiple company coordination has not been automated yet but may well be a reality in the near future.

Some companies have been developing central "control rooms" which are designed to provide information about company operations on a real-time basis. A console provides a means for management to interrogate the system with questions on factors such as (1) the amount of overtime by project charged for the current month and for the year-to-date, (2) the schedule status of project XYZ, and (3) the turnover rate among research personnel. Most of these systems are not real-time in the same sense as the foregoing examples because the data are collected and processed periodically. Charts and graphs are developed from the data processed in the latest batch and become the current information stored in the system. On the other hand, it is conceivable that data could be collected on a real-time basis and illustrations developed and displayed by the system each time an inquiry is directed to it. The charts and graphs would be produced as a part of the real-time inquiry processing operation itself.

The use of a complete model of the information-decision system for a given firm would allow top management to check the repercussions of alternative policies. Such interrogation, or *fast simulation,* of the company's operations would provide a valuable tool for decision makers, allowing some insight into the impact of alternative decisions without committing resources in an experimental situation.[18]

THE COMPUTER UTILITY

For many organizations a computer installation has been considered a prestige factor. Increasingly, however, management is finding that it is more economical to buy data processing service from outside. This has been particularly true for those companies that cannot justify even a small-scale computer. In addition, technological changes in second and third generation computers, plus significant improvements in data transmission, have caused reevaluation of this problem on the part of medium and large companies. Computer utilities are growing rapidly and it is estimated

[18]For example, see: James B. Boulden, "Instant Modeling," in Albert N. Schrieber (ed.), *Corporate Simulation Models,* Graduate School of Business Administration, University of Washington, Seattle, 1970, pp. 578–599.

that they will represent about one-half of the computing capacity in the United States by 1975.[19]

The computer utility has three principal features:

1. It provides computer services to users remote from the central computer. Data are transmitted over telephone wires.
2. It can instantly respond to user requests, thereby providing real-time computer service.
3. It is sufficiently versatile to match and in some cases exceed the capabilities of private computers.[20]

The computer utility has the potential to provide real-time systems for small business, industrywide information retrieval, on-line programming for scientific uses, computer-aided instruction, and a checkless society. It has been cited as "the greatest single advance in information handling since the computer." Computer utilities could provide universal computer service in business, government, science and education. And it could be as commonplace, by the end of this century, as the telephone service of today.[21]

A number of factors will affect the growth of computer utilities in the future. For example, real-time computer systems provide useful information for operational decision making. Timely information allows better control of the flow of material through a production and distribution system and allows maintenance of minimal inventories of raw materials and finished goods without decreasing customer service. Improved service should result in a competitive advantage and increased sales. Interactive decision simulation and problem solving provides another potential benefit to management.

The cost of computation decreases as the size and speed of computers increase. Therefore, the service of a computer utility may be less expensive than operating one's own computer installation. However, this cost/benefit analysis must include the cost of transmitting data to and from the central computing facility.

As the technology of real-time systems increases, the attract-

[19]"Computer Utilities: No Easy Road Ahead," *EDP Analyzer*, October, 1967, p. 13.
[20]William M. Zani, "The Computer Utility," *California Management Review*, Fall 1970, p. 31.
[21]For detailed predictions of the impact of computer utilities, see Ibid. p. 32.

iveness of computer utilities will improve. As flexible software systems are developed to meet a variety of user requirements, a computer utility will become even more attractive than currently.

Foremost among the factors restraining the growth of computer utilities is the difficulty of providing a total range of services for users. If a company has to provide some of its own service in-house, it may not be economical to use an outside organization for part of the overall system. Thus, it will be important for computer utilities to provide a wide range of processing methods, such as real-time, remote-access batch, and traditional batch processing systems.

So far, it has been difficult to evaluate real-time systems quantitatively. Emphasis has been placed on qualitative improvements such as "better" managerial decision making. "Until new evaluation techniques become more widely understood and accepted, the difficulties in evaluating operational savings will restrain the growth of the computer utility."[22]

When the computer is not on an organization's own premises, there is typically an uneasy feeling about equipment breakdown and/or the security of its data. Finally, a data processing manager may lobby against the use of a computer utility because it may decrease the size and scope of the operation under his control.

All in all, the computer utilities offer a significant opportunity for many organizations to improve data processing and management information-decision systems. However, there are significant problems which will restrain their growth for the foreseeable future. To gain widespread use, computer utilities must:

1. Overcome some perceived and actual problems related to the reliability of systems and the security of data
2. Wait for large numbers of people to be trained on how to use real-time systems effectively
3. Develop their system on large third or most likely fourth generation computers in order to gain significant economies of scale
4. Overcome the high cost of data transmission
5. Overcome problems and costs related to the development of flexible application systems that will meet many different requirements
6. And, above all, provide complete business systems to replace the small- to medium-size computers.[23]

[22]Ibid, p. 35.
[23]Ibid, p. 36.

CURRENT AND FUTURE DEVELOPMENTS

Electronic data processing systems of the future will depend primarily upon progress in two areas: (1) computer technology and (2) innovations in information-decision system design. There seems to be little doubt about technological progress. Although the transaction speed in most electronic computers is already incredible, product-research people assert that machines many times faster will be available in the future. With proper programming and clean input data, the electronic computer leaves little to be desired in the way of accuracy. Memory sizes undoubtedly will be increased manyfold in order to provide space for storing entire files of information. This will facilitate real-time processing, depending upon improvements in the input-output phases. Thus the technological or hardware aspects of the electronic data processing system of the future will probably leave little to be desired. The software aspects, on the other hand, have not been developed to the same degree of sophistication. Our ability to capitalize on the potential capabilities is still as questionable as it was in the late 1950s.

> . . . While *technological* progress itself can be revolutionary and make all these possible, *methodological* progress is by its very nature evolutionary. We cannot expect to achieve the rosy picture of the integrated data processing applications, the "fast time" business simulation, "optimum" production scheduling and automatic "decision making" functions by an explosive and revolutionary breakthrough. It is going to take a long, evolutionary process, involving hard and persistent work on the part of all of us, before we shall be able to use computers for all the tasks they are technically capable of performing.[24]

Methodological progress involves human beings, who often are resistant to change. New concepts of systems of information flow require organizational adjustments and realigned concepts of authority and responsibility. Integrated data processing and/or real-time processing for an entire system will require centralization of the processing phase of the complete data processing cycle. However, this does not necessarily mean centralization of decision making since data may originate at distant points, be processed, and returned in terms of pertinent information for managerial decision making in diverse locations within the organization.

---

[24]Michael J. Kami, "Electronic Data Processing: Promise and Problems," *California Management Review,* Fall 1958, p. 77.

Of particular emphasis in some current and more future systems is the concept of fast response. That is, the system provides information to decision makers in a matter of seconds or minutes. The ultimate in this approach involves real-time, on-line systems where the data base is updated simultaneously with organizational activities and pertinent changes in the environment. Decision makers have immediate access to such real-time information via many kinds of input-output devices including visual consoles. Pertinent statistics or graphic information could be obtained in response to a managerial inquiry.

> For senior management, however, the mechanism of communication with the processing system must be far more capable of doing what the telephone does for him now. It must permit him to interact with the processor without having to learn a new language or code, without having to know how to type, without having to wait until the processor noisily hammers out its message to him one printed character after another. The typewriters, teletypes, and even the vast arrays of push-buttons that so often accompany current and popular impressions of direct access management systems are still of much value, but only in the hands of the skilled technicians whose jobs require their special capabilities.[25]

The Browsing Era

"A partnership or conversational mode, or browsing technique between man and computer is still in the early formative stages. However, just enough evidence has already appeared to document the beginning of the browsing era."[26]

Time-sharing centers (computer utilities) in many locations all over the country are currently providing engineers, scientists, professors, students, and managers with a new kind of analytical capability. The decision maker actually evolves a problem-solving technique as he goes along. There is no necessity for him to be a programmer or to know anything about the detailed language of the machine. To illustrate, several specific examples are described:

> The designer can browse through selections of design shapes, sizes, and techniques. The partnership of the relatively large memory capacity and computing capability of the computer with

[25]Joseph Spiegel, John K. Summers, and Edward M. Bennett, "AESOP: A General-purpose Approach to Real-time Direct Access Management Information Systems," *Systems & Procedures Journal,* July–August 1967, p. 39.
[26]Richard E. Sprague, "The New Era in Information Systems," *Systems & Procedures Journal,* July–August 1967, p. 26.

the ingenuity and inventiveness of man produces a new level of creativity.

In the field of education, even more startling and "far out" things are happening. Students using terminals connected on-line to a computer can study and learn using automated teaching or programmed learning techniques.

Library research using browsing methods will revolutionize the library itself as well as the way in which researchers use library facilities.

Doctors and medical researchers are using time-shared concepts to aid in diagnosis and laboratory analysis. Two-way partnership communication and browsing are important in this situation.

One final technique which will evolve in the Browsing Era is a form of browsing by executives which might be labelled "what if". Managers, either individually or in groups, will ask "what if" types of questions and browse through many alternatives in direct management language communication with the system. Again, the conversational mode is the important capability in doing this, and the currency of the information dealt with is not nearly so important as the fast response.[27]

While there is a great deal of optimism with regard to the potential for automated systems there is also a need for caution. Pessimistic points of view suggest that "they will never work." However, in an era of accelerating technology such as our society has witnessed over the past several decades, this would seem to be a dangerous assumption. While we may remain skeptical, we should recall our attitude toward Buck Rogers and his space ships of the 1930s.

A better approach is to evaluate such systems in terms of the kinds of decisions managers make and the kind of activities they engage in. For example, Dearden divides top management's functions into six general categories—management control, strategic planning, personal planning, coordination, operating control, and personal appearances.[28] He concludes that real-time methods can be useful in certain types of operating systems, particularly logistic systems. And, depending on the amount of time the executive spends in direct controlling of organizational activities, a fast-response system may also be useful in this regard. For the other functions, however, he is convinced that real-time, fast-response systems would not be particularly beneficial.

[27]Ibid., pp. 26–28.
[28]John Dearden, "Myth of Real-time Management Information," *Harvard Business Review*, May–June 1966, p. 125.

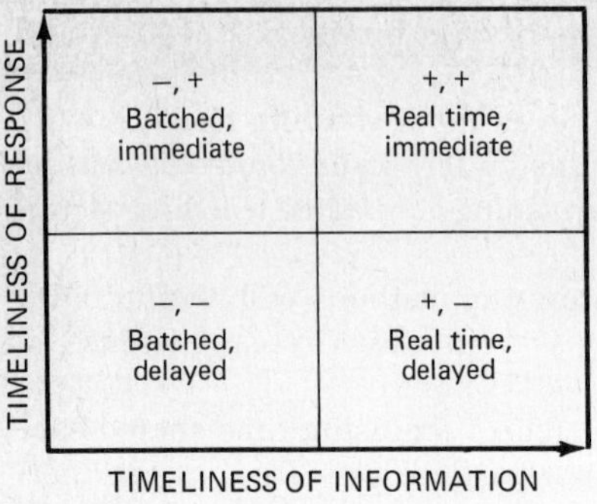

FIGURE 15-4. Timeliness of response versus timeliness of information in management information-decision systems.

It is important to distinguish types of decisions and design the system accordingly. For example, the browsing concept relies heavily on fast-response systems. However, this does not necessarily require that all information provided by the system has to be on a real-time basis. Some information might be inserted into the data base as events take place. Other information might be fed in daily, weekly, monthly, or annually. A decision maker may want real-time information but be willing to wait several days or weeks for the information to be developed. Figure 15-4 shows a matrix of timeliness of information versus timeliness of response. Obviously, the most difficult task is to provide real-time information on a fast-response basis. The important thing for managers and systems designers is to identify the needs of the organization and employ available technology to satisfy those needs.

Interorganizational Systems

The integration of data processing systems among separate organizations is forecast by Kaufman:

> ... Management, during the first decade of the computer, has generally faced major problems in introducing electronic data processing into relatively simple systems environments. So far, attempts to achieve highly integrated, companywide, so-called "total systems" have been largely unsuccessful, although the concept is useful and provides a practical goal for many data processing programs. In fact, as the second computer decade begins, some authorities are sufficiently disenchanted to reject the "total system" approach outright as unsound, recommending instead concentration or more limited but probably more manageable consolidations.
>
> Nevertheless, major new technological developments are confronting us with the possibility that our earlier "total system"

thinking may have fallen short conceptually of the real meaning of "total." Notwithstanding past experience with intracompany integration, there would now appear to be broader, but still practical, systems which are worth considering. All business is involved in constant interconnection and intercommunication with other organizations—whether suppliers, customers, or competitors. In effect, each company system functions within a still larger "total system." Thus, company boundaries are not the only, or even the most meaningful, system boundaries. Therefore, even though internal systems may still be far from totally integrated, perceptive management needs to begin to consider the new possibilities for coordinating data processing *outside* its own organizational limits.[29]

There are examples of time-sharing arrangements where input-output devices are located on the premises of several companies with access to the same central processing unit (a computer utility, e.g.). Small computers might be installed also; in such cases there is a communication system among computers. This approach could eliminate the duplication of files which frequently occurs among companies or entities which are all part of a macro information system. Source data would need to be recorded only once because all parts of the system would have access to it immediately; repeated transcriptions would not be necessary when data output from one organization became input for another. The objective is to eliminate as much data processing as possible by having the effects of a transaction reflected simultaneously in the files of all entities involved.

A central clearing system is shown in Figure 15–5. In this case the data processing center, which might be a banking system, maintains a complete data storehouse covering individuals and and organizations that are part of the system. The paperwork involved in invoicing and writing checks could be eliminated. Claims could be entered directly into the system with debits and credits made to the appropriate account of the other participant(s) involved in the transaction. Systems such as the one described will probably be slow in coming; they represent a significant conceptual adjustment. On the other hand, the hardware and software packages undoubtedly could be developed. A breakthrough will depend on the creativity of systems designers and the propensity of users to accept innovation.

Kaufman sums up his view of the future as follows:

[29]Felix Kaufman, "Data Systems That Cross Company Boundaries," *Harvard Business Review*, January–February 1966, p. 141.

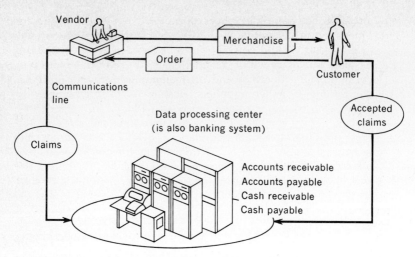

In this system, a data processing center would be used to clear claims (equivalent to invoices) against accepted claims (equivalent to payments). Paper would be largely eliminated as a carrier of information.

FIGURE 15-5. Account billing and payment with a central clearing system. (Source: Felix Kaufman, "Data Systems That Cross Company Boundaries," *Harvard Business Review,* January-February 1966, p. 151.)

> Theoretically, an end result of . . . [thinking beyond total systems] . . . might be a single data processing system for all the affairs of our economy. Clearly—and unfortunately, from many points of view—there are many obstacles to the achievement of such a system.[30]

SUMMARY

Automated information flow represents the office counterpart to production automation. Data processing provides a good example of the application of the systems approach in industry.

In describing data processing several significant points were stressed. First, data must be screened by the processing system in order to develop pertinent information for managerial decision making. Thus we recognize a significant difference between *data* and *information*. Second, the concept of data reduction was defined as the processing of vast amounts of scientific data usually gathered from experimental or test situations. Third, most business data processing involves file maintenance applications

[30]Ibid., p. 152.

and includes four basic steps—collect, process, analyze, and decide. It was emphasized that data processing takes place regardless of the tools of implementation, whether paper and pencils or large-scale electronic digital computers.

The evolution of data processing equipment was traced to show how newer, more elaborate equipment facilitates the design of sophisticated systems. However, parallel improvements are needed in computer software if full benefit is to be realized in data processing applications.

Some examples were presented of typical electronic data processing applications: payroll, inventory, and accounts payable. Examples of integrated data processing—tying separate applications together into an overall system for the entire organization—also were presented.

Real-time processing, updating a master file or description of the current situation with every transaction, was illustrated with examples such as SAGE and airline reservation systems. When fast response (in seconds) is coupled with real-time information, managers have a powerful aid for decision making. However, such sophisticated systems are expensive and should be justified on the basis of a thorough cost/benefit analysis.

Time-sharing computer utilities are growing rapidly and have the potential of providing organizations with a significant opportunity to improve data processing applications. However, a number of problems were cited which must be resolved before the full benefit of this approach can be achieved.

Current and future developments in data processing systems were discussed in detail. The relationship between technological and methodological progress was stressed. The "browsing era" and interorganizational systems were described as examples of what can and might be done. Progress in both hardware and software design, plus creativity on part of systems designers, will allow the development of innovative managerial information-decision systems.

QUESTIONS

1. Relate data processing systems to automation.
2. What function does a data processing system perform in developing meaningful information for managerial decision making?
3. Compare and contrast scientific and business data processing.
4. Briefly describe four basic phases of the data processing cycle.
5. Trace the evolution of data processing hardware. Why is the electronic computer a significant addition to the list?

6. Trace the evolution of data processing software. What contribution does it make?
7. What major problems have occurred as organizations have attempted to implement electronic data processing systems? Give examples from your own experience.
8. Describe an EDP application not discussed in the chapter.
9. What is the essence of integrated data processing (IDP)? What is the likelihood of automating total systems of information flow?
10. What is the essence of real-time data processing? Cite some examples of how it might work in systems with which you are familiar.
11. Pick any example of information flow and describe a "cloud nine" data processing system for the future.

Consolidated
Producers *

Consolidated Producers was a major producer of mechanical and sheet metal parts of a proprietary nature and also was a subcontractor manufacturing to the designs and specifications of others. James Homer had been the coordinator for the electronic data-processing center of Consolidated Producers for six years. During this period several different tasks had been programmed on the computer, e.g., payroll, manufacturing scheduling, and certain applications of inventory control. Top management, however, was not yet convinced of the feasibility of expanding the electronic data-processing (EDP) program. Their uncertainty was based on three issues: (1) there was a lack of understanding about electronic data-processing systems among middle management, (2) Homer often was unable to satisfy middle management's requests for new information by pointing out that their requests would require reprogramming, and (3) there was no specific evidence that the machines were paying for themselves.

Homer attempted to meet the first criticism by an informal educational program for interested executives. He explained that "data processing systems ordinarily consist of a combination of units including input, storage, processing, and output devices. The devices may vary but typically the operations can be performed either by paper and pencil or by machines."

The transfer of the data-processing function from manual to electrical accounting machines and electronic computers had been gradual

*Source: Albert N. Schrieber, Richard A. Johnson, Robert C. Meier, William T. Newell, and Henry C. Fischer, *Cases in Manufacturing Management,* McGraw-Hill Book Company, New York, 1965, pp. 104–110.

at Consolidated Producers. During the 1930s the company used a manual system. Information was recorded and reproduced by hand or typed, transactions were posted by hand, calculations were made with adding machines and desk calculators, and information was stored as paper forms in filing cabinets.

During the 1940s the company introduced electrical accounting machines (EAM), sometimes referred to as punched-card accounting. The basic element in this system was the punched card. The holes in the cards actuated the machines to perform various operations for keeping records. Some of the operations performed included reading, printing, adding, subtracting, multiplying, dividing, comparing, classifying, and summarizing. The initial step in this data-processing system was to transfer information from printed or handwritten documents to punched cards. That was done with the card punch machine. Other electrical-mechanical machines verified the information, printed the information on the face of the card, sorted the cards by selected characteristics, matched or merged similar cards from different decks, calculated the arithmetic data on the cards, and returned the punched information back into the printed word in the form of invoices, reports, purchase orders, checks, etc.

"The computer," Homer stated, "distinguishes an electronic data processing system from an EAM system. The computer is able to store information in the form of an electronic code and select and use this information when it is needed. "Further," Homer continued, "the computer can follow a sequence of instructions (the program) from beginning to end; and these instructions can require the computer to choose between alternatives."

Most of the same peripheral equipment was used to receive or expel information in the EDP system as in the EAM system. New and faster equipment, however, had been designed (e.g., magnetic tape input and output, high-speed printers, etc.) to keep pace with the tremendous processing speed, accuracy, and reliability of the computer.

James Homer responded to management's second criticism by stating:

> The EDP system has been damned by some for its inflexibility and praised by others for its flexibility. This paradox stems from characteristics which are common to large-scale EDP efforts, particularly those in the field of manufacturing control. Unlike payroll computations, the basic policies relating to manufacturing control are subject to considerable fluctuation. This is caused by the need to respond to changed conditions in shop load, labor market, vendor relations, customer needs, clerical manpower restrictions, and sales contingencies, to name but a few. The biggest single factor contributing to system inflexibility is caused by the time required to define a change with the precision needed by EDP and to translate the definition into machine instructions: in other words, to reprogram.

An EDP system cannot operate effectively without careful planning. The equipment is uncompromising and intolerant of value judgements which somehow exist in the less sophisticated manual system. This aspect of EDP does not apply to changes in quantities or revision of parameters. It applies particularly to changes involving processes of logic and decision.

Management has an inherent horror of becoming subservient to the EDP system or, more precisely, of being forced by circumstances to be dependent on the EDP programmer's estimate of how long it will take to reprogram what to the manager is a simple, straightforward, and very necessary change in ground rules. All too frequently the reprogramming estimate is so long that the manager will override the request to reprogram and supplement the current EDP output by manual means. When this happens, the suspicion may remain in the manager's mind that the reprogramming time was not estimated honestly, and further, the manager may be frustrated because he cannot prove his suspicions.

There have been times, however, when the EDP system has been able to extract data which have proved significant. The data were prepared in hours in contrast to the typically long flow time requirement or to being unavailable by manual methods.

The final criticism, that of proving savings from EDP installations, often was very difficult to resolve. Manual and EDP systems were different and usually not directly comparable. That is, the EDP systems not only replaced the manual systems but produced more and different kinds of information faster. Homer pointed out, therefore, that the machines were doing a larger and more effective job than the manual system they replaced. The methods of cost analysis, however, usually failed to give full credit to the larger quantity and higher quality of work performed by the machines, and often the actual cost savings could not be proved.

There had been at least one application in Consolidated Producers, however, where the actual results were measured. It had involved the transfer of an existing program from EAM to EDP based on an International Business Machines Corporation (IBM) 1401 data-processing system.

The 1401 system was completely transistorized and could perform the basic functions of reading, printing, comparing, adding, subtracting, editing, storage, etc., and variations of these functions. There were five interrelated units in the 1401 card system:

1. The IBM 1401 processing unit which contained 1,400 positions of alphameric core storage, each storing six characters of information (expandable to 2,000, 4,000, 8,000, 12,000 or 16,000 positions), and the circuitry that performed the machine logic.
2. The IBM 1402 card read-punch unit containing the read-feed section which could read 800 cards per minute and the punch section which could punch 250 cards per minute, each card containing up to 80 characters of information.

3. The IBM 1403 printer unit which was capable of printing as many as 600 lines per minute, with a print span of 100 to 132 print positions of alphabetic and numerical data per line.

4. The IBM 729 magnetic-tape units which handled $\frac{1}{2}$ inch-wide plastic tape coated with metallic oxide that could be magnetized in tiny spots to store 200 to 556 characters per inch and could be processed at speeds up to 112.5 inches per second to read or write up to 62,500 characters per second. A $\frac{1}{2}$ inch-diameter tape containing 2,400 feet could store up to 14,000,000 characters.

5. IBM 1405 magnetic-disk storage units which contained thin metal disks 24 inches in diameter, coated on both sides with a metallic oxide on which information could be recorded by means of magnetic spots located in concentric tracks. Access arms containing reading heads could move to any position on the disks which were revolving at 1,200 rpm. Thus, the information stored could be written or read on a random access basis rather than on a sequential basis as was the case with the tapes. The 50 disks in the unit had a storage capacity of 20 million alphameric characters, and data could be read or re-corded at the rate of 22,500 characters per second.

The savings forecast in transferring the application to the 1401 card system were summarized as follows:

EAM systems cost:

Total basic lease cost/month	$ 4,378.00
Average extra shift lease cost/month	1,607.86
Total manpower costs (including support group)/month	9,372.00
	$15,357.86

Anticipated EDP systems costs with 1401:

Total basic lease cost/month	$ 5,474.50
Average extra shift lease cost/month	289.92
Total manpower costs (including support group)/month	4,998.40
	$10,762.82

Total savings/month	$ 4,595.04
Total savings/year	$55,140.48
Reprogramming costs	$28,450.00

The management of Consolidated Producers had approved this conversion to the 1401 computer. The actual costs of the program were summarized two years later as follows:

Systems cost with 1401:

Total basic lease cost/month	$ 6,487.00
Total manpower costs (including support group)/month	3,456.50
	$ 9,943.50

Total savings/month	$ 5,414.36
Total savings/year	$64,972.32
Reprogramming costs	$56,343.60

One additional piece of equipment had been ordered to support the 1401. The rental cost of this piece of supporting equipment had not appeared in the original estimate of costs. The 1401 equipment had been scheduled to arrive on March 1 and the program scheduled to be in operation by April 1. Actually, the equipment arrived April 1, and it was August 1 before the program was functioning as planned. Once the program was in operation, however, it proved to be more effective than the estimate, and several workers were transferred to other assignments.

Later in the same year, Homer proposed an integrated data-processing system to maintain perpetual inventory records, initiate reorders, and perform many other administrative and control functions. His estimate of costs and savings was based on the following data.

Twenty-four systems and programming personnel would be required for 21 months, twelve manufacturing conversion personnel for 2 months, ten material conversion personnel for 6 months, and five engineering conversion personnel for 2 months. The pay scale for these people averaged $550 a month. Machine time for testing and parallel operations would cost $69,200; the conversion key punching, $34,000; and the operation of peripheral machines during the implementation, $120,000.

The rental on the new equipment would cost $48,200 a month, and the manpower cost to operate the equipment (including support machines) would be $54,000 a month. This operation would eliminate the rental cost of machines which were renting for $24,000 a month and reduce the manpower requirement for different clerical operations by 210 people, whose average pay was $475 a month.

This new system involved the control of parts and materials (COPAM) and was designed to assist in the attainment of such objectives as: reduced flow time, increased inventory turnover, uniformity of systems, reduced paper work by personnel in the line organizations, closer integration among departments, and simplification of operation procedures. Consequently, there were many benefits to be gained which could not be measured in dollars and cents.

Management had reviewed the presentation of this proposed new system with skepticism: First, would the system work? And second, would the savings be sufficient to justify the high conversion cost? One area of concern was the electronic data processing system which was being used to record shop time for timekeeping and cost control. This system had been in operation for over a year and was still troublesome. The greatest problem was related to the need to have the workers insert the correct information input at the work stations. The men in the shop and their foremen seemed to have little concern for using care in inserting the correct data in the system. In spite of this difficulty, however, the accountants pointed out that the EDP system allowed them to account for more than 85 per cent of the costs incurred in the shop. Prior to the introduction of the system, the reverse had been true, i.e., only 15 per cent of the costs were accountable directly, while the remainder had to be prorated by formula. If the costs were not charged to the correct order, however, the additional information was of limited value.

Many of the supervisors of the company were opposed to the new system. Homer felt this opposition was caused by (1) their unwillingness to learn and use a new system, (2) their dislike of reducing the size of their work group, and (3) their reluctance to delegate any of their decision-making authority to the machine.

No employee of the company had ever lost his job because of EDP. Every employee who had been replaced by machines was transferred to another group or assigned to perform other services in the same group. The total work force of the company was approximately the same as it had been during the past five years. The output was slightly higher.

John Olson, the manager of the purchasing department, wondered if he could depend on the new system to give him an accurate account of inventories. Years ago the company had used a system of perpetual parts inventory. Clerks were stationed in every store area to account for the receipt and issue of parts. A separate ledger page was maintained for each part and when parts arrived the ledger was credited with the quantity received. The ledger was debited with the quantity of every issue of the part. When the mimimum inventory levels were reached, the clerk initiated a reorder for parts.

This system had not worked effectively. There were countless situations when the balance shown on the ledger record did not agree with the bin count. Consequently, it became necessary to check the quantities in the bins frequently to make sure the inventory recorded on the ledgers actually existed. Finally, the company decided to drop the ledger record and depend on the storekeepers to maintain inventory levels. The new system was based on bundling a quantity of parts as a safety stock. Whenever a storekeeper had to break open the safety stock to fill a parts requisition, he issued a request to purchase a new supply of parts. This system had worked well and was still in use.

Homer believed that COPAM would be a successful system providing that the basic policies and conditions upon which the system was designed would remain constant. Moreover, he stated that Consolidated Producers could not hope to retain its position as a major concern in the industry if it did not adopt and use new tools and techniques to improve its operating efficiency.

QUESTIONS

1. How long would it take Consolidated Producers to recover the costs of developing the COPAM program? Is this a reasonable period of time?

2. Would this be a good return on the investment? Make whatever assumptions you feel are necessary.
3. How much confidence can be placed in the accuracy of the cost estimate? What might cause errors and how serious might these errors be? How can the estimate be improved?
4. What is the significant difference between setting up an EDP program for payroll computation and for manufacturing control?
5. What is meant by changes in parameters in contrast to changes in logic?
6. Is there any way to measure the value of reduced flow time, increased inventory turnover, and other intangible benefits attributed to the proposed system?
7. What advantages of the manual system might be lost in the changeover to EDP?
8. Is it possible to design an effective control system when the decentralized units are not responsible for correct input?
9. Can a company achieve the cost advantage of machine efficiency when the total work force is not reduced?
10. What are the advantages of EDP? The disadvantages?
11. What are the advantages of integrated data processing (IDP)? The disadvantages?

PART 4

We now move forward into a new era in the
handling of systems; an era in which man
will base his understanding of control on
the archetypal viable system of cerebral
behavior, as he has already learned to base
his knowledge of power on the archetypal
energy system of hydrogen-helium fusion.
I believe the outcome may be just as far-
reaching and much more constructive. Let
us hope that we can play our own parts with
sufficient insight and sensitivity that we do
not annihilate the very equilibria we seek
to reinforce.

S. Beer, *Below the Twilight Arch:
A Mythology of Systems*

The Future

INTRODUCTION We have set forth the theoretical framework
for a general systems theory and outlined its relationship to organization theory and management practice in Part 1. In Parts 2 and 3,
ideas and techniques for implementation were presented, followed by examples of managerial applications illustrating the
systems approach. In Part 4, we consider the future.

Because of the widely diverse application of systems theory,
it is difficult to discern a precise pattern of future utilization based
on past experience. However, we anticipate that managers will
utilize *systems theory and concepts* more and more to integrate

their operations. They really have no choice; they must if they are to survive in a dynamic environment and meet the growing demands which are being placed upon them.

Past experience with the systems approach provides a limited basis for evaluating future trends. Nevertheless, in Chapter 16 we shall "crystal-ball," using past experience and judgment to point up some of the most important applications, innovations, and problems which may arise from the utilization of the systems approach.

The Systems Approach in the Future

A fundamental view of this book is that organizations are open, dynamic man-machine systems. They are in constant interaction with their environment. The systems approach provides a philosophical basis for understanding these organizations, a generalized model for their design and analysis, and a practical means for their management. We have related systems concepts to the managerial processes of planning, organizing, controlling, and communicating and have utilized them in the design and analysis of systems. Managerial applications of the systems approach have been illustrated. This chapter looks to the future. We shall discuss some of the possible applications of the systems approach and their effects upon the management of many types of organizations. The following topics are discussed:

> The present forecasts the future
> The systems approach revisited
> Application in diverse organizations
> The systems approach in interorganizational relationships
> The systems approach and environmental relationships
> A new managerial role
> Epilogue

THE PRESENT FORECASTS THE FUTURE

We have emphasized that the systems approach is a way of thinking about the job of managing. It provides a framework for visualizing internal and external environmental factors as an integrated whole. A system has been defined as "an organized or complex whole; an assemblage or combination of things or parts forming a complex or unitary whole." Certainly this definition fits most modern business enterprises, hospitals, universities, and other organizations. The systems approach provides a framework for studying the management of complex organizations and sets forth concepts which will improve their effectiveness and efficiency.

Many examples of the application of the systems approach in business and other organizations have been given, such as distribution systems, producing systems, program management, planning-programming-budgeting systems, and data processing systems. Examples have been given to illustrate the design and analysis of complex systems. In the future, all these applications and techniques for the implementation of the systems approach will have significant impacts.

There will be no drastic revolution in management functions or organizations to encompass the systems approach. Rather, its adaptation to organizations has been and will continue to be an evolutionary process. Many of the examples cited throughout this book indicate that rudimentary applications of the systems approach occurred early in industrial history. Increasingly, managers have become more sophisticated in its use. This is the book's fundamental thesis: business and other organizations will utilize systems theory and concepts more and more to integrate their operations. They have no real choice if they are to survive in a dynamic environment and meet growing demands.

Although there are historical examples of the application of the systems approach, it has been only within the past two decades that this concept has been emphasized. Because of this recent development we do not pretend to have the "last word" on the systems approach. We have become increasingly aware of the growing number of applications in many types of organizations over the past several years. In the future many more applications will become apparent. Yet, even though the systems approach is still in its infancy, it does provide the basic conceptual framework for organizations and their management in the future. Beckett suggests:

Granted that systems theory is unfinished—granted even that it is in its infancy—it is nevertheless an intellectually valid and a conceptually useful instrument or approach by means of which the subject of management can be studied—and now more clearly understood than ever before. To employ an approach that is strengthened by underlying theoretical integrity is to recognize and avoid the shortcomings of much traditionally popular but still superficial management thought. With a grasp of systems theory one can perceive that unless systems interrelationships are understood and reckoned with, solutions can be at best superficial and at worst destructive. Without a grasp on systems concepts and an ability to deal with complex systems interrelationships, the danger of coming to the wrong conclusions, and taking the wrong action, is very great—so great that the possibilities of finding the right solution may be fewer than those of finding the wrong ones.[1]

It is difficult to make exact predictions as to the future applications and implications of the systems approach. The impact will be substantial and will be nearly universal. Analysis of past experience and evaluation of current trends point to some of the most important future applications, innovations, and problems arising from this approach. We shall review the general nature of the systems approach and then investigate future applications and implications.

THE SYSTEMS APPROACH REVISITED

In Chapters 1 and 6 we suggested that the systems approach draws heavily upon the underlying body of knowledge from general systems theory which has relevance for a wide variety of scientific endeavors and practical applications. The systems approach involves applying relevant concepts from general systems theory in order to facilitate the understanding of organization theory and management practice. But, the broad term *systems approach* is used in many different ways and we found it meaningful to refine these ideas by describing systems philosophy, systems analysis, and systems management.

In the broadest or most general sense we have *systems philosophy*. This refers to "a way of thinking" about phenomena in terms of wholes—including parts, components, or subsystems and with emphasis upon their interrelationships. According to Churchman, "Systems are made up of sets of components that

[1]John A. Beckett, *Management Dynamics: The New Synthesis,* McGraw-Hill Book Company, New York, 1971, p. 213.

work together for the overall objective of the whole. The systems approach is simply a way of thinking about these total systems and their components."[2] Systems philosophy represents a broad conceptual viewpoint at a high level of abstraction.

Systems analysis is a method or technique used in problem solving or decision making. It involves awareness of a problem, identification of relevant alternatives and variables, analysis and synthesis of the various factors, and determination of an optimal (at least better) solution or program of action. Systems analysis is generally directed toward the operational problems of the organization with a view to achievement of specific objectives and efficient utilization of resources.

Systems management involves the application of systems concepts to managing organizations. The viewpoint is pragmatic; the method is synthesis (the art of building an organization as a system through the assemblage or combination of parts); and the task is to coordinate operations into an integrative whole. Systems management is vitally concerned with the appropriate design of the organization to achieve maximum operational efficiency as well as enhancing the well-being of human participants.

We have utilized these three frames of reference throughout the book. Systems philosophy was considered primarily in Part 1, systems design and analysis in Part 2, and systems management in Part 3. In the future they will become even more meaningful. Systems philosophy based upon general systems theory will provide the basic conceptual foundation for all sciences. Anatol Rapoport emphasizes its importance in the behavioral sciences:

> The systems approach to the study of man can be appreciated as an effort to restore meaning (in terms of intuitively grasped understanding of wholes) while adhering to the principles of *disciplined* generalizations and rigorous deduction. It is, in short, an attempt to make the study of man both scientific and meaningful.[3]

We would expand this viewpoint to include not only the behavioral sciences, but all social and physical sciences as well.

Systems analysis will find increasing application in helping to solve many of the technological, economic, and social problems facing man. For example, the techniques of systems analysis

[2]C. West Churchman, *The Systems Approach,* Dell Publishing Co., Inc., New York, 1968, p. 11.
[3]Walter Buckley (ed.), *Modern Systems Research for the Behavioral Scientist,* Aldine Publishing Company, Chicago, 1968, p. xxii.

will be used extensively in investigating ecological and environmental relationships. Meeting the challenges of air and water pollution will be facilitated by systems analysis techniques.

Systems management, involving the application of systems concepts to managing organizations, will continue to extend its influence beyond business. We see increasing application of systems management in organizations such as hospitals, universities, and governmental agencies. Managers in these organizations will be vitally concerned with the appropriate design of the system to enhance the achievement of organizational objectives.

APPLICATION IN DIVERSE ORGANIZATIONS

One of the basic themes throughout this book is that modern society involves continual growth and evolution of complex organizations in widely different forms in order to perform diverse social roles. Society is not static; it is continually changing and adapting. "New social forms emerge, old ones modify their forms, change their traditional functions, and acquire new meaning. One of the more significant and important of these developments is the emergence of many varieties of large-scale organizations on which society increasingly depends."[4] There has been an emergence of complex organizations in every field of endeavor. The growth of corporations, unions, trade associations, hospitals, educational institutions, and governmental agencies has resulted from the need for integrating human activities into more encompassing organizational forms.

The systems approach will be used increasingly for all organizational types. We have found that the general model which views the organization as a sociotechnical system with interrelated subsystems—goals and values, technology, structure, psychosocial, and managerial—to be useful for understanding all organizational types.

Throughout this book we have stressed the application of the systems approach to different types of organizations. Concepts of systems design and techniques of systems analysis are appropriate to all organizations. Development of information-decision systems, utilization of concepts of material, information, and energy flows, and adoption of the program management form are evident in a wide variety of organizations.

[4]W. Lloyd Warner (ed.), *The Emergent American Society: Large-Scale Organizations,* Yale University Press, New Haven, Conn., 1967, vol. I, p. vii.

The application of the systems approach to future organizational problems will not be simple. Sayles and Chandler suggest that the problems faced by the National Aeronautics and Space Administration in its space programs are not as complicated as those of other sociotechnical programs. They say:

> But compared to some of the socio-technical programs on the horizons, NASA had a simple life. . . . As one moves into the socio-technical area this luxury disappears. The Department of Housing and Urban Development does not control housing. It encounters vested interests wherever it turns. An environmental control agency will have complex relationships with industry, which will be a contractor, a user, and an element the agency is regulating . . . Many of these programs will have to deal with political complexities NASA never dreamed of—interfaces that are more readily identified than managed. Dramatic goals to mobilize public opinion and focus diverse professionals, such as landing on the moon, may be hard to come by. The day New York City gets fresh air may be of great significance to man on earth, but it does not have the same impact. . . . We would still insist that these large systems can be understood and managed. And indeed management and organizational skills will be many times more critical in these inherently unwieldy public-private systems than in more traditional organizations.[5]

The systems approach provides the best means for dealing with these complex organizational and managerial problems. It does not restrict us to thinking about organizations as purely mechanistic-bureaucratic structures but we can consider them as open, problem-solving systems. In the future, organizations of all types must respond to technological and social changes. The open-systems approach provides a basis for understanding these adaptive processes.[6]

THE SYSTEMS APPROACH IN INTERORGANIZATIONAL RELATIONSHIPS

We have emphasized the application of the systems approach in individual organizations. We have also suggested its appropriateness for dealing with interorganizational relationships. In particular, discussion of distribution systems and planning-

---

[5]Leonard R. Sayles and Margaret K. Chandler, *Managing Large Systems: Organizations for the Future,* Harper & Row Publishers, Incorporated, New York, 1971, p. 320.
[6]Melvyn L. Cadwallader, "The Cybernetic Analysis of Change in Complex Social Organizations," in Buckley, op. cit., pp. 437–440.

programming-budgeting systems emphasized interorganizational relationships. In the future, the systems approach will be of fundamental importance in providing a means for interorganizational coordination. We are coming to recognize that "all formal organizations are embedded in an environment of other organizations as well as in a complex of norms, values, and collectivities of the society at large. . . . The phenomena and problems of interorganizational relations are part of the general class of boundary-relations problems confronting all types of social systems, including formal organizations."[7]

As we give greater consideration to the interdependence and integration among organizations, the systems approach provides the most appropriate model for dealing with the emerging complexities. In interorganizational analysis we are primarily expanding the boundaries of the system under consideration from that of the individual organization to encompass numerous organizations. As our society becomes more complex and interlocking, it is necessary to expand the boundaries of the system under consideration.

> The interdependencies of modern life are reflected in the growing emphasis on *systems*. The term is not to be escaped: systems management, urban systems, the systems approach. Most frequently, regrettably, the implicit or explicit meaning is simply technical relationships: airplanes and airports, distribution channels, and inventory. But most environmental and technical interrelationships also involve organizational interrelationships. To be sure, in the past organizations had relationships with one another. However, most were static or impersonal, defined by rather rigid legal agreements (setting forth mutual responsibilities) or governed by the invisible hand of the marketplace or the more visible hand of the government regulator. Only recently have we come to recognize that most of our contemporary "problem" areas require both the close collaboration of many institutions and rapid, dynamic mutual adaptation.
>
> We easily observe this in the growing concern over health services, the court system, and many other areas of public and private investment.[8]

The systems approach is an important development which will help in interorganizational coordination. For example, program management has been used as a means for improving inte-

---

[7]William M. Evan, "The Organization-set: Toward a Theory of Interorganizational Relations," in James D. Thompson (ed.), *Approaches to Organizational Design,* University of Pittsburgh Press, Pittsburgh, Pa., 1966, p. 175.
[8]Sayles and Chandler, op. cit., p. 316.

gration within the organization and for better interorganizational coordination. This approach will be utilized to deal with many important social and economic problems. Each participating organization will assign personnel to participate with the counterparts from other organizations on a particular program. In the past, this frequently has been accomplished through informal communication and ad hoc committee arrangements. In the future, these approaches will become more formalized.

Advancements in information technology, aided by developments in the electronic computer, will help improve communication systems across organizational boundaries. Traditionally, the concern has been with developing internal communication systems. In the future, development of systems of information flow among organizations will be emphasized. This trend is already emerging in the banking system with the movement toward a "checkless society."

THE SYSTEMS APPROACH AND ENVIRONMENTAL RELATIONSHIPS

We have stressed the view that the organization can be thought of as a subsystem of the broader sociocultural environment in which it operates. The systems approach provides a model for thinking about these relationships. All organizations receive inputs, transform these in some way, and return outputs to the environment.

Over the past decade there has been a growing concern over the relationships between man, his organizations, and his environment. The expansion of studies of the ecosystem, the concern over the deterioration of the natural environment, the questions raised about the impacts of technology, and the development of such areas as environmental sciences and environmental administration are indicative of these concerns. Broadly speaking, we are recognizing that man is just a subsystem of the universe and that his actions may have significant adverse implications for his environment, other living organisms, and all of mankind.

> It is quite clear that life on this planet depends on a delicate ecological balance among many forms of life at all levels of complexity. Each organism contributes to and takes from its surroundings in such a way that an overall equilibrium is maintained. Upset this equilibrium at any point and monumental consequences ensue. Each organism, and each group of diverse organisms, must somehow achieve an environment that all find at least reasonably

congenial if it is to survive. Only today, and slowly, is man coming to recognize that this great imperative of nature applies as much to him as to the creatures from whose study he has gained this knowledge. We can no longer blindly change the world about us, ignoring the consequences of change, without threatening our own survival as a species.[9]

While it is true that we are slowly recognizing that man has the capacity to destroy his environment and perhaps even himself as a species, we are having great difficulties in doing anything to prevent these possibilities. One of the primary reasons is that we are used to thinking in closed-system terms. We have no developed conceptual models which allow us to consider all of the consequences of our actions. We typically have only looked at very limited and partial views of the inputs and outputs of our systems. For example, in business we have typically used "profits" as an indicator of the social efficiency of the organization. We have failed to recognize that many costs—such as environmental pollution, dissatisfaction of organizational participants, and other adverse consequences—are social costs which are not accounted for in the typical profit-and-loss statement.

The open-systems approach provides us with a more appropriate model for dealing with these environmental relationships. But, applying this approach to many of our complex social, technological, and environmental problems will not be easy. DeGreene suggests the following steps:

> Applying the systems approach to the sociosphere involves three steps: (1) recognizing that society's problems *can* be approached in systems terms; (2) defining subsystems, interrelationships, information forms and needs, inputs, throughputs, outputs, missions, constraints and so forth; and (3) pursuing specific programs, e.g., information gathering, modeling, and simulation, directed toward better understanding.[10]

We are well on the way to accepting his first point and are gradually making progress on the next two. In the future we will become much more sophisticated in applying the systems approach to complex problems.

[9]Harold M. Proshansky, William H. Ittelson, and Leanne G. Rivlin (eds.), *Environmental Psychology: Man and His Physical Setting,* Holt, Rinehart and Winston, Inc., New York, 1970, pp. 1–2.
[10]Kenyon B. DeGreene (ed.), *Systems Psychology,* McGraw-Hill Book Company, New York, 1970, p. 561.

Measurement of Organizational Performance

One of the most important problems facing organizations of the future will be the evaluation of their performance in broader systems terms. For the business organization "profits," as determined by the marketplace, have served as a gross measure of overall performance. There is growing concern that traditional financial accounting measures only certain aspects of the performance of the organization and does not adequately consider many other vital factors. Profits alone do not fully indicate such things as well-being and satisfaction of the human participants within the organization, nor the full impact of the business upon its environment.

Nonprofit organizations such as universities, hospitals, and public agencies have even greater problems of measurement and evaluation of performance. These organizations do not have profits as the gross measurement. It is frequently difficult to establish specific goals which can be used as a basis for measurement of performance in many of our social programs such as urban renewal, alleviation of poverty, and health care.

The systems approach will provide a better means for measurement of organizational and social performance. We have seen that systems analysis, cost-benefit analysis and the planning-programming-budgeting systems are being used to help in the establishment of goals, to evaluate alternative means for achieving these goals, and to measure the organization's performance toward their accomplishment. These techniques will become more useful and important in the future.

New measurements of performance will be developed for the macro level of society. In the past sophisticated measurements in the economic-technical sector have been used. In the future a system of national social indicators and a program of social system accounting will be developed. These systems will help in evaluating society's performance across a broader spectrum of activities.

A NEW MANAGERIAL ROLE

As a result of the application of the systems approach, dramatic changes may take place in the role of managers. First, and perhaps most important, will be the change in the way the manager conceptualizes his function.

Unlike the traditional specialist, the new systems manager will be a super-generalist. As a systems man he will be concerned with the optimization of overall organizational objectives. He will be a problem-solver instead of a technically oriented machine-man or specialist. Whether or not the systems manager of the future will be an updated experienced manager of today or a distinctly new breed is immaterial; in any case an almost radical orientation toward the job will be required, for the successful manager of the future must utilize the systems approach to the management problems that face him in an ever growing complex business world. The systems approach is not something like a suit of clothes that can be donned at will; it is rather a way of life itself, a way of thinking, a conceptual frame of reference that must permeate one's every decision and outlook. [11]

Management must deal with the dynamics of change and provide coordination for the overall system. We do not agree with some writers who suggest that computerized information-decision systems will take over many managerial functions. While this new technology will help in dealing with the routine, programmable decision-making activities, it will not eliminate the more important function of management in dealing with the nonprogrammable, innovative, and creative aspects of organizations.

Increasingly, management has become an intellectual activity and involved more effective use of knowledge. Management systems will require more participants with advanced education. The introduction of a number of specialists oriented toward the performance of their particular skills may create major managerial problems. In the future, one of the more difficult managerial tasks will be the integration of these diverse specialists, professionals, and scientists into an effective organization.

A Flexible Managerial System

In the future, organizations will tend toward a flexible managerial system. Many of the participants in the managerial system will be performing their activities on a wider variety of programs. Positions and functions will not be as clearly described as in the past. Rather, their activities will be dictated by the forces of change and the requirements of specific programs. In the operating subsystem managers will have to be flexible in meeting change. In the co-

[11]Peter P. Schoderbek (ed.), *Management Systems,* 2d ed., John Wiley & Sons, Inc., New York, 1971, pp. 540–541.

ordinative and strategic subsystems even more adaptability will be required because of the problems of integration of organizational activities and the dynamics of the environment. In all three subsystems—the operating, the coordinative, and the strategic—the managerial task in most organizations of the future will emphasize innovation and creativity.

The Situational View of Management

The systems approach provides a basic frame of reference for the emerging "situational" or "contingency" view of management.[12] Management is not just a set of principles which can be pulled out of the hat and applied to every situation. The nature of the technology, the variations in human participants and the wide diversity in environmental relationships make the management of each organization somewhat unique. Management is not a set of "everlasting truths" applied indiscriminately from a "patented" bottle of knowledge. It requires the understanding of many complex interrelationships, the design of a sociotechnical system to operate effectively and efficiently, the satisfaction of the human participants, and the continuous adaptation of the system in a changing environment. The systems approach provides the basic conceptual framework for this managerial role.

EPILOGUE

In discussing various approaches to the study of management, Koontz states:

> From the orderly analysis of management at the shop-room level by Frederick Taylor and the reflective distillation of experience from the general management point of view by Henri Fayol, we now see these and other early beginnings overgrown and entangled by a jungle of approaches and approachers to management theory.
>
> There are the behavioralists, born of the Hawthorne experiments and the awakened interest in human relations during the 1930's and 1940's, who see management as a complex of interpersonal relationships and the basis of management theory the tentative tenets of the new and undeveloped science of psychology. There are also those who see management theory as simply a manifestation of the institutional and cultural aspects of sociology. Still others, observing that the central core of management is

---

[12]Robert J. Mockler, "Situational Theory of Management," *Harvard Business Review*, May–June 1971, pp. 146–155.

decision-making, branch in all directions from this core to encompass everything in organization life. Then, there are mathematicians who think of management primarily as an exercise in logical relationships expressed in symbols and the omnipresent and ever revered model. But the entanglement of growth reaches its ultimate when the study of management is regarded as a study of one of a number of systems and subsystems, with an understandable tendency for the researcher to be dissatisfied until he has encompassed the entire physical and cultural universe as a management system.[13]

We plead guilty as charged, because we have shown how the management process can be applied to the organization as a system. We also suggest that recognition should be given to systems of systems, leading ultimately to the entire physiocultural universe. This latter aspect was portrayed in the prologue to Part 1:

> All philosophers find
> Some favorite system to their mind
> In every point to make it fit
> Will force all nature to submit.

The point that must be emphasized is that the systems approach is primarily a "way of thinking," a mental frame of reference which can be utilized by management in performing its traditional primary functions of planning, organizing, and controlling operations. It is not in conflict with the newer approaches and techniques of management—in fact the systems approach provides the general model for their development. As Simon says:

> The term "systems," therefore, does not denote an approach to management theory that is antithetical to, or even distinct from, empirical observation, development of behavioral theories, use of a decision-making frame of analysis, or application of mathematical techniques. It denotes a concern, in the conduct of all these activities, with complexity and with the necessity for developing tools that are especially adapted to handling complexity.[14]

These functions and new techniques will continue to be fundamental in the management process. The systems approach provides a better framework for carrying out and integrating these activities.

However, the systems approach does not provide a ten-step

---

[13]Harold Koontz, "The Management Theory Jungle," *Journal of the Academy of Management,* December 1961, pp. 174–175.

[14]Herbert A. Simon, "Approaching the Theory of Management," in Harold Koontz (ed.), *Toward a Unified Theory of Management,* McGraw-Hill Book Company, New York, 1964, pp. 84–85.

algorithm, the application of which ensures success. It is not a clearly defined bundle of techniques and is not limited in application to particular industries or functional departments. It is not only automation of the factory or electronic data processing in the office. Rather, it is a broad frame of reference which views the organization as a total system and seeks to achieve the objectives of that system by clearly understanding and relating subsystem performance to the whole. In the future, the systems approach as a "way of thinking" will become more and more pervasive in the managerial process.

So far the primary reasons for the emergence and application of the systems approach have been the advancing technologies and increasing industrial complexities within our society. These forces will continue, possibly accelerating in the future. The systems approach will allow more effective adaptation to changing scientific and technological environments.

Rapid changes over the past two decades have forced managers to reevaluate their ideas regarding the role of the organization within society as a whole. And so it will be in the future. One of the fundamental theses of this book has been that the organization must be considered as a subsystem of a larger environmental system.

Within organizations the application of systems concepts will foster significant changes in the managerial process of planning, organizing, and controlling. The systems approach, hopefully, can provide a means of "getting out of the rut."

> For men are prone to go it blind
> Along the calf-path of the mind,
> And work away from sun to sun
> To do what other men have done.

One of the major changes within organizations will be the breakdown of traditional functional specialization geared to optimizing performance of particular departments. There will be growing use of organizational structures designed around projects and information-decision systems. The systems approach calls for integration, into a separate organizational system, of activities related to particular projects or programs. This approach currently is being implemented in some of the more advanced technology industries.

The application of the systems approach to organizations should not be viewed as a dehumanizing force. Rather, its application will provide greater opportunities for human expression and self-fulfillment. Concerted application of the systems approach will continue the trend whereby man has been able to create known and systematic relationships out of the seeming chaos of his natural environment. A careful scrutiny, on the other hand, reveals the generally systematic relationships in nature. This would seem to suggest the need to recognize natural man-machine systems arranged to accomplish specific human objectives. The systems approach, as applied in organizations, will release man's physical and mental processes from the more difficult and mundane activities in order that he may direct his efforts toward higher-level, creative and rewarding tasks.

> The writers against religion, whilst
> they oppose every system, are wisely
> careful never to set up any of their own.
>
> Edmund Burke, *A Vindication of
> National Society*

QUESTIONS

1. How will the dynamic environment affect organizations of the future? Do you think organizations will become more "open" or "closed" in relation to their environment? Give examples.
2. What are some of the ways in which the systems approach will affect management in the future?
3. Why will the problems of interorganizational relationships be of increasing importance in the future? What means might be used to improve interorganizational coordination?
4. How will the systems approach affect the integration of scientists, professionals, and other specialists into the organization?
5. What will be some of the impacts of application of the systems approach on our society and culture?
6. Why will the organization of the future be concerned with establishing new measures for evaluation of performance? What types of measures might be used?
7. How does the systems approach provide a new "way of thinking"?
8. Make a list of the ways in which the systems approach will affect organizational participants.

Bibliography

Ackoff, Russell L. (ed.): *Progress in Operations Research,* John Wiley & Sons, Inc., New York, 1961.
———: "Towards A System of Systems Concepts," *Management Science,* July 1971, pp. 661–671.
Alexis, Marcus, and Charles Z. Wilson: *Organizational Decision Making,* Prentice-Hall, Inc., Englewood Cliffs, N.J., 1967.
The Analysis and Evaluation of Public Expenditures: The PPB System, A Compendium of Papers Submitted to the Subcommittee on Economy in Government of the Joint Economic Committee, 91st Cong., 1st Sess., 1969.
Andersen, Theodore A.: "Coordinating Strategic and Operational Planning," *Business Horizons,* Summer 1965, pp. 49–58.
Andrew, Gwen: "An Analytic System Model for Organization Theory," *Academy of Management Journal,* September 1965, pp. 190–198.
Anshen, Melvin, and George L. Bach (eds.): *Management and Corporations 1985,* McGraw-Hill Book Company, New York, 1960.
Ansoff, H. Igor: *Corporate Strategy,* McGraw-Hill Book Company, New York, 1965.
Anthony, Robert N.: *Planning and Control Systems: A Framework for Analysis,* Harvard Graduate School of Business Administration, Boston, 1965.
Archer, Stephen H.: "The Structure of Management Decision Theory," *Academy of Management Journal,* December 1964, pp. 269–287.
Argyris, Chris: *Integrating the Individual and the Organization,* John Wiley & Sons, Inc., New York, 1964.
Ashburn, Anderson: "Detroit Automation," *Annals of the American Academy of Political and Social Science,* March 1962, pp. 21–28.
√ Ashby, W. Ross: *An Introduction to Cybernetics,* John Wiley & Sons, Inc., New York, 1956.
Barnett, John H.: "Information Systems: Breaking the Barrier," *Journal of Systems Management,* May 1969, pp. 8–10.
Bartlett, Hale C. (ed.): *Readings in Physical Distribution,* 2d ed., Interstate Printers and Publishers, Danville, Ill., 1970.
Bauer, Raymond A. (ed.): *Social Indicators,* The M.I.T. Press, Cambridge, Mass., 1966.

Beckett, John A.: *Management Dynamics: The New Synthesis*, McGraw-Hill Book Company, New York, 1971.

Beckhard, Richard: *Organization Development: Strategies and Models*, Addison-Wesley Publishing Company, Reading, Mass., 1969.

Bedford, Norton M., and Mohamed Onsi: "Measuring the Value of Information—An Information Theory Approach," *Management Services*, January–February, 1966, pp. 15–22.

Beer, Stafford: *Cybernetics and Management*, John Wiley & Sons, Inc., New York, 1959.

Bellman, Richard: "Control Theory," *Scientific American*, September 1964, pp. 186–200.

Bennis, Warren G. (ed.): *American Bureaucracy*, Aldine Publishing Company, Chicago, 1970.

——: *Changing Organizations*, McGraw-Hill Book Company, New York, 1966.

——, Kenneth D. Benne, and Robert Chin (eds.): *The Planning of Change*, 2d ed., Holt, Rinehart and Winston, Inc., New York, 1969.

Bentley, W.H.: "Management Aspects of Numerical Control," *Automation*, October 1960, pp. 64–70.

Berelson, Bernard: *The Behavioral Sciences Today*, Harper & Row, Publishers, Incorporated, New York, 1964.

——, and Gary A. Steiner: *Human Behavior: An Inventory of Scientific Findings*, Harcourt, Brace & World, Inc., New York, 1964.

Berkeley, Edmund C.: "The International Impact of Computers and Automation," *Computers and Automation*, May 1965, pp. 17–18.

Berkwitt, George J.: "Management Rediscovers CPM," *Dun's Review*, May 1971 pp. 57–59.

Black, Guy: "Systems Analysis in Government Operations," *Management Science*, October 1967, pp. B-41–B-58.

Blake, Robert R., and Jane S. Mouton: *Corporate Excellence through Grid Organization Development: A Systems Approach*, Gulf Publishing Company, Houston, 1968.

Blau, Peter M., and W. Richard Scott: *Formal Organizations*, Chandler Publishing Company, San Francisco, 1962.

Blumberg, Donald F.: "New Directions for Computer Technology and Applications—A Long Range Prediction," *Computers and Automation*, January 1964, pp. 8–17.

Boguslaw, Robert: *The New Utopians*, Prentice-Hall, Inc., Englewood Cliffs, N.J., 1965.

Boore, William F., and Jerry R. Murphy: *The Computer Sampler—Management Perspectives on the Computer*, McGraw-Hill Book Company, New York, 1968.

Borko, H. (ed.): *Computer Applications in the Behavioral Sciences*, Prentice-Hall, Inc., Englewood Cliffs, N.J., 1962.

Boulding, Kenneth E.: "General Systems Theory: The Skeleton of Science," *Management Science*, April 1956, pp. 197–208.

——: *The Meaning of the 20th Century*, Harper & Row, Publishers, Incorporated, New York, 1965.

Bowen, Howard R., and Gorth L. Mangum (eds.): *Automation and Progress*, Prentice-Hall, Inc., Englewood Cliffs, N.J., 1966.

Brady, Rodney H.: "Computers in Top-level Decision Making," *Harvard Business Review*, July–August 1967, pp. 67–76.

Branch, Melville C.: *Planning: Aspects and Applications,* John Wiley & Sons, Inc., New York, 1966.

Bright, James R.: *Automation and Management,* Harvard University, Graduate School of Business Administration, Boston, 1958.

Brown, Warren B.: "Systems, Boundaries, and Information Flow," *Academy of Management Journal,* December 1966, pp. 318–327.

Bruner, William G., Jr.: "Systems Design: A Broader Role of Industrial Engineering," *Journal of Industrial Engineering,* March–April 1962, pp. 91–93.

Buckley, Walter (ed.): *Modern Systems Research for the Behavioral Scientist,* Aldine Publishing Co., Chicago, 1968.

Burck, Gilbert: *The Computer Age and Its Potential for Management,* Harper & Row, Publishers, Incorporated, New York, 1965.

Burlingame, John F.: "Information Technology and Decentralization," *Harvard Business Review,* November–December 1961, pp. 121–126.

Burns, Tom, and G. M. Stalker: *The Management of Innovation,* Tavistock Publications, London, 1961.

Business Week, "Computer Move into the Machine Shop," Sept. 19, 1970, pp. 88–90.

Caples, William G.: "Automation in Theory and Practice," *Business Topics,* Autumn 1960, pp. 7–19.

Caspari, John A.: "Fundamental Concepts of Information Theory," *Management Accounting,* June 1968, pp. 8–10.

Chamberlain, Neil W.: *Enterprise and Environment: The Firm in Time and Place,* McGraw-Hill Book Company, New York, 1968.

Chandler, Alfred D., Jr.: *Strategy and Structure,* The M.I.T. Press, Cambridge, Mass., 1962.

Churchman, C. West: *The Systems Approach,* Dell Publishing Co., Inc., New York, 1968.

———, Russell L. Ackoff, and E. Leonard Arnoff: *Introduction to Operations Research,* John Wiley & Sons, Inc., New York, 1957.

Cleland, David I.: "Why Project Management?", *Business Horizons,* Winter 1964, pp. 81–88.

——— and William R. King: *Systems Analysis and Project Management,* McGraw-Hill Book Company, New York, 1968.

Clough, Donald J.: *Concepts in Management Science,* Prentice-Hall, Inc., Englewood Cliffs, N.J., 1963.

Colm, Gerhard: *Integration of National Planning and Budgeting,* National Planning Association, Washinton, D.C., 1968.

Cook, Desmond L.: *Program Evaluation and Review Technique—Application in Education,* U.S. Department of Health, Education, and Welfare, Government Printing Office, Washington, D.C., 1966.

Culbertson, James T.: "Automation: Its Evolution and Future Direction," *Computers and Automation,* November 1960, pp. 14–18, and December 1960, pp. 34–36.

Cyert, R. M., and James G. March: *A Behavioral Theory of the Firm,* Prentice-Hall, Inc., Englewood Cliffs, N.J., 1963.

Dalton, Gene W., Paul R. Lawrence, and Jay W. Lorsch: *Organizational Structure and Design,* Richard D. Irwin, Inc., and The Dorsey Press, Homewood, Ill., 1970.

Daniel, D. Ronald: "Management Information Crisis," *Harvard Business Review,* September–October 1961, pp. 111–121.

———: "Team at the Top," *Harvard Business Review,* March–April 1965, pp. 74–82.

Daniel, Norman E., and J. Richard Jones: *Business Logistics Concepts and Viewpoints,* Allyn and Bacon, Inc., Boston, 1969.

Dearden, John: "How to Organize Information Systems," *Harvard Business Review,* March–April 1966, pp. 65–73.

————: "Myth of Real-time Management Information," *Harvard Business Review,* May–June 1966, pp. 123–132.

Dechert, Charles R.: "The Development of Cybernetics," *The American Behavioral Scientist,* June 1965, pp. 15–20.

DeGreene, Kenyon B. (ed.): *Systems Psychology,* McGraw-Hill Book Company, New York, 1970.

Deutsch, Karl W.: "On Communication Models in the Social Sciences," *Public Opinion Quarterly,* Fall 1952, pp. 356–380.

Dickson, Gary W., and John K. Simmons: "The Behavioral Side of MIS," *Business Horizons,* August 1970, pp. 59–91.

Diebold, John: *Beyond Automation,* McGraw-Hill Book Company, New York, 1964.

————: *Business Decision and Technological Change,* Praeger Publishers, New York, 1970.

Dorfman, Robert: "Operations Research," *American Economic Review,* September 1960, pp. 575–623.

Dorsey, John T.: "A Communication Model for Administration," *Administrative Science Quarterly,* December 1957, pp. 307–324.

Drew, Elizabeth B.: "HEW Grapples with PPBS," *The Public Interest,* Summer 1967, pp. 9–29.

Drucker, Peter F.: *The Practice of Management,* Harper & Row, Publishers, Incorporated, New York, 1954.

————: *Technology, Management and Society,* Harper & Row, Publishers, Incorporated, New York, 1970.

Dusenbury, Warren: "CPM for New Product Introduction," *Harvard Business Review,* July–August 1967, pp. 124–139.

Dutton, John M., and William H. Starbuck (eds.): *Computer Simulation of Human Behavior,* John Wiley & Sons, Inc., New York, 1971.

Dyer, James S.: "The Use of PPBS in a Public System of Higher Education: Is It Cost-Effective?" *Academy of Management Journal,* September 1970. pp. 285–299.

Eckman, Donald P. (ed.): *Systems: Research and Design,* John Wiley & Sons, Inc., New York, 1961.

Economic Analysis and the Efficiency of Government, Report of the Subcommittee on Economy in Government of the Joint Economic Committee, 91st Cong., 2d Sess., February 1970.

Eddington, Sir Arthur: *The Nature of the Physical World,* University of Michigan Press, Ann Arbor, Mich., 1958.

Eilon, Samuel: "Some Notes on Information Processing," *The Journal of Management Studies,* May 1968, pp. 139–153.

Ellis, David O., and Fred J. Ludwig: *Systems Philosophy,* Prentice-Hall, Inc., Englewood Cliffs, N.J., 1962.

Ellul, Jacques: *The Technological Society,* John Wilkinson (trans.), Alfred A. Knopf, Inc., New York, 1964.

Emery, F. E. (ed.): *Systems Thinking,* Penguin Books Ltd., Harmondsworth, Middlesex, England, 1969.

Emshoff, James R.: *Analysis of Behavioral Systems,* The Macmillan Company, New York, 1971.

Enke, Stephen (ed.): *Defense Management*, Prentice-Hall, Inc., Englewood Cliffs, N.J., 1967.

Enthoven, Alain C.: "Systems Analysis and Decision Making," *Military Review*, January 1963, pp. 7–17.

Ernst, Martin L.: "Operations Research and the Large Strategic Problem," *Operations Research*, July–August 1961, pp. 437–445.

Etzioni, Amitai: *Modern Organizations*, Prentice-Hall, Inc., Englewood Cliffs, N.J., 1964.

Evans, Marshall K., and Lou R. Hague: "Master Plan for Information Systems," *Harvard Business Review*, January–February 1962, pp. 92–103.

Ewell, James M.: "The Total Systems Concept and How to Organize for It," *Computers and Automation*, September 1961, pp. 9–13.

Fabun, Don: *The Dynamics of Change*, Prentice-Hall, Inc., Englewood Cliffs, N.J., 1967.

Feigenbaum, Edward A., and Julian Feldman (eds.): *Computers and Thought*, McGraw-Hill Book Company, New York, 1963.

Fiedler, Fred E.: *A Theory of Leadership Effectiveness*, McGraw-Hill Book Company, New York, 1967.

Flagle, C. D., W. H. Huggins, and R. H. Roy (eds.): *Operations Research and Systems Engineering*, The Johns Hopkins Press, Baltimore, 1960.

Flood, Merrill M.: "System Engineering," *Management Technology*, Institute of Management Sciences, Monograph 1, January 1960, pp. 21–35.

Forrester, Jay W.: *Industrial Dynamics*, The M.I.T. Press, Cambridge, Mass., and John Wiley & Sons, Inc., New York, 1961.

———: *Urban Dynamics*, The M.I.T. Press, Cambridge, Mass., 1969.

———: *World Dynamics*, Wright-Allen Press, Inc., Cambridge, Mass., 1971.

French, Wendell: "Processes vis-à-vis Systems: Toward a Model of the Enterprise and Administration," *Academy of Management Journal*, March 1963, pp. 46–57.

———: *The Personnel Management Process*, 2d ed., Houghton Mifflin Company, Boston, 1970.

Gagné, Robert M. (ed.): *Psychological Principles in Systems Development*, Holt, Rinehart and Winston, Inc., New York, 1962.

Galbraith, John Kenneth: *The New Industrial State*, Houghton Mifflin Company, Boston, 1967.

Gale, John R.: "Why Management Information Systems Fail," *Financial Executive*, August 1968, pp. 44–48.

Gallagher, James D.: *Management Information Systems and the Computer*, American Management Association, Inc., New York, 1961.

Golovin, Nicholas E.: "Social Change and the 'Evaluative Function' in Government," *Management Science*, June 1969, pp. B-461–B-480.

Gore, William J.: *Administrative Decision-Making*, John Wiley & Sons, Inc., New York, 1964.

Greenberger, Martin (ed.): *Management and the Computer of the Future*, The M.I.T. Press, Cambridge, Mass., and John Wiley & Sons, Inc., New York, 1962.

Gross, Bertram M.: *Organizations and Their Managing*, The Free Press, New York, 1968.

Grusky, Oscar, and George A. Miller (eds.): *The Sociology of Organizations*, The Free Press, New York, 1970.

Gutenberg, Arthur W.: "A Perspective on Management Control Theory," *Evolving Concepts of Management*, Proceedings of the 24th Annual Meeting of the Academy of Management, Chicago, December 1964, pp. 82–92.

Haberstroh, Chadwick J.: "Controls as an Organizational Process," *Management Science,* January 1960, pp. 165–171.

Hagstrom, Warren O.: "Traditional and Modern Forms of Scientific Teamwork," *Administrative Science Quarterly,* December 1964, pp. 241–263.

Haire, Mason: *Psychology in Management,* McGraw-Hill Book Company, 2d ed., New York, 1964.

———— (ed.): *Modern Organization Theory,* John Wiley & Sons, Inc., New York, 1959.

Hall, Richard H.: "The Concept of Bureaucracy: An Empirical Assessment," *American Journal of Sociology,* July 1963, pp. 32–41.

Hamelman, Paul W.: "Missions, Matrices and University Management," *Academy of Management Journal,* March 1970, pp. 35–47.

Hammerton, J. C.: "Automatic Machine Scheduling," *Computers and Automation,* May 1961, pp. 17–22.

Hare, Van Court, Jr.: *Systems Analysis: A Diagnostic Approach,* Harcourt, Brace & World, Inc., New York, 1967.

Harvey, Allan: "Are Total Systems Practical?" *Business Automation,* June 1969, pp. 72–76.

Harvey, Edward: "Technology and the Structure of Organizations," *American Sociological Review,* April 1968, pp. 247–259.

Hayes, Robert H.: "Qualitative Insights from Quantitative Methods," *Harvard Business Review,* July–August 1969, pp. 108–117.

Head, Robert V.: *Real-Time Business Systems,* Holt, Rinehart and Winston, Inc., New York, 1965.

Heany, Donald F.: *Development of Information Systems,* The Ronald Press Company, New York, 1968.

————: "Is TIMS Talking to Itself?", *Management Science,* December 1965, pp. B-146–B-155.

Herrmann, Cyril C.: "Systems Approach to City Planning," *Harvard Business Review,* September–October 1966, pp. 71–80.

Hertz, David B.: "Mobilizing Management Science Resources," *Management Science,* January 1965, pp. 361–367.

————: "The Unity of Science and Management," *Management Science,* April 1965, pp. B-89–B-97.

Heslen, Robert: "Choosing an Automatic Program for Numerical Control," *Control Engineering,* April 1962, pp. 109–113.

Hickey, Albert E., Jr.: "The Systems Approach: Can Engineers Use the Scientific Method?", *IRE Transactions on Engineering Management,* June 1960, pp. 72–80.

Higginson, M. Valliant: *Managing with EDP: A Look at the State of the Art,* American Management Association, New York, 1965.

Hitch, Charles J.: *Decision-Making for Defense,* University of California Press, Berkeley, Calif., 1965.

Holden, I. R., and P. K. McIllory: *Network Planning in Management Control Systems,* Hutchinson Educational Ltd., London, 1970.

Holt, Herbert, and Robert C. Ferber: "The Psychological Transition from Management Scientist to Manager," *Management Science,* April 1964, pp. 409–420.

Hopeman, Richard J.: *Systems Analysis and Operations Management,* Charles E. Merrill Publishing Co., Columbus, Ohio, 1969.

Hopkins, Robert C.: "Possible Applications of Information Theory to Management Control," *IRE Transactions on Engineering Management,* March 1961, pp. 40–48.

Horvath, William J.: "The Systems Approach to the National Health Problem," *Management Science,* June 1966, pp. B-391–B-395.

Hower, Ralph M., and Charles D. Orth: *Managers and Scientists*, Division of Research, Harvard Graduate School of Business Administration, Boston 1963.

Hunt, Raymond G.: "Technology and Organization", *Academy of Management Journal*, September 1970, pp. 235–252.

"Impact of Automation," *U.S. Department of Labor Bulletin 1287*, 1960.

Jaffe, A. J., and Joseph Froomkin: *Technology and Jobs*, Frederick A. Praeger, Inc., New York, 1968.

Jodka, John: "PERT: A Control Concept Using Computers," *Computers and Automation*, March 1962, pp. 16–18.

Johnson, Richard A.: *Employees—Automation—Management*, Bureau of Business Research, University of Washington, Seattle, Washington, 1961.

——, Fremont E. Kast, and James E. Rosenzweig: "Designing Management Systems," *The Business Quarterly*, Summer 1964, pp. 9–66.

——, ——, and ——: "Systems Theory and Management," *Management Science*, January 1964, pp. 367–384.

——, William T. Newell, and Roger C. Vergin: *Operations Management—A Systems Concept*, Houghton Mifflin Company, Boston, 1972.

Kahn, Alfred J.: *Theory and Practice of Social Planning*, Russell Sage Foundation, New York, 1969.

Kanter, Jerome: *Management Guide to Computer System Selection and Use*, Prentice-Hall, Inc., Englewood Cliffs, N.J., 1970

Kast, Fremont E.: "A Dynamic Planning Model," *Business Horizons*, Spring 1968, pp. 55–60.

—— and James E. Rosenzweig: "Management and Accelerating Technology," *California Management Review*, Winter 1963, pp. 39–40.

—— and ——: "Minimizing the Planning Gap," *Advanced Management*, October 1960, pp. 20–23.

—— and ——: *Organization and Management: A Systems Approach*, McGraw-Hill Book Company, New York, 1970.

—— and ——, (eds.): *Science, Technology, and Management*, McGraw-Hill Book Company, New York, 1963.

Katz, Daniel, and Robert L. Kahn: *The Social Psychology of Organizations*, John Wiley & Sons, Inc., New York, 1966.

Kaufman, Felix: "Data Systems That Cross Company Boundaries," *Harvard Business Review*, January–February 1966, pp. 141–155.

Keegan, Warren J.: "The Acquisition of Global Information," *Management Review*, June 1968, pp. 54–56.

Kelly, Joseph F.: *Computerized Management Information Systems*, The Macmillan Company, New York, 1970.

Klasson, Charles R., and Kenneth W. Olm: "Managerial Implications of Integrated Business Operations," *California Management Review*, Fall 1965, pp. 21–31.

Knowles, Henry P., and Borje O. Saxberg: "Human Relations and the Nature of Man," *Harvard Business Review*, March–April 1967, pp. 22, 40ff.

Kompass, E. J.: "Information Systems in Control Engineering," *Control Engineering*, January 1961, pp. 103–106.

Koontz, Harold (ed.): *Toward a Unified Theory of Management*, McGraw-Hill Book Company, New York, 1964.

Kornhauser, William: *Scientists in Industry*, University of California Press, Berkeley, Calif., 1963.

Krauss, Leonard I.: *Administering and Controlling the Company Data Processing Function*, Prentice-Hall, Inc., Englewood Cliffs, N.J., 1969.

Lach, E. L.: "The Total Systems Concept," *Systems and Procedures,* November 1960, pp. 6–7.

Lawrence, Paul R., and Jay W. Lorsch: *Organization and Environment,* Harvard Graduate School of Business Administration, Boston, 1967.

—— and ——: *Studies in Organization Design,* Richard D. Irwin, Inc., and the Dorsey Press, Homewood, Ill., 1970.

Leavitt, Harold J.: "Applied Organizational Change in Industry: Structural, Technological and Humanistic Approaches," in James G. March (ed.), *Handbook of Organizations,* Rand McNally & Company, Chicago, 1965, pp. 1114–1170.

——: *Managerial Psychology,* 2d ed., University of Chicago Press, Chicago, 1964.

LeBreton, Preston P., and Dale A. Henning: *Planning Theory,* Prentice-Hall, Inc., Englewood Cliffs, N.J., 1961.

—— (ed.): *Comparative Administrative Theory,* University of Washington Press, Seattle, 1968.

Levin, Richard I., and Charles A Kirkpatrick: *Planning and Control with PERT/CPM,* McGraw-Hill Book Company, New York, 1966.

Levinson,Harry: "Reciprocation: The Relationship between Man and Organization," *Administrative Science Quarterly,* March 1965, pp. 370–390.

Likert, Rensis: *The Human Organization,* McGraw-Hill Book Company, New York, 1967.

Lippitt, Gordon L.: *Organization Renewal,* Appleton Century Crofts, New York, 1969.

Lipperman, Lawrence L.: *Advanced Business Systems,* AMA Research Study 86, American Management Association, New York, 1968.

Lipstreu, Otis, and Kenneth A. Reed: "A New Look at the Organizational Implications of Automation," *Academy of Management Journal,* March 1965, pp. 24–31.

Litterer, Joseph A.: *The Analysis of Organizations,* John Wiley & Sons, Inc., New York, 1965.

Litwak, Eugene: "Models of Bureaucracy Which Permit Conflict," *American Journal of Sociology,* September 1961, pp. 177–184.

Litwin, George H., and Robert A. Stringer, Jr.: *Motivation and Organizational Climate,* Division of Research, Graduate School of Business Adminstration, Harvard University, Boston, 1968.

Lombard, George F. F.: "Relativism in Organizations," *Harvard Business Review,* March–April 1971, pp. 55–65.

Luce, R. Duncan, and Howard Raiffa: *Games and Decisions,* John Wiley & Sons, Inc., New York, 1957.

Lyden, Fremont J., and Ernest G. Miller (eds.): *Planning-Programming-Budgeting: A Systems Approach to Management,* Markham Publishing Company, Chicago, 1967.

Malcolm, D. C., and A. J. Rowe: "Computer-based Control Systems," *California Management Review,* Spring 1961, pp. 4–15.

——, ——, and Lorimer F. McConnell (eds.): *Management Control Systems,* John Wiley & Sons, Inc., New York, 1960

Management 2000, The American Foundation for Management Research, Inc., New York, 1968.

Mann, Floyd C., and Richard L. Hoffmann: *Automation and the Worker,* Holt, Rinehart and Company, Inc., New York, 1960.

—— and Lawrence K. Williams: "Observations on the Dynamics of a Change to Electronic Data-Processing Equipment," *Administrative Science Quarterly,* September 1960, pp. 217–256.

March, James G. (ed.): *Handbook of Organizations,* Rand McNally & Company, Chicago, 1965.

—— and Herbert A. Simon: *Organizations,* John Wiley & Sons, Inc., New York, 1958.

Maurer, John G.: *Readings in Organization Theory: Open-Systems Approaches,* Random House, Inc., New York, 1971.

McCracken, Daniel D.: "The Software Turmoil," *Datamation,* January 1962, pp. 21–22.

McDonough, Adrian M.: *Information Economics and Management Systems,* McGraw-Hill Book Company, New York, 1963.

McGarrah, R. E.: *Production and Logistics Management,* John Wiley & Sons, Inc., New York, 1963.

McGregor, Douglas: *The Human Side of Enterprise,* McGraw-Hill Book Company, New York, 1960.

——: *The Professional Manager,* ed. by Warren G. Bennis and Caroline McGregor, McGraw-Hill Book Company, New York, 1967.

McGuire, Joseph W.: *Theories of Business Behavior,* Prentice Hall, Inc., Englewood Cliffs, N.J., 1964.

McHale, John: "Science, Technology, and Change," *The Annals of the American Academy of Political and Social Science,* September 1967, pp. 120–140.

McKean, Roland N.: *Efficiency in Government through Systems Analysis,* John Wiley & Sons, Inc., New York, 1958.

McRainey, J. H., and L. D. Miller: "Numerical Control," *Automation,* August 1960, pp. 70–100.

Meier, Robert C., William T. Newell, and Harold L. Pazer: *Simulation in Business and Economics,* Prentice-Hall, Inc., Englewood Cliffs, N.J., 1969.

Melitz, Peter W.: "Impact of Electronic Data Processing on Managers," *Advanced Management,* April 1961, pp. 4–6.

Mesarovic, Mihajlo D. (ed.): *Views on General Systems Theory,* John Wiley & Sons, Inc., New York, 1964.

Mesthene, Emmanuel G.: *Technological Change: Its Impact on Man and Society,* The New American Library, Inc., New York, 1970.

Michael, Donald N.: "Some Long-range Implications of Computer Technology for Human Behavior in Organizations," *The American Behavioral Scientist,* April 1966, pp. 29–35.

Miller, David W., and Martin K. Starr: *The Structure of Human Decisions,* Prentice-Hall, Inc., Englewood Cliffs, N.J., 1960.

Miller, E. J., and A. K. Rice: *Systems of Organization,* Tavistock Publications, London, 1967.

Miller, Ernest C.: *Advanced Techniques for Strategic Planning,* American Management Association, Inc., New York, 1971.

Miller, J. James: "Automation, Job Creation, and Unemployment," *Academy of Management Journal,* December 1964, pp. 300–307.

Miller, James G.: "Living Systems: Basic Concepts," *Behavioral Science,* July 1965, pp. 193–237.

Miller, Robert W.: "How to Plan and Control with PERT," *Harvard Business Review,* March–April 1962, pp. 93–104.

Mishkin, Eli, and Ludwig Braun, Jr.: *Adaptive Control Systems,* McGraw-Hill Book Company, New York, 1961.

Mockler, Robert J. (ed.): *Readings in Management Control,* Appleton Century Crofts, New York, 1970.

Morris, William T.: "On the Art of Modeling," *Management Science,* August 1967, pp. B-707–B-717.

Murphy, Gardner: "Toward a Field Theory of Communication," *Journal of Communication,* December 1961, pp. 196–201.

Myers, Charles A. (ed.): *The Impact of Computers on Management,* The M.I.T. Press, Cambridge, Mass., 1967.

Myers, M. Scott: "The Human Factor in Management Systems," *California Management Review,* Fall 1971, pp. 5–10.

Neuschel, Richard F.: *Management by System,* McGraw-Hill Book Company, New York, 1960.

Newman, William H., Charles E. Summer, and E. Kirby Warren: *The Process of Management,* 3d ed., Prentice-Hall, Inc., Englewood Cliffs, N.J., 1972.

Nichols, Gerald E.: "On the Nature of Management Information," *Management Accounting,* April 1969, pp. 9–15.

Optner, Stanford L.: *Systems Analysis for Business Management,* 2d ed., Prentice-Hall, Inc., Englewood Cliffs, N.J., 1968.

Ordway, Frederick I., III, (ed.): *Advances in Space Science and Technology,* vol. 7, Academic Press Inc., New York, 1965.

Parsons, Talcott: *Structure and Process in Modern Societies,* The Free Press, New York, 1960.

Perrow, Charles: *Organizational Analysis: A Sociological View,* Wadsworth Publishing Company, Inc., Belmont, Calif., 1970.

Petit, Thomas A.: "A Behavioral Theory of Management," *Academy of Mangement Journal,* December 1967, pp. 341–350.

Pfiffner, John M., and Frank P. Sherwood: *Administrative Organization,* Prentice-Hall, Inc., Englewood Cliffs, N.J., 1960.

The Planning-Programming-Budgeting System: Progress and Potentials, Report of the Subcommittee on Economy in Government of the Joint Economic Committee, 90th Cong., 1st Sess., December 1967.

Porter, Lyman W., and Edward E. Lawler, III: *Managerial Attitudes and Performance,* Richard D. Irwin, Inc., Homewood, Ill., 1968.

Presthus, Robert: *The Organizational Society,* Alfred A. Knopf, Inc., New York, 1962.

Program Planning and Control System, Department of the Navy, Special Projects Office, 1960.

Proshansky, Harold M., William H. Ittelson, and Leanne G. Rivlin: *Environmental Psychology: Man and His Physical Setting,* Holt, Rinehart and Winston, Inc., New York, 1970.

Putnam, Arnold O., E. Robert Barlow, and Gabriel N. Stilan: *Unified Operations Management,* McGraw-Hill Book Company, New York, 1963.

Quade, E. S. (ed.): *Analysis for Military Decisions,* The Rand Corporation, Santa Monica, Calif., 1964.

Quinn, James Brian: "Technological Forecasting," *Harvard Business Review,* March–April 1967, pp. 89–106.

Rader, Louis T.: "Roadblocks to Progress in the Management Sciences and Operations Research," *Management Science,* February 1965, pp. C-1–C-5.

Reagan, Philip H.: "Multi-machine Automation by Direct Numerical Control," *Computer Decision,* July 1970, pp. 32–35.

Reeser, Clayton: "Some Potential Human Problems of the Project Form of Organization," *Academy of Management Journal,* December 1969, pp. 459–467.

Reintjes, J. E.: "The Intellectual Foundations of Automation," *Annals of the American Academy of Political and Social Science,* March 1962, pp. 1–9.

Rickover, Hyman G.: "A Humanistic Technology," *The American Behavioral Scientist,* January 1965, pp. 3–8.

Roberts, Edward B.: "Industrial Dynamics and the Design of Management Control Systems," *Management Technology,* December 1963, pp. 100–118.

Roman, Daniel D.: *Research and Development Management: The Economics and Administration of Technology,* Appleton Century Crofts, New York, 1968.

Rosenzweig, James E.: "The Weapon System Management Concept and Electronic Data Processing," *Management Science,* January 1960, pp. 149–164.

————: "Managers and Management Scientists: Two Cultures," *Business Horizons,* Fall 1967, pp. 79–86.

Ross, Joel E.: *Management by Information System,* Prentice-Hall, Inc., Englewood Cliffs, N.J., 1970.

Rubenstein, Albert H.: "Organizational Factors Affecting Research and Development Decision-Making in Large Decentralized Companies," *Management Science,* July 1964, pp. 618–633.

———— and Chadwick J. Haberstroh (eds.): *Some Theories of Organizations,* rev. ed., Richard D. Irwin, Inc., and The Dorsey Press, Homewood, Ill., 1966.

Ruesch, Jurgen, and Gregory Bateson: *Communication,* W. W. Norton & Company, Inc., New York, 1951.

Rush, Harold M. F.: *Behavioral Science: Concepts and Managerial Applications,* Personnel Policy Study No. 216, National Industrial Conference Board, Inc., New York, 1969.

Samuel, Arthur L.: "Artificial Intelligence: A Frontier of Automation," *Annals of the American Academy of Political and Social Science,* March 1962, pp. 10–20.

Saxberg, Borje O., and John W. Slocum, Jr.: "The Management of Scientific Manpower," *Management Science,* April 1968, pp. B-473–B-489.

Sayles, Leonard R., and Margaret K. Chandler: *Managing Large Systems,* Harper & Row, Publisher, Incorporated, New York, 1971.

Schoderbek, Peter P.: *Management Systems,* 2d ed., John Wiley & Sons, Inc., New York, 1971.

Schrieber, Albert N. (ed.): *Corporate Simulation Models,* Graduate School of Business Administration, University of Washington, Seattle, 1970.

Schwitter, Joseph P.: "Computer Effect upon Management Jobs," *Academy of Management Journal,* September 1965, pp. 233–236.

Scott, Ellis L., and Roger W. Bolz (eds.): *Automation and Society,* The Center for the Study of Automation and Society, Athens, Ga., 1969.

Scott, William G.: "Organizational Theory: An Overview and an Appraisal," *Journal of the Academy of Management,* April 1961, pp. 7–26.

————: *Organization Theory: A Behavioral Analysis for Management,* Richard D. Irwin, Inc., and The Dorsey Press, Homewood, Ill., 1967.

Seiler, John A.: *Systems Analysis in Organizational Behavior,* Richard D. Irwin, Inc., and The Dorsey Press, Homewood, Ill., 1967.

Seligman, Ben B.: *Most Notorious Victory: Man in an Age of Automation,* The Free Press, New York, 1966.

Shannon, Claude, and Warren Weaver: *The Mathematical Theory of Communication,* University of Illinois Press, Urbana, Ill., 1949.

Shenton, D. W., and H. Gleixner: "Automated Material Control," *Automation,* January 1961, pp. 50–59.

Shepard, Jon M.: *Automation and Alienation—A Study of Office and Factory Workers,* The M.I.T. Press, Cambridge, Mass., 1971.

Shubik, Martin: "Simulation of Industry and Firm," *American Economic Review,* December 1960, pp. 908–919.

Shultz, George P., and Thomas L. Whisler (eds.): *Management Organization and the Computer,* The Free Press, New York, 1960.

Shycon, Harvey N., and Richard B. Maffei, "Simulation: Tool for Better Distribution" *Harvard Business Review,* November–December 1960, pp. 65–75.

Simon, Herbert A.: *Administrative Behavior,* The Macmillan Company, New York, 1959.

———: *The New Science of Management Decision,* Harper & Row, Publishers, Incorporated, New York, 1960.

———: *The Shape of Automation for Men and Management,* Harper & Row, Publishers, Incorporated, New York, 1965.

Smalter, Donald J.: "Influence of Department of Defense on Corporate Planning," *Management Technology,* December 1964, pp. 115–138.

Smith, Christopher F.: "Graphic Systems for Computers," *Computers and Automation,* November 1965, pp. 14–16.

Snow, C. P.: *The Two Cultures and the Scientific Revolution,* Cambridge University Press, London, 1959.

Sprague, Richard E.: "The New Era in Information Systems," *Systems & Procedures Journal,* July–August 1967, pp. 26–28.

Starr, Martin K.: "The Politics of Management Science," *Interfaces,* June 1971, pp. 31–37.

Steiner, Gary A. (ed.): *The Creative Organization,* The University of Chicago Press, Chicago, 1965.

Steiner, George A. (ed.): *Managerial Long-range Planning,* McGraw-Hill Book Company, New York, 1963.

———: *Top Management Planning,* The Macmillan Company, New York, 1969.

——— and William G. Ryan: *Industrial Project Management,* The Macmillan Company, New York, 1968.

Stewart, John M.: "Making Project Management Work," *Business Horizons,* Fall 1965, pp. 54–68.

Stoller, David S., and Richard L. Van Horn: *Design of a Management Information System,* Institute of Management Sciences, Monograph 1, January 1960, pp. 86–91.

Stout, Thomas M.: "Process Control: Past, Present, and Future," *Annals of the American Academy of Political and Social Science,* March 1962, pp. 29–37.

Summer, Charles E. Jr., and Jeremiah J. O'Connell: *The Managerial Mind,* Richard D. Irwin, Inc., Homewood, Ill., 1964.

Sutermeister, Robert A.: *People and Productivity,* 2d ed., McGraw-Hill Book Company, New York, 1969.

Tagiuri, Renato: "Value Orientations and the Relationship of Managers and Scientists," *Administrative Science Quarterly,* June 1965, pp. 39–51.

Tannenbaum, Arnold: *Control in Organizations,* McGraw-Hill Book Company, New York, 1968.

Terreberry, Shirley: "The Evolution of Organizational Environments," *Administrative Science Quarterly,* March 1968, pp. 590–613.

Thome, P. G., and R. G. Willard: "The Systems Approach to a Unified Concept of Planning," *Aerospace Management,* Fall–Winter 1966, pp. 25–44.

Thompson, James D. (ed.): *Approaches to Organizational Design,* The University of Pittsburgh Press, Pittsburgh, Pa., 1966.

————: *Organizations in Action,* McGraw-Hill Book Company, New York, 1967.

Thompson, Victor A.: "Bureaucracy and Innovation," *Administrative Science Quarterly,* June 1965, pp. 1–20.

Thurston, Philip H.: "Who Should Control Information Systems?", *Harvard Business Review,* November–December 1962, pp. 135–139.

Tilles, Seymour, "The Manager's Job—A Systems Approach," *Harvard Business Review,* January–February 1963, pp. 73–81.

Toffler, Alvin: *Future Shock,* Random House, Inc., New York, 1970.

Vergin, Roger C., and Andrew J. Grimes: "Management Myths and EDP," *California Management Review,* Fall 1964, pp. 59–70.

von Bertalanffy, Ludwig: "General System Theory: A New Approach to Unity of Science," *Human Biology,* December 1951, pp. 303–361.

————: *General System Theory,* George Braziller, New York, 1968.

Walker, Charles R. (ed.): *Technology, Industry, and Man,* McGraw-Hill Book Company, New York, 1968.

Warren, E. Kirby: *Long-range Planning: The Executive Viewpoint,* Prentice-Hall, Inc., Englewood Cliffs, N.J., 1966.

Webb, James E.: *Space Age Management,* McGraw-Hill Book Company, New York, 1969.

Weiner, Milton G.: "Observations on the Growth of Information-Processing Centers," in Albert H. Rubenstein and Chadwick J. Haberstroh (eds.), *Some Theories of Organization,* The Dorsey Press, Inc., and Richard D. Irwin, Inc., Homewood, Ill., 1960.

Weinwurm, George F.: "Computer Management Control Systems through the Looking Glass," *Management Science,* July 1961, pp. 411–419.

Whisler, Thomas L.: *Information Technology and Organizational Change,* Wadsworth Publishing Company, Inc., Belmont, Calif., 1970.

Wiener, Norbert: *The Human Use of Human Beings,* Houghton Mifflin Company, Boston, 1954.

Weist, Jerome D., and Ferdinand K. Levy: *A Management Guide to PERT/CPM,* Prentice-Hall, Inc., Englewood Cliffs, N.J., 1969.

Wildavsky, Aaron: "Rescuing Policy Analysis from PPBS," *Public Administration Review,* March–April 1969, pp. 189–202.

Wilemon, David L., and John P. Cicero: "The Project Manager—Anomalies and Ambiguities," *Academy of Management Journal,* September 1970, pp. 269–282.

Wilensky, Harold L.: *Organizational Intelligence,* Basic Books, Inc., Publishers, New York, 1967.

Wilson, Charles Z., and Marcus Alexis: "Basic Frameworks for Decisions," *Journal of the Academy of Management,* August 1962, pp. 150–164.

Woodward, Joan: *Industrial Organization: Theory and Practice,* Oxford University Press, Fair Lawn N.J., 1965.

Wyman, Forrest P.: *Simulation Modeling: A Guide to Using SIMSCRIPT,* John Wiley & Sons, Inc., New York, 1970.

Yarmolinsky, Adam: *The Military Establishment,* Harper & Row, Publishers, Incorporated, New York, 1971.

Young, Stanley: *Management: A Systems Analysis,* Scott, Foresman and Company, Glenview, Ill., 1969.

Zani, William M.: "The Computer Utility," *California Management Review,* Fall 1970, pp. 31–37.

Name Index

Subject Index

Page numbers in *italics* indicate cases.